INTRODUCTION TO
POLICING

9781529713633
Bundle: Intro to Policing 3E

How to access your e-book via Kortext

-Go to www.kortext.com.
-Click on the 'Login' button.
-Enter your Access Code in the relevant box.
-Enter your personal details to set up an account.
-Access your book online!
-Download the App for offline access.

Access Code

Sara Miller McCune founded SAGE Publishing in 1965 to support the dissemination of usable knowledge and educate a global community. SAGE publishes more than 1000 journals and over 800 new books each year, spanning a wide range of subject areas. Our growing selection of library products includes archives, data, case studies and video. SAGE remains majority owned by our founder and after her lifetime will become owned by a charitable trust that secures the company's continued independence.

Los Angeles | London | New Delhi | Singapore | Washington DC | Melbourne

MICHAEL ROWE

INTRODUCTION TO POLICING

3RD EDITION

Los Angeles | London | New Delhi
Singapore | Washington DC | Melbourne

Los Angeles | London | New Delhi
Singapore | Washington DC | Melbourne

SAGE Publications Ltd
1 Oliver's Yard
55 City Road
London EC1Y 1SP

SAGE Publications Inc.
2455 Teller Road
Thousand Oaks, California 91320

SAGE Publications India Pvt Ltd
B 1/I 1 Mohan Cooperative Industrial Area
Mathura Road
New Delhi 110 044

SAGE Publications Asia-Pacific Pte Ltd
3 Church Street
#10-04 Samsung Hub
Singapore 049483

Editor: Natalie Aguilera
Assistant editor: Delayna Spencer
Production editor: Sarah Cooke
Copyeditor: Solveig Gardner Servian
Proofreader: Fabienne Pedroletti
Indexer: Martin Hargreaves
Marketing manager: Susheel Gokarakonda
Cover design: Stephanie Guyaz
Typeset by: C&M Digitals (P) Ltd, Chennai, India
Printed in the UK

Library of Congress Control Number: 2017958642

British Library Cataloguing in Publication data

A catalogue record for this book is available from
the British Library

ISBN 978–1-47397–294–0
ISBN 978–1-47397–295–7 (pbk)

Contents

Detailed Contents

Preface

Preparing a third edition of this book has provided an opportunity to reflect on changes in debates about policing since the initial proposal for this text was developed in the early 2000s. At that time, shortly after the publication of the Lawrence Report of 1999, issues relating to diversity and the policing of racist attacks were high on the agenda. The police were in a period of expansion: officer numbers in England and Wales had risen and the new role of Police Community Support Officer seemed to provide an opportunity for expanding capacity as police increasingly worked in multi-agency partnerships with other public sector organisations. The problem of antisocial behaviour was salient and had led to the development of reassurance Neighbourhood Policing. A decade or more later, inevitably, the challenges facing policing have changed. Cybercrime, terrorism and the investigation of historical sex abuse cases are among the most difficult problems facing police across the world as the twenty-first century matures. In England and Wales, police have gone through an extended period of financial pressure; officer numbers have fallen back to the level they were at two decades ago. Police and Crime Commissioners (PCCs), since 2012, have added a new dimension to police governance and are often powerful local actors in the wider criminal justice sector.

What is also notable is the considerable continuity across the period. Fundamental questions about police accountability have not been resolved by the introduction of PCCs. In many countries, related concerns about the investigation of complaints against the police persist, and the use of (sometimes deadly) force against members of the public remains controversial. Other matters, the pluralisation and privatisation of policing are obvious examples, also continue to unfold. What becomes apparent through the preparation of three versions of this book over a period of a decade is that final chapters are never written. Revised and updated though this edition is, it can only offer insight into debates that stretch into the future. Many of the questions addressed in the chapters here relate to fundamental debates about power and politics, rights and ethics, the liberty of citizens and the security of the state. These remain – and will continue to remain – fascinating and challenging. If this contribution offers some insight into those, then the goal will have been achieved.

Online Resources

Introduction to Policing 3e is supported by a wealth of online resources for both students and lecturers to aid study and support teaching, which are available at https://study.sagepub.com/rowe3e

FOR STUDENTS

Weblinks direct you to relevant resources to broaden your understanding of chapter topics and expand your knowledge.

A **flashcard glossary**, which features terms from the book, is an ideal tool to help you get to grips with policing, key terms and revise for exams.

Find **chapter summaries, annotated further reading and study questions** from the book to help you master the topic of policing.

Self-check questions and answers allow you to test your knowledge to help you prepare for assignments and exams.

Free access to **scholarly journal articles**, chosen to deepen your knowledge and reinforce your learning of key topics.

Author-selected video from the **SAGE Criminology and Criminal Justice Video Collection** to foster understanding and facilitate learning.

FOR LECTURERS

Lecturer's notes outline the key learning objectives covered in each chapter and provide you with suggested activities/examples to use in class or for assignments.

PowerPoint slides featuring figures and tables from the book, which can be downloaded and customised for use in your own presentations.

1
WHAT IS POLICING?

CONTENTS

LEARNING OBJECTIVES

More than four decades ago, the American sociologist Egon Bittner (1974: 17) observed that the police service was one of the 'best known but least understood' of public institutions. The numerous studies and accounts that have emerged in the intervening period might mean that the police service is today even better known, although perhaps still less well understood. Crime and policing, including allegations of malpractice and corruption as well as heroism and selflessness, continue to feature heavily in the press, and the television schedules and cinema programmes are replete with cop shows. Familiarity, however, should not be confused with understanding, and this chapter aims to:

- outline theoretical perspectives on what 'policing' is

- give an overview of what the police service does

- distinguish between the relatively narrow activities associated with the institution of the police service from broader social processes of policing in broader terms.

KEY TERMS

bureaucracy; crime control; information work; law-enforcement; national identity; police and policing; service role; sovereignty and use of force

INTRODUCTION

In Britain, perhaps more than most countries, the police service forms part of the historical landscape and the police officer is elevated to the status of national symbol and is a ubiquitous part of the cultural framework (McLaughlin, 2007a). Colls (2002) showed how rhetoric surrounding the law, and its application to all without fear or favour, played an important role in the very development of the British state through much of the Middle Ages. Clearly the law has often not been cast or applied in the interests of the whole population, but mythological accounts can be powerful narratives that shape national identity. Loader (1997: 2) suggested that the police are 'a principal means by which English society tells stories about itself … an interpretive lens through which people make sense of, and give order to, their world.'

Before attempting to answer the question 'what is policing?', a points of clarification needs to be made. Most important is the need to distinguish between the narrow set of functions performed by the institution of the police service and the broader processes of social regulation and reproduction that govern everyday lives. The wider account of policing as a social function stresses that many institutions that do not have any formal role in the regulation of social life in practice contribute to the development of social norms and standards of behaviour that underpin the ordinary social interaction of everyday activity. The word 'policing' is etymologically related to 'politics', the governance of the city or state, and was used in broad terms to signify social regulation in the widest sense. Box 1.1 outlines the development of the term. 'Policing' did not come to be associated with the particular activities of a specific institution (*the* police) until relatively recently in many societies. The historical development of the police in Britain is described in the next chapter, which shows that demand for a particular organisation to police society emerged in Britain during the eighteenth century.

Box 1.1

The Changing Meaning of 'policing'

[T]he Greek politeia meant all matters affecting the survival and well-being of the state (*polis*). The word and the idea were developed by the Romans (the Latin politia can be translated as the state), largely disappeared with their Empire, but were resurrected in the medieval universities to justify the authority of a prince over his territories. By the early eighteenth in continental Europe *la police* and *die Politzey* were being used in the sense of the internal administration, welfare, protection, and surveillance of a territory. The word 'police' was not popular in England as it smacked of absolutism ... but the word was increasingly used towards the end of the eighteenth century.

(Emsley, 1996: 3)

Schools provide a good example of the broader process of social regulation as they play a central role in the socialisation of young people by preparing them for adult life. This is not the primary function of the education system, of course, but recent debates about the development of the study of citizenship within schools indicates that preparing young people for their post-school lives is increasingly recognised as an important secondary role. For these reasons it is readily apparent that the education system plays a central role in the policing of society, if that is conceived in terms of the broad process of social regulation. Many other agencies also contribute to this process in ways that are less obvious: religious groups, health providers, and the business sector – to take three examples – contribute in various ways to the organisation of social life and could be regarded as part of the process of policing. Increasingly these 'third party' agencies have been corralled into formal frameworks of regulation and are legally obliged to monitor client behaviour and report suspicious activities to law-enforcement agencies (Mazerolle and Ransley, 2005). Some might argue that the media plays a central role in shaping subjective interpretation of the world and the place of the individual within it and so are important agents of policing in this wider sense. In Chapter 10 the increasing range of institutions engaged in police networks is considered in more detail.

The difficulty of theorising policing in these broad terms is that it becomes difficult to know where the category can be closed. Informal social control and self-policing (such as where citizens are encouraged to report concerns that their friends, family, neighbours or acquaintances are being 'radicalised') are important forms of regulation, and it is often noted that almost no policing activity can occur without some public engagement. While clearly this demonstrates that policing is not just the business of the formal police service and that other institutions play a crucial role in developing, for example, public perceptions of criminal or deviant behaviour, but the same could be said for almost any and every aspect of social life. For this reason, much of this book will focus on the narrow approach to policing and concentrate primarily on the activities of the police service, and so this initial discussion of 'what is policing?' is also cast relatively narrow. Other agencies, both in the private and the public sector, play an increasingly important role in the business of policing and where relevant these are included in the discussion and analysis in chapters that follow. Since the police service cannot be understood in isolation from broader social developments, the wider dynamics of policing are crucial to many of the topics featured throughout the book. For the purposes of understanding 'what is policing?', though, it is to the narrower role of the police service that the analysis now turns.

Even a narrow focus on the institution of the police raises the dilemma of how to answer the question, and two perspectives are taken here. This chapter addresses the question literally by exploring what it is that the police do. Chapter 2 explores the question in historical terms by charting the myriad factors that led to the establishment of the modern police service in the nineteenth century.

WHAT IS POLICING?

Attempts to define policing have focused upon a range of different aspects of the diverse roles that the service performs. Chapter 2 provides an alternative approach by considering the historical development of the police service in Britain. In this section various other perspectives are discussed. First, a traditional 'common sense' definition of police work – that it is primarily a matter of law-enforcement – is considered. Although this approach does not account for the many other aspects of police work that do not, directly or indirectly, relate to crime control and law-enforcement, it has the advantage of providing a relatively clear, concise definition. Other perspectives that seek to reflect the wider activities performed by the police are then considered. One approach has been to define the police service in terms of its recourse to the use of force, and the power of the police service over ordinary citizens. Certainly, the police service exerts coercive power over citizens not available to many other agencies. However, approaches based on the centrality of force as a source of police power over citizens need to account for the coercive power exercised by other institutions which use force. Moreover, studies suggest that a characteristic of police work is to under-enforce the law and to use persuasion and negotiation rather then physical force, although the potential to do so remains.

Another approach to understanding policing focuses on the routine functions performed by officers. These perspectives tend to note the breadth and diversity of tasks that the police perform, many of which are characterised by a broader public service ethos not related to crime control. In contrast to the law-enforcement model, this has the advantage of reflecting the realities of police work, but tends to result in definitions that are so broad that they lack focus. A further perspective suggests that law-enforcement is only part of the police role, which is characterised more broadly by the bureaucratic and administrative responsibilities of officers. The gathering, interrogation and communication of intelligence relating to crime, disorder and antisocial behaviour has, it is argued, become the defining characteristic of police work. A final perspective is an institutional one that relates to the role of the police service in terms of the broader functions of the criminal justice system.

Each of these approaches to understanding policing is explored in greater detail in the discussion below. These are separated into different categories in an effort to illustrate different ways of considering policing. It is not suggested that anyone of them ought to be chosen at the expense of the others.

a narrow, law-enforcement approach

In an effort to cut bureaucracy and return control of the police to local communities the coalition government proposed a series of measures in a 2010 consultation document *Policing in the 21st Century: Reconnecting Police and the People*. Among proposals regarding measures to free police from the burden of red-tape, reconnect with communities and enhance democratic accountability the government established that 'the key priority for police is to cut crime'. The predominance of the law-enforcement approach to policing in government policy has featured across a number of policy and political developments, including in the elections for Police and Crime Commissioners that were first held in

November 2012, more analysis of which is contained in Chapter 4. The crime-fighting mandate of police has been axiomatic in public discussion of policing for sometime. In November 2005 the Commissioner of the Metropolitan Police delivered the annual BBC Dimbleby Lecture, and suggested that increasing social diversity, debates about moral relativism, and social fragmentation meant that policing could no longer be left to the police to decide on their own (Blair, 2005). The time had come, Sir Ian Blair rather portentously argued, for the public to decide what kind of police service that it wanted. A series of controversies had been at the forefront of popular debate and a period of considered reflection about the nature of policing and how it might be properly developed in difficult times would be appropriate.

As McLaughlin (2007a) noted, however, much of the press response to Sir Ian's bid for dialogue was characterised by two, related, reactions. First, media commentators poured scorn on the Commissioner claiming that his invitation amounted to a tacit admission that he did not know what the role of the police was. Blair was portrayed as a liberal intellectual – more concerned with political correctness than police work – who was so out of touch that he no longer even knew what the service was for. Second, the newspapers gave a simple and relatively narrow definition of what the police service is for: catching criminals. The *Daily Telegraph* (2005), for example, told Sir Ian in no uncertain terms "'What kind of police service do we want?'" The answer is obvious: one that better protects us from crime.'

Clearly political, policy and popular cultural understanding of the police are often centred around their crime-fighting role. Although the following discussion will demonstrate that policing is about much more than crime-fighting it is not surprising that the news media suggests otherwise given that it is this that features so heavily in all types of media coverage. Both fictional and factual representations of crime and policing tend to focus disproportionately on violent offending and the police response to it. Media coverage of policing is significant since many people get information about crime trends, and the response to it, indirectly through newspapers and television, and because mediated images influence debate about future directions for the police service and the 'state of the nation' more generally (Mawby, 2003a). Clearly generalising about the media coverage of the police, as though this were a coherent or univocal phenomenon, is unhelpful and it should be remembered that ideas about crime and insecurity are communicated in complex and unpredictable ways (Innes, 2004; Lee, 2007). Nonetheless, media coverage of policing often focuses upon the crime-fighting work that officers do. Television shows may give a false impression of the nature and extent of crime for reasons of narrative and drama. These considerations also influence media representations in documentary programmes and 'infotainment' shows that purport to represent the 'reality' of police work, but nonetheless give a selective and partial account. Reiner (2003: 269) noted that the police are subject to occasional negative media coverage and the exposure of police deviance has been a recurring theme. On balance, though, he argued that:

The overall picture of crime and control presented in the media, whether fiction or news, is thus highly favourable to the police image. Crime is represented as a serious threat to vulnerable individual victims, but one that the police routinely tackle successfully because of their prowess and heroism. The police accordingly appear as the seldom-failing guardians of the public in general, essential bulwarks of the social order.

Media coverage of the police, clearly, is disproportionately focused on their law-enforcement duties. As Mawby (2003b) noted, research suggests that media accounts are the authoritative narrative of policing for large sections of the public.

If these representations are important in terms of public attitudes, it seems equally likely that they have implications for those who work for the police – and for new recruits – who might find themselves working in an environment radically different from that which they had been encouraged by the media to expect. What is also important is that popular cultural representations offer a wholly unrealistic conception of policing. The crime-fighting mandate does provide one answer to the question 'What is policing?'. This might be a somewhat narrow conceptualisation of policing, but clearly apprehending offenders and preventing crime are central elements of police activity. Even this narrow perspective of police work, though, raises important questions. The range of acts that contravene the criminal law is huge and diverse. The 1996 Police Act, for example, outlaws the act of 'causing disaffection among police officers'; the Malicious Damages Act 1861 outlaws the placing of wooden obstacles on railway tracks; the Companies Act 1985 makes 'failing to keep accounting records open to inspection' a criminal offence. Box 1.2 outlines some of the circumstances defined as criminal by the 1351 Treason Act.

Box 1.2

The 1351 Treason Act

[W]hen a man doth compass or imagine the death of our Lord the King, or of our lady his Queen, or of their eldest son and heir; or if a man do violate the King's companion, or the King's eldest daughter unmarried, or the wife of the King's eldest son and heir; or if a man do levy war against our lord the King in his realm, or be adherent to the King's enemies in his realm, giving them aid and comfort in the realm, or elsewhere and thereof be provably attainted of open deed by the people of their condition … and if a man slea the chancellor, treasurer or the King's justices … assigned to hear and determine being in their places doing their offices. (www.legislation.gov.uk)

That legal prohibitions on various activities are introduced or repealed over time is one reason why a crime-centred definition of policing needs to be adopted with caution. Furthermore, the breach of certain criminal laws, including most of those examples cited above, may never feature in the work of most police officers. The 'black letter' of the criminal law provides only a very weak indication of what police officers actually do: this is partly because individual officers operate with considerable discretion but also a result of the principle of operational independence, which means that Chief Constables are able to exercise their discretion in terms of establishing which criminal activities will be prioritised. Not only does the differential enforcement of the law mean that police activity cannot simply be read from statute it also provides the conceptual space that criminological analysis seeks to fill by exploring the circumstances in which individual officers and the police service collectively enforce certain laws but not others. At various stages in this book the differential enforcement of the law is considered. The significance of officer discretion is discussed in Chapter 6 where the broader topic of police occupational subculture and its impact on police work is considered. Chapter 7 explores why hate crimes, such as racist violence, have tended to be under-policed. Chapter 11 considers the extent to which the surveillance and law-enforcement powers of the police have been expanded by CCTV and similar technologies.

Against a context of concerns about changing crime problems, reductions in public expenditure, questions about public confidence in the police, and prospects of structural reforms that might have included police services being merged or even privatised, an independent commission reviewed twenty-first century policing. In a report published in 2013, the Independent Police Complaints Commission wrestled with the role and mandate of the police, pointing out that many foundational principles remained important but needed to be updated. The Commission (IPCC, 2013: 31) identified eight key principles of policing:

1. The basic mission of the police is to improve the safety and well-being of the people by promoting measures to prevent crime, harm and disorder.

2. The police must undertake their basic mission with the approval of, and in collaboration with, the public and other agencies.

3. The police must seek to carry out their tasks in ways that contribute to social cohesion and solidarity.

4. The police must treat all those with whom they come in to contact with fairness and respect.

5. The police must be answerable to law and democratically responsive to the people they serve.

6. The police must be organised to achieve the optimal balance between effectiveness, cost-efficiency, accountability and responsiveness.

7. All police work should be informed by the best available evidence.

8. Policing is undertaken by many providers, but it remains a public good.

This definition of police work is broadly consistent with other influential statements made since modern police services were established in the nineteenth century. The relative unanimity around the role of the police service, though, cannot disguise the enormous complexities and contradictions contained within them. As principles they might be appropriate but enacting these would demonstrate that there may be contradictions between some of them, such as enforcing the law and maintaining public order, and priorities need to be established within this broad framework. Many of the tensions surrounding these eight principles are discussed throughout the rest of this book.

the centrality of 'force' to policing

Other efforts to define the police and the policing role more widely have focused upon the police monopoly in the legitimate use of force. If the police embody the state, then Max Weber's classic definition of state sovereignty as the possession of a legitimate use of force over a given territory is clearly an important feature of the police role. Bittner (1974) and Klockars (1985) have argued that it is the ability to use force against fellow citizens that is the defining characteristic of the police officer. Like definitions that focus upon law-enforcement, the emphasis on police use of force reveals important properties of police work but, similarly, are subject to important caveats that muddy the waters. First, research evidence makes it very clear that police officers tend to under-utilise their capacity to use force to resolve conflict. Although there are clearly occasions when the police use of force is properly subject to legal, political and media scrutiny – recent examples include the police response to the summer riots in London and other cities in July 2011 and the furore surrounding the shooting of Jean Charles de Menezes at Stockwell Park tube station in the aftermath of the July 2005 terrorist attacks in London – negotiation and persuasion characterise most police–public interaction. In part the doctrine of the use of minimum force has been an important component of securing police legitimacy (Reiner, 2000). Moreover, the police service finds that its monopoly status – never absolute in any case – is increasingly eroded as other agencies are afforded recourse to the use of force. Other state employees, such as customs officers and environmental health officers, also have legal powers to detain people and property. Additionally, quasi-public agencies, such as bailiffs employed by the courts, also have powers to enter property and can use force in a limited way in order to do so.

the practice of policing

Attempts to identify the role of the police reviewed thus far have been based on abstract, normative considerations of what the principles of the police ought to be. Another, more rigorous examination of what the police service does can be gleaned from various research studies that have explored the realities of routine police work and found that service-oriented work and order-maintenance – a much more nebulous concept than crime control – characterise much of what officers do. Among the first accounts of police work was Bittner's (1974) review of policing studies, including that of Reiss (1971) and Niederhoffer (1969), in the USA that led him to the view that 'when one looks at what policemen actually do, one finds that criminal law enforcement is something that most of them do with the frequency located somewhere between virtually never and very rarely' (Bittner, 1974: 22). Earlier, Banton's (1964: 2) study of the British police led him to the view that 'the police are relatively unimportant in the enforcement of law'. More time was spent performing a wide range of public service roles, Bittner suggested, that had little in common except that there was no other agency that might be expected to perform the function. Although not greatly helpful to those seeking to understand what policing actually is, Bittner's (1974: 30) observation amply illustrates the breadth of the police task: 'no human problem exists, or is imaginable, about which it could be said with finality that this certainly could not become the proper business of the police.'

The service roles performed by the police are widely noted in studies of routine police work. Much traffic policing, for example, is directed toward keeping roads clear so that vehicles keep moving and public safety is enhanced. This might involve some law-enforcement activity but, as with other areas of police work, it has been widely established that officers tend to under-enforce the law and to use other strategies – most obviously negotiation – in order to ensure public co-operation. Bayley's (1994) study of routine police work in Australia, Canada, England and Wales, Japan, and the USA suggested that patrol work accounts for most of what officers spend their time doing, and that most of this is directed – especially in urban areas – by dispatchers who in turn are responding to calls for help from the general public. Bayley (1994: 30) estimated that no more than seven to ten per cent of such calls relate to crime, and even that small proportion includes much that is of a non-serious nature. Against this background, much routine policing is about patrol work, such that officers might be understood as 'tour guides in the museum of human frailty' whose role is to

> 'sort out' situations by listening patiently to endless stories about fancied slights, old grievances, new insults, mismatched expectations, infidelity, dishonesty and abuse. They hear all about the petty, mundane, tedious, hapless, sordid details of individual lives. Patient listening and gentle counselling are undoubtedly what patrol officers do most of the time.
>
> (Bayley, 1994: 31–2)

While it might be that officers spend much of their time performing roles that appear to have little or nothing to do with crime-fighting, the distinction between law-enforcement and crime-control models of policing is not so clear-cut as first it might appear. Bittner (1974) presented an imaginary traffic police officer to illustrate the complex priorities that might make the general service role a priority over crime control in some circumstances, as the extract in Box 1.3 demonstrates. Popular representations of police work might present a narrow range of crime-fighting activity as typical of policing but the apparently peripheral service work might have broader implications for community relations and law-enforcement. A BBC documentary that explored the contemporary nature of British policing was told, by the director of the Police Foundation, of an officer who responded to an elderly lady who requested assistance in opening a tin of cat food (BBC, 2006a). Clearly this illustration is only one remove from the cliché of emergency services rescuing cats from trees, and has as little to do with crime control as can be imagined. Nonetheless, the Foundation's director pointed to the value of such a service as it provides assurance to the person who receives it, and helps to shore up the legitimacy of the service. It also provides further illustration of the challenge of arriving at a clear and concise definition of the police function.

Box 1.3

The Competing Priorities Facing Bittner's Traffic Cop

One of the most common experiences of urban life is the sight of a patrolman directing traffic at a busy street intersection. This service is quite expensive and the assignment is generally disliked among policemen. Nevertheless it is provided on a regular basis … Despite its seriousness and presumed necessity, despite the fact that assignments are planned ahead and specifically funded, no assignment to a traffic control post is ever presumed to be absolutely fixed … no matter how important the post might be, it is always possible for something else to come up than can distract the patrolman's attention and cause him to suspend attending to the assigned task … It is virtually certain that any normally competent patrolman would abandon the traffic post to which he was assigned without hesitation and without regard for the state of the traffic he was supposed to monitor, if it came to his attention that a crime was being committed somewhere at a distance not too far for him to reach in time either to arrest the crime in its course, or to arrest its perpetrator … But if the crime that came to the attention of the officer had been something like a conspiracy by a board of directors of a commercial concern to issue stock with the intention of defrauding investors, or a landlord criminally extorting payments from a tenant, or a used-car dealer culpably turning back an odometer on an automobile he was preparing for sale, the patrolman would scarcely lift his gaze, let alone move into action. The real reason why the patrolman moved out was not the fact that what was taking place was a crime in general terms, but because the particular crime was a member of a class of problems *the treatment of which will not abide*. In fact, the patrolman who unhesitatingly left his post to pursue an assailant would have left his post with just as little hesitation as to pull a drowning person out of the water, to prevent someone from jumping off the roof of a building, to protect a severely disoriented person from harm, to save people in a burning structure, to disperse a crowd hampering the rescue mission of an ambulance, to take steps to prevent a possible disaster that might result from broken gas lines or water mains, and so on almost endlessly, and entirely without regard to the substantive nature of the problem, as long as it could be said that it involved *something-that-ought-not-to-be-happening-and-about-which-someone-had-better-do-something-now!*

(Bittner, 1974, emphasis in original)

There has been considerable oscillation between the twin polices of crime control and service provision in political terms during the last few decades. Some Chief Constables have strongly advocated a community policing model predicated upon the co-provision of services with other agencies and with the public more generally (Alderson, 1984) and the development of the police 'Statement of Common Purposes and Values' placed a clear emphasis on the service role (Reiner, 2000: 110–1). Recent reductions in expenditure on policing have led to attempts to distinguish between 'frontline', 'mid-office' and 'back-office' police functions, and reviews of police pay and conditions have also led to a refocus on the proper balance between various roles that offices perform (HMIC, 2011a, 2011b; Winsor, 2011). The tension between service provision and crime-fighting – two possible answers to the question 'what is policing?' – turns out to be misplaced if policing is understood in terms of order maintenance; a strategic role that encompasses all of the activities alluded to in the discussion so far. Conceptualising police work in terms of broader processes of social regulation not only helps understand the sheer breadth of activities that the public police actually carry out, it also allows for the complementary contributions made to this process by other agencies.

police as bureaucrats

If policing is to be understood on the basis of the various tasks and functions that officers perform, then a fundamental reassessment of the role is required in the light of the amount of administration that officers do. Although studies of police work often bear out that officers engage in risky pursuits of offenders and confront danger, these are exceptional events for most officers, although the potential for such encounters might mean that they shape officer perceptions of people and situations (Reiner, 2000). The routines of police work are characterised by administrative and procedural work which might not be understood as 'real' policing by police subculture or media representation, but is centrally important in terms of the proportion of time devoted to it. The administrative burden on police officers is often cited as a priority to be tackled by reform programmes and innovative technological solutions that promise to ease the load – some of these are discussed in Chapter 11. While record-keeping and form-filling are often associated with attempts to micro-manage officer behaviour and hold their managers to account in terms of targets and performance management regimes, the extent of police administration has partly been determined by demands to ensure that powers are discharged fairly, and that legal procedures, for example, relating to the continuity of evidence, are being adhered to. The background to some of these requirements is outlined in Chapter 3, in which police powers are discussed, and in Chapter 7, where considerations relating to diversity issues are reviewed. Efforts to reduce the administrative burden on police officers have sometimes involved civilianisation of roles previously fulfilled by officers, and the employment of Police Community Support Officers (PCSOs) who can perform ancillary functions and allow police to attend to 'frontline' policing tasks. The scope and extent of the pluralisation of policing is discussed in Chapter 10.

For whatever reason, though, it is clear that a quantitative answer to the question 'what is policing?' might lead to the conclusion that it is an administrative role. Certainly, Ericson and Haggerty's (1997) study of police work in Canada noted the considerable bureaucratic responsibility that officers faced – they identified, for example, that officers attending the scene of a road traffic accident were required to complete a dozen different forms. The extent of this aspect of police work led Ericson and Haggerty (1997) to argue that police officers had become 'knowledge workers' whose primary role was to communicate risk within the police service, the criminal justice system and to a host of other agencies. Similarly, a Home Office funded study of policing in Britain also found that officers were required to spend much of their time on activities that kept them away from patrol work (PA Consulting Group, 2001). The research, based on analysis of diaries completed by officers, concluded that 43 per cent of officer time was spent inside police stations, most of which was either devoted to the custody process, which took an average of 3.5 hours per prisoner, or was spent completing paperwork. Box 1.4 gives an overview of some of the bureaucratic requirements on officers. The Home Office (2010b) has sought to reduce police administration through abolition of many of the targets and performance management indicators that were previously applied to policing and commitments to protect 'frontline' policing during a period of financial austerity have downgraded 'backroom' activities. The extent to which resources devoted to apparently bureaucratic tasks are essential to underpin policing practice that is based on scientific evidence, and professional expertise is considered at various points throughout this book.

Box 1.4

Routine Police Work?

But what accounts for the time operational officers spend in the police station? The two main culprits are the time taken to process prisoners and prepare prosecutions, and the other paperwork which the police must produce. Arresting someone – no matter whether they are a petty criminal or a serious offender – keeps officers off the beat for an average of 3.5 hours – often for far longer. At busy times there are bottlenecks in custody and frequent delays in carrying out finger-printing, photographing and criminal record checks. Delays are generally the same for a simple shop-lift as for a much more serious matter. Where a solicitor, appropriate adult or interpreter is required, this can trigger a further wait of on average an hour. If CCTV or an identity parade is involved further substantial delays can ensue.

Other paperwork includes crime reports, intelligence reports, forms to log recovered property, missing person details, information required for special force initiatives as well as paperwork connected with the shift administration and the officer in question. Often one event (e.g. a crime) can trigger the recording of the same information on multiple separate records. Where forms are available electronically, little officer time is actually saved because the IT system applications are mostly antiquated and do not talk to each other.

(PA Consultancy, 2001: vi)

an institutional perspective

The distinction between policing and the police has often been overlooked in academic analysis of policing. Although that is changing, as discussion in Chapter 10 indicates, it is less clear that media or political debate about policing has broadened. A narrow response to the question 'what is policing?' retains an institutional approach and regards policing as a key agency within the broader criminal justice system. As will be demonstrated throughout this book, the police service might be the 'state in uniform', the pre-eminent visible embodiment of sovereignty and the rule of law, but it is not the only agency influencing and regulating social conflict and cohesion

For much analysis of the performance, equity and efficiency of the criminal justice system concern about policing begins and ends with the actions of the public police, which, while only a small component within the complex justice system, plays a crucial role as a 'gateway agency' to the rest of the system. Even though a recurring theme of this chapter and this book is that policing is a process continued beyond the public police, it is clear that little done by other agencies feeds into the criminal justice system without an input from the police service. For this reason alone it might be important to remember that even though 'policing' and 'the police' are no longer synonymous, it continues to be the case that the public institution of the police occupies most attention in wider debates about law-enforcement, order maintenance and the almost boundless rank of tasks associated with policing.

CONCLUSION

The chapter has addressed the question 'What is policing?' in terms of the underlying principles of the police service and the wide range of roles performed by officers. While policing as a social function is broader than this, the initial focus has been on the public institution of the police service. It was shown that the media and other popular representations that suggest that policing is primarily about crime-fighting are seriously misleading, not least because they underplay the broader order maintenance and service work that officers do. The following chapter considers the history of the police, and the ways in which it has developed. Just as this chapter emphasises that policing is about much more than the law-enforcement activities of the public police service, so too the discussion in Chapter 2 suggests that policing needs to be understood in broader terms.

chapter summary

- The police have become a cultural symbol and an important element of narratives of national identity.

- Police and policing are distinct concepts. Policing relates to broad processes of social regulation underpinning everyday life, as performed by a wide range of agencies. Historically, 'policing' has been understood in these broad terms and not associated with the activities of a particular organisation.

- A narrower definition, equating policing to the activities of the institution of the police, might lack breadth but it is clearer and more concise perspective.

- Often, policing is understood in terms of law-enforcement, certainly this has been a common perspective in media coverage. Fictional and documentary images of police work tend to centre on crime-fighting, portraying the police as the 'thin blue line' between social order and chaos.

- The law-enforcement perspective is flawed since police officers use considerable discretion when applying the law, and many laws are rarely enforced by most officers. Moreover, police services perform a wide range of activities that do not relate to law-enforcement.

- Other definitions focus upon the police monopoly use of force. Traditionally state sovereignty has been understood in these terms and considering the police as the 'state in uniform' leads to this definition being transferred to the police service. In reality force tends to be under-used and negotiation characterises police encounters with the public, although the potential for coercive force might shape these interactions.

- Fulfilling police public-service roles might enhance legitimacy, secure public confidence, and so contribute to crime control and law-enforcement.

- Police officers are required to perform a wide variety of administrative tasks, to the extent that some have characterised policing as a form of 'knowledge work'. Moves to civilianise police duties and develop technological methods to reduce the bureaucratic burden have been widely pursued.

- Policing can also be understood in institutional terms as a key element of the criminal justice system. Although much of the order-maintenance and service-oriented functions of the police service do not contribute to the criminal justice system more widely, discussion of the efficacy and efficiency of the system more generally tends to relate to the police service, the 'gateway' agency, in some respect.

self-check questions (with answers at the back of the book)

1. How can narrow and broader definitions of policing be characterised?

2. What agencies, apart from the police service, play a role in regulating social life?

3. Why did Mawby (2003a) argue that media images of policing are important?

4. Who provided a 'classic' definition of state sovereignty?

5. Why might the 'use of force' offer only a limited understanding of the police function?

6. In what, very broad, terms did Bittner (1974) define the police task?

7. What proportion of public calls to the police did Bayley (1994) find were related to crime?

8. How did Ericson and Haggerty (1997) characterise police officers?

9. What two factors explain, according to research published in 2001, the significant amount of time officers spend within the police station?

10. What relation does the police service have to the criminal justice system more generally?

study questions

1. What are the difficulties in distinguishing between a narrow and a broad definition of policing?

2. To what extent is the use of force a good basis for defining policing?

3. What is policing?

annotated further reading

Bittner's (1974) article 'Florence Nightingale in Pursuit of Willy Sutton ...' is an early account of the complexities and contradictions inherent in the police function that provides a compelling argument against a narrow 'law-enforcement' definition of the role of the police.

The first chapter of Waddington's (1999) *Policing Citizens* contains a useful discussion of the question that has framed this chapter: 'What is policing?' Waddington explores the force-service dichotomy and similarities and specificities of police work across the world.

Chapters 3 and 4 of McLaughlin's (2007) *The New Policing* provide an excellent account of the development of 'police studies', focusing on traditional perspectives (including that of Bittner) that emerged in the USA in the 1960s and somewhat latter in the UK, and 'new perspectives' that consider the changing terrain of policing in post-modern, post-industrial global society.

annotated listings of links to relevant websites

A good starting point for general information on the roles, responsibilities and development of the police in Scotland is available from the homepage of Police Scotland, in particular the strategy *Policing 2026*, www.scotland.police.uk/about-us/policing-2026/. Similar information relating to England and Wales can be found at the Home Office website, www.homeoffice.gov.uk/police/, and at the Northern Ireland Policing Board website, www. nipolicingboard.org.uk/.

The full text of Sir Ian Blair's Dimbleby lecture *What Kind of Police Service do we Want?* can be found at http://news.bbc.co.uk/2/hi/uk_news/4443386.stm.

The Independent Police Complaints Commission reviewed a broad range of aspects of contemporary policing, including the mandate and tasks of police in their historical context. The Commission report is available at www.lse.ac.uk/socialPolicy/Researchcentresandgroups/mannheim/pdf/PolicingforabetterBritain.pdf.

annotated links to journal articles

Brodeur's article identified an important distinction between 'high' and 'low' policing: the former being that associated with the development and protection of nation states and the latter with law-enforcement, crime investigation and public safety:

Brodeur, J.P. (1983) 'High and Low Policing: Remarks about the Policing of Political Activities', *Social Problems*, 3: 507–520.

Loader outlined the social, political and cultural significance of policing and emphasised the importance of understanding the broader dimensions of police work:

Loader, I. (1997) 'Policing and the Social: Questions of Symbolic Power', *British Journal of Sociology*, 48 (1): 1–18.

In an article that considers the impact of financial austerity on British policing, Millie reviewed the distinction between narrow and broad approaches to the police mandate and argued that there might be advantages to a relatively narrow definition:

Millie, A. (2013) 'The Policing Task and the Expansion (and Contraction) of British Policing', *Criminology and Criminal Justice*, 13: 143–60.

Zedner considered claims that policing is entering a new era in the context of the historical development of the service, and suggested that emerging patterns have longer precedents than is often recognised:

Zedner, L. (2006) 'Policing Before and After the Police – The Historical Antecedents of Contemporary Crime Control', *British Journal of Criminology*, 46: 78–96.

2

HISTORICAL ORIGINS AND DEVELOPMENT OF THE POLICE IN ENGLAND AND WALES

CONTENTS

LEARNING OBJECTIVES

While Chapter 1 sought to explain policing in terms of the various roles and functions of the service and the principles, the focus of this chapter is to explore the historical development of the police service in England and Wales up to the end of the nineteenth century. Various perspectives that account for these trends are explored in the second part of the chapter. One such, the 'conservative' perspective, suggests that the establishment of the police service in London in 1829 was an innovative – but natural and logical – response to changing social, economic and political circumstances. Alternatively, 'revisionist' accounts explain the establishment of the police in terms of containing threats of political violence and maintaining order among the industrial working class more generally. Although they reach contrasting conclusions, both accounts indicate that the history of the police service needs to be understood against the wider background of the period: just as contemporary police reforms discussed elsewhere in the book are often a reflection of more fundamental social change. The objectives of the chapter are to:

* examine the foundation and development of the police service in Britain
* outline the changing social, political and economic context that shaped the establishment of the police service
* explore interpretations of these processes.

KEY TERMS

attitudes to order; establishment and development of police services; historical interpretation; military; police and policing; political unrest; public involvement in policing; underlying principles and urban crime

INTRODUCTION

Various countries might claim to have established the first police service, and these competing claims partly reflect the breadth of the functions that might be defined as 'policing'. As was noted in Chapter 1, the word 'policing' developed in relation to general patterns of social regulation, which suggests that is has been continued in one form or another since there have been states or governments. Given the extent of policing history it might be wondered why so much discussion of the historical development of policing relates to the British experience. Clearly policing traditions in other countries continue to be researched and discussed, and comparative accounts note national specificities that reinforce the danger of an ethnocentric perspective that views everything from a limited and partial British vantage point (Mawby, 1999). That the focus of the following discussion is almost exclusively on the development of the police of England and Wales reflects the importance of these arrangements in global terms, as British colonialism exported policing systems – alongside the common law tradition to which it is related – to many countries. This did not mean that a single vision – in terms of principle or practice – of policing prevailed across the British empire, or that the Metropolitan Police model outlined below was uprooted and transplanted around the imperial system. Clearly, as in other matters, colonial administrators were often able to adapt the institutional arrangements available to them to suit the particular circumstances that they faced. Nonetheless, the principles of policing that evolved in nineteenth-century Britain have provided a framework that has spread and endured in many countries. David Bayley (1985, cited in Mawby 2003b) argued that modern policing can be distinguished from earlier forms as it is characterised by specialisation, professionalism and publicness, organising principles central to the creation of the Metropolitan Police.

A BRIEF HISTORY OF THE POLICE IN ENGLAND AND WALES

While certain dates, events and characters tend to feature in most histories of the police in England and Wales, there is little consensus on how to explain the development of the professional service in the nineteenth century. Facts might be sacred but it is not self-evident which of them are important, relevant, or can be safely disregarded. It is, for example, a fact that the Metropolitan Police (dubbed the 'new police') was established in 1829 following legislation that was steered through parliament by the Home Secretary, Sir Robert Peel. It is unlikely that there is a history of British policing that does not mention this. There is far less agreement, however, about how significant these facts are in terms of understanding why policing emerged in the ways that it did. Providing an historical overview of the major milestones that have shaped the police in England and Wales while doing justice to the historical controversies about structure and agency, the dangers of teleology, and the importance of locating these developments in their broader context is the challenge addressed in the discussion that follows.

As Emsley (1996: 4) has noted, until relatively recently historical accounts of the development of the British police have only been found in the memoirs of former Chief Constables, senior politicians and civil servants. These accounts reinforced the established perspective that modern policing systems developed in London in the

early decades of the nineteenth century and then, as the wisdom of these arrangements came to be more widely recognised, were slowly expanded across the rest
of the country. Orthodox accounts, such as those by Lee (1901) and Reith (1948),
regard the establishment of the Metropolitan Police in 1829 as an important stage
in the gradual evolution of policing that could be traced back to the Anglo-Saxon
era during which a peaceable settled community was directly responsible for its own
policing. Lee (1901: ix) introduced his account of the history of the English police in
terms that exemplify what Reiner (2000: 15) described as the 'palpably conservative'
tone of many early histories:

> **Our English police system ... rests on foundations designed with the full approval of the people ... and has been slowly moulded by the careful hand of experience, developing as a rule along the line of least resistance, now in advance of the general intelligence of the country, now lagging far behind, but always in the long run adjusting itself to the popular temper.**

The consensual view places great emphasis on a strong historical theme of community
participation that runs, it is claimed, through English police history from the Anglo-
Saxon era to the present. Although many historical accounts tend to regard the
establishment of the Metropolitan Police in 1829 as a pivotal point, it is clear that
there are many features that have endured from earlier periods. Mawby (1999: 30)
noted that policing in England between the 1740s and 1850s were characterised by
self-policing, community engagement in street patrols, and that the private sector provided many policing services: all features of twenty-first century police reform. The
grassroots engagement of the public in police activity has been central to much of
the discourse and practice of policing in Britain. By the end of the first millennium the
population was organised into groups of ten households, known as 'tythings', which
were themselves grouped together into larger 'hundreds' and supervised by a
'hundredman' who was accountable to the 'shire reeve', or sherrif. When a crime
occurred it was the direct duty of all to pursue and apprehend the offender and to
present him to the authorities. The subsequent organisation of policing and direct
involvement of local people in its operation reflects the early traditions established by
the Statute of Winchester in 1285. Ascoli (1979: 16) argued that the Statute was 'one
of the most important, and certainly one of the most durable, of all constitutional
measures'. Some of the key provisions of the Statute are outlined in Box 2.1; notable
among them are the direct involvement of all people in the maintenance of law and
order and also that the role of the unpaid part-time constable was to bring offenders
before the courts, not to dispense justice summarily. The principle that those accused
of offending should be tried by their peers – as encoded in Magna Carta – is one on
which the jury system continues to rely.

Box 2.1

The Statute of Winchester, 1285

- Purpose was 'to abate the power of felons'
- duty of everyone to maintain the King's Peace, and it was open to any citizen to arrest an offender
- the unpaid, part-time constable had a special duty assisted by the watchman
- hue and cry was to be raised to apprehend offenders
- penalties were imposed against those who did not comply with the compulsory pursuit of criminals
- everyone was required to keep arms for preserving peace and apprehending criminals
- town gates were closed between sunset and sunrise and strangers not allowed to enter
- the constable had a duty to present the offender at the court leet.

(Derived from Ascoli, 1979 and Critchley, 1978)

The term 'constable' seems to have first been used during the Norman period, but was central to the provisions of the Statute of Winchester, and, again, it is clear that the principles that underpinned the office continue to resonate. Unlike their modern counterparts, though, constables in the thirteenth century were unpaid, and expected to carry out their duties in addition to other paid employment. However, the unpaid status of the constable reflected a continuing principle, which is that the police officer ought to represent the 'citizen in uniform'. This principle is tested by contemporary debates about police professionalism and proposals for officers to have specialist high-level qualifications. These requirements are in tension with the common law principle that a constable 'is only a person who is paid to perform as a matter of duty acts which if he were so minded he might have done voluntarily' (Stephens, 1964, cited in Ascoli, 1979: 18). The longevity of the provisions of the Statue have been widely noted in traditional police histories; Critchley (1978: 7), for example, noted that it 'was the only general public measure of any consequence enacted to regulate the policing of the country between the Norman Conquest and the Metropolitan Police Act, 1829, so that for nearly 600 years it laid down the basic principles.'

urban lawlessness

It is when it comes to explaining the transition from these 'pre-modern' policing arrangements to the establishment of the Metropolitan Police in 1829 that competing theoretical perspectives emerge. Traditional accounts suggest, implicitly or otherwise, that the process by which a professional institution came to be invested with responsibility for law-enforcement and order maintenance was a rational response to changing social circumstances. The twin processes of industrialisation and urbanisation, it is held, accelerated the crime problem while at the same time rendered prevailing provisions ever less effective. Certainly those directly responsible for establishing the 'new police' in 1829 couched their arguments in terms of the need to stem the rising tide of street crime. Home Secretary Peel argued in parliament that the Metropolitan Police ought to be established because of crime levels were accelerating even faster than the urban population was growing (Bailey, 1981: 13; Emsley, 1996: 25). Not only did the growth of urban areas foster problems such as public drunkenness, street disorder, prostitution and the like, it also eroded the informal social controls that had existed in pre-industrial society (Hay, 1975). There had been a number of attempts to modernise policing arrangements from the mid-eighteenth century onwards, and often these were advocated in terms of the need to develop new arrangements to meet the particular challenges of new times. Sir John Fielding oversaw the work of the Bow Street Runners from the 1740s onwards and was a committed advocate of reform of the policing system, although not along the lines eventually followed (Emsley, 1996: 248). He associated the crime problems of the period with illegal drinking establishments, and painted a picture familiar to those who have followed more recent debates about 'binge drinking':

> **At the ale-house the idle meet to game and quarrel; here the gamblers form their strategms; here the pick-pockets hide themselves till dusk, and gangs of thieves form their plots and routs; here conspirators contrive their hellish devices; and here the combinations of journeymen are made to execute their silly schemes.**
>
> **(Sharpe, 1984: 104)**

Reith (1948) also noted the role that alcohol played in rising street crime and disorder and noted that the policing authorities of the time were implicated in this as many deputy constables were also retailers of cheap gin. Reith also suggested that 'the poverty and destitution of many of the slum-warren and cellar dwellers was such that they were compelled to live by theft and other forms of crime' (1948: 6).

political unrest and the limits of the military

Not only was crime growing as a general social problem but political unrest was also posing renewed challenges to the authorities. The 'hunger riots' of the mid-eighteenth century and the political unrest that occasionally accompanied campaigns for democratic reform in the nineteenth century both demonstrated that the military were unable to secure public order in ways that were both effective and publicly acceptable.

The limitations of the military's capacity to maintain order were brought into sharp focus at the Chartist rally held at St Peter's Field in Manchester in 1819. Thousands of people gathered to hear Henry Hunt press the demands for universal suffrage, annual Parliaments and free elections in what has been described as the 'most numerous meeting that ever took place in Great Britain' (Marlow, 1971). As the authorities sought to arrest Hunt and other leading figures appearing at the rally the crowd panicked and many were trampled underfoot by the yeomanry who, under the guidance of local magistrates, were responsible for upholding order.

The actions of the military, which resulted in the deaths of 15 people and injury to hundreds, were quickly condemned in the local and the national press, who quickly coined the phrase 'Peterloo Massacre'. While public outrage at such events, and others such as the Gordon Riots of 1780, highlighted the ineffectiveness of the military when it came to the maintenance of law and order in such circumstances it would be simplistic to suggest that the disproportionality of the response to these challenges that was the main spur for seeking other means by which crowd control could be exercised. Emsley (1996: 60) pointed out that one reason why the loss of life and injuries inflicted at Peterloo caused such outcry was because they were so rare, and that those responsible for deploying the army were well aware of the dangers of over-reaction and the public vilification that might ensue. The continued use of the military also became untenable for practical as well as political reasons since their physical isolation in barracks away from urban areas meant that they could not be quickly mobilised in response to disorder (Reith, 1948). Furthermore, the use of the police service as a legitimate and effective alternative to the deployment of troops against 'the mob' was not wholly successful as concerns about the policing of public disorder continued through the nineteenth and into the twentieth century. Fielding (2005) noted that concerns about the inability of the military to respond to the Gordon Riots in the 1780s recurred a century later in respect to the policing of political protests in Trafalgar Square, most notably the 'Bloody Sunday' riots in November 1887.

the 'demand for order'

Whether in terms of general urban lawlessness or emerging challenges of political and industrial disorders, the above perspectives suggest that policing developed in response to changing social and political conditions. Another perspective suggests that the development of policing reflected wider demands for a more regulated and orderly society. Thompson (1968) argued that disorder was often regarded as a relatively legitimate means by which political and economic grievances could be advanced in pre-democratic and pre-industrial British society, but that this discourse shifted as society became urbanised and industrialised. Similarly, Silver (1967) demonstrated that perceptions of crime and lawlessness chimed with more fundamental insecurities about threats to social order in more general terms, often relating to the moral depravity of immigrants and the 'dangerous classes'.

The breadth of the activities ascribed to the mid-nineteenth century police reflected their role as 'domestic missionaries', charged with tackling behaviour regarded as an affront to the moral and ethical sensibilities of the middle classes. The police service, authors such as Storch (1976, see Box 2.2) argued, developed in tandem with efforts at social reform intended to improve the standing of the urban masses, such as the Temperance Movement that sought to tackle alcoholism. Similarly, Dunning et al. (1987) noted the important role of the police service in the regulation of the leisure pursuits of working-class communities in the early years of the twentieth century, through, for example, suppressing informal street gambling.

Box 2.2

The Policeman as Domestic Missionary

[T]he initiatives of the police authorities in these areas of course cannot be viewed apart from the attitudes, prejudices, and momentary reformist enthusiasms of the municipalities, magistrates, and local elites who employed them. This was especially the case outside of London where the police were much less independent of local control than in the metropolis. For this reason police actions must be considered as forming the cutting edge of a wider and larger effort in northern industrial towns to impose new standards of urban discipline. It was the boroughs, after all who charged the police with the monitoring and suppression of popular activities and recreations considered conductive to immorality, disorder, or crime; it was the police who had to discharge that mandate as best they could or at least convince those to who they were responsible that they were doing so … In February 1836, the Leeds council requested the mayor to direct the police to give information 'as shall lead to the conviction of all … persons as shall continue to prophane the Lord's day', to pay particular attention to drinking places on Saturday nights, to strictly enforce proper closing times, and to 'observe those who resort to the public house or use sports in time of divine service'.'

Storch (1976: 483)

---

establishing the Metropolitan Police

It was against this background of changing threats of crime and disorder that the Metropolitan Police was established in 1829. By June 1830 the Metropolitan Police comprised two Commissioners, 17 Superintendents – one for each division – 68 Inspectors, 323 Sergeants and 2,906 Constables (Lee, 1901: 236). The legislation that initiated the force left the detail of these arrangements to the first Commissioners, Charles Rowan and Richard Mayne, who devised the recruitment and training methods, the style of the uniform, pay and conditions, and other provisions. Many of the decisions made by Rowan and Mayne appear to have been intended to overcome the widespread opposition to the establishment of the Metropolitan Police. The initial instructions given to police officers by the Commissioners stressed the importance of civility and caution when it came to interaction with the public. While this emphasis seems to have been designed to assuage public opinion it was also understood to bring practical benefits, since a 'quiet and determined manner' would cause an officer to 'excite the well-disposed of the bystanders to assist him, if he requires them' (Critchely, 1978: 53).

In addition to shaping officers' demeanour in an effort to overcome suspicion of and hostility to the new police, other practical details were attended to. The symbolic value of the police uniform in signalling the presence of the police on the streets, for example, was recognised by the Commissioners, who were also mindful that suspicion of officers acting as undercover agents would be overcome by visible uniforms (Reynolds, 1988: 151). In practice the wearing of uniform by most officers did not preclude surveillance activity, which was conducted against Chartists and particularly developed by the establishment of the Special Branch in the wake of Fenian bombing campaigns in the 1860s and 1880s (Emsley, 2003: 75). For general public relations, though, it was considered important that uniforms were blue in colour and so distinct from the red tunics used by the military. The desire to avoid the trappings of militarism also partly explains the relatively unarmed nature of the new police, who were equipped only with wooden truncheons, although cutlasses and pistols were available for emergencies (Emsley, 1996: 26). In other respects, though, perceived benefits of militarism were incorporated into the new policing arrangements, as the centrality of drill in police training and the billeting of officers in section houses to help maintain discipline testify (Reith, 1948: 32). In operational terms the focus of the new police was firmly on establishing a symbolic presence on the streets, reflecting a fundamental belief in the preventative value of patrol work. That two-thirds of officers were deployed on night-time patrols suggests that the Metropolitan Police were continuing the long-established role of watch and ward. Reith's (1948: 32) description of the specifications intended to guide officers on patrol suggests that this long-established role was subject to bureaucratic regulation under the new policing arrangements:

The men were not permitted to sit down or to lean against anything or to have any kind of rest. They were expected to patrol their beats, steadily and constantly, for nine consecutive hours, at the steady rate of two and a half miles per hour.

Public opposition to the new policing arrangements did not abate once the Metropolitan Police force had been established. Some local authorities were concerned that the new police were more expensive and less effective than previous arrangements and complained that the local watch committees had been deprived of their role in the governance of the police, a function that had been taken over by the Home Office, and yet were required to continue funding the new institution and that the cost of doing so had greatly increased (Emsley, 1996; Palmer, 1988; Reynolds, 1998). Early criticism of the new police also related to the inability of the Metropolitan Police to meet public demands for visible patrols, which suggests that the perceived lack of 'bobbies on the beat' has been a concern as long as there have been bobbies. In the early 1830s a parish official from Southwark reported to the Home Secretary that local inhabitants were dissatisfied with the new arrangements as they never saw an officer on patrol, and in 1830 a public meeting in Shoreditch resolved

> [t]hat an experience of nine months under the system of the New Police has fully proved that its operations are inimical to the interests of the parish containing up to 60,000 inhabitants for so far from being better protected one half of the parish is never visited by the New Police.
>
> (Reynolds, 1998: 158)

The apparently poor quality of police recruits might have meant that their presence on the streets did little to improve public perceptions. Bailey (1981: 48) argued that an early feature of the force was 'inefficiency, indiscipline (notably drunkenness) and a massive turnover of constables' that was so great that within four years of the establishment of the Metropolitan Police only one-sixth of the 3,000 original recruits were still in post (Critchley, 1978: 54; Reiner, 2000: 20). Opposition is also evident from the list of negative epithets used to describe the new police – Reiner (2000: 48) lists vivid terms such as 'Crushers', 'Peel's Bloody Gang', 'Blue Locusts', 'Jenny Darbies' and 'Raw Lobsters' – and from the real threat of physical violence that officers routinely faced. Ascoli (1979: 95) argued that officers faced a 'baptism of fire' and that physical assault was 'commonplace', which suggests that officers were not over-reacting when they adopted the habit of carrying their wooden rattles in the chest pocket of their uniforms in order to protect the heart in the event of being stabbed (Reith, 1948: 41). Such makeshift forms of protection were not enough to prevent the first murder of a police officer, as PC Long was fatally stabbed in August 1830 (Ascoli, 1979: 95). In 1833 a police charge on a protest meeting at Cold Bath Fields in Clerkenwell, London, organised by the National Political Union, led to disorders in which 'the police were stoned, baton charges ensued, and three policemen were stabbed, one of whom was killed outright' (Critchley, 1978: 55). It is a mark of the public mood about the actions of the new police that the subsequent coroner's inquest into PC Culley's death returned a verdict of justifiable homicide, although this was subsequently overturned following an appeal by the government.

Public concern about the Metropolitan Police emanated, Reith (1948: 45) argued, from wide swathes of society. While it might be easily imagined that criminals were against more organised policing, the range of groups Reith found to be opposed to the new police is so broad that it might be wondered if there were any sections of society not against the new arrangements. For different reasons Reith suggested that hostility was shared among the labouring classes, artisans and small shopkeepers, affluent shop-keepers, merchants and industrialists, titled, aristocratic landowners and that even King George IV made public comments against the Metropolitan Police.

Given this breadth and depth it is remarkable how quickly public opposition to the new police appears to have subsided. As Reiner (2000) noted, orthodox accounts of police history suggest that the deaths of officers such as Long and Culley helped to turn public opinion in favour of the police. Critchley (1978: 55–6) certainly took the view that securing public consent could be attributed to

the way in which 3,000 unarmed policemen, cautiously feeling their way against a hostile public, brought peace and security to London, in place of the turmoil and lawlessness of centuries.

Although, as Reiner (2000: 29) noted, Storch (1975), Cohen (1979) and Brogden (1982) have argued that opposition to the police has continued among many sections of society and that anti-police riots have been a recurrent feature of police history, it does seem that the ferocity of anti-police feeling decreased during the 1830s. Contemporary research findings suggest that support for the police is closely aligned to perceptions that they operate in a procedurally just way (Hough et al., 2013). On that basis, it seems likely that growing familiarity with the new police role, and improvements in how officers discharged their duties, might have enhanced support among many sections of the population Palmer (1988: 313) suggested that 'the unthinkable was slowly becoming the acceptable' by the mid-1830s, which might have been due in part to a decrease in violent protest as political reform progressed during this period. No doubt the government's agreement, in 1833, to contribute to the financing of the police, which effectively reduced the local police rates, helped overcome the opposition from parish authorities (Palmer, 1988: 313). In addition, it seems that the police came to be regarded as efficient in terms of dealing with the problem of crime. Reith (1948: 53) suggested that the Metropolitan Police were credited with decreasing burglary and street disorder and that this success led to demands from adjacent areas that the new policing arrangements be extended to them. Those arguing for new policing to be developed outside of the capital often suggested that the success of the Metropolitan Police had led to criminal activity being displaced into areas not previously troubled by significant problems.

expansion and consolidation

The process by which police forces came to be established across the country as a whole began as a matter of enablement whereby county and borough authorities were given the opportunity to establish police forces should they so wish to do. While the Municipal Corporations Act 1835 required that Watch Committees be established, their remit was to oversee police organisations deemed suitable to local requirements, which sometimes meant that little changed in terms of the routine arrangements of night-watchmen and other officials (Emsley, 2003: 70; Wall, 1998: 27). Further legislation extended this opportunity to county authorities in 1839 and 1840, but control over Chief Constables in rural areas remained in the hands of local magistrates, rather than elected Watch Committees, and in that context chief officers enjoyed greater autonomy and a higher social status than their counterparts in urban areas (Wall, 1998). Although many accounts of the historical development of the police in mid-nineteenth century Britain tend to present an unfolding process whereby the metropolitan model was rolled out across the country, at the same time that constabularies were being established steps were also taken in the opposite direction that sought to improve the efficiency of 'pre-modern' policing arrangements (Wall, 1998: 25). That established policing arrangements existed in conjunction with the new police for some time demonstrates that different local authorities embraced the new arrangements more eagerly than others (Bailey, 1981: 12; Reynolds, 1988: 4). Critchley (1978: 90) noted the patchwork of arrangements in the following terms:

> **Outside London two different systems of policing existed for some years side by side. In some rural areas, as in a few large boroughs, the new professional police were well entrenched, but tens of thousands of acres of rural England continued to rely on the old system of parish constables, augmented here and there by a paid watchman or two, employed under the Lighting and Watching Act, or local improvement powers.**

It was not until the 1850s that arrangements were put in place that established a uniform policing system across the England and Wales. The County and Borough Police Act 1856 required that each county establish a police force under the direction of the magistracy. The Act also provided central funding for one-quarter of the cost of pay and clothing providing that Her Majesty's Inspectorate of Constabulary (HMIC) were satisfied that the force was being run efficiently. To this end the inspectors were required to report annually to Parliament (Emsley, 2003: 71). Bailey (1981: 15) suggested that HMIC faced an 'uphill struggle' in their early efforts to promote consistency in the practices of the 200 or so forces that existed after the 1856 legislation but that the system of inspection helped to secure the consent of the middle classes by imposing a raft of service roles on the police, including the inspection of weights and measures, the inspection of lodging houses, and the enforcement of the licensing and vagrancy laws.

The 1856 Act established a framework that provided the basis for policing in England and Wales that persisted until the 1960s and introduced a mixture of local and central control in terms of the management and financing of the new police. Wall (1998: 42–3) identified three salient features in the emergence of the Metropolitan, borough and county forces during the middle decades of the nineteenth century. First, there was no coherent concept of police professionalism or of the tasks and duties that officers should perform. Second, local factors determined the management structures of forces and the nature of officers recruited to senior positions. Third, the priorities of each force were determined, to a large degree, by the particular concerns and priorities of local power elites. While initial opposition, as has been outlined, was entrenched and broadly cast the latter half of the nineteenth century saw the police elevated to a 'sacred status' in British political, social and cultural life as they adopted the role of 'an all purpose emergency service upon which the local townsfolk relied when in trouble' (Wall, 1998: 45). While serious resistance to the police service continued to be a feature among many communities and incidents of anti-police violence recurred on a regular basis, by the mid-nineteenth century police forces were established as a central feature of the landscape of the state.

PERSPECTIVES ON THE DEVELOPMENT OF THE POLICE

Reiner (2000) distinguished between orthodox and revisionist accounts of the history of the British police, and this section begins by outlining these perspectives, exploring the assumptions behind them, and suggesting that – despite the differences between them – there are important similarities in these approaches. The discussion then moves on to consider other perspectives on and interpretations of the development of policing in England and Wales. Emsley (1996: xi) offered a cautionary reminder to those seeking to explain the historical development of institutions, namely of the need to avoid the problem that 'the text can finish as a celebration of a steady progress to the present'; a warning echoed in the discussion that follows that stresses that the police service did not unfold along pre-ordained lines solely according to a plan conceived by Home Secretary Peel or by Commissioners Rowan and Mayne.

orthodox and revisionist accounts

Early accounts of the historical development of the police are primarily found in the memoirs of politicians or senior officers who were in various ways responsible for establishing policy and practice for the emerging institutions. As Emsley (1996) and Rawlings (2002) have noted police historians such as Lee (1901), Reith (1948), Critchley (1978) and Ascoli (1979) implicitly or explicitly regard the Metropolitan Police as a beneficent legacy of far-sighted reformers such as Peel, Rowan and Mayne. The establishment of the new police is explained in terms of the inability of the inefficient system of parish constables and watchmen that was unable to respond to increasing problems of crime, especially street crime. In this respect orthodox police histories broadly accept the rationale for the new policing arrangements that were advanced by those campaigning for reform in the first decades of the nineteenth century. As was noted earlier, the Metropolitan Police Bill was presented to parliament as the most effective way to deal with a burgeoning crime problem. Orthodox accounts suggest that those who opposed the introduction of the Metropolitan Police, many and varied though they were, were motivated either by romantic loyalty to a system that had served well but was increasingly anachronistic or by misplaced fear that the new arrangements would drastically curtail civil liberties. As the reality of the new policing arrangements began to emerge, and their successes in reducing crime became apparent, orthodox histories suggest that critics were silenced: Reiner (2000: 19) noted that 'in the orthodox view, opposition to the police might have been nasty and brutish, but it was blessedly short'.

Rising crime and the apparent decreasing capacity of the authorities to respond to it were attributed, by both police reformers and orthodox police historians, to the social dislocation wrought by the combined forces of industrialisation and urbanisation. The Metropolitan Police is often presented as the epitome of English pragmatic genius, whereby new constitutional arrangements were introduced in a way that continued principles and traditions whose pedigree was all but lost in the mists of time. Reiner (2000: 16) noted the tendency for orthodox accounts to read as 'jingoistic eulogies' for the police service and the introductory remarks provided by Lee (1901) and Reith (1948) ably demonstrate this, as the former noted that 'our English police system … rests on foundations designed with the full approval of the people … and has been slowly moulded by the careful hand of experience' (Lee, 1901: ix) and the latter struck a modest tone in his preface (Reith, 1948):

> someone suggested that I should write a brief account of the story of the police which could be made easily available to the general public and provide for foreigners answers to the innumerable, eager questions which they customarily ask, following their first experiences of the methods and behaviour of our police.

In addition to the problems posed by street crime, orthodox histories of the police explain the establishment of the new police in terms of the need to respond to the incipient threat posed by public disorder. The impact of the 1819 'Peterloo Massacre' on public and political opinion has already been mentioned, but his was only one of a number of disturbances that suggested that the military could not provide an appropriate response. Reith (1948: 10) argued that urbanisation meant that, from the mid-1700s onwards, it became increasingly easy for citizens to raise a mob (with an indication of the 'prospect of loot') in pursuit of their private grievances. Clearly though the threat of public disorder was not entirely a manifestation of lawlessness and 'mob rule' since unrest relating to a range of social and political grievances were frequent occurrences during this period. Rawlings (2002: 110–12) argued that the practical difficulties of using the military to suppress disorders were compounded by fears that soldiers might side with protestors and 'the mob' rather than the authorities. The use of police officers, orthodox accounts suggest, offered the prospect of a more disciplined and timely response to disorders and, as with crime more generally, the possibility of effectively preventing disturbances in the first place.

Conventional accounts suggest that the Metropolitan Police service overcame the life-threatening public opposition that beset it during in infancy and came to be recognised, in adulthood, as an imitable model to be extended country-wide such that the constable came to embody the national character. Subsequent revisionist interpretations of police history have emphasised the enduring opposition to the police among sections of the population that have been the focus of intrusive coercion. Reiner (2000: 29) noted that police historians such as Storch (1975), Cohen (1979) and Brogden (1982) explored the lineage of opposition that endured from the early days of the Metropolitan Police, as was described in the previous section, throughout the nineteenth and the twentieth centuries. Dunning et al. (1987) showed that opposition to the police among working-class communities in the first half of the twentieth century was centred as much on efforts by constables to regulate everyday social activities – such as gambling and drinking in public places – as it was on the control or suppression of mass political activity. Underlying perspectives that draw attention to the enduring uneasy relationship between the police and marginalised communities is an explanation of the origins of the police service that also starkly diverges from orthodox accounts.

Although conventional accounts acknowledge that the role of the new police was, at least in part, to respond to heightened challenges to public order, revisionist accounts explain this in terms of the establishment's need to suppress nascent working-class activism. Much of this related to the Chartist movement in the early period of the new police, although the actual threats to public order were exacerbated by anticipation that the revolutionary fervour alive in many European countries during the 1840s and 1850s would spread to Britain (Rawlings, 2002: 162–4). Revisionist explanations of the suppression of political unrest mirror a general account that explains the development of the new police in terms of the changing demands of industrial capitalism. It was not only the police role in responding to public disorder that can be explained in terms of changing class relations but also the broader role in maintaining discipline and order among the working-class more generally. From this perspective, as was suggested in Box 2.2, Storch (1976: 481) described the police role as a 'domestic missionary' that ought to be understood in the context of other efforts to regulate the behaviour of the masses:

In northern industrial towns of England these police functions must be viewed as a direct complement to the attempts of urban middle-class elites – by means of Sabbath, educational, temperance, and recreational reform – to mould a labouring class amenable to new disciplines of both work and leisure. The other side of the coin of middle-class voluntaristic moral and social reform … was the policeman's truncheon.

limits to orthodox and revisionist perspectives

The orthodox and revisionist accounts clearly have distinct theoretical foundations. Whereas the former presents the establishment of the new police as a rational and enlightened response to a growing problem of crime and lawlessness, the latter directs attention to the capacity that the police offered the state when it came to the suppression of political disorder and the regulation of the dangerous classes. Despite the clear divergence in terms of the analysis offered by orthodox and revisionist interpretations they share framework in that they are, as Styles (1987) described them, 'problem-response' models that see the police service as a reaction to changing social circumstances. One difficulty with historical narratives of the police service is the tendency toward a teleological account that presents each development as though a step toward some pre-determined final position. In practice the police services established in the mid-nineteenth century did not always mirror the intentions of those politicians and policy-makers who legislated for them. Not only did the process of getting the various pieces of legislation through parliament lead to negotiation and compromise over the exact role and structure of the new police forces but financial constraints meant that, in practice, the activities of the police were sometimes curtailed (Emsley, 1996). The need to recognise the multiplicity of causes is further demonstrated by Reynolds' (1998: 4) argument that local and national leaders had different reasons for extending the new policing arrangements across the country. As well as considering the complexity of the historical development of the police this tends to be under-played by orthodox and revisionist perspectives it is important to consider other contributions to the process that do not relate easily to either account. Bailey (1981) provided several examples of such factors, including the transition from imposing the death sentence for many offences to the use of transportation. Since this meant that the severity of punishment for many offences decreased it was considered important to maintain deterrence by increasing the prospect of being caught, and the new police offered greater institutional capacity to apprehend offenders. Additionally, Bailey (1981: 11) argued that the development of the modern police must be understood in the context of the expansion and bureaucratisation of the state regulation, which meant that:

No longer was the enforcement of the criminal law made to rely upon the private initiative of thief-takers, voluntary associations for self-protection and contractor-gaolers. Instead, the

responsibility was progressively delegated to the agents of a professional police and prison system. In the realm of criminal justice, laissez-faire retreated before the imposition of a widespread apparatus of law and order.

old wine in new bottles?

Another perspective on the historical development of the modern police service is that which stresses the continuities and similarities between the old and new arrangements. Zedner (2006) warned that while the identification of historical epochs provides a useful way of distinguishing different features of particular periods, it can be misleading since the focus tends to be on points of difference rather than continuities. A number of authors (Styles, 1987; Emsley, 1996; Reynolds, 1998) have argued that the establishment of the Metropolitan Police in 1829 represented less of a break with old policing styles than has often been assumed in both orthodox and revisionist accounts. Reynolds (1998: 162) argued that many of the working practices of the Metropolitan Police, such as the crime prevention focus, the employment of full-time officers and the bureaucratic organisation – all of which are celebrated in historical accounts – actually pre-date the establishment of the 'new police'. Emsley (2003: 68) noted that the first instructions issued to police constables in 1829 detailed some of the duties that had been inherited from the old watchmen, such as powers to apprehend those suspected of criminal activity, as well as vagrants and prostitutes, and the power to demand the names of people such that they could be summoned to appear before the magistrates in connection with offences relating to the licensing laws, for example. Not only had some tasks transferred from old to new police, there were also clear continuity in personnel, since many of the officers first employed by the Metropolitan Police previously had been night watchmen or constables employed by the parishes. Moreover Reiner (2000: 41) emphasised that the social background of officers was similar to that of those employed under the earlier arrangements. More generally, Styles (1987) explored many of the features held to distinguish the Metropolitan Police from the preceding arrangements and suggested that many of these were apparent long before the supposed watershed of 1829. That the Metropolitan Police were salaried, professional, organised, state-appointed, preventative and uniformed did not, Styles (1987) noted, actually distinguish them from the police arrangements of the preceding decades. For example, watchmen in the eighteenth century were salaried and while they might not have been professional in terms of their training or career structure, the same could be said of the Metropolitan Police for most of its early decades. One aspect of the Metropolitan Police that literally distinguished it from its forebears was that officers were uniformed. Styles (1987) argued that it is highly significant since the distinguishing feature of the new police was that it was presented and perceived as innovative. Coupled with the efforts of the first Commissioners to secure popular support by promoting the service-orientation of the new police, it seems that concerns with public opinion, legitimacy and the benefits of high visibility policing have a longer history than contemporary commentators on the police might realise.

CONCLUSION

Whether radical or traditional, perspectives on the history of policing in Britain tend to relate the development of the Metropolitan Police Service in 1829 – a model of professional specialism that has been influential in many societies – to the changing political, economic, and social context of the period. Other perspectives suggest that concentrating on the circumstances in which the 'new police' were established detracts attention from considerable continuities in terms of personnel and activities. Moreover, many features of policing in the period before the establishment of the Metropolitan Police mirror contemporary patterns, trends and controversies. Public engagement in police work and the diverse range of agencies engaged in policing were core characteristics of the 'old' policing and, as later chapters indicate, are enduring concerns in the twenty-first century.

chapter summary

- The model developed in London in the nineteenth century has influenced policing in many parts of the world. Policing systems characterised by specialisation and professionalism can be traced back to the establishment of the Metropolitan Police, created in 1829.

- Traditional histories of policing tended to be written by retired senior officers, politicians and civil servants, which partly accounts for a conservative tone that explains the development of the modern police service in terms of a natural evolution of arrangements long established in British history.

- Anglo-Saxon policing was characterised by the direct involvement of ordinary people. The 1285 Statute of Winchester provided a framework for policing until the eighteenth century.

- From the mid-1700s problems of urban lawlessness and political unrest exposed the inadequacy of established informal and unprofessional policing arrangements and the use of the military to quell public disorder.

- The demand for order increased during this period and the new police was shaped by social reform intended to regulate what was perceived as the problematic behaviour of the 'dangerous' classes.

- In 1829 the Metropolitan Police was established with two Commissioners, 17 Superintendents, 69 Inspectors, 323 Sergeants and 2,906 Constables. The service-orientation of the new police was intended to overcome public suspicion and to cultivate co-operation.

- Public opposition was not abated by these measures. The financial burden on local watch committees, the inability of the police to meet new demands for patrols, and the poor quality of officers led to sustained antipathy to the Metropolitan Police.

- From the middle of the eighteenth century anti-police sentiment was overcome. Central government contributed greater resources and it was perceived that the Metropolitan Police were becoming more effective.

- Government legislation and local demand meant that the 'new policing' model expanded during the mid-nineteenth century.

- Orthodox accounts outline the development of policing in the nineteenth century in terms of a natural, if inspired, response to changing problems of crime and disorder and a growing realisation that established arrangements were ill-suited to the emerging urban and industrial landscape. The 'genius' of the new arrangements, orthodox histories suggest, was that they incorporated long-standing traditions of local policing that reflected the demands of the public.

- Revisionist perspectives explain the development of the 'new police' as an attempt to control increasing working-class activism that emerged alongside urbanisation and industrialisation.

- Both orthodox and revisionist accounts interpret the development of the police in terms of response to changing social conditions. Others have argued that policing developed in the nineteenth century in a piecemeal fashion and cannot be understood as the coherent or consistent expression of a particular programme.

- Another perspective notes that the distinction between traditional 'old police' and the 'new police' of the nineteenth century is less marked than many accounts have suggested. In personnel terms and in the general roles police were expected to fulfil, considerable continuities can be identified.

self-check questions (with answers at the back of the book)

1. What features characterised policing in England between the 1740s and 1850s?

2. Name the constitutional arrangement that enshrined the key features of policing from the thirteenth century until the establishment of the 'new police' in the nineteenth century.

3. To what did Sir John Fielding attribute the crime problems of the 1740s?

4. Who addressed the Chartist rally at St Peter's Field, Manchester 1819 that fuelled concern about using the military to control crowds?

5. How did Storch characterise the role of the police in the mid-nineteenth century?

6. What measures were introduced in an effort to overcome public suspicion of the 'new police' in the early nineteenth century?

7. What proportion of the 3,000 officers recruited to the Metropolitan Police when it was established in 1829 is it estimated were still in post four years later?

8. What legislation required counties to establish a police force?

9. How do orthodox perspectives explain dissatisfaction with the use of the military to respond to political and social unrest?

10. How do revisionist accounts tend to explain the development of the 'new police'?

study questions

1. What characteristics of the pre-modern police continue to inform current approaches to policing?

2. Compare and contrast the orthodox and revisionist accounts of police history.

3. In what terms have both the orthodox and revisionist accounts been criticised?

annotated further reading

Reiner's (2000) *Politics of the Police* has been a hugely influential book exploring perspectives on the development of policing, analysing the myths and realities associated with the 'golden age' of policing in Britain in the post-war period, and the politics of law and order. Part One of the book provides an account of the foundation and development of the police service. Reiner argues that legitimacy was established because the service operated bureaucratically, according to the rule of law, with a strategy of minimal force and non-partisanship, with accountability, performed a service role, sought to prevent crime problems, and was relatively effective. He also argues that the 'golden age' that was achieved in the post-Second World War period was partly related to the broader context of the welfare state and consensus politics.

Rawlings' (2002) *Policing – A Short History* outlines and analyses the history of the police service from the Anglo-Saxon period until the end of the twentieth century. While examining the ways in which policing arrangements have developed in relation to wider patterns of social change, the book also makes clear that some contemporary concerns, for example about the criminalisation of the poor and the role of private security firms, are very long-standing indeed.

annotated listings of links to relevant websites

Useful resources relating to the development of the modern police service, including a time-line of key developments from 1829 to the present day, can be found at www.metpolicehistory.co.uk/, the website of the Friends of the Metropolitan Police Service.

An article by Chris Williams ('Britain's Police Forces: Forever Removed from Democratic Control?', 2003) examines tension between the principles of local control and the direction of the police service by central government. Williams argues that contemporary debates about central and local direction, considered at greater length in Chapter 4, can be traced back to the nineteenth century.

James Sharpe examines the history of crime in the centuries before the establishment of the 'new police' and the apparent decreasing effectiveness of the 'old police' to respond to emerging challenges. His paper, *The History of Crime in England, 1550–1914* (1995), can be found at www.ehs.org.uk/the-society/assets/sharpe20b.pdf.

annotated links to journal articles

The contested and controversial development of policing in England is explored in Storch's account of the mid-nineteenth century experience:

Storch, R. (1975) 'The Plague of Blue Locusts: Police Reform and Popular Resistance in Northern England 1840–57', *International Review of Social History*, 20: 61–90.

An analysis of the social background of police recruits in the first century or so of modern policing is provided in Emsley and Clapson's article:

Emsely, C. and Clapson, R. (1994) 'Recruiting the English Policeman C. 1840–1940', *Policing and Society*, 3: 269–8.5

Brogden explored the influence of colonial policing on the domestic development of policing in England, suggesting that transnational and global influences are not solely of recent significance:

Brogden, M. (1987) 'The Emergence of the Police: The Colonial Dimension', *British Journal of Criminology*, 27: 4–14.

Myths and popular cultural representations of policing in the 'golden age' of the 1950s abound, and McLaughlin critically examines the creation of the iconic Dixon of Dock Green:

McLaughlin, E. (2005) 'From Reel to Ideal: The Blue Lamp and the Popular Cultural Construction of the English Bobby', *Crime, Media, Culture*, 1(1): 11–30.

3

POLICE POWERS: THE LEGAL FRAMEWORK

CONTENTS

LEARNING OBJECTIVES

A common response to real or imagined threats from criminals, terrorists or those committing antisocial behaviour is that the police, courts, and criminal justice system in general need to be given new powers in order to provide an effective response to novel and emerging challenges. Clearly changes in criminal opportunity can mean that legal powers available to police need to be refined in the light of novel and emerging threats. In the field of cybercrime, stalking or terrorism, the legal powers available to the police – in terms of seizing assets or conducting surveillance – have developed in recent years. Many of the legal frameworks surrounding those are outlined in other chapters. The focus here is on the 1984 Police and Criminal Evidence Act, on the key laws that shape police interactions with the public. While other laws are also significant, it is also acknowledged that the effectiveness of policing and law-enforcement is shaped by organisational, political and cultural factors that are only indirectly related to formal legal powers. Although the suggestion that the police can more effectively fulfil their role if they have improved legal powers seems no more than common sense and might have some appeal to the police service and to politicians eager to establish their law and order credentials, the link between the two is far from straightforward. With this in mind this chapter aims to:

- examine the development and consolidation of police powers into the 1984 Police and Criminal Evidence Act

- outline police powers in respect of stop and search; entry, search and seizure; arrest; detention; questioning and treatment; documentary evidence in criminal proceedings; complaints and discipline, and other matters

- demonstrate that police powers derive from much more than the legal frameworks that stipulate what officers can, and cannot do. The institutional and political power of the service also shapes the role of the police.

KEY TERMS

warrests; citizens' arrest; institutional and symbolic power of police; Judges' Rules; Police and Criminal Evidence Act 1984; police custody; Protection of Freedoms Act 2012; rights of suspects; stop and search; Terrorism Act 2000 and warrants

INTRODUCTION

Parliamentary interest in the powers of the police is a relatively recent phenomenon, for most of their history the powers of British police officers have remained ill-defined in legal terms. In part this seems to have been a reflection of the wider tendency to conceptualise the police constable as nothing more than the 'citizen in uniform' that has been integral to the process of legitimating the police service. Since the officer was of equal standing to the ordinary citizen it was not considered necessary to grant the police extraordinary legal powers that would differentiate constables from the rest of the community. Leigh (1985: 5) noted that the tradition had been that the 'constable's duties were wide, but his powers were limited'. While Commissioner of the Metropolitan Police, Sir Robert Mark had suggested that the only power the police had over the ordinary citizen was the power to inconvenience them (Judge, 1986: 175). The 1929 Royal Commission on Police Powers and Procedure explained the relative silence of Britain's unwritten constitution on the topic of police power in the following terms:

> **The police of this country have never been recognized, either by the law or by tradition, as a force distinct from the general body of citizens. Despite the imposition of many extraneous duties on the police by legislation or administrative action, the principle remains that the policeman, in the view of the common law, is only a person paid to perform, as a matter of duty, acts which if he were so minded he might have done voluntarily ... Indeed a policeman possesses few powers not enjoyed by the ordinary citizen, and public opinion, expressed in Parliament and elsewhere, has shown great jealousy of any attempts to give increased authority to the police.**
>
> **(Robilliard and McEwan, 1986: 2)**

This chapter explores the ways in which the powers of the British police service have been developed and increasingly codified since the last decades of the twentieth century. In particular some of the provisions of the Police and Criminal Evidence Act 1984 (PACE), which continues to provide the framework from which many police powers are derived, are outlined. Some PACE powers were amended by the Protection of Freedoms Act 2012 and those changes are also outlined. The chapter moves on to consider the broader context of debates about the legal powers of the police. It is suggested that there are various reasons why the 'black letter of the law' provides only a weak explanation of what the police service actually does and, furthermore, that much of the real power of the police derives not from the statute books but from the institutional and political framework in which the service operates. In this sense the concept of police 'power' needs to be considered in more complex and nuanced terms.

THE CONSOLIDATION OF POLICE POWERS

In keeping with the conception of the constable as a 'citizen in uniform', police powers have remained uncodified and developed only in a piecemeal fashion on the basis of case law. Prior to the Police and Criminal Evidence Act 1984 police powers were derived from individual pieces of legislation, Home Office directives, case law, and the 'Judges Rules' – introduced in 1912 to govern the treatment of those held in police custody. In legal terms police constables are independent officers of the Crown – rather than employees – with personal discretion in terms of when, where and how they enforce the law. Although accountable to senior officers and the local police authority, constables cannot be given direct orders in relation to the application of the law. Since officers are not technically employees they cannot be dismissed (although the 2011 Winsor Review suggested that this be changed), unless they are in breach of specific disciplinary rules and are subject to various legal obligations that extend into their private lives in ways that do not apply to conventional employees. On this basis, the police regulations issued by the Home Office in 1952 stipulated that 'every constable must devote his whole time to the police service' and required that chief officers' permission be granted if a constable resided at premises where a business was conducted by family members. More recently the requirement that officers refrain from activity 'likely to interfere with the impartial discharge of his duties or which is likely to give rise to the impression amongst members of the public that it may so interfere', as the regulations put it, has been used to prohibit officers joining extremist political parties such as the British National Party (ACPO, 2003).

The powers that police officers have, over and above those available to the ordinary citizen, were, until the 1980s, derived from individual pieces of legislation. One implication of this was that the powers available to officers were neither clearly defined nor consistent across the country. For example, the 1824 Vagrancy Act, which predated the establishment of the Metropolitan Police, gave constables in London powers to stop and search people in the streets but these did not extend to all officers in other parts of the country. However, officers in some other cities had similar powers, as granted, for example, by the Liverpool Corporation Act 1921 or the Manchester Police Act 1944. Although legislation such as the Firearms Act 1968 and the Misuse of Drugs Act 1971 gave powers to search people in particular circumstances there was no general law that gave the police power to search for offensive weapons or stolen goods. It was in response to a series of public scandals that the Police and Criminal Evidence Act 1984 was introduced, replacing the Judges Rules that had guided police behaviour for decades (see Box 3.1).

Box 3.1

The Judges' Rules

For many years it had been apparent that stipulations in the Judges' Rules, for example to provide legal advice to people in custody, were often regarded by officers as advisory rather than binding. Zander (2005) argued that this disregard for the Judges' Rules might have

(Continued)

stemmed from the arbitrary and isolated manner in which they were developed, a process from which the police had been excluded. Additionally, Judge (1986) noted that the non-statutory nature of the Rules also undermined their status among police officers who sometimes felt they were inimical to the investigation process. The particular circumstances by which the Judges' Rules were replaced stemmed from the wrongful imprisonment of three boys who had falsely confessed to the 1972 murder of Maxwell Confait. An inquiry into the episode found that the youths had been denied the right to legal advice, improperly questioned, and that there had been improprieties in the charging process (Reiner, 2000: 65). The report also found that officers had been unaware of what was required of them under the Judges Rules and recommended that a Royal Commission be established to consider further reforms (Reiner, 2000: 65). The subsequent Royal Commission on Criminal Procedure was established in 1978 with a brief to strike the appropriate balance between promoting the interests of the public by prosecuting offenders and protecting the rights of those suspected or accused of an offence.

police power versus the rights of the suspect

Although there was a case for creating a single statutory basis for police powers as an exercise in good legal and administrative housekeeping, the proposals contained in the Police and Criminal Evidence Bill 1982 generated huge controversy. The passage of the bill was delayed by a general election but was eventually enacted as the 1984 Police and Criminal Evidence Act. Described by Reiner (2000: 176) as 'the single most significant landmark in the modern development of police powers', most of the provisions of the Act took effect from 1986. Opposition to the Act came from two distinct camps. Essentially a 'law and order' lobby welcomed the extension of police powers contained within the Act, but argued that establishing a statutory framework of rights for those in custody would erode the power of the police and weigh the scales of justice too far in the interests of suspects. Former Metropolitan Police Commissioner, Sir David McNee, for example, claimed that the new regulations concerning the interviewing of suspects in custody 'gives virtually no assistance to police and every assistance to a suspect wishing to hide his guilt' (Koffman, 1985: 12). The Chief Constable of Merseyside, Kenneth Oxford, represented ACPO during consultations over the Bill, and argued that it was a widely misunderstood piece of legislation and that those aspects of PACE that extended police powers effectively did little more than codify prevailing police practices into law. However, Oxford argued that those parts of the Act relating to police treatment of suspects in custody were cause for concern and that 'I and my fellow chief constables feel the balance has been tipped too far in favour of the wrongdoers against the interests of the law-abiding citizen and an effective police service' (Oxford, 1986: 68).

In the other camp were those who opposed the extensions of police power contained in the Bill and doubted that the accompanying procedural safeguards would be meaningful in practice. Opposition was raised to the extension of police powers in terms of stopping and searching individuals, taking fingerprints and other 'non-intimate' samples, and searching premises. All of these provisions have been reviewed and amended at various stages since PACE was originally established, and the Codes of Practice that cover the implementation of the various provisions provide one method of doing this. There are eight Codes, providing detailed guidance on PACE (and related) powers relating the core areas discussed below (stop and search, arrest, detention and so on). Other primary legislation has also impacted on PACE. The Criminal Justice Act 1988, for example, expanded the definition of an offensive weapon to encompass most knives and bladed objects. Further the Crime and Security Act 2010 meant that DNA and other intimate samples could not be retained in cases where the suspect was not charged.

PACE IN PRACTICE

From a vantage point three decades after the Act came into force, neither sets of objections appear to have been borne out by experience. Although various concerns have emerged about the extent to which the Act has proved effective there is little evidence that PACE has hampered the ability of the police to go about their duties; indeed some of the provisions required by the Act, for example to tape record interviews with suspects, have come to be valued by officers who find it in their interests to have an objective record of their interrogation. While concerns continue to be expressed about the impact that police stop and search procedures has upon some sections of the community, these tend to relate to the manner in which officers interact with the public rather than the legal powers at their disposal (Stone and Pettigrew, 2000). Zander (2005: xiv) noted that a Home Office review of PACE that gathered evidence from police, prosecutors, lawyers, civil liberties and human rights groups – as well as public consultation – came to the view that the core framework of PACE had considerable support.

PACE has had an impact in a number of ways. First, the Act itself provides a clear framework for police powers in relation to individual citizens in respect of the following key areas, each of which form separate sections of the Act:

- stop and search
- entry, search and seizure
- arrest
- detention
- questioning and treatment
- documentary evidence in criminal proceedings

- complaints and discipline
- other miscellaneous matters.

The following paragraphs detail some of the key police powers defined by PACE. By no means do they amount to an exhaustive, or legally definitive, account of police powers. Such a task is very effectively performed by Zander's (2005) analysis of the legal nuances relating to powers granted to the police by PACE. In more general terms texts by English and Card (2015) and by Jason-Lloyd (2005) provide excellent reviews of police powers, including but not limited to those established by PACE. Instead, general principles relating to police powers regarding stop and search, entry, search and seizure, arrest, and the treatment of those in custody are outlined.

police powers to stop and search

Section 1 of PACE authorises the stop and search of a person or a vehicle for stolen or prohibited articles if a constable has 'reasonable suspicion' for suspecting that such items will be found. These powers apply in any public place, which is defined as a place to which the public has access rather than in terms of strict legal ownership of land. The Code of Practice (see Box 3.2) that provides more detailed advice stipulates what constitutes 'reasonable' in this context and makes it clear that there must be some objective basis for it. Information or a description received from a witness to a crime or a person being seen to act covertly or warily might be grounds for reasonable suspicion, but this can never be justified purely on the grounds of personal appearance. The Code advises that the Equality Act 2010 prohibits officers from discriminating on the grounds of 'protected characteristics' including race, age, gender, disability or sexual orientation and that police have a duty to eliminate discrimination, harassment and victimisation and to foster good relations. The extent to which these clauses are met is considered further in Chapter 7.

Box 3.2

Extract from PACE Code A, 2015

Principles Governing Stop and Search

1.1 Powers to stop and search must be used fairly, responsibly, with respect for people being searched and without unlawful discrimination. Under the Equality Act 2010, section 149, when police officers are carrying out their functions, they also have a duty to have due regard to the need to eliminate unlawful discrimination, harassment and

---

victimisation, to advance equality of opportunity between people who share a 'relevant protected characteristic' and people who do not share it, and to take steps to foster good relations between those persons (see Notes 1 and 1A). The Children Act 2004, section 11, also requires chief police officers and other specified persons and bodies to ensure that in the discharge of their functions they have regard to the need to safeguard and promote the welfare of all persons under the age of 18.

1.2 The intrusion on the liberty of the person stopped or searched must be brief and detention for the purposes of a search must take place at or near the location of the stop.

1.3 If these fundamental principles are not observed the use of powers to stop and search may be drawn into question. Failure to use the powers in the proper manner reduces their effectiveness. Stop and search can play an important role in the detection and prevention of crime, and using the powers fairly makes them more effective. Codes of practice – Code A Exercise by police of officers' statutory powers of stop and search.

1.4 The primary purpose of stop and search powers is to enable officers to allay or confirm suspicions about individuals without exercising their power of arrest. Officers may be required to justify the use or authorisation of such powers, in relation both to individual searches and the overall pattern of their activity in this regard, to their supervisory officers or in court. Any misuse of the powers is likely to be harmful to policing and lead to mistrust of the police. Officers must also be able to explain their actions to the member of the public searched. The misuse of these powers can lead to disciplinary action.

1.5 An officer must not search a person, even with his or her consent, where no power to search is applicable. Even where a person is prepared to submit to a search voluntarily, the person must not be searched unless the necessary legal power exists, and the search must be in accordance with the relevant power and the provisions of this Code. The only exception, where an officer does not require a specific power, applies to searches of persons entering sports grounds or other premises carried out with their consent given as a condition of entry.

1.6 Evidence obtained from a search to which this Code applies may be open to challenge if the provisions of this Code are not observed.

(Home Office, 2014)

The powers extend to any vehicle, including aircraft, and to any items contained within the vehicle. Stolen or prohibited articles are defined in particular terms in the Codes of Practice. Stolen items include those being handled by the person stopped, even if they were not actually stolen by that person. Prohibited articles fall into two main categories: those that are offensive weapons of some kind, and those that might be used for the commission of a criminal act. Offensive weapons fall into three categories. First, those items that are specifically designed for this purpose, such as a flick knife or a cosh. Second, articles that might not be designed to be offensive weapons but which have been adapted in some way for that purpose such as, for example, a screwdriver that has been sharpened. Third, the potentially very wide category of any item that is intended to be used as an offensive weapon, which could, of course, include everyday items that could, if so intended, be used in a violent manner.

Section 1 of the Act outlines that these powers are available to officers:

(a) In any place to which at the time when he proposes to exercise the power the public or any section of the public has access, on payment or otherwise, as of right or by virtue of express or implies permission, or

(b) in any other place to which people have ready access at the time when he proposes to exercise the power but which is not a dwelling.

In these terms, public space is defined broadly in relation to the nature and extent of public access, rather than in terms of property ownership. A football ground, for example, maybe privately owned but, since the public have access to it, even though they are required to pay for the privilege, they constitute public places under the terms of the Act. By referring to public places as those to which people have 'ready access' it is not necessary that people have a legal right to be present, merely that the place is readily accessible, which means that those trespassing on private land are liable to be stopped and searched. While the Act expressly limits the powers to spaces that are not dwellings, it stipulates that those who the officer believes are not residents of the property and do not have permission – even if only implicit – to be on the property are susceptible to being stopped and searched. The Act does not give the police power to stop and search people on their own private land.

It should be noted that the tendency to talk about 'stop and search' in unitary terms is somewhat misleading since there is a distinction between the two in the Act and associated Codes of Practice. While an officer needs reasonable suspicion to stop an individual in order that to conduct a search they must not do so until the person stopped has been questioned and given an opportunity to explain their behaviour or presence in the area. The response to these questions might confirm the officer's suspicion or reveal grounds to believe that the person is in possession of other types of prohibitive item. In either case the person stopped can then be searched. Alternatively, though, the explanation might be credible and the person eliminated from the investigation. If the officer decides that a search is necessary, then this must be carried out at or nearby to the place where the person was stopped. While consent ought to be sought for the search, force can be used if this is not given or if the person resists. The search should be restricted, the Code of Practice stipulates, to a 'superficial examination of outerclothing' and a constable is only permitted to require the removal of outer garments, jackets and gloves. It is permissible for an officer to search inside pockets, feel inside collars or cuffs, socks and shoes but any more intimate search many only be conducted away from the public space in a police van or at a police station. More intimate searches must only be conducted by officers of the same sex as the person stopped and no-one of the opposite sex is allowed in the vicinity unless specifically requested by the member of the public.

PACE required from its inception that officers make a record of all searches at the time that they were made unless it were 'wholly impracticable' to do so. In such circumstances the officer must make a record as soon as is possible afterwards. The Crime and Security Act 2010 reduced the amount of information that needs to be recorded. Seven points need to be included: the object of the search, the ground for suspicion, date, time, place, the person's self-defined ethnic origin, and the identity of the officer involved. There is no requirement for officers to record minor or informal encounters or those in which a person is asked to account for their behaviour, possession of any item or presence in a particular location but is not searched.

additional powers to stop and search

While PACE was intended to consolidate earlier legislation relating to stop and search there have been subsequent pieces of legislation that have given additional powers. Among the highest profile of these have been the Criminal Justice and Public Order Act (CJPOA) 1994 and the Terrorism Act 2000 (TA), although the use of both has dropped considerably in recent years. Section 60 of the CJPOA permits senior officers to authorise officers to search anyone present in a designated place where it is reasonably anticipated that incidents involving serious violence may take place. The Act explicitly states that this means that an officer can stop any person or vehicle within the area whether or not there is reasonable suspicion that they are carrying a prohibited weapon or might be intent on violent activity. The removal of the requirement for reasonable suspicion is a significant break with the PACE framework and was originally introduced to deal with public order situations where, it was argued, this had been a major impediment to the police (Jason-Lloyd, 2005: 47). Although these powers are only available to officers under certain circumstances, since they must be authorised by an Inspector, and subsequently ratified by a Superintendent, and can only apply for a period of 24 hours, subject to one extension of a further 24 hours, they offer officers very broad grounds to conduct stop and searches outwith the framework of checks and balances introduced by PACE. Concerns have been expressed that these powers have become part of the routine policing of town and city centres and that increasing numbers of people are being subject to stops and searches where the test of 'reasonable' suspicion has not been met (Rowe, 2004: 95–6). The over-use of 'section 60' stop and searches was cited as a causal factor of the 2011 summer disorders. The numbers of section 60 searches has declined significantly: the highest annual count in the last decade was 150,174 in 2008/09 but by 2015/16 this had fallen to 974 (Home Office, 2016a).

This decrease might reflect a combination of political pressure to reduce the use of these powers, an increased sense within the service that they might be disproportionate, and a legal landscape that was challenging stop and search powers exercised in similar ways, as outlined in the next paragraph.

Similarly sections 44, 45 and 46 of the Terrorism Act 2000 allows for stop and searches of people and vehicles to be authorised by an officer above the rank of Assistant Chief Constable in a given area for a limited period. These stops must be conducted for the purposes of uncovering items connected with a terrorist attack and the authorisation can only be given if there is specific intelligence or information to suggest that a terrorist attack is planned in the area concerned. The code of practice governing the Act stipulates that care should be taken not to unnecessarily target these powers against those of a specific ethnic background; again the Equality Act 2010 applies to this form of stop and search, although – as with PACE stop and searches – evidence reviewed in Chapter 7 suggests disproportionality is highly apparent in terms of the ethnicity of those subject to these powers. However, following a 2010 European Court ruling, and accusations from civil liberties groups and the Independent Reviewer of Terrorism Legislation that the police were abusing their powers, the s44 arrangements were replaced and no stops and searches have subsequently been carried out under these powers. The Protection of Freedoms Act 2012 rewrote parts of the Terrorism Act 2000 and imposed greater restrictions on police powers to stop and search without reasonable suspicion. These included tightening of the circumstances in which such powers can be used (they can no longer be deployed for general purposes of deterrence of public reassurance, for example). Requirements for oversight were enhanced and the time period for which permission to carry out stop and searches without reasonable suspicion can be granted was reduced. Schedule 7 of the Terrorism Act 2000 gives police powers to stop and search individuals at ports and airports, and to detain individuals for up to six hours. No 'reasonable suspicion' is required in relation to the individual concerned. In the year to September 2016, there were over 21,500 examinations carried out under Schedule 7, a 25 per cent reduction on the previous year, but still a major concern in terms of police relations with minority communities, especially since few arrests result (StopWatch, 2014; Blackwood et al., 2013).

PACE powers of entry, search and seizure

The police powers to search outlined above apply only to public places; powers to enter private property are outlined sections 8, 17, 18 and 32 of PACE. Police enter private property either with a warrant issued by a magistrate or, under specified circumstances, without a warrant. Other legislation also allows the police to enter premises: the Misuse of Drugs Act 1971, for example, grants officers power to enter the business premises of someone who produces or supplies controlled drugs to examine records and stocks; the Road Traffic Act 1988 affords officers the power to enter premises to take a breath test following an accident that has led to personal injury (Jason-Lloyd, 2005: 95). The PACE provisions stipulate that a magistrate can issue a warrant granting an officer the power to enter premises if it is not possible to gain entry with consent. A warrant is issued to enable officers to look for material relating to a serious arrestable offence which is likely to be of substantial value to the investigation and be relevant evidence. Certain items are identified as legally privileged and so cannot be included in such searches; for example, communication between a client and professional legal advisor. Further items, including journalistic documents, medical records, items held in confidence for business purposes, is treated as either 'excluded material' or 'special procedure material' and cannot be searched under the a general warrant, although other authorisation can be sought to search these.

In addition to identifying materials not included by search warrants, PACE introduced other safeguards in terms of the steps that officers must take when making an application to the magistrate. It is required that the police identify the nature of the evidence that they expect to find, the crime(s) to which it may relate. If the premises is multi-occupancy then only those parts of it relating to the individual identified in the warrant may be searched. The code of practice issued under the terms of PACE make detailed stipulation about the conduct of searches; for example, that questions asked during the process must relate to the conduct of the search itself and must not become an interview about the alleged offence (Zander, 2005: 67). While force may be used to gain entry this must only be done when and to the extent necessary.

other powers of entry

Additionally the police continue to have a wide range of powers of entry that do not require a warrant. Section 17 of PACE covers powers of entry for the purposes of executing a warrant for arrest, arresting someone for committing an arrestable offence, arresting a youth or child remanded to local authority care, recapturing someone who is unlawfully at large, or to 'save life or limb' or prevent serious damage to property. In addition police officers have common-law powers to enter property to prevent or respond to a breach of the peace. Officers must give an explanation of why they are entering a property, unless it would be 'impossible, impractical or undersirable' to do so (English and Card, 2015: 76). Officers must have reasonable grounds to believe that the person they are seeking is at the property and, if the property is multi-occupancy then the officer(s) can only enter those parts where the person may be.

Section 18 of PACE grants powers to enter premises of any person arrested for an arrestable offence if it is believed that a search of the premises would reveal material related to that offence, or one similar to it. Searching the home of someone arrested for burglary in order to find stolen goods or proceeds from burglaries, for example, is permitted but a search for drugs (unrelated to the burglary) would not be (English and Card, 2015: 77). These searches must be authorised by an Inspector and the basis for the search must be explained to the occupier of the property. The same conditions apply to the searches of multiple occupancy premises as outlined in relation to section 17 searches. Further powers of entry and search are provided by section 32 of PACE, which stipulates that officers might, after making an arrest, enter and search the premises where the person was immediately before or when they were arrested. Such action can only be taken if it is reasonably believed that evidence of the offence for which the arrest was made will be found. As with all of the provisions described here the term 'premises' has been interpreted very widely by the courts (Zander, 2005).

police powers of arrest

Again, a legal distinction is made between arrests carried out as a result of a warrant and those made without warrant. Section 24 of PACE outlines officers powers of arrest for 'arrestable offences', of which there are three categories, as outlined in Box 3.3.

Box 3.3

Police Powers of Arrest

Police officers can arrest without a warrant in circumstances relating to:

- offences for which the punishment is fixed by law, currently only the offence of murder falls into this category

- offences for which a convicted person over the age of 18, who has no previous convictions, would be liable for a sentence greater than five years' imprisonment – this category includes a large number of offences, such as theft, burglary, assault, robbery, indecent assault and common law offences such as kidnapping and attempting to pervert the course of justice (Zander, 2005: 95)

- a miscellaneous list of offences that, although not punished with a sentence greater than five years, are considered serious in some aspect, including acts criminalised by the Wireless Telegraphy Act 1949, the Wildlife and Countryside Act 1981, the Football (Offences) Act 1991 and the Sexual Offences Act 2003 (Jason-Lloyd, 2005: 64–8).

An arrest can be legally made by any person, police officer or otherwise, who reasonably believes that an offence in one of these three categories is in the process of being committed. The key to the legality of an arrest in such circumstances is the reasonable belief that an offence is being committed, even if it turns out not to be the case. In circumstances were an arrestable offence has already been committed, any person can make a lawful arrest of the guilty offender. However, unlike a situation in which a crime is in progress, in these circumstances if a person is subsequently acquitted of the alleged offence then the arrest itself is rendered illegal if carried out by a member of the public other than a police officer. As English and Card (2015: 60) point out, it is reasonable for the law to allow a private citizen to intervene and arrest an offender in the act of committing a crime – even if only on the basis of reasonable belief that the person is committing an offence, but a 'citizen's arrest' under other circumstances is hazardous as compensation for wrongful arrest might be claimed. While PACE only gives police officers, not ordinary citizens, power to arrest to prevent an arrestable offence from being committed, other legislation, namely the Criminal Law Act 1967, gives anyone the right to intervene using reasonable force to prevent crime or lawfully arrest an offender (Jason-Lloyd, 2005: 70–71).

The police do not have direct power of arrest for offences not classified as 'arrestable'; instead these – usually more minor – offences ought to be dealt with by reporting them and summoning the suspected person to court. However, section 25 of PACE outlines some general conditions of arrest that mean that, if an officer is unable to obtain a reliable name and address of the person suspected of committing such an offence, then an arrest might be made. The same section of the Act also allows for a person to be arrested in order to prevent them causing harm to themselves or to prevent damage to property.

Only a minority of arrests are made under the terms of a warrant issued by a magistrate and these are issued in only limited circumstances, such as when the identity of an offender is known but the person cannot be located or when an individual has failed to attend court in response to a summons (Jason-Lloyd, 2005: 85). Once a warrant has been issued it remains in force until it is executed, which can be done by any police officer and by civilian enforcement officers. Since 2004 arrest warrants issued in certain other EU countries can be enforced in the UK, although the increasing use of these provisions to extradite UK citizens to other member states has led the government in 2012 to announce a review of the provisions of the European Arrest Warrant (House of Commons, 2013).

For an arrest to be legal certain procedures must be followed by the police. Prime among these is the need to inform the person of the grounds for their arrest immediately or as soon as is practically possible. Section 28 of PACE outlines these requirements, which are a long-standing feature of common law. Handcuffs or other means of restraint must only be used if there is reason to believe that the person arrested is likely to use violence or to escape. The person must be issued with a caution, although minor deviation from it does not render the arrest illegal (see Box 3.4).

Box 3.4

The Police Caution

'You do not have to say anything. But, it may harm your defence if you do not mention when questioned something which you later rely on in court. Anything you do say may be given in evidence.'

Following arrest a person must be taken to a 'designated police station', essentially one that has the necessary facilities to keep people in custody, immediately. In areas where there is not a designated police station in the immediate vicinity then the person can be held for up to six hours before being taken to such a station. In the following section the powers of the police during the detention process are outlined.

police powers of detention

Concern about police abuse of the Judges' Rules that had lightly regulated police behaviour in relation to those held in custody was a central factor in the development of the provisions enacted by PACE. The safeguards introduced from 1986, when PACE came into force, were often cited as demonstration that the abuses of police power revealed by miscarriage of justice cases uncovered in the 1980s were historical remnants of police malpractice impossible in the contemporary period, a claim that does not entirely bear scrutiny (Reiner, 2000: 66–7).

One of the main innovations introduced by PACE is the role of custody officer, who has legal responsibility for keeping people in custody, ensuring that their rights are safeguarded, and for the eventual release of the person, whether they be remanded in custody, or released on bail or unconditionally. Formally the custody officer has to decide if there is sufficient evidence to justify a charge against a person who has been arrested and brought to a police station, although the Crown Prosecution Service is ultimately responsible for prosecuting cases. In practice, individuals are seldom charged immediately upon arrival at the police station and it is more usual for the custody officer to book an individual into custody so that they can be subject to further interview (Zander, 2005: 123–4). Although PACE stipulates that the detention of a person is only legal if it is necessary to allow further enquiries to be made, for example, to prevent that person from destroying evidence or interfering with witnesses, in practice it seems likely that custody officers authorise detention at a lower threshold in circumstances where it makes the process of investigation more straightforward (Zander, 2005: 124). As part of this booking in process the custody officer is required to advise the person of their right to legal advice and to make a phone call to allow someone to be informed of their arrest. The custody officer records and takes charge of the personal property of a person when they are booked into custody. If the person is under 17, or has special needs of some kind, then it is up to the custody officer to see that an 'appropriate adult' is brought in to represent the interests of that person. Additionally the custody officer completes a risk assessment of each person, asking them questions about any problems that they have with drugs or alcohol, and assessing if they are likely to harm themselves. The custody officer is responsible for ensuring that a detailed record is kept of decisions applying to each person detained, including those relating to the periodic review of the basis of their detention that should be completed every six to nine hours.

Although the Judges' Rules had stipulated that private legal advice should be made available to anyone in taken into custody, it was widely accepted that this principle was neither well-known nor frequently practised. PACE stipulates that free legal advice be made available to anyone in custody at any time, and that such advice ought to be communicated in private. A duty solicitor scheme operates such that advice is available, perhaps via telephone, at all times, although the quality of legal advice provided in this way has been cause for concern (Zander, 2005: 187). Delaying the person's access to legal advice is only permitted in relation to serious crimes and with the authorisation of a Superintendent if there are reasonable grounds for believing that informing a solicitor that the person is in custody would serve to alert others who might be implicated in the crime, would harm relevant evidence, or would allow the disposal of proceeds arising from the offence. Other changes introduced by PACE include the tape, or more recently video, recording of police interviews, and the stipulation of the ways in which interviews must be conducted. PACE also requires that those in custody are given proper periods of rest, and are provided with regular meals. Clearly many of these provisions have been introduced to ensure that police powers are not disproportionate to individuals' rights and the broader interests of justice. As was noted earlier, many objections to PACE suggested that these requirements would tip the balance too far in the interests of the suspect and would hamper the police fight against crime.

A cartoon published in *Police* magazine in March 1984 showed two harassed officers trying to complete a mountain of paperwork while overlooked by a collection of stereotypes, including a bowler-hatted bureaucrat, a doctor and a social worker. In the corner a waiter is laying a table, opposite a comfortable sofa and slippers, in anticipation of the arrival of the prisoner. Overlooking the whole scene, from a balcony are ten lay visitors, one of whom is equipped with binoculars! Such nightmares of a politically correct future have not been borne out, and it is notable that, as Morgan and Newburn (1997) and Dixon (1997) have noted, some of the provisions that were greeted with suspicion have come to be accepted as routine practice. The value of recording interviews has come to be recognised by many in the police service since it has reduced arguments in court about what was said by whom and in what way (Reiner, 2000: 180). In his introduction to Zander's (2005: v) account of police powers, the former Chief Justice, Lord Judge, argued that greater regulation of police detention powers and procedures for interviewing suspects has developed a situation such that

> **there is rarely any significant dispute about what actually happened at a police station, and in particular what was said by the defendant and the context in which his words were spoken. The result is a trial process which gets closer to the truth.**

POLICE POWER: THE WIDER CONTEXT

The previous paragraphs have reviewed various police powers in relatively narrow legal terms. There are several reasons for believing, however, that these provide only a weak indication of what the police service actually does. Not only is this because the majority of police work is not related to law-enforcement, as Chapter 1 made clear, or because police officers do not abide by these legal requirements, although sometimes that is the case, as Reiner's (2000: 173) 'law of inevitable increment – whatever powers the police have they will exceed by a given margin' attests. In addition the statute books only reveal a partial picture of police powers. As the following discussion demonstrates, the notion of 'police powers' needs to be considered in more nuanced terms because power is derived from many sources other than the law and many of the legal powers given to the police have come to encompass other agencies.

That policing is about more than the activities of the police service was firmly established in Chapter 1, and a recurring theme of this book is to explore the range of agencies, public and private sector, that contribute in various ways to policing in this broad sense. Related processes of social transformation and political reform have meant that policing is now a fragmented activity, provided for by different actors at different levels and in different places. The diversity or plurality of policing, as Johnston (2000) has argued, is inextricably linked to changing practices and processes of governance, whereby central government rules 'at a distance' via complex networks and coalitions of state, private and civil partnerships. Against this background the policing 'family' has been extended in Britain (for more details, see Chapter 8), and some of the powers detailed in the previous section have been granted, in full or part, to civilians within the police service or to other agencies altogether. Not only have some police powers, for example those relating to detention, been partially extended to civilians within the police service, such as Community Support Officers and civilian investigating officers, but also to other agencies altogether. Landlords, for example, are required by the Immigration Act 2014 to check the immigration status of new tenants and a range of businesses are required by the Proceeds of Crime Act 2002 to report to the National Crime Agency 'suspicious activities' – financial transactions that might be related to proceeds of crime, money laundering or the financing of terrorism. The granting of formal powers more widely across a network of agencies complements structural transformations in the nature of space, which has meant that the powers of the public police have become relatively marginal to the practices of policing because the private sector explicitly has assumed a more central place in process of social regulation (Mazerolle and Ransley, 2005). Although, as was seen in much of the earlier discussion, PACE provisions mean that the legal powers of the police service tend to apply to places defined as public in terms of access rather than ownership, increasingly private security regimes act as gatekeepers and regulators of large swathes of land in urban areas and so assume greater significance in the routine organisation of social life that bears little relation to the specific individual powers of police officers (Wakefield, 2004; Coleman et al., 2005).

Not only does consideration of police power need to address the implications of extending legal provisions to a wide range of agencies, it must also be noted that only a proportion of what the public police service does is related to their formal statutory powers. Chapter 1 noted that David Bayley's comparative analysis led him to the estimate that only between seven and ten per cent of routine police work is related to crime, which suggests that formal legal powers of the type described in previous paragraphs are only even notionally significant a small proportion of the time (Bayley, 1985). A focus on the legal framework of police powers reflects a jurisprudential approach to policing that fails to address the cultural and sociological determinants of police practice. Central to a proper understanding of policing are the informal skills associated with the negotiation of complexities and contradictions of human relations. Although it might not be immediately apparent that the persuasive skills of a police officer, for example to convince a member of the public to behave in a certain manner. is related to the specific power granted by the law to that officer, the more that power is understood in broad and complex terms the more it becomes clear that it infuses all police work. The legal and constitutional position afforded to the police officer is but a very narrow element of that officer's power. As a plethora of social theorists have argued, power must be conceived as a relatively elusive and multi-faceted construct (Lukes, 2005). While legal frameworks such as that laid down by PACE suggest that the police ought to operate on the basis of consent, and only invoke more formal legal powers where to do so is unavoidable, it is clear that even the most consensual of interactions between police officer and citizen unfold against a background of unequal power dynamics.

One reason why it is important to preserve the legitimacy of the police service is that this helps to invest the individual officer with the authority that makes it easier to perform routine duties. Such authority becomes a resource that officers can use in the 'production of intended effects', which is how Bertrand Russell defined power (Barry, 1981: 80). On a micro level officers have other related resources at their disposal that provide additional opportunities to exercise power. The organisational and logistical possibilities provided by the communication systems and resources at their disposal also amount to another source of power, since these enhance the coercive potential of the individual officer and the police service as an organisation. The constable politely requesting that a street corner beggar 'moves on' does so in the knowledge that both parties are aware that this may be an offer that cannot be refused.

These informal and non-statutory powers available to individual police officers reflect other forms of power that accrue to the police service institutionally. As theorists such as Foucault (1981), Lukes (1974; 2005) and Bourdieu (1991) have argued, power is also constituted by the ability to shape knowledge and discourse and so influence subjective readings of the world. Much of the power of the police service institutionally stems from their status and ability to provide authoritative narratives on a wide range of social issues, most particularly those relating to crime, disorder and social conflict but, inter alia, family structure, personal morality, sexuality, and 'deviance' in many forms. Ericson and Haggarty (1997) identified the central role that police agencies play as communicators of knowledge and information among networks of private and public agencies. Loader and Mulcahy (2001a, 2001b) have detailed the changing ways in which senior police officers have exercised their collective 'power of legitimate naming', whereby they have been able to

> **authorize, categorize, evoke, represent, reinforce and undermine elements of the wider culture, whose presence as interpreters of social institutions, conflicts and hierarchies presupposes something significant about the ownership and framing of relevant issues, and whose individual and collective utterances circulate meanings that contribute in potentially telling ways to the formation of opinion and belief.**
>
> **(Loader and Mulcahy, 2001a: 42)**

Although chief police officers, especially those in rural parts of England and Wales (Wall, 1998), have always part of elite networks with powers of influence, Loader and Mulcahy traced how this broad form of police power extended from the 1970s as senior police officers have developed an increasing corporate voice under the auspices of the Association of Chief Police Officers, since 2015 the National Police Chiefs' Council. However, the exercise of 'soft power' by senior officers is increasingly challenged as their ability to shape the political agenda around policing is contested on multiple social media platforms. More formally, local Police and Crime Commissioners also provide a strong local 'voice' in terms of highlighting and prioritising crime and policing issues (Loader, 2016). Both these elements are considered in more detail in Chapter 4.

Case law and revisions to instruments such as the PACE Codes of Practice always provide for re-interpretation of police powers as defined in relatively narrow legal terms but, these developments aside, the 'law in books' is relatively fixed and stark: either an officer has the legal power do to something or not. For the reasons outlined in these final paragraphs this provides only a weak guide to police power in practice, since other factors such as institutional power and the authority of the police in general terms are also crucial determinants of what the police do. These powers, though, must be endlessly reproduced and vary according to context to an extent that they cannot be taken for granted. The power of the police cannot be understood without reference to the statute book but, equally, cannot be understood apart from the broader social context in which policing is practised.

CONCLUSION

Political debate about policing often centres around whether officers have sufficient legal powers to confront the ever-changing problems of crime and disorder apparently confronting society. The chapter has explored reasons why police powers became increasingly codified in Britain and reviewed the arguments that surrounded the Police and Criminal Evidence Act 1984. A 'pro-law and order' lobby argued that the new law would tie the hands of the police and put too much emphasis on protecting the rights of suspects. Others argued that PACE would damage civil liberties by giving extensive new powers to the police. Most of the research evidence now tends to suggest that the PACE framework, once hugely controversial, has come to be widely accepted. Just as the previous chapter argued that the concept of policing needs to be understood in broad terms, this chapter has shown that police powers also need to be considered widely. Although the law is a necessary part of much policing it does not provide an adequate explanation of the routine activities of police officers. The cultural, political and organisational powers of the police service are considerable.

chapter summary

- Historically the principle that police officers are 'citizens in uniform' has meant that the legal powers afforded to them have been broadly those available to members of the public.

- The Police and Criminal Evidence Act 1984 codified many of the powers that police officers have over citizens, in terms of stop and search; entry, search and seizure; arrest; detention; questioning and treatment; documentary evidence in criminal proceedings; complaints and discipline, and other matters.

- Police officers are independent officers of the Crown. Although accountable to senior officers and the range of bodies that govern the police service, officers exercise their discretion independently.

- PACE gives police officers power to stop and search a member of the public where they have 'reasonable suspicion'. The Equality Act 2010 determines that police ought to operate in ways that challenge inequality.

- Persons stopped, whether searched or not, should be provided with a record of the encounter that includes information about the circumstances that informed the officer's decision, the identity of the officer, and the means by which they might complain about their experience.

- Section 60 of the Criminal Justice and Public Order Act 1994 and the Terrorism Act 2000 permit the stop and searching of members of the public for much more general reasons. Section 60 enables officers to stop and search any individual present in places where it is anticipated that incidents of serious violence might take place. The use of these powers has decreased dramatically since 2008/09. The Terrorism Act 2000 enables officers to stop and search individuals at times and places were it is anticipated there might be terrorist activity.

- PACE stipulates that officers can enter private premises, without being invited, if in possession of a warrant. Officers can enter without a warrant in order to effect an arrest, to recapture someone unlawfully at large, or to save life and limb. As with stop and search powers, they must have 'reasonable grounds' to support their decision.

- Officers can arrest a person without a warrant if they are suspected of committing an 'arrestable' offence. If any person, police officer or civilian believes such a crime is in the process of being committed, they can legally arrest the suspected perpetrator.

- Custody officers are legally responsible for deciding if there is sufficient evidence to hold an individual once they have been arrested and for ensuing that the rights of those in custody are observed.

- Discussion of the formal legal powers of police officers needs to be broadened, partly to recognise that a range of other agencies – policing in more general terms – share some of these provisions, and also because police power also derives from institutional framework and resources, and from the symbolic authority of the service. Additionally the police service is powerful in that it can shape public and political discourse about contemporary issues.

self-check questions (with answers at the back of the book)

1. How did Sir Robert Mark characterise the power of the police over the citizen?

2. What was introduced in 1912 to govern the treatment of those held in custody?

3. What is the general condition for the police powers to stop and search an individual under section 1 of PACE?

4. How does PACE define a 'public place'?

5. What legislation prohibits police officers from discriminating on grounds such as race, gender or disability?

6. What documents cannot be searched under the terms of general search warrant?

7. Under what circumstances can magistrates issue a warrant for arrest?

8. What conditions does PACE stipulate justify detaining an individual in custody prior to their being charged with an offence?

9. Why does a concentration on the legal powers granted to the police provide only a partial understanding of police work?

10. How did Loader and Mulcahy characterise the power of senior police officers to identify and define crime problems?

study questions

1. What are the main principles underlying police powers defined in the Police and Criminal Evidence Act 1984?

2. For what reasons is the 'law in books' (Dixon, 1997) an imperfect guide to police activity?

3. Apart from the law, what are the other bases of police powers?

annotated further reading

Much more detailed and legally authoritative guides to police powers are available in two magisterial volumes. English and Card's (2015) *Police Law* reviews the general principles underpinning the police as well as specific nature of police legal powers in relation to the treatment of suspects, traffic, drinking and drug-taking, public order and myriad other criminal matters. Another invaluable reference is Zander's (2005) *Police and Criminal Evidence Act 1984*, which contains a useful background essay as well as a full copy of the eight Codes of Practice.

Loader and Mulcahy (2001a, 2001b) argue that police power needs to be understood in broader terms, deriving not only from the law but also the institutional, political, social and cultural position of the service in general and senior officers in particular. The development of the Association of Chief Police Officers as a corporate voice for the police service, they argue, has greatly extended the power of senior officers to define crime problems and identify the most appropriate solutions to them.

annotated listings of links to relevant websites

A UK government publication provides an overview of police powers, at https://www.gov.uk/government/publications/police-powers-and-procedures-in-england-and-wales-201112-user-guide.

The codes of practice that provide detailed guidance on police powers can be found at www. gov.uk/guidance/police-and-criminal-evidence-act-1984-pace-codes-of-practice.

The campaign group StopWatch provides a host of background research and information, as well as practical advice, relating to the use and abuse of police stop and search powers. The campaign website is at www.stop-watch.org/.

annotated links to journal articles

The Police and Criminal Evidence Act 1984 regulates the treatment of suspects in police custody, and Skinns' article explored potential changes to detention periods and considers how they might compare to periods before the Act was introduced:

Skinns, L. (2010) 'Stop the Clock? Predictors of Detention without Charge in Police Custody Areas', *Criminology and Criminal Justice*, 10: 303–320.

In two companion pieces, Loader and Mulcahy encouraged a conceptualisation of police powers that recognises that they have considerable influence that is only partially based on the legal status and powers of the office of constable. The political, social and ideological power of the police is explored through both articles:

Loader, I. and Mulcahy, A. (2001a) 'The Power of Legitimate Naming: Part I—Chief Constables as Social Commentators in Post-War England', *British Journal of Criminology*, 41: 41–55.
Loader, I. and Mulcahy, A. (2001b) 'The Power of Legitimate Naming: Part II—Making Sense of the Elite Police Voice', *British Journal of Criminology*, 41: 22–65.

Bowling and Phillips provide a critical review of police stop and search practices, an aspect of powers that are among the most controversial aspects of contemporary police work:

Bowling, B. and Phillips, C. (2007) 'Disproportionate and Discriminatory: Reviewing the Evidence on Police Stop and Search', *Modern Law Review*, 70: 236–961.

4

WHO GUARDS THE GUARDS?

CONTENTS

LEARNING OBJECTIVES

Discussion of the governance of policing has focused primarily on the formal democratic and legal arrangements under which police services have been regulated. Issues relating to funding and the general direction and control of police services in England and Wales have been governed by arrangements that purport to ensure operational independence and accountability to both central government and local agencies. The chapter reviews these developments but also explores issues of accountability in broader terms by considering, for example, efforts to promote ethical codes and human rights policing. The chapter concludes by examining the prospects for democratic accountability in a period when policing is increasingly pluralised. In particular, the chapter aims to:

- critically examine disciplinary systems intended to regulate individual police officer behaviour and broader mechanism to provide democratic oversight of policing

- review efforts to influence policing by the promotion of professionalism, ethical and human rights

- consider the implications of increasing diversity of agencies engaged in policing for fundamental principles of democratic accountability.

KEY TERMS

accountability; complaints; ethics; human rights; legitimacy; police governance and Police and Crime Commissioners

INTRODUCTION

The question 'Who guards the guards?' is among the oldest of political philosophy. Holding police officers to account for their (in)actions raises legal, moral and political questions about social regulation and has important implications for the legitimacy of the police service. Reiner (2000) has argued that during the 'golden age' of British policing in the 1950s and 1960s the extent of public scrutiny of police behaviour might have been minimal compared to what has followed. Nonetheless, the image and authority of the 'bobby on the beat' during that period were secure due to, among other things, an 'almost mythical process of identification with the British people' (Reiner, 2000: 55). The ties that bound the police and the public might have loosened as strategies to hold the police to account have developed over subsequent decades.

APPROACHES TO ACCOUNTABILITY

Accountability relates to political and other processes that seek to influence the performance and priorities of the police service. This includes systems designed to investigate complaints about police malpractice, and reviews of police performance, which may be couched in terms of statistical information about crime patterns, clear-up rates, time taken to respond to emergency calls, financial scrutiny, or public satisfaction with local policing provisions. A recurring theme of this book is the increasing importance of considering policing as a process of social regulation, which engages a diverse range of local, national and international actors. Similarly, accountability is better understood as a multifaceted set of processes, some of which are formal and institutional and others more ad hoc. This discussion will begin by focusing on these issues as they relate to the public police before moving on to consider wider questions about the accountability of plural policing. See also Box 4.1 for an overview of what accountability means in relation to the police force.

Box 4.1

Accountability

What does 'accountability' mean? In this discussion, it is understood in two ways: first, as holding the police to account, in terms of interrogating the actions of individual officers; and second, in terms of controlling the general direction of policing (i.e. governance). An important example of the former, in recent Britain, has been the investigation of the shooting of Jean Charles de Menezes at Stockwell tube station, London, in July 2005. The latter dimension of accountability relates to the broader control and direction of policing, in terms of funding, establishing priorities, and reviewing performance across the service as a whole.

One of the problems with many mechanisms of accountability is that they provide models for police activity based upon rules, regulations and hierarchies of decision making and responsibility – none of which necessarily have much influence in terms of understanding what police officers actually do. As discussed previously, police work is diverse and sometimes unpredictable and so any system based upon procedural frameworks is unlikely to cover more than a small proportion of the activities officers actually carry out (see Chapter 1 for a discussion of the unpredictable and heterogeneous nature of police work). Moreover, as is discussed in Chapter 6, police culture is often held to influence the exercise of discretion that is central to police work. Also, features of police culture, such as group solidarity and insularity, have often been seen to frustrate the integrity and transparency of attempts to hold individual officers to account. The implications of these challenges to the accountability of the police are considered in the following section, which discusses the investigation of police complaints.

CONTROLLING THE CONSTABLE

A long-term trend in the investigation of complaints against the police in Britain has been the development, over several decades, of an independent system. Until the Police Act 1964, there was no systematic means for investigating public complaints about officer conduct. The 1964 Act continued the tradition whereby complaints were dealt with internally by forces about whom the allegation had been made. Concern about this system of self-regulation led the Police Act 1976 to establish the Police Complaints Board, under which more serious complaints were investigated by officers from another force, which was intended to ensure a degree of independence by distancing the investigator from the investigated. However, by the early 1980s a range of problems were identified by those who advocated a more transparent system with greater independence. Among these factors a series of high-profile anti-corruption initiatives introduced in the late 1970s following long-term perception that the Metropolitan Police Service, and in particular some squads of detectives, were undermined by corruption. Somewhat differently, concern about police racism that surfaced, among other places, in Lord Scarman's report into the 1981 Brixton disorders noted that a greater degree of independence would enhance public confidence in the system for investigating complaints against the police. In the mid-1980s an element of independence was introduced into the oversight of police investigations, although these continued to be carried out by police officers. As Prenzler (2000) has noted, the establishment of the Police Complaints Authority (PCA) in Britain during the mid-1980s followed an international trend towards civilian oversight of the investigation of complaints. The PCA managed the investigation of more serious complaints against the police, although these continued to be conducted by police officers. It was often held that complaints were best examined by police officers as it was they who had the necessary professional and investigatory skills. As the range of agencies involved in the conduct of investigations, in both civil and criminal matters, has extended in recent years, the notion that the police were uniquely placed to conduct such forensic examinations became increasingly untenable.

In addition to using civilians to investigate complaints, the Independent Police Complaints Commission (IPCC) system differs from earlier arrangements as it is charged with investigating complaints made against non-sworn staff employed by the police, including Police Community Support Officers and civilian staff. Arrangements introduced by the Police Reform Act 2002 claim a number of other advantages over previous regimes. First, any party can record a complaint about perceived misconduct, not just the person directly 'victimised'. Witnesses or third parties can record a complaint and so start an investigation. Second, complaints can be recorded directly with the IPCC who can then pass details to the relevant police force. This means that complainants do not have to approach directly the force about which they are complaining. Both of these reforms are intended to make it less intimidating to make a complaint against the police. A third change is that a system of 'local resolution' has been introduced such that complaints can be resolved relatively quickly in cases where the complainant is content to receive a formal apology from the police service. These are most obviously intended for situations where officers have been uncivil to members of the public, who then feel satisfied with an apology and do not wish to pursue their complaint further. Research evidence on the nature of complaints against the police suggests that many fall into this category such that a speedy resolution is most appropriate. Prenzler and Porter (2016) noted that research evidence suggests that these alternative dispute resolution practices tend to be quicker, cheaper and more satisfying for those involved.

A fourth aspect that distinguishes the IPCC from previous arrangements is that it can investigate issues of concern that transcend specific allegations of misconduct against particular officers by examining matters of policy and organisational practice that give rise to public concern about policing. This is referred to as the 'guardianship role'. The Home Office (2005a: 3) advised local chief officers that complaints about the 'direction and control' of policing will relate to at least one of the following four categories, but that these do not compromise the operational independence of chief officers:

- operational policing policies (where there is no issue of conduct)
- organisational decisions
- general policing standards in the force
- operational management decisions (where there is no issue of conduct).

The broader guardianship role extends to the complaints system itself, as the IPCC is charged with increasing public confidence in the integrity of the system itself. However, it seems that the extent to which the IPCC has been able to pursue this wider remit has been limited, perhaps by the extensive case load it has been pursuing relating to specific concerns about individual officers. While research commissioned by the IPCC suggests that public confidence has been enhanced by the independence of the new regime for investigating complaints, confidence in the system tends to be related to wider attitudes toward the police service in general: those with a negative view of the police were less likely to trust the complaints system and less inclined to make a complaint (IPCC, 2007). A common challenge to police complaints systems, Prenzler (2000) argued, is to avoid 'capture' by the police service itself. He showed that there are a number of ways that this commonly occurs, including the tendency to employ former officers to investigate complaints. The IPCC system seeks to avoid this danger, as ex-officers cannot be employed. Even so, if confidence in the complaints system itself is related to wider perspectives on the police service more generally, then it might be that the IPPC has only limited scope to enhance the reputation of the complaints system. This might explain why the IPCC found that high levels of confidence in the complaints system among the general population were not shared by many groups that might experience more difficult relations with police. Data from an IPPC (2014) survey found that 53 per cent of adults agreed that the IPCC improved the way in which the police deal with complaints, a proportion that was slightly higher among males than females, younger adults (15–24 year olds) compared to older people, and among BME groups compared to the white population.

Figure 4.1 shows the number of complaints against individual officers recorded by the IPCC in 2015/16, and the longer-term trend. Clearly there has been an increase in the number of cases recorded over the period, but a fairly stable state in recent years. To some extent it is likely that these fluctuations are related to changes in reporting and recording practices rather than an increase in misconduct.

As the figure indicates, the 34,247 complainants recorded in 2015/16 returns to the position around the turn of the decade. The overall pattern for the 43 police services in

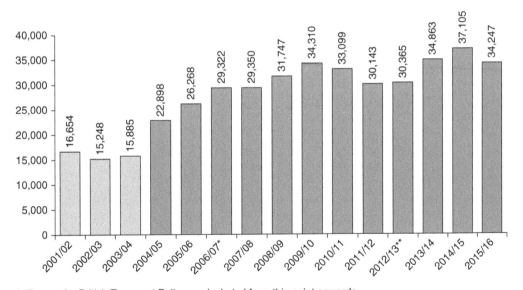

* Figures for British Transport Police are included from this point onwards.
** The definition of a complaint was broadened from this point onwards to include direction and control (applies to complaints received on or after 22 November 2012).

Figure 4.1   Complaint cases recorded 2001/02 – 2015/16 (IPCC, 2106)

England and Wales (plus British Transport Police) masks significant differences between services: North Yorkshire Police, at one end of the spectrum, saw a 44 per cent reduction in the year to 2015/16, while, at the other end of the spectrum, West Yorkshire Police saw a 49 per cent increase. The reduction in complaints in 2015/16 needs to be understood in terms of decreasing officer numbers; indeed the figure for that year amounted to 276 complaints per 1,000 staff, and increase since the 2011/12 ratio of 213 per 1000 personnel, and 225 in 2010/11. The nature of complaints is illustrated in Figure 4.2.

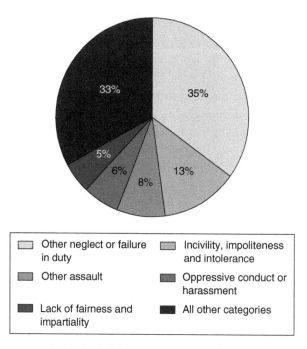

Figure 4.2 Allegations recorded in 2015/16 by category (IPCC, 2016)

There are a number of potential outcomes to a complaint against the police. 'Local resolution' involves the complaint being settled via mediation between the local police service and the complainant, and may involve a local officer investigating the circumstances surrounding the complaint. With the agreement of the complainant this process might result in an apology and the identification of measures to prevent a similar incident from recurring. In 2015/16, 38 per cent of allegations were finalised following local resolution. Other outcomes include the withdrawal or discontinuation of the complaint, the former with the consent of the complainant and the latter in circumstances were they are unco-operative or vexatious. The IPCC can give forces permission to dispense with a complaint when there is insufficient evidence or it is judged to be an abuse of the complaints process. See Box 4.2 for an overview of the IPCC functions.

Of those 31,333 complaints investigated in 2014/15, 14 per cent were upheld, a proportion broadly similar to previous years. Again there was considerable variation between police services, and the IPCC (2015: 5) reported that the proportion upheld varied from 7 to 27 per cent.

Box 4.2

The Independent Police Complaints Commission (IPCC)

The IPCC varies from earlier systems in a range of key respects:

- complaints investigated by independent, non-police staff
- 'third parties' can register complaints
- complaints can be reported directly to the IPCC, not necessarily the police service subject to the complaint
- 'local resolution' possible if the complainant is prepared to accept an apology
- IPCC has a 'guardianship role' to look at concerns beyond individual incidents
- IPCC is responsible for improving public confidence in the complaints system.

In addition to local resolution, other possible outcomes arising from a complaint are:

- withdrawal, at the instigation of the complainant
- discontinuation, if the complainant is unco-operative or vexatious
- formal investigation.

ETHICS, HUMAN RIGHTS AND POLICING

The arrangements described in the previous section provide a framework for dealing with allegations of officer misbehaviour or the inappropriate direction and control of police services locally. Essentially they are both retrospective and negative, as they seek to redress past failures of one kind or another. Other efforts to 'guard the guards' have been developed in relation to British policing in the recent past that are future-oriented and seek to improve policing standards. This section reviews two of sets of initiatives: those that seek to encourage an ethical framework for the police service, and the impact that human rights legislation has on policing.

ethics and policing

The idea of ethical policing has become increasingly salient in Britain in recent years. As a means of controlling the actions of police officers and ensuring their accountability it might be considered that the promotion of police codes of ethics seeks to positively develop policing. The introduction of codes of ethics for the police needs to be understood, in the British case at least, in the wider context of professionalisation of policing – described by Chan (2003) as an important contemporary logic of police reform (see Chapter 12 for further discussion). A central characteristic of professions is that an established ethical code of practice provides a framework for self-regulation. Proponents of professionalism within policing, such as the College of Policing, have regarded ethical practice as an important priority. Moreover, wider concern about political corruption, standards in public life, and abuse of power have impacted on British policing. A series of miscarriages of justice – many of which implicated the criminal justice system in general as well as the police service in particular – coupled with incidents of public disorder and a growing sense that increased public expenditure on the police had not 'produced dividends' in terms of reducing crime combined to undermine police legitimacy (Reiner, 2000: 66–7). Controversies surrounding the Hillsborough disaster and the disorder at Orgreave during the 1984/85 miners' strike, and corrupt relations between police and journalists, have also contributed to concerns about the probity of policing. Advocates of ethical standards for the police often explicitly identify their potential to reverse these trends by increasing accountability and enhancing public confidence (Neyroud, 2003). This is particularly evident in the context of police reform in Northern Ireland as part of the broader peace process, which is discussed at greater length below. The development of a police code of ethics was clearly articulated in terms of the need to garner support for the police service from across the various ethno-religious communities of Northern Ireland. The Police Service of Northern Ireland (PSNI) Code of Ethics was launched in 2003 and replaced the previous disciplinary code that had regulated police conduct. The Code was promoted as the basis of a tacit contract between the police and the public whereby the former afford the latter respect in return for co-operation:

> **The ability of police officers to carry out their functions and duties depends on approval from the public for their existence, actions and behaviour. In simple terms, effective policing requires the support and willing co-operation of the public. Public confidence in the police is closely related to officers' attitudes and behaviour towards the public, in particular their respect for individuals' fundamental rights and freedom as enshrined in the European Convention on Human Rights.**
>
> **(Northern Ireland Policing Board, 2003:4)**

The globalisation of policing discourse – revisited in various contexts in this book – extends to questions of governance and accountability. Many of the ethical codes developed in liberal democratic societies provide a similar vision of the normative police officer, as the examples presented in Box 4.3 demonstrates. Both codes refer to the public and private activities of officers in ways that do not apply to most other employees. The privileged position of police officers in the information society is reflected in the stricture that notes the confidentiality of personal data contained in police systems (Ericson and Haggerty, 1997).

Advocates of ethical policing often argue that the development of such codes is an important means of enhancing the professional status of police officers. If the police service is to establish itself on professional terms similar to other public sector occupations it needs to develop an ethical framework that mirrors those applicable in the medical professions, the legal system or the civil service. Not only might codes of ethics provide a sharper management tool to deal with instances of misconduct, their development can also encourage the development of an organisational culture that allows for performance monitoring and early interventions that can help officers reflect upon and improve their own practice. Neyroud (2003) argued, for example, that the development of ethical policing was a central strategy for the broader promotion of police professionalism. This would, he argued, be one method of reshaping the exercise of police discretion such that the negative influence of police occupational subculture was reduced (Westmarland and Rowe, 2016). The traditional attempt to closely regulate officer decision-making is increasingly inappropriate to the contemporary environment, hence 'rule-bound bureaucracy' ought to be replaced by 'flexible professional practice' (Neyroud and Beckley, 2001: 86).

policing and human rights

Discussion of policing and human rights in Britain during recent years has often portrayed the latter as a politically correct restraint on the provision of effective policing.

Contrary to popular media-driven discourse, the argument that human rights provisions are antithetical to effective and legitimate policing does not withstand scrutiny. The Human Rights Act 1998 effectively incorporated into British law the provisions of the European Convention on Human Rights (ECHR). The ECHR defines a series of human rights that the British state is bound to observe. Among these are the right to life (article 2), the right not to be tortured or subject to inhuman or degrading treatment (article 3), the right to liberty and the security of the person (article 5), the right to a fair public hearing (article 6), the right to freedom of expression (article 10) and the right to peacefully assemble with others (article 11). Very many of these provisions have implications for policing. In respect of some of the topics covered, the police were already obliged to cover the regulations set out by PACE (see Chapter 3 for more on PACE). Not only have the police had to observe controls on operational behaviour for some time, there are other reasons to reconsider the popular discourse that suggests human rights provisions shackle police officers. First, the ECHR makes very clear, by listing them in each case, that the rights identified are not absolute, there are circumstances in which they can be over-ridden. For example, individuals have the right to privacy, but Article 8 makes it clear that the need to protect an individual can be outweighed by the wider interests of society and so this right can be set aside as long as this

is in accordance with the law and is necessary in a democratic society in the interests of national security, public safety or the economic well-being of the country, for the prevention of disorder or crime, for the protection of health or morals, or for the protection of the rights and freedoms of others.

Clearly these circumstances might include a wide range of situations in which it is permissible for the police service, or other public authorities, to conduct surveillance on those suspected of criminal activity. The test of such actions is couched in terms of the need to demonstrate that the contravention of rights in any case is necessary and proportionate. In practice these provisions mean that police surveillance operations have to be authorised by senior officers who are required to certify that operations are justified in that the information sought cannot be gained via other means (i.e. the surveillance is 'necessary'), is reasonable in relation to the desired outcome and will not intrude upon the privacy of unrelated individuals (i.e. it is 'proportionate').

These requirements clearly seek to affect the behaviour of police officers individually and collectively and so provide a framework of police accountability similar to that which governs the investigation of complaints against the police. It does not seek to restrict the activities of police officers but to limit these in ways consistent with the principles of policing in a liberal democratic society. Human rights legislation is often presented negatively, as conferring 'rights' upon criminals that restrict the ability of the police to tackle them. However, it provides an important discourse in terms of the broader mandate of a democratic police service. As Crawshaw et al. (1998: 225, cited in Sheptycki, 2000: 6) have noted, 'not only are the police required to protect human rights when exercising their powers, they are required to protect human rights as one of their functions'.

Developing policing as a means of protecting and enhancing democracy and the respect of human rights has been a major component of international efforts to transform policing in transitional societies, such as countries of the former Soviet Union and South Africa. Robertson (2005) outlined the centrality of police reform to the promotion of open government and human rights in Ukraine and Russia, although she noted that such efforts might have an impact in some localities but will not improve police–public relations more widely unless there is a broader commitment to democratic reform and the rule of law. Similarly Newburn and Sparks (2004, cited in Robertson, 2005) have argued that commitment to criminal justice reform and the promotion of human rights might often be related to efforts by emerging states to gain acceptance in international forums rather than genuine commitment to change. Stenning and Shearing (2005) suggested that the pluralisation of policing networks has led to a move away from a conceptualisation of the police role in terms of law-enforcement and crime control toward a broader remit defined in terms of the promotion of harm reduction, security and safety. One implication of this has been that policing networks are coming to be assessed against global norms. Bayley's (2015) review of recent history of police reform and human rights began by contrasting the acceleration of human rights as a benchmark for reform across many transitional societies with the poor quality of the outcomes. He noted that 'most of the world's people are still wretchedly policed' (Bayley, 2015: 540).

The UN's record in such places as Haiti, Somalia, Eastern Congo, Bosnia and East Timor is mixed to say the least, while bilateral efforts are also suffering from perceived underachievement leading to acute donor fatigue. America's prodigiously expensive police reform in Iraq and Afghanistan, for example, costing tens of billions of dollars, is widely regarded as a failure. Furthermore, a strong argument can be made that police reform has increasingly been aimed more at enhancing security, counterterrorism, in particular, of donors than at advancing democratic, rights-based policing in host nations.

policing, human rights and police reform in Northern Ireland

The scope for human rights discourse to transcend embedded conflicts about policing and security was a key driver of police reform in Northern Ireland. The transformation of policing in Northern Ireland has been a major component of the ongoing peace process. The Independent Commission on Policing for Northern Ireland (ICPNI), chaired by Chris Patten, reported in 1999, and provided a radical agenda for the development of policing that sought to make local boards responsible for the direction of policing, in broad terms. The Commission boldly stated that the role of the police be cast in terms far beyond law-enforcement and crime control:

> It is a central proposition of this report that the fundamental purpose of policing should be ... the protection and vindication of the human rights of all. Our consultations showed clear agreement across the communities in Northern Ireland that people want the police to protect their human rights from infringement by others, and to respect their human rights in the exercise of that duty. Article 28 of the Universal Declaration of Human Rights states: 'everyone is entitled to a social and international order in which the rights and freedoms set forth in this Declaration can be fully realised'. The role of the police is to help achieve that social and international order. They must, for example, uphold the laws that safeguard the lives of citizens. There should be no conflict between human rights and policing. Policing means protecting human rights.

> (ICPNI, 1999: 28)

Internationally developed approaches to conflict resolution based around restorative justice have been implemented in an effort to overcome prevailing forms of informal justice exercised by Loyalist and Republican paramilitary groups (Silke and Taylor, 2000). Often these systems of informal community policing have been understood as efforts of paramilitary groups to exercise control over territories and populations. However, McEvoy and Mika (2002) noted that such explanations overlook the unpalatable truth that the swift and brutal punishments produced often have proved popular with the public. Advocacy groups such as Amnesty International and Human Rights Watch criticised punishment violence and persuaded political parties to explore other forms of criminal justice. In addition to providing a framework through which paramilitary policing could be criticised, an international discourse of human rights also created conceptual space whereby the various parties to the conflict in Northern Ireland could engage in dialogue (McEvoy and Mika, 2002). Kempa and Johnston (2005: 188) argued that, perhaps counter-intuitively, this process entails developing a broad political debate – including agendas on human rights – about the future of policing:

> Recent experience in Northern Ireland suggests that an adaptive way forward lies in a deliberate effort to 'repoliticise' the policing debate. This does not mean encouraging partisan contests over resources and symbolic issues. It means creating opportunities for groups to come together and encouraging them to approach the policing issue in terms of broader normative questions regarding the appropriate nature of the polity in uncertain global times.

As has been demonstrated in the previous paragraphs, reference to ethical principles and human rights relate to debates about 'guarding the guards' in two distinct senses. First, in retrospective negative terms, both concepts provide standards against which previous police behaviour can be assessed. In this sense they contribute toward disciplinary regimes. Second, though, discussion of ethics and human rights can be used in a more progressive sense as a framework for orienting the future development of police services and policing in a broader sense. The macro-governance of the British police is further considered in the following section, before the chapter concludes by exploring the challenges of governing policing in the broader sense of a social process of regulation.

GOVERNING THE BRITISH POLICE

As was shown in Chapter 2 the police in Britain have always been governed by a combination of local and central agencies. Forces were established across England and Wales in the middle of the nineteenth century partly as a result of local demand for professional police institutions capable of tackling crime, and partly as a result of central government efforts to establish a standard pattern of policing across the country as a whole. The combination of central and local governance of police was enshrined in the Police Act 1964, and continue since the introduction of Police and Crime Commissioners in 2012. The 1964 Act divided the governance of the police between three parties: the Chief Constable (or Commissioner in the case of the Metropolitan Police); the police authority, representing local citizens; and the Home Office, on behalf of central government. The Police Reform and Social Responsibility Act 2011 developed these arrangements through the abolition of the local police authorities, which are replaced by directly elected Police and Crime Commissioners (PCCs), who are overseen by Police and Crime Panels.

The role of PCCs incorporates much of what was performed under previous arrangements by local police authorities. PCCs set the level of council tax precept that contributes to police funding, have the power to appoint and dismiss chief officers, and are responsible for consulting with local communities to help establish policing priorities. Where PCCs have a greater role than predecessor police authorities is in relation to the wider community safety and local criminal justice arena. Funding for services such as statutory drug intervention programmes and services for victims has been devolved from central government to PCCs who can commission such work from the local public, private or charitable sector. The work of PCCs is supported by local Police and Crime Panels (PCPs) comprised of local councillors drawn from the authorities covered by each police service area. PCPs are intended as a check and balance on PCCs that will also help to ensure that information about the performance of the local PCC is available to voters as part of the four-year electoral cycle.

The impact of PCCs remains to be seen. The introduction of the new component in the democratic infrastructure of the state was met initially, in electoral terms at least, with apparent public apathy – at least in terms of turnout at the first round of elections in 2012. In some areas it seems likely that the role of the PCC will be performed by directly elected Mayors (as will happen in Manchester from 2017). As Reiner (2013) noted, predictions of future trends are made more difficult since political and social developments are likely to mean that the PCC model will not necessarily unfold neatly in accordance with the intentions of the architects of these new arrangements. Crawford (2012) reminded us that there are now multiple local experiments established in police accountability and it seems unlikely that each will develop in a uniform way. One of the key tensions is that police accountability continues to be operated in different directions: both 'downwards' to local communities as well as 'upwards' to central government (Murphy et al., 2016).

Nonetheless, it seems likely that PCCs will face challenges on a number of fronts. Key among these will be the fuzzy boundaries of the notion of constabulary independence. While police continue in legal terms to have independence, the concentration of powers into one office-holder, who has the power to dismiss chief officers, poses a considerable risk that PCCs will become embroiled in operational decision making (Lister, 2013). Another problem relates to the sheer size and complexity of the electorates that PCCs are supposed to represent. Although the problem of democratic representation is not confined to PCC electorates it is exacerbated by the size and scale of populations in many police service areas: the PCC for West Yorkshire, for example, represents 2.2 million people and covers 23 parliamentary constituencies (Sampson, 2012: 5).

A further problem is that it is not clear that PCCs will do anything to address democratic deficits in terms of a lack of accountability of private sector or hybrid forms of policing (Lister and Rowe, 2015) (as discussed below and in Chapter 10). Neither will PCCs address the lack of accountability applied to regional, national and transnational policing arrangements (some of which are discussed in Chapter 8).

ACCOUNTABILITY AND PLURAL POLICING

The discussion so far has focused upon the public police service and how it might be held accountable, whether in terms of responding to the alleged misconduct of an individual officer or more broadly when it comes to governance and direction. However, the proliferation of agencies involved in the provision of security raises important questions about accountability in an era of plural policing. In an early study, Shearing and Stenning (1983) argued that for much of the long history of private policing in North America questions about social justice and accountability had been marginalised by a conceptualisation of the sector as the junior partner to the public police. As long as the private security industry was held to be less significant, in terms of the number of people employed and the roles that they carried out, there were few concerns about regulation and it was held that this could be left to the market mechanisms in the form of contracts between security companies and their customers (Shearing and Stenning, 1983). While Shearing and Stenning demonstrated that it may never have been true that the private sector was the junior partner, the more important concern that they raised related to the increasing importance of the private sector in an era when the state monopoly on policing was rapidly unravelling. Clearly Shearing and Stenning's predicton that private policing would play an increasing role in the regulation of human relations was a prescient one. What their discussion did not anticipate, however, is the increasingly blurred boundary between public and private policing. It has not been the case that the role of the public sector has shrunk under the challenge of the private. As is shown in Chapter 10, the picture has become more complex than a simple binary of public and private suggests. Loader (2000: 324) argued the need to reconsider governance in the following terms:

> **[W]e can no longer solely concern ourselves with how the public police can be made accountable to government, whether by legal, democratic or – as has been prominent of late – managerialist means. The pluralization of policing has generated a situation in which established intra-organizational modes of accountability (and their supporting structures of thought) are rendered limited and inadequate, and where novel policing forms are fast outstripping the capacity of existing institutional arrangements to monitor and control them. The world of plural policing remains, at best, weakly or obscurely accountable.**

In this final section of the chapter we will explore the nature of accountability in the context of plural policing and the various means that have been used to develop systems to regulate the mixed economy of policing. White (2016) noted that private policing has been regulated variously by legal and statutory arrangements, via market-based mechanisms, and through critical public discourse. Private policing in Britain was largely unregulated until the Private Security Industry Act 2001. The primary requirement introduced by the Act was that all personnel – officers, managers and directors of companies – be licensed. White (2010) suggested that the new regulatory regime had two principal objectives: to reduce criminality and raise standards in the industry.

Additionally, the Act established the Security Industry Authority (SIA) that oversees the process of regulation and licensing and the provision of training that will, it is claimed, help to transform the industry and enhance public legitimacy. The Authority has powers to inspect private security businesses and check that personnel have the necessary licenses. White (2010: 156) noted that although the Authority failed deliver on some functions it had removed licences from 35,000 individuals and had become 'a credible enforcer or regulation'. The SIA survived a government review of public bodies ('the bonfire of the Quangos') in 2010 but reforms announced in 2013 mean that the future role of the SIA will be to licence security businesses rather than individuals: accredited security businesses will then be responsible for ensuring that they employ appropriate staff.

Following White's (2016) argument that critical public discourse has played a role in holding the private security industry to account, it might be increasingly important to consider informal means by which police more broadly are regulated. Social media and camera-phone technology mean that police are routinely exposed to unregulated informal systems of oversight directly operated by the public. The consequences of such forms of 'sousveillance' (Mann et al., 2003) remain under-researched and the potential that they might have as a corrective on misconduct could be limited since there is no clear route to disciplinary action against those apparently caught engaging in problematic behaviour. Nonetheless, some research evidence into the impact of body-worn cameras suggests that technology can have an impact on the behaviour of officers, and so it seems likely that devices operated by the public might also have an effect (Reiner, 2016).

The end of the cold war and peace process in Northern Ireland might have led to an enhanced role for the security services in policing, particularly in the context of intelligence gathering and transnational organised crime. While parliament and the government provide for the accountability of these agencies in constitutional terms, this is clearly much narrower than the systems outlined in previous sections of this chapter as they apply to the public police. It is argued in Chapter 8 that one of the major challenges relating to transnational and global policing is that there is a paucity of accountability and oversight mechanisms. In part this is because of a lack of legal and regulatory framework, but this is exacerbated by a lack of 'global civil society' that can provide a normative context for governance. Domestically there are a range of agencies outside of the public police service and private security industry involved in a host of policing activities including fraud, human trafficking and terrorism. Box 4.4 outlines one mechanism by which some of these activities are made transparent and accountable, but it is clear that much of the general oversight and governance of these activities is carried on through broader democratic process. Parliamentary oversight of security services, for example, is an expression of accountability as are the interventions of specialist offices such as PCCs or the IPCC.

Box 4.4

Governing the Extended Police Family

Other parties in emerging policing networks are also subject to oversight. For example, the Regulation of Investigatory Powers Act 2000 (RIPA) established the Investigatory Powers Tribunal (IPT) to oversee surveillance and intelligence gathering. The Tribunal determines the legality of intelligence and surveillance undertaken by MI5, MI6 and GCHQ and their roles in monitoring terrorism and criminal activity. As with the SIA, the Tribunal's remit only extends to individual complaints relating to alleged infractions of the rules. The IPT does not appear to have power to hold to account services in broader terms. It does not hold agencies that have investigatory powers to account in terms of the general control and direction.

CONCLUSION

What emerges from this review is that narrow mechanisms of accountability exist in respect to some of the agencies involved in policing networks. These tend to only relate to allegations of misconduct against specified personnel and do not extend, as with the public police, to broader questions about policies and priorities. Moreover, systems of accountability and governance have been developed to oversee specific agencies and institutions within particular jurisdictions. These regimes become increasingly unable to hold accountable policing networks as they develop in a global context. To use the language of much contemporary analysis, existing arrangements focus upon nodes rather than networks of policing. Loader (2000) argued that questions about social justice, accountability, governance and legitimacy are made more urgent in the developing environment of contemporary global policing. Prevailing systems have focused on police institutions developed in the context of modern sovereign states and as such do not translate to diverse and dispersed networks that transcend national boundaries. The response to this changing policing terrain has been the evolution of hybrid mechanisms of governance, including, among others, a reliance on licensing, registration, rules concerning insurance coverage, self-regulation, the establishment of minimum standards and marketplace accountability to customers (Wood and Shearing, 2007: 133). Loader (2000) noted that many of these mechanisms allow little or no room for consideration of fundamental principles of justice or the pursuit of the public interest. He proposed the establishment of local, regional and national policing commissions charged with controlling the public, voluntary and commercial nodes within policing networks. These commissions would hold these networks to democratic account in the interests of public justice, defined in terms of recognising the diverse interests and demands of the public, respect for human rights, and an equitable distribution of policing resources.

chapter summary

- Police accountability has two dimensions. First, efforts to hold individual officers to account. IPCC investigations into fatal incidents involving the police are good illustrations of this form of accountability. The second aspect of accountability relates to governance in broader terms of the direction, principles and overall performance of the police service.

- The international trend towards the wholly independent investigation of complaints was exemplified in the Police Reform Act 2002, which established the Independent Police Complaints Commission (IPCC). The IPCC provisions allow for the wholly independent investigation of complaints.

- Other approaches seek to develop police professional standards. Codes of ethics are developed in an effort to promote a normative framework to which officers should aspire. Emphasising ethical police performance has also been seen as a method to enhance police legitimacy and improve public confidence.

- Similarly, human rights provisions have provided a framework to control police operations. While citizens have the right to privacy, for example, the police can contravene this with surveillance operations, providing that these are 'necessary' (no alternatives are available) and 'proportionate' (in relation to the gravity of the matter at hand).

- Police reform in the context of international development has centred around the promotion of human rights. In this context, human rights agendas have not only focused on controlling what officers are permitted to do, they also establish a range of objectives that the police are expected to secure.

- The governance of British police is shared between central government, Police and Crime Commissioners, Police and Crime Panels, and Chief Constables. While Chief Constables have operational responsibility and independence, the PCCs, PCPs and central government are responsible for financial provisions and establishing the policy and direction of police services.

- The establishment of the office of PCC in 2012 was predicated on government claims that a system of democratic accountability (via a locally elected PCC) was replacing bureaucratic accountability through public service management.

- The PCC role faces serious challenges relating to the difficulty of a single individual representing large and complex communities that might not have a coherent or consistent set of needs and demands. There might also be a danger of PCCs compromising the operational independence of police, especially as PCCs have power to dismiss chief officers.

- Developments in the governance and accountability of the public police do not easily extend to the emerging context of plural policing. While legislation requires that private security personnel are licensed and the Security Industry Authority can inspect companies, concerns continue about the extent to which the sector more widely is accountable and effectively regulated. Certainly questions about the direction and control of the private security industry continue to be resolved by the market mechanism, which marginalises public interest and social justice questions.

self-check questions (with answers at the back of the book)

1. Prior to the Police Reform Act 2002, which agencies and groups had advocated the establishment of an independent system to investigate complaints against the police?

2. What does the 'local resolution' of a complaint against the police entail?

3. When was the Code of Ethics of the Police Service of Northern Ireland first established?

4. Under the terms of the European Convention on Human Rights, what conditions need to be met if individual rights are to be set aside?

5. What did the Patten Commission into policing in Northern Ireland suggest was the main purpose of the police?

6. What piece of legislation established the office of Police and Crime Commissioner (PCC)?

7. What form of accountability did the government claim was introduced via the establishment of PCCs?

8. Why did Shearing and Stenning (1983) suggest that concern about the role of private security had been marginalised in the USA, prior to the 1980s?

9. What is the primary requirement of the 2001 Private Security Industry Act?

10. What concerns did Loader (2000) suggest are made more salient by the changing environment of international policing?

study questions

1. What have been the key arguments in favour of developing an independent system of investigating complaints against the police?

2. How might an emphasis on ethics and human rights impact upon policing?

3. Although the position of local police authorities might have been eroded in recent years, why is it simplistic to argue there has been an unchecked process of centralisation. Can Police and Crime Commissioners provide effective oversight of policing?

annotated further reading

Dixon and Smith's (1998) article, 'Laying Down the Law', analyses changing combinations of systems of accountability applied to the British police. Three key cases that tested aspects of police accountability are reviewed and developments such as operational independence, liability for losses experienced by the public due to police negligence, and the increasing role of civil law proceedings against police are examined.

Neyroud and Beckley's (2001) *Policing, Ethics and Human Rights* explores the development of a human rights/ethics based approach to policing developed in Britain in response to miscarriages of justice, and perceptions of police racism and incompetence. The book distinguishes between personal, operational and organisational ethics and argues that each of these will become increasingly important in the development of professional policing as demands on the service become increasingly complex and performance is subject to greater public scrutiny.

White's (2010) *The Politics of Private Security: Regulation, Reform and Re-Legitimation* provides an excellent account of developing approaches to regulating private security in

Britain and the continuing challenges faced. His (2016) 'Private Security and the Politics of Accountablity' analysis of the governance of private security provides a new framework to capture the breadth of different modes of accountability. Loader and Walker's (2007) *Civilising Security* makes a strong case for enhancing democratic oversight of policing activities in broad terms.

annotated listings of links to relevant websites

The website of the Independent Police Complaints Commission (ipcc.gov.uk) contains many resources, including performance statistics, reports into specific complaints, and links to other agencies and useful police-related resources and organisations.

The Association of Police and Crime Commissioners can be found at www.apccs.police. uk/, which contains links to the individual websites of Police and Crime Commissioners alongside much other background information to the office.

Information about ethics in policing can be found at the web page of the College of Policing, www.college.police.uk/What-we-do/Ethics/Pages/Code-of-Ethics.aspx.

annotated links to journal articles

An article by Chan provides a critical review of different strategies for accountability:

Chan, J. (1999) 'Governing Police Practice: Limits of the New Accountability', *British Journal of Sociology*, 50 (2): 251–70.

The introduction of the office of Police and Crime Commissioners is analysed in a several journal articles, including:

Lister, S. (2013) 'The New Politics of the Police: Police and Crime Commissioners and the "Operational Independence" of the Police', *Policing*, 7 (3): 239–47.

Sampson, F. (2012) 'Hail to the Chief?—How far does the Introduction of Elected Police Commissioners Herald a US-Style Politicization of Policing for the UK?', *Policing*, 1–12.

The relationship between private security and the state and the implications that this has for the legitimacy of the sector and reviewed in White's article:

White, A. (2013) 'The New Political Economy of Private Security', *Theoretical Criminology*, 17: 85–101.

5

COMMUNITY POLICING

CONTENTS

Community policing is a nebulous concept used to describe a range of programmes and initiatives from those that closely involve members of the public in the routines of the police service to those that seem to represent little more than a public relations exercise intended to secure legitimacy. In many respects it might be tempting to reject the phrase entirely on the grounds either that it is tautologous (what else, apart from 'the community' in some shape or form, could be policed?) or that it is applied to such a wide spectrum of policing styles and practices that it is virtually meaningless. However, the ubiquity and resilience of promises to deliver community policing means that this temptation has been resisted. This chapter aims to:

- explore the multiple ways in which community policing has been defined and practised
- consider links between community policing, law-enforcement and public legitimacy
- outline some of the key challenges facing efforts to develop community policing.

KEY TERMS

consent; consultation; co-production; legitimacy and Neighbourhood Policing

INTRODUCTION

Even though the principle of community policing is problematic, it remains a vital starting point in how we think about the relationship between the police and the public. As indicated in Chapter 1, the idea that the public confer consent on the power that holds power over them is an important organising principle for the police in many societies. Difficult though it may be to implement – and many of the obstacles are outlined later in the chapter – community policing in some form remains the only viable way for the police to retain public support and is a vital prerequisite for attempts to reduce crime. Alongside moral and ethical arguments for embracing the principles of community policing lies a pragmatic case based upon the need to cultivate public support so that problems of crime and disorder can be addressed. Recent research suggests that perceptions of procedural justice are important to public support for police and the principle of the rule of law and might be secured more effectively through high-visibility community policing (Hough et al., 2010). Bradford (2017) indicates that fair and just treatment by the police shapes the extent to which individuals are identified, and self-identity, as part of the mainstream community, which also points to the ways in which policing can contribute to the development of communities. In terms of trust and confidence in the police, Van Damme (2017) found that positive contact with officers was central to not only moral identification with the police but also a wider sense of obligation to obey the law.

The chapter begins by considering the wide ranges of approaches to the concept of community policing, and the implications that these variously have for the development and delivery of policing programmes. The discussion continues by exploring the various efforts to develop community policing that have been made in Britain, the USA, South Africa and elsewhere during recent decades, and considers the social and political context against which such programmes have been introduced. In the penultimate section the chapter considers some of the generic problems that have hampered the effective delivery of community policing. The conclusion argues that although the principles of community policing might never be wholly realised in practice they continue to provide an important philosophy around which policing ought to be organised.

DEFINING 'COMMUNITY POLICING'

As will be seen below, definitions of community policing often seem vague, and more than a little aspirational. Even so, there are core themes common to many outlines of the principles and practices of community policing. Some of these focus on the ways in which policing is produced – the processes through which the activities of the police are co-ordinated and delivered. The following section describes these in some detail, in the context of Britain and the USA. Following that, another perspective is outlined, which focus instead on understanding community policing in terms of the different outcomes that are produced compared to other models of policing.

process-led approaches

As has been noted, the ubiquity of community policing and the ease with which it is endorsed by police services with fundamentally different histories and characteristics might lead one to conclude that the concept contains little concrete meaning. Indeed some advocates of community policing have argued that the term ought to remain somewhat vague since it should provide a general framework rather than a detailed programme of activity (Moore, 1992; Eck and Rosenbaum, 1994/2000). Skogan (2006a) acknowledged that community policing has been widely endorsed by the police services of the USA and that a very diverse range of activities have been developed under this rubric. He suggested that community policing is a process rather than a product and embraces three key elements: citizen involvement, problem-solving and decentralisation (Skogan, 2006a: 28). The first of these was emphasised in the influential work in the

USA by Trojanowicz and Bucqueroux (1990, cited in Tilley, 2003: 314), who outlined the principles of community policing in the following terms:

> **Community policing is both a philosophy and organisation strategy to allow community residents and police to work together in new ways to solve problems of crime, fear of crime, physical and social disorder and neighbourhood decay.**

Clearly this approach is broadly similar to that later described by Skolnick, although it is interesting that the extract above makes no reference to decentralisation. The notion that policing ought to be jointly directed and produced by the public and the police service emerges though as a core similarity between these two definitions, and is one found in almost all accounts of community policing. Another perspective from the USA is offered in Skogan's study of community policing in Chicago. Skogan (2006b: 5) noted that practices of community policing incorporate a very wide range of practices but that at its core community policing is a 'process rather than a product'. Box 5.1 summarises Skogan's definition.

Box 5.1

Community Policing as Process and Product

In some places community policing is in the hands of special neighbourhood officers, whereas in other cities it involves the transformation of the entire police department. In some communities, residents participate in aggressive Neighbourhood Watch patrols ... though in many more communities public involvement is limited to asking citizens to call 911 quickly when they see something suspicious. Departments also point to a long list of activities they have underway ... officers patrol on foot ... and on horses, bicycles or even Segways ... However, community policing is not defined by these kinds of activities ... Community policing is not a set of specific projects; rather, it involves changing decision-making processes and creating new cultures within police departments. It is an organizational strategy that leaves setting priorities and the means of achieving them largely to residents and the police who service in their neighbourhoods. Community policing is a process rather than a product.

(Skogan, 2006b: 5)

Again it is clear that this typology shares much in common with those already outlined, however, it is notable that the definition of community policing has been broadened somewhat to refer to the internal organisation and culture of the police service. It might also be significant that while the first element emphasises the value of public input into policing the following three aspects all foreground the police department itself, suggesting that they continue to be 'first among equals' in relation to the public. The primacy of the police service among multi-agency partnerships and the power that this affords them in terms of defining agendas concerning crime and antisocial behaviour has been noted in the British context and will be explored in more detail later in the chapter when a range of obstacles to the effective development of community policing are outlined.

Although they do not always explicitly acknowledge it, the definitions of community policing described above all relate to the experience of the USA, from where Brogden (1999) has argued the dominant discourse for police reform across much of the rest of the world has emerged. He suggested that the apparent failures of community policing in many contexts has partly been due to poor implementation but is also explained by the 'alien legal, cultural and organizational history' that pertains outside of the USA (Brogden, 1999: 167). Definitionally, if not operationally, though, it seems that British perspectives on community policing are broadly similar to those developed in the USA. Weatheritt (1987) argued that the term 'community policing' in the British context had been used to describe a wide range of programmes and that it tended to be used to denote projects of which authors approved. Some of the core characteristics of community policing initiatives in Britain are similar to those identified in the USA. Smith (1987), for example, argued that community policing, in common with other efforts to develop a community orientation for social policy, had three central features: decentralisation, partnership, and the incorporation of the informal and voluntary sectors.

outcome-led approaches

While the definitions outlined in the previous section focus on the structures and systems by which policing is delivered, other commentators have instead emphasised that community policing encompasses a broader set of policing outcomes that go beyond a focus of crime control and law-enforcement. Along these lines Friedman's (1992) study led to the view that what defined the broad range of activities brought together under the umbrella of community policing was that they 'aimed at achieving more effective and efficient crime control, reduced fear of crime, improved quality of life, improved police services and police legitimacy'. An early proponent of community policing in Britain was John Alderson, who, when Chief Constable of Devon and Cornwall police, promoted objectives for the police service, as outlined in Box 5.2, many of which go far beyond the traditional definitions of policing that were outlined in Chapter 1.

Box 5.2

Alderson's Model of Community Policing

- To contribute to liberty, equality and fraternity.
- To help reconcile freedom with security and to uphold the law.
- To uphold and protect human rights and thus help achieve human dignity.
- To dispel criminogenic social conditions, through co-operative social action.
- To help create trust in communities.
- To strengthen security and feelings of security.
- To investigate, detect and activate the prosecution of crimes.
- To facilitate free movement along public thoroughfares.
- To curb public disorder.
- To deal with crises and help those in distress involving other agencies where needed.

(Alderson, 1979, cited in Tilley, 2003: 314)

Clearly any list of this kind raises further questions. It might be wondered, for example, what are the 'criminogenic social conditions' that the police ought to be seeking to dispel. Whatever difficulties might arise with this definition of the police role, though, it is clear that a highly ambitious and wide-ranging scope for the police service was envisioned, and that this has often been at odds with political rhetoric, from all sides, during the intervening quarter of a century that has stressed the need for the police to vigorously pursue a more narrow goal of 'cracking down' on crime.

community policing as a means to recover public consent

Waddington (1999a: 207) argued that Alderson's advocacy of community policing can only be properly understood as rejection of the technocratic professionalism of policing that had occurred in England and Wales during the late 1960s. In the interests of economy, efficiency and modernisation policing had been transformed in that period into Unit Beat Policing, a key feature of which was that officers were deployed in cars and so were able to cover larger geographical areas. Along with other developments, such as the closure of many 'police houses' and the replacement of police telephone boxes with two-way radios, the drive to promote a more efficient system of policing had the unintended consequence of separating police officers from the public. While traditional police patrol work came to be regarded as inefficient in terms of tackling crime, it had secured a relatively high public profile for the police. They became a regular presence in the community, which provided some symbolic reassurance for the wider society. Police efforts to become more professional in the 1960s meant that officers became increasingly separated from the people they were supposed to serve. Constables were not able to develop personal relations with the public when they drove past them in cars as they did when walking around on the beat. Brain (2010: 40) described the impact that changes in the delivery of policing had on public perceptions as traditional models were

gradually abandoned in favour of officers patrolling solely in 'panda' cars enhanced by 'incident' or 'immediate' response cars, generally double-crewed by the more experienced members of the shift. Middle England began to lament the absence of the 'bobby on the beat' ... Many politicians and members of the public wanted to see the return in real life of *Dixon of Dock Green*, a possibly unique example of a fictional character of only partial authenticity becoming the mainspring of political and policy initiatives.

It was against this background of decreasing routine contact between the police and the public that advocates such as Alderson were introducing measures that sought to reintroduce the police into community life. That such aims underpin the contemporary drive towards Neighbourhood Policing in England and Wales suggests that earlier demands for community policing remained unrealised to some extent. Brain (2010) noted that the term 'neighbourhood policing' was used in preference to 'community policing' since the latter was strongly associated with failed efforts to develop local policing. The nature of Neighbourhood Policing and some of the key challenges for efforts to reinvigorate community policing in the twenty-first century are considered later in this chapter. The extent to which contemporary drives toward evidence-based policing might be in tension with principles of community policing are also considered.

Efforts to define community policing remain problematic. Some have argued that the term is subject to such a range of uses, and abuses, that it ought to be dispensed with altogether. Tilley (2003: 315) noted that his review of the literature on community policing led him to the view that '"community policing" is widely endorsed, though at the same time widely seen to be close to meaninglessness'. Perhaps the most reliable way of conceptualising community policing is provided by Brogden and Nijhar's (2005: 2) approach, which is to define the concept in terms of *what it is not*:

It is not military-style policing with a central bureaucracy obedient to directive legislation which minimises discretion. It is not policing that is autonomous of public consent and accountability. It is not policing that is committed primarily to reactive crime-fighting strategies. It is not policing that is measured by output in terms of professional efficiency. Rather it is policing which is determined by strategies, tactics and outcomes based on community consent.

PRACTISING COMMUNITY POLICING

Just as the principles of community policing are wide ranging, so too are the practices introduced in its name. Ekblom (1986) noted that community policing in England and Wales incorporated the deployment of specialist community constables and liaison officers, a range of means of promoting consultation through surveys and community meetings, and police working in conjunction with other agencies. Similar approaches were further promoted by New Labour as multi-agency partnership approaches to crime prevention and community safety, advocated since the early 1990s (Home Office, 1991). Programmes such as reassurance policing and, subsequently, Neighbourhood Policing placed considerable emphasis on the co-production of policing and on responding to the priorities of local communities (Innes, 2004; Brain, 2010). A review of Neighbourhood Policing programmes suggested the following key characteristics (Flanagan, 2007, 2008 in Turley et al., 2012):

- strong Community Safety Partnership (CSP) leadership and priority setting
- understanding local neighbourhoods through information sharing, mapping and resource allocation
- strong community engagement
- dedicated, multi-agency teams with a Neighbourhood Manager, accommodated in the same place where possible
- joint tasking arrangements
- better information to the public
- joint performance measures, monitoring and improvement processes
- financial planning and pooling of budgets to support outcomes.

The establishment of Police and Crime Commissioners (PCCs) in 2012 (discussed at greater length in Chapter 4) was grounded in the coalition government's 'localism agenda' and was intended to help re-connect policing to the community. PCCs have been promoted as local champions able to advocate on behalf of the public and ensure that the police reflect their priorities. PCCs have an important role in commissioning services previously funded directly by the Community Safety Partnerships that have formed an important part of the local architecture of community safety and community policing, extending to the development of community penalties for offenders. In this way PCCs offer the potential to further integrate police with other local agencies working within probation, drug and alcohol counselling, family, housing, health and education services.

Although the nature of initiatives designed to deliver community policing are extremely diverse they can be considered as falling into two broad categories: those initiatives designed to increase consultation between the police and the public, and those designed to enhance collaboration (Bennett, 1994). Those schemes designed to increase consultation may involve the police questioning the public to find out how well (or badly) they are doing their job, a process that may not, necessarily, effect subsequent operational decisions. It can mean more than this, and involve officers consulting with the community in order to discover what their priorities are and what types of crime they wish to see the police concentrate upon. Alternatively it may mean that the police develop means to make themselves formally accountable to the local community by ensuring that they explain and justify their actions to local people. Making data available online that shows crime trends down to the street level is one way in which local communities might access information such that they can interact in a more equal and meaningful way with police, a development considered further in Chapter 11.

police–community consultation

A key formal method whereby the police consult local communities has been via community meetings. Section 106 of the Police and Criminal Evidence Act 1984 (PACE) required that the police establish consultative groups to identify public priorities for policing. Often police services established a number of these committees, commonly one for each division of the force. Research has suggested that these committees did not, for a number of reasons, tend to fulfil their role effectively, as is discussed further in Chapter 4. Partly this seems to be due to the police themselves: the meetings tended to be held on police premises and very much under the direction of the force itself with few resources committed to them. Without support from the force in general it was difficult for these meetings to influence policing across the whole constabulary, and there is a perception that the meetings become little more than 'talking shops', providing the chance for grievances and concerns to be aired but little more. Keith (1988) argued that the PACE provisions confused consultation with accountability and that unequal power relations between the parties were fundamentally problematic, a criticism that applies more widely to other aspects of community policing.

Another, more general, problem is that the members of the public who attend do not appear to be representative of the population: as a whole they tend to be white, middle-class, middle-aged males. Similarly, Crawford (2012) argued that PCCs might not represent an authentic voice of local public demands and that 'there are risks that policing agendas influenced by majoritarian sensibilities may be captured by those with the loudest voices, the largest political influence and the deepest pockets'. Those 'hard to reach groups' who are actually more likely to come into conflict with the police are unlikely to participate in consultation (Jones and Newburn, 2001). As McLaughlin

(1991: 116) has argued, these efforts to identify issues of concern to local communities are unlikely to incorporate those for whom 'the police were the problem'.

There are, however, other methods whereby the police can liaise with the public including, increasingly, in online social media environments (Schneider, 2016). Often this occurs more informally and through individual officers whose role it is to work with minority groups, in schools and youth projects, among the elderly, and with other groups in the community. Innes and Innes (2011) found that police visibility is closely linked to public confidence and police legitimacy. Formal methods of consultation also exist as the police work with other public agencies including local government, business, educational and charitable groups. As these opportunities are often and informal and usually based on personal contacts and interactions it is very difficult to ascertain how effective they are. Since the Crime and Disorder Act 1998 gave, for the first time, local authorities statutory responsibility to tackle problems that had previously been the domain of the police service the already developing trend toward multi-agency partnerships has accelerated further. While such networks often seem to have been undermined by institutional and organisational problems, relating agencies having competing agendas, being relatively unequal in terms of power and commitment to projects, and being dominated by a small cohort of agencies. Edwards and Hughes (2002) stressed that the nature and quality of partnerships varies from place to place and is often contingent on local factors that are difficult to predict or to generalise about. They noted that 'partnerships can provide opportunities for building stable, long-term, exchange relationships built on trust and co-operation, yet they can also create opportunities for destabilising, short-term, self-interested competitive behaviour' (Edwards and Hughes, 2002: 146). Fraught and unpredictable though such mechanisms might be on occasion, they do offer at least the prospect of the police service liaising with and consulting other agencies and contribute to a process whereby the police are not isolated and atomised from other institutions but become engaged and integrated with them. More recently, the promotion of the Total Place initiative has meant that criminal justice agencies have been encouraged to develop creative partnerships and to identify ways of collaborating on the delivery of public sector services. One benefit of this, it is claimed, is a reduction in the duplication of expenditure and can 'do more with less' resources. The reduction of 20 per cent in police budgets over 2010–15 also forced police services to connect with other public and private partners (HMIC, 2011a, 2011b).

police–community collaboration

Police–community collaboration refers to developments designed to directly involve local people in the policing of their own neighbourhoods. These approaches rely upon the idea that the incorporation of the community directly into policing will help to prevent crime in the first place and to increase chances of arresting criminals. Initiatives such as Neighbourhood Watch, discussed more fully below, where residents provide informal surveillance of their localities such that their mutual security is increased, have been introduced with this end in mind. Neighbourhood Watch schemes were introduced in Britain in the mid-1980s and quickly flourished. By the mid-1990s it was estimated that there were 115,000 schemes across England and Wales, and it is estimated that some 3.3 million people lived in areas covered by Neighbourhood Watch. The rapid expansion of Neighbourhood Watch has led to the establishment of similar schemes designed to promote effective communication as a method of crime prevention in a range of niche areas. For example, Business Watch, Office Watch, Vehicle Watch, Boat Watch, Shop Watch, Farm Watch, Pub Watch, School Watch, Golf Watch, Post Office Watch, Church Watch, Bed and Breakfast Watch, Child Watch, and Horse Watch have been among the programmes introduced to extend community policing beyond residential neighbourhoods. In many respects the development of these elements of community policing foreshadowed government emphasis on activities that directly engage the public in service delivery and require police to 'see like a citizen' in terms of approaches to their role (Holdaway, 2013).

While Neighbourhood Watch has undoubtedly been a success in terms of the number of schemes established and has become a ubiquitous feature of the urban landscape, it is difficult to discern the impact it has had on levels of crime. To some extent this lack of clarity reflects the huge diversity of activity encompassed under the umbrella of Neighbourhood Watch and that many schemes become dormant after an initial burst of energy. Furthermore the range of neighbourhoods in which schemes have been established is considerable and it is difficult to develop robust evaluation methodologies that can attribute changing crime patterns to the introduction of a scheme. Comparing the performance of Neighbourhood Watch in these circumstances is very problematic. Most of the evidence from the UK experience seems to be that Neighbourhood Watch schemes seem to have some initial impact in reducing offending when introduced into areas that had previously experienced high volumes of crime. Bennett (1990, cited in Fleming, 2005) found that crime levels actually rose in some areas where Neighbourhood Watch had been introduced, a trend he attributed to schemes established in middle-class areas with relatively low crime rates that encouraged local residents to report incidents to the police that would not previously have been recorded. Since Neighbourhood Watch claims that crime prevention and detection are among its key objectives it is reasonable, if difficult, to seek to establish the extent to which these goals are being met. However, as Fleming (2005) has argued, it seems likely that schemes can also play an important role in developing communication between police and public and providing for enhanced reassurance. Given the increasing recognition that the fear of crime is as important as the reality of crime levels in terms of the deleterious effect that it can have on peoples' quality of life, it is clear that any benefits Neighbourhood Watch can bring in this regard are likely to mean that it continues to be a feature of community policing. However, while the co-production of policing intends to promote reassurance it might be argued that risk and danger are communicated when community police officers, for example, inform local residents about crime problems in their area, and that the posters, window-stickers and street signs that constitute the paraphernalia of Neighbourhood Watch schemes might reinforce rather than assuage public fear of crime (Lee, 2007). The impact of surveillance technology and communication relating to risks of crime is considered further in Chapter 11.

community policing and reassurance

That the police need to focus on providing reassurance to the public is the central principle underlying Neighbourhood Policing. At the heart of these developments is the conundrum that public concern and fear about crime has risen despite a sustained reduction in crime levels. Recorded crime levels in Britain fell consistently since the mid-1990s. In 2015–16 police recorded 4,673,175 offences in England and Wales, an eight per cent rise on the previous year but 16 per cent lower than the total a decade earlier. The Crime Survey of England and Wales (CSEW) estimated there were 6.2 million incidents of crime in the survey year ending September 2016, a slight decrease that was not statistically significant (ONS, 2017). The CSEW also found that public perception of crime trends did not appear to recognise falling crime as in 2015/16, 60 per cent stated that they thought crime had risen during the previous two years (ONS, 2017). One implication of this 'reassurance gap' is that fear of crime is relatively autonomous of actual patterns of offending. Additionally it suggests that fear of crime has wider implications for community cohesion and ought to be addressed by the police, criminal justice system and other agencies. Innes (2004: 156) argued that the divergent trends in crime rates and fear of crime contributed to the development of 'reassurance policing' that is predicated on renewing connections between policing and communities

as was being made evident, public perceptions of security/insecurity are not and never have been, solely dependent upon the police's efficacy in preventing and detecting crime. Nor are they determined by the recorded crime rate ... In the academy, this situation stimulated careful and detailed investigation of the fear of crime concept and the instruments that had been used to measure it. These investigations identified a number of problems with both the concept and the survey measures in which the concept had become grounded ... In policy-making circles, attention began to focus upon the 'reassurance gap'. In essence, the notion of a reassurance gap sought to diagnose why people did not believe that they were becoming safer in terms of the declining objective risk of being a victim of crime. The resulting diagnosis suggested that fear was only ever partially a function of objective victimization risk, and that in fact expressions of fear involve complex, situated, adaptive and subjective appraisals of risk.

The reassurance policing programme developed in England and Wales was based upon a threefold strategy comprising 'high visibility patrols performed by officers who are known to the local public; the targeting of "signal crimes" and "signal disorders"; and informal social control performed by communities' (Innes, 2004: 151). Like other aspects of community policing, the reassurance strategy can also be understood as a reaction against other forms of policing, in particular the intelligence-based approach that saw officers target known offenders, cultivate informants and develop crime mapping techniques that would provide a basis for effective intervention against crime. While such methods might have contributed to the fall in crime noted by the BCS, it has been argued that they removed the police from the public arena and reduced the symbolic authority they provided (Sparks et al., 2001). Police Community Support Officers (PCSOs) were introduced under the terms of police reform legislation in the early 2000s and were intended to provide for reassurance through patrol work and to provide support to police officers. More recently there has been a 'rediscovery' of the role of voluntary special constables: in September 2012 there were 19,159 'specials' compared to 14,411 PCSOs. Although the number of specials had fallen in the preceding 12 months, the drop had been lower than for PCSOs or for sworn constables. The Neighbourhood Policing programme is one manifestation, the Home Office claims, of a more fundamental shift toward 'citizen-focused' policing. This is defined as 'a way of working in which an in-depth understanding of the needs and expectations of individuals and local communities is routinely reflected in decision-making, service delivery and practice' (Home Office, 2005b: 7). The programme seeks to reintegrate the police service into the routine activity of community life and, although the Home Office (2005b) recognized the fallacy of nostalgia for a bygone golden age of policing, the programme claims it will strengthen police relations with the public such that residents are familiar with local officers and are able to communicate with them easily. In that way, informal opportunities for consultation and accountability will be developed, as routine police work is embedded in ordinary community life.

The Neighbourhood Policing programme promises to provide for both police–community consultation and co-production. The general purpose of NP is to 'tackle crime and the fear of crime better and bring the police closer to communities' and underpinning this is the stated commitment to a 'visible and accessible police ... who stay in the job long enough to build lasting and trusting relationships with the communities they serve'. In turn the community is envisaged as being best placed to help shape and participate in the solutions to community safety priorities and in turn need to be empowered to hold the police and other partners to account if they do address acute or persistent problems of crime and antisocial behaviour. Finally the programme is seen as part of the broader movement from reactive policing to being more proactive – 'using local information and real time intelligence to better target crime hotspots, increase detections and bring more offenders to justice' (Home Office, 2006a: 4). In recent years these have been made operational in the form of local crime maps that provide information about crime incidents to the public via the web, as is discussed more fully in Chapter 11. Box 5.3 gives an overview of Neighbourhood Policing.

Box 5.3

Neighbourhood Policing

The purpose of Neighbourhood Policing is to tackle crime and fear of crime better and bring the police closer to communities. Its key principles are:

- *Visible and accessible police* – local people seeing and having regular contact with the same officers – week in and week out – who stay in the job long enough to build lasting and trusting relationships with the communities they serve.
- *Influence* – over community safety priorities in their communities which might be dealing with persistent burglaries; clearing up graffiti and vandalism or tackling open drug dealing or gun crime. Local people who are closest to the problems in their communities are often best placed to help shape and participate in the solutions to them.
- *Interventions* – joint action with communities and partners to solve problems and harness everyone's strengths.
- *Answers* – sustainable solutions to problems and feedback on results. People will know the names, numbers and email addresses of their Neighbourhood Policing teams. They will also know who is responsible for what in terms of reducing crime, tackling anti-social behaviour and keeping the areas where they live and work safe. The Government is legislating to make it possible for local people, through the Community Call for Action, to trigger action by the police and other partners to address acute or persistent problems of crime or anti-social behaviour.

(Home Office, 2006a: 4)

Important elements of the NP agenda include a recommitment to the delivery of high-visibility frontline policing that both leads and encompasses diverse partners from among the extended police family described more fully in Chapter 8. Additionally the programme seeks to re-establish connections between the police and local communities that were lost as the Unit Beat Policing re-organised and professionalised the service in the 1960s and 1970s. By pledging that individual officers will become familiar characters in the local landscape the programme seeks to re-embed police into the fabric of communities. Notions of consultation and responsiveness are, as with earlier reassurance policing projects, seen as vital to the integration of police and local communities.

The new policing settlement promises to enhance three core principles identified in the HMIC report (HMIC, 2001) that has shaped the development of reassurance policing: namely, visibility, familiarity and accessibility. Many of the assumptions, implicit or explicit, that underpin the Neighbourhood Policing programme have applied to community policing projects more generally. The experience of those programmes, and concerns about the viability of communities as a policing resource, have led to the identification of a range of practical and conceptual challenges for community policing, and it is to these that the following section turns.

CHALLENGES FOR COMMUNITY POLICING

While programmes appealing to the principles of community policing have been persistent features of global policing developments for many years, it is clear that they have faced a range of challenges and rarely have lived up to the claims made for them. In this section some of the common problems that have beset community policing will be reviewed. Some of these relate to internal policing issues, such as culture and the difficulties of reconciling contrary objectives, while others relate to the lack of a 'model community' and the problematic wider context in which community policing is introduced.

not real police work?

Research evidence suggests that police officers do not tend to regard the role of community policing with very much esteem. Foot patrol, one of the three central planks of Neighbourhood Policing, tends to be considered by officers as a low-status aspect of policing – not a 'real' part of the job. The origins, nature and implications of police subculture is discussed at greater length in Chapter 6. This subcultural resistance to community policing cannot simply be attributed to recalcitrant or retrogressive attitudes among junior ranks. Chan (1997) has shown that police working culture needs to be understood in terms of wider institutional and organisational contexts. The failure of the police service to properly resource community policing, or to protect community police officers from being reassigned to other duties (factors that partly explain the establishment of the PCSO as a dedicated patrol role) reinforces perceptions that community policing is marginal to the 'core' business. Pressure for officers to meet performance indicators, such as ensuring a speedy response to calls from the public, also detract from foot patrol and community policing work that does not lead to tangible results in terms of measurable 'sanctioned detections'.

Another way in which police culture may be detrimental to the principle of community policing refers not to the internal organisation of the force but rather to outside relations with the general public. Reiner (1978) argued that the nature of police work – the boredom, unsociable hours, occasional periods of danger, and the routine exposure to shocking and traumatic events – cultivates a sense among officers that they are separate and isolated from broader society. He argued that this encourages the police to regard the public with some suspicion and to rely upon stereotypes of different social groups in order to understand the world outside the police station. Efforts to broaden the diversity of police staff, as discussed in Chapters 5 and 7, are intended to address some of these problems. The extent to which the legitimate professional interests of officers can be reconciled with elements of the Neighbourhood Policing Plan, such as the pledge that officers will remain in post for longer periods of time and so develop stronger relations with local people, remains to be seen.

transplant failure

Apart from internal factors that have hindered the effective development of community policing programmes are a range of contextual challenges relating to the nature of contemporary communities and the broader environment in which programmes are introduced are likely to pose important challenges. Brogden and Nijhar (2005) argued that community-oriented policing (COP) has become a core component of western interventions in societies in transition. USA and British government policy to developing nations, for example, have placed considerable emphasis on the importance of police reform and tackling crime to more general processes of political, social and economic development, and these initiatives have usually been framed in terms of community policing. In developing nations, in post-apartheid South Africa and post-communist Eastern Europe community policing became central to social transformation (Hills, 2000; Van der Spuy, 2000; Beck and Chistyakova, 2004). A central component of such developments, Goldsmith and Harris (2017) noted in their study of Australian policing in Papua New Guinea, the Solomon Islands and Timor Leste, has been the development of community relationships on the basis of trust. This, they noted, was made more difficult given prevailing cultural and political power relations and the lack of capacity within local communities. Alongside a range of problems relating to the implementation of community policing, Brogden and Nijhar (2005) found that models of COP devised and practised in the USA have been exported around the world and introduced into countries with wholly different social traditions and contexts. For these reasons they argue:

> The four primary components of community policing in the West that are most evident in the export drive – community forums, neighbourhood watch schemes, problem-solving and beat patrolling – have not worked anything like as successfully as appears in the international sales literature. For the most part, where such schemes have been established by the

police and by local business elites in Africa and in the Indian sub-continent, they have simply exacerbated social schisms. For the most part COP materials are shoddy goods, with few health warnings attached. They have invariably not been tailored to the particular needs of African, Asian, Latin American and East European societies.

(Brogden and Nijhar, 2005: 231)

As is mentioned in Chapter 8 in relation to human rights and international development, one reason why community policing has not transplanted effectively to developing countries is that its adoption is primarily occasioned by the need to access international aid, and so the roots of community policing run shallow in these circumstances. There is a more general conundrum, which has implications for developed and developing countries alike, that community policing is intended, among other things, to contribute to the development of social cohesion and capital – qualities that are prerequisites for successful community policing.

imperfect communities

While Neighbourhood Policing and the advent of PCCs are intended to increase the influence of the public voice in shaping policing priorities, the status of public demands in the overall determination of policing priorities remains ambiguous. While being seen to take seriously issues of concern to local communities will continue to be an important feature of the community policing agenda, it is clear that this does not impose absolute obligations upon local police managers. The increasing salience of various forms of social diversity might mean that local communities will not produce coherent agendas or priorities to which Neighbourhood Police teams can respond. Even where there is some consensus, it might be that issues of social justice, among other things, make it proper that the police service retains professional independence such that it might not act upon certain demands. Tension between community policing and local accountability on the one hand, and the development of professional and scientific strategies on the other, is discussed at greater length in Chapter 12. Crawford and Lister (2004) noted that local communities have often demanded that police officers provide reassurance by moving on young people congregated in public spaces and that this raises important questions relating to social justice and equity. Moreover there is a danger that Neighbourhood Policing programmes repeat more general tendencies to afford a spurious 'grassroots authenticity' to locally identified priorities (Hughes and Rowe, 2007). It might be that local residents' perceptions of issues most serious to them do not equate to actual risks or harm measured in more objective terms. Furthermore, as Lee (2007) argues, there is often a feedback loop such that community perceptions of crime and security issues iterate with agendas established by the police, local media and broader political discourse. Hughes and Rowe (2007) describe the relational nature of local knowledge in the following terms:

In some circumstances, police and community knowledge can exist in symbiotic relation such that one can reinforce and complement the other to produce authoritative local common sense that underpins local governance. Alternative perspectives, among hard-to-reach or marginalised groups, for example, might be driven out of local consultation processes.

policing and social cohesion

The broader remit that community policing programmes develop for the service might also raise significant challenges. As several of the definitions outlined earlier in this chapter made clear, and the Neighbourhood Policing programme reaffirms, community policing promises to engage the police in developing social cohesion. Predominantly with reference to the USA, Weisburd et al. (2010) noted that crime-prone locales are also characterised by low levels of social capital and collective efficacy. Subsequently a key part of police intervention has to be about developing the capacity of communities to exercise informal social control. Even working in partnership with other agencies, the capacity of the police service to positively improve the quality of life of disadvantaged communities is likely to remain limited. While crime and antisocial behaviour might have serious deleterious effects on the quality of life of those living in some neighbourhoods, and the police might be able to take some steps to tackle some important causal factors, it seems unlikely that the police service will have the capacity to address structural problems that might generate insecurity. Crawford (2003) and Newburn (2003) have argued that efforts to broaden the remit of the police service reflect a more general, problematic, trend whereby central government in Britain has sought criminal justice responses to non-criminal justice problems.

CONCLUSION

Community policing faces a series of challenges in terms of the viability of the police service to meet a much wider remit that requires them to build social capital and enhance 'quality of life' issues. The idea that local communities are appropriate or viable sites for determining and promoting policing priorities has also been critically explored, and it has been suggested that this might raise profound concerns relating to social justice. In many respects these concerns, while important, represent limits to the aspirations of community policing programmes but do not mean that devolved, service-oriented, inclusive models of policing ought to be abandoned. While the 'community' might not exist in the idealised form often implied in policy statements, the partnership approaches that characterise contemporary policing developments offer opportunities for engagement that might prove worthwhile on occasion.

In recent years the development of evidence-based policing (EBP) has seen an emphasis on the use of scientific method, research and evaluation in order to develop a body of knowledge upon which reliable police interventions can be based. Such approaches can provide a strong logic for the deployment of resources and tactics to deal with particular problems of crime and disorder. However, it is unclear how they can be reconciled with a philosophy of community policing that suggest services ought to be developed in consultation with local communities. The most obvious test of this relates to the provision of visible foot patrols. While statistical and research evidence suggests this is likely to be demanded by many communities and (as has been argued in this chapter) is closely related to public trust and confidence, other evidence tends to suggest that foot patrol is not the most effective way of responding to crime. Since policing communicates messages about social identity, community, belonging and embeddedness it seems likely that political social and cultural pressures to provide certain forms of policing (such as foot patrol) are likely to out-weigh efforts to embed EBP across the whole of policing. Similar tensions between public accountability and scientific professional expertise are evident in other sectors – creating 'super hospitals' that can more effectively treat patients but at the expense of closing local facilities is one example – but it seems likely that such debates will figure more frequently as the use of EBP to shape service delivery becomes more common.

Further questions about the future prospects of community policing relate to the tensions that surround contradictory processes of centralisation and devolution. While Neighbourhood Policing and similar programmes focus on devolving responsibility to the local level, these sit alongside the creation of new forms of centralised policing services – such as the National Crime Agency and the College of Policing – that exert considerable influence and yet are not locally accountable. In more general terms, it is maintained by some that while contemporary nation states have devolved various functions to other agencies, in this context responsibility for policing has been relinquished to local Basic Command Units, there has nonetheless been an increase in the regulatory power of the state which has assumed greater capacity to 'steer' the provision of services even if it is no longer directly responsible for 'rowing' (Johnston and Shearing, 2003).

Bowling and Foster's (2002) analysis of British policing concludes by outlining the contrasting trends with an increasing emphasis on devolution and community orientation that seems to be undermined by concurrent processes whereby the governance of the police is becoming increasingly centralised and powers available to them being extended. Moreover, transnational and global policing see the increasing removal of control and consultation from the realm of local communities. While the problems facing community policing have been outlined in this chapter, it is clear that they also need to be understood in the wider context of trends moving in other directions. For this reason Bowling and Foster's (2002: 1021) uncertainty about how these complex patterns will unfold in the future provide a suitable note on which to end this discussion:

On the one hand, the rise of community policing, the development of multi-agency partnerships, changing loci of responsibility, new developments in police accountability – such as the implementation of an independent police complaints system, the Human Rights Act 1998, the Race Relations (Amendment) Act 2000, and the Freedom of Information Act 2000 – together with a new willingness to take account of research findings, suggest that openness, accountability of policing to the public will increase. On the other hand, a raft of recent legislation, including the Criminal Justice and Public Order Act 1994, the Crime and Disorder Act 1998, the Regulation of Investigatory Powers Act 2000, and the Terrorism Act 2001, has extended *policing* powers, and the sphere of police influence, in new and unwelcome directions ... These shifts mirror a greater separation of public policing functions at the national and transnational level, which has been established without any significant public discussion.

chapter summary

- The principle that the police service ought to seek the consent of the community and to meet public expectations is important in terms of legitimacy and operational effectiveness.

- Community policing can be defined in terms of principles, such as devolution of power and responsibility to the local level, public consultation and the involvement of citizens.

- Other approaches explain community policing in terms of the type of outcomes that it produces. Rather than conceiving of policing primarily in terms of crime control and law, community policing establishes outcomes relating to fear of crime, quality of service, improving life chances for local communities, and so establishes a much broader remit for the police.

- Another approach stresses that community policing programmes have developed, in Britain, as a reaction to dissatisfaction that had developed from the late 1960s, as changing police practices had led to deterioration in community relations. Coupled with concerns about malpractice and rising crime rates, these created deteriorating prospects for the police and community policing was pursued in order to salvage police legitimacy.

- In practice, community policing often entails enhanced consultation with local communities. This can be a formal legal requirement or a matter of providing for informal contacts for officers to consult local people as part of their routine work.

- Community policing has aimed to bridge the reassurance gap, whereby that declining levels of crime, noted by the Crime Survey of England and Wales, have not been mirrored in public perceptions, which have held that crime rates continue to rise.

- In addition to providing for high-visibility policing, the Neighbourhood Policing programme claimed to give communities influence over local agendas, opportunities for joint interventions to tackle problems, and make police answerable. This related to government commitment to principles of localism.

- Community policing has often marginalised by dominant subcultural understanding of what constitutes 'real police work', which tends to be defined in narrow crime control, law-enforcement terms. Such cultural values reflect a more general organisational tendency to under-resource and under-value community policing.

- Community policing projects have been exported from the USA and Britain to many developing countries; often these have been less than successful as they have been introduced into social, political and economic contexts that are not conducive to developing civil society relations with the police service.

- Further challenges relate to the nature of communities, which tend to offer fragmented, contradictory and imperfect knowledge of local crime problems. It is unlikely that community consultation, no matter how effective, would produce a coherent programme of action.

- Community policing programmes cast the role of the police service in broad terms, often relating to enhancing social cohesion or improving the quality of life for local residents. This poses challenges, since the police service, or criminal justice agencies more widely, might not be well placed to address criminogenic factors.

- The development of evidence-based policing models might be in tension with approaches based on consultation and 'agenda setting' with local communities. More fundamentally, the devolution of policing to local levels has been in tension with the growing importance of key national and transnational policing arrangements.

self-check questions (with answers at the back of the book)

1. What three elements did Skogan (2006a and b) suggest characterise community policing initiatives in the USA?

2. How did Weatheritt (1987) suggest the term 'community policing' had been used in Britain?

3. Identify four aspects of Alderson's (1979) model of community policing.

4. What was the name of the policing model introduced alongside panda cars, two-way radios and other innovations in the late 1960s?

5. What legislation required that the police, in partnership with other agencies, conduct audits to establish the community safety needs of local communities?

6. How many people was it estimated lived in areas covered by Neighbourhood Watch schemes?

7. What did a 2001 HMIC report establish as the three core features of reassurance policing?

8. What features of police work explain the tendency for officers to be culturally isolated from the wider community?

9. Why might local residents' perceptions of crime risks not be reliable?

10. What trend appears to contradict moves to devolve policing closer to local communities?

study questions

1. Is community policing best understood as a philosophy or a programme?

2. Do the contradictions and fragmentation of communities fundamentally undermine community policing projects?

3. Does central government control of the police service undermine the democratic credentials of Neighbourhood Policing?

annotated further reading

The development of community policing in the Anglo-American context, in the Pacific Rim and in the European Union is reviewed by Brogden and Nijhar (2005), who identify ten myths associated with much debate of this approach to police work. Brogden and Nijhar (2005) argue that community policing models have tended to fail when transported to developing countries that do not share the social and political context of north America in which they were developed.

A special edition of the journal *Criminology and Criminal Justice* (2007, vol. 7, no. 4) explores the development of Neighbourhood Policing in Britain, and the implications of social diversity and central government control for efforts to reinvigorate community policing. Articles in the journal explore community policing as it applies to minority ethnic communities in rural areas; to new travellers; to lesbian, gay, bisexual and transgender communities; and to virtual communities.

Roberg et al.'s (2005) *Police and Society* provides a good overview of the foundations and administration of the police in the USA, the behaviour of officers, and a range of controversies and challenges faced in the context of policing a diverse and fragmented society. The book contains a chapter that reviews the transition toward community policing and the associated philosophy, strategy and tactics.

annotated listings of links to relevant websites

One of the most extensive, sustained and researched experiments in community policing has been conducted in Chicago. Data on the project, known as the Chicago Alternative Policing

Strategy (CAPS), including background papers and the results of research can be found at the Institute for Policy Research at Northwestern University: www.northwestern.edu/ipr/publications/policing.html.

Current developments in community policing in England and Wales largely focus upon the Neighbourhood Policing programme, details of which can be found at www.gov.uk/government/publications/delivering-neighbourhood-policing-in-partnership.

The philosophy and practice of community policing has often developed in the USA, information on the operation and principles of many examples can be found at http://cops.usdoj.gov/html/cp_topics/Community-Policing-Topics.asp.

annotated links to journal articles

A 2007 special edition of the journal *Criminology and Criminal Justice* explored a range of challenges relating to the development of community policing. All the articles in this edition also relate to themes explored in this chapter. Among the topics explored in the pieces below are the difficulties of policing diverse and complex communities, the position of minorities in rural areas, virtual online communities, and the policing of lesbian, gay, bisexual and transgender communities:

Hughes, G. and Rowe, M. (2007) 'Neighbourhood Policing and Community Safety: Researching the Instabilities of the Local Governance of Crime, Disorder and Security in Contemporary UK', *Criminology and Criminal Justice*, 7: 317–46.

Garland, J. and Chakraborti, N. (2007) '"Protean Times?": Exploring the Relationships between Policing, Community and "Race" in Rural England', *Criminology and Criminal Justice*, 7: 347–65.

Wall, D.S. and Williams, M. (2007) 'Policing Diversity in the Digital Age: Maintaining Order in Virtual Communities', *Criminology and Criminal Justice*, 7: 391–415.

Moran, L. (2007) '"Invisible Minorities": Challenging Community and Neighbourhood Models of Policing', *Criminology and Criminal Justice*, 7: 417–41.

6

POLICE CULTURE

CONTENTS

LEARNING OBJECTIVES

Although media portrayal of police work often presents officers as the brave 'thin blue line' protecting society from threats of crime, disorder and anarchy, images of corruption, deviance, racism and sexism have become common themes in popular cultural representations of policing. Integral to the television show *Life on Mars*, in which a contemporary cop travelled back in time to the 1970s, is the lead character's impatience with the casual sexism, rule-breaking and excessive drinking of his colleagues. While the drama relies upon the idea that modern police work has been transformed from the unreconstructed insularity and machismo of earlier periods, contemporary scandals and exposés of the 'reality' of policing often focus on the problematic working culture of the junior ranks. This chapter explores the nature of police culture and the implications that this has for the delivery of policing. In particular, the chapter aims to:

- illustrate the nature of police culture in broad terms, and in more detail, in relation to racism, sexism and homophobia
- consider whether police culture originates from the socio-economic background from which officers are recruited or emerges from the nature of police work
- examine debates about the link between police culture and police behaviour, and the significance of these debates in the context of plural policing.

KEY TERMS

deviance; discretion; ethics; homophobia; institutional change and reform; organisational subculture; racism and sexism

---

INTRODUCTION

In the earlier discussion about the nature of policing and police work it was noted that policing is a contested activity that can be understood and interpreted in contrasting ways. Very often policing has been considered in narrow and relatively simple terms as law-enforcement. Although sociological accounts have long emphasised that this is only a marginal aspect of police work, popular culture often represents the 'cops and robbers' tradition familiar from myriad television shows, films, music and literature.

As was explained in Chapter 1, law-enforcement perspectives on policing have often been mirrored in academic analysis, which – until the last few decades – tended to focus upon legal frameworks, institutional arrangements and resources. This conceptualisation began to shift once research into policing began to establish that individual officers had considerable scope to interpret and apply the law selectively. The 'discovery' of police discretion underpins debate about the origins, nature and impact of police subculture, and is the starting point for discussion in this chapter. While many occupations and professions are known to produce particular cultural patterns that develop among the working lives of employees, discussion of the 'working personality' of police officers is particularly important because it is often held that this helps to shape the ways in which policing is applied in practice. Having reviewed the nature of officer discretion the chapter will continue by considering the origins and nature of police culture.

POLICE DISCRETION

With limited resources it is clear that police officers, from the most junior to the most senior, prioritise which laws to enforce and to what extent they will be enforced in particular circumstances. Reiner (2000) noted that this is both a necessary and a desirable state of affairs. Noting that it is practically impossible for the police to enforce all laws on all occasions, Reiner also highlighted that it would not be normatively acceptable for them so to do. Furthermore, the application of any law requires interpretation in the context of particular circumstances, and this inevitably entails a degree of subjectivity on the part of the officer. That officers use their judgement as they decide when to use the full extent of their legal powers and when to rely upon informal means to resolve the conflicts and disputes that they routinely face is sometimes a matter of practical consideration. More than this though, it is also desirable, as the blanket enforcement of all laws on all occasions would have a deleterious effect on public confidence in the police and the criminal justice system more generally (Wilson, 1968).

As has been said, employees in many occupations are expected to exercise discretion when doing their jobs. Health care providers consider the particular characteristics of individual patients before embarking on a programme of treatment, or deciding that none should be offered. Educators properly take into account mitigating circumstances when deciding on the grade awarded to a student. Research suggests, though, that the exercise of discretion in the delivery of policing is markedly different from other contexts for a number of reasons. First, police officers occupy an unusual – although not unique – position in that they embody the symbolic power of the sovereign state and have recourse to the legitimate use of force against fellow citizens. For many analysts this is the defining characteristic of the public police (Bittner, 1974). Although regulation and governance are increasingly diffuse and are exercised by complex and shifting networks of local, national and global actors (as is outlined in more detail in Chapters 8 and 10) it remains the case that the police officer continues to occupy a symbolic position in terms of relations of power between state and citizen. For that reason, as research evidence demonstrated that police officers use their discretion in law-enforcement, concern began to be expressed that the selective application of the law undermined democratic governance (Neyroud and Beckley, 2001: x). Police officers, the conventional model held, were expected to enforce laws produced by the democratic nation state 'without fear or favour'; that they did so selectively on the basis of their own judgement, it was argued, corrupted the proper constitutional framework.

A second reason why discretion in police work is somewhat distinct from that practised by other workers also relates to the particular context of the police institution. Although the scope of information technology and the reach of performance-monitoring regimes have shone some light into the darkness, it continues to be the case that officers exercise their discretion in conditions of relative invisibility. Moreover it is junior officers, with relatively little experience, who are more likely to be deployed on routine patrol work and to have direct, possibly problematic, encounters with the public. One commentator on police work famously noted that police work is unlike other types of employment since 'the police department has the special property ... that within it discretion increases as one moves down the hierarchy' (Wilson, 1968: 7).

The sheer diversity and unpredictability of police work means that individual officers will often be exercising their discretion in circumstances distanced from their supervisors. Although police officers might have targets set in terms of the number of sanctioned detections they are required to achieve, might be encouraged to participate in foot patrol, or to visit vulnerable premises or communities, they retain considerable autonomy over how they discharge their duties. Police work can be considered relatively invisible since it is carried out in places and at times removed from supervision and scrutiny of more senior officers, the extent to which technological developments have reduced the scope of officer discretion is considered in more detail in Chapter 11. Debates about the abuse of police discretion often focus on claims that officers over-police certain communities. For example, it has been widely claimed that racist aspects of police subculture lead officers to stop and search young black males more often than the white community. Clearly, if this claim can be substantiated, this would constitute an abuse of police powers. In response to these concerns police organisations in Britain have, for some years, monitored officers' stop and search activity in an effort to identify officers who, deliberately or otherwise, disproportionately target some groups in this way. Similarly efforts to improve the police response to domestic violence have sometimes focused on encouraging officers to arrest suspects and not to use their discretion in order to seek an informal 'resolution' of these conflicts. Carswell (2006) noted that officers' reluctance to intervene had often been rooted in cultural perspectives on gender relations within marriage and that the private sphere was beyond the proper intervention of the state. Rowe (2007a) highlighted that efforts to address these shortcomings often require an officer to arrest perpetrators, and so seek to limit, or remove altogether, discretion. Grant and Rowe (2011) noted that measures to delimit officer discretion in response to domestic violence were only partially successful since officers inevitably were required to interpret and subjectively apply guidelines provided to them. In other words, officer discretion was curtailed but not eliminated, partly since it is an integral part of police work.

Technological developments and the administrative requirements to record encounters with the public and to account for time spent on duty offer police supervisors enhanced opportunities to scrutinise police behaviour (Ericson and Haggerty, 1997). While these efforts seek to limit the scope for officers to abuse their discretion by over-policing some groups, it is much more difficult to interrogate circumstances in which officers 'turn a blind eye' or use their discretion not to invoke their full legal powers. As McLaughlin (2007b) recounts, the 2003 BBC television documentary *The Secret Policeman* provided clear evidence that some police recruits continued to hold violent racist attitudes, and that police probationer training was not effectively challenging such racism. One of the key passages from the undercover exposé involved a police recruit recounting how his hatred of Asian people had led him to target an Asian man for motoring violations. Additionally the probationary officer noted that he had used his discretion to ignore similar offences committed by a white female driver. Both of these illustrate the use of police discretion. Clearly the former incident amounted to an abuse of police power since the officer's decision was based, he admitted, on extraneous factors (i.e. the ethnicity of the driver). That was a decision to intervene, though, and the procedures that the officer would have been required to complete meant that it was possible, in principle, for his supervisor to review the circumstances and details of the encounter. The second incident also involved the officer using his discretion. Again, this appears to have involved an abuse of police discretion since it too was based on the ethnicity, and maybe the gender, of the driver concerned. In this case, however, the result was a decision not to intervene and as such is beyond the scrutiny of supervisory officers who are unlikely to directly observe the officer's behaviour.

It is partly due to the difficulties of reviewing police decision making that some argue that the most effective way of ensuring that officers do not abuse their discretionary powers is to develop robust ethical frameworks that encourage officers to become reflective practitioners who can be relied upon to act professionally and responsibly. Neyroud and Beckley (2001) argued that the most effective way to prevent the abuse of police discretion is to develop the professionalism of officers by establishing a stronger ethical framework for police practice. Additionally, models of scientific or evidence-based policing seek to develop professional practice such that discretion is exercised on the basis of expert knowledge of the impact of different intervention options (Weisburd and Neyroud, 2011). Culturally-based decision making derived from informal craft knowledge; custom and tradition is replaced by officers using modern technology and scientific analysis to underpin their practice.

While the exercise of discretion is a central and legitimate aspect of police work, it is widely held that it is often unduly influenced by working cultures that encourage stereotyping and prejudice to enter into officer decision making in ways that are unacceptable. Long-standing concerns that the police service fails to provide an appropriate service to minority groups and to women have drawn attention to the negative impact of police culture (Rowe, 2004; Westmarland, 2002). Walklate (1995: 104) noted the close association between discretion and police culture in the following terms:

> Police officers deal with … discretion, and the confusion it sometimes generates, through the construction of collectively understood and often taken-for-granted norms and values, frequently referred to in the academic literature as 'cop culture'. Co-operation and solidarity have frequently been commented upon as being key features of this 'cop culture' … On occasions, that culture has been seen as the source of all policing ills. Indeed, the solidarity engendered by it had been known to provide 'cover' for rather less than legitimate policing activities. Understanding the nature and impact of this culture on how the task of policing is performed is crucial to an understanding of how, in routine practice, the central task of policing is interpreted.

THE NATURE OF POLICE CULTURE

The 'working personality' of the police officer has been a recurring theme in sociological studies of the police since such research began in Britain and the USA in the early 1960s. Since that time successive studies of police work, especially those in an anthropological or ethnographic tradition, have explored the ways in which officers understand the world around them and conceive of their role within it (Skolnick, 1966; Reiner, 1978; Punch, 1979). Not surprisingly each of these studies places a different emphasis on particular aspects of police culture and each reaches its own conclusions. However, there is a remarkable and persistent unanimity on some key features of police culture (see Box 6.1).

Box 6.1

Reiner's (2000) Seven Components of Police Subculture

- A sense of mission
- Suspicion
- Isolation/solidarity
- Conservatism
- Machismo
- Pragmatism
- Racial prejudice.

Writing about emerging sociological studies in the USA, Balch (1972) suggested police culture was understood in the following terms:

> In the last few years a great deal has been written about the police mentality. If we can believe everything we read in magazines, journals, and sociology books, the typical policeman is cynical, suspicious, conservative, and thoroughly bigoted. This is not a flattering picture to be sure, but it recurs again and again in the popular and 'scientific' literature on the police. Perhaps there is something about the police system itself that generates a suspicious, conservative world-view. Or perhaps certain personality types are inadvertently recruited for police work. Either explanation is plausible, and both may be correct.

Paoline et al. (2000) described police occupational culture in the following terms, relating it to the nature of police work:

> Officers cope with the danger and uncertainty of their occupational environment by *being suspicious* and *maintaining the edge* ... Officers cope with the organizational environment by taking a *lay-low* or *cover-your-ass* attitude and adopting a *crimefighter* or *law-enforcement* orientation ...

> The problems that officers confront in their working environment, as well as the coping mechanisms prescribed by the police culture: *social isolation* and *group loyalty* ... The dangerousness of their occupational environment prompts officers to distance themselves from the rest of society ... The unique elements of their coercive authority separates them further from the public.

Such findings are often reflected in newsmedia reports of police deviance. The 2003 BBC television exposé of racism among police probationers has already been referred to; another under-cover documentary portrayed police officers watching pornographic material while on duty, denigrating the account of a victim of rape, and boasting that they had driven past a man lying injured in the road because they had wanted to make it back to the police station in order to watch a major football match on television (Channel 4, 2006). The same documentary recorded officers playing 'hide and seek' while on vehicle patrol and ignoring radio calls for help while they went to fetch take-away meals. As Cockroft (2012) has noted, the notion of 'police culture' often has informed media explanations of police deviance, and has featured more prominently in public debate that many other social scientific concepts.

racism and police culture

Although not all aspects of police culture are inherently negative, the norms and values outlined here are often used to explain enduring concerns about police racism, sexism and homophobia. In his report into the 1981 disorders in Brixton, Lord Scarman argued that the police service in Britain was not institutionally racist but that there was clearly a problem of racial prejudice among a proportion of junior officers (Scarman, 1981). Often this explanation of police racism is referred to as a 'rotten apples' perspective, which associates the problem with the negative prejudices and stereotyping of a small minority of officers that has a disproportionate impact on the organisation as a whole. Although the 1950s and 1960s often have been portrayed as a 'golden age' of British policing it is increasingly apparent that even during that hallowed era police officers displayed virulent racist attitudes toward migrants from the Caribbean, and later from the Indian sub-continent (McLaughlin, 2007a: 171). Furthermore, Whitfield (2007) demonstrates that racist attitudes during this period were not confined to retrograde junior officers but extended up to senior officers who, among other things, were privately opposed to the appointment of 'coloured' police officers.

In 2012 newspapers reported that a black man in London had recorded racist abuse he had received from officers in a police van after he had been arrested on suspicion of driving while under the influence of drugs. In addition to recording officers' use of racist language the man claimed that he had been subject to physical assault. In October 2012, at a second court hearing, the officer against whom the allegations were made was cleared by the judge after a jury failed to reach a decision in relation to a charges of racially aggravated public order. As well as raising concerns about the use of racist language – which the defending officer denied was his intent – the case raised questions about the effectiveness of police disciplinary procedures and the management of complaints (*Guardian*, 2012a). This indicates that problematic consequences relating to occupational culture are institutional matters even if they are demonstrated by only a minority of staff.

In November 2006, Hertfordshire police disciplined 140 staff who had circulated a racist email containing footage of a black man being decapitated as he fell onto railings following a police pursuit. Eight of those disciplined were sergeants and seven civilian supervisors (Butt, 2006), which suggests that the racist subcultures permeate supervisory roles. Apart from the contemporary references to information technology, such incidents litter accounts of police relations with minority ethnic communities and have done so for decades. These examples have been selected because they represent something of the wider context of debates about racism and police culture, and, more specifically, as they indicate that these concerns relate both to external relations between the police and the public, and to internal personnel matters. Prior to the publication of the Lawrence Report (McPherson, 1999), it was often held that the nature of workplace banter and the use of racist and derogatory language more generally behind the scenes of the police station was not necessarily of primary importance. The off-stage characteristics of police subculture, such as sending 'inappropriate' emails, was not closely associated with the professional discharge of police duties. Whether this perspective is tenable, and the relationship between police culture and performance more generally, is considered at greater length later in this chapter.

This brief review of the debates about racism and police subculture reflects a tendency to consider these issues in relatively narrow terms associated with the individual deviance of police staff. Often this is demonstrated by senior officers' response, which is usually to identify and discipline those responsible and to devise strategies to ensure that such problems do not recur. The quest to develop effective psychological tests that might identify applicants to the police service who have authoritarian or prejudiced personalities is often cited by senior officers promising that the lessons of the past will be learnt. For example, it has been reported that new technologies tantalise employers with their apparent capacity to use MRI scans that can identify neural activity in parts of the brain that indicate that an individual has racist values (Russo, 2007). Sociologically such techno-solutions raise profound questions about the nature and definition of racism and whether it can be isolated to particular chemical processes in the brain or is an emergent property of social relations that develop in particular contexts and power dynamics.

While understandable in institutional terms, conceptualising police culture only in terms of the deviant behaviour of retrograde officers and staff who transgress against official policy is of limited use. Discourse that presents racism as a pathological problem associated with flawed individuals has become commonplace in public debates about the problem. While it might appear to further antiracist agendas, the creation of racist 'folk devils' by the mass media serves to marginalise analysis of racialisation in its broader social context. The condemnatory couplet of 'racist copper' has become a recurring image in popular culture representation, which serves to keep the problem of racism on the agenda but does nothing to develop understanding in the context of cultural and institutional dynamics. The racism of police culture must also be understood more broadly in terms of the normative whiteness of police services. Efforts to promote cultural diversity, for example through the establishment of staff associations such as the Black Police Association or the Muslim Police Association, have the unintended consequence of underlining the marginality and specificity of officers and civilian staff of a minority ethnic background. Affording these groups particular status reaffirms the 'whiteness' of the mainstream of police organisations, described by Loftus (2008) as the dominant 'white space' of policing. This promotes the 'balkanisation' of police staff into narrow enclaves of identity politics and has created an environment in which 'cultural wars' can gain ground (McLaughlin, 2007b). Furthermore, the provision of diversity training programmes or development of tougher sanctions against racist officers and other police staff does not address some of the more fundamental challenges of reshaping police culture such that it becomes more appropriate to an increasingly diverse social, political and cultural context.

As was noted in Chapter 1, police work has, in the British context at least, had metaphorical qualities that have provided a cultural lens through which national identity has been focused. As the notions of 'Englishness' and 'Britishness' become increasingly contested and complex, police culture needs to be reworked if the embedded problems of racialisation – which go far beyond instances of police deviance – are to be addressed. The relationship between police culture and efforts to reform the service are considered further toward the end of this chapter.

sexism and police culture

Sexist attitudes and machismo have been widely noted elements of police culture and, like other topics discussed here, have been identified as problematic both internally in terms of staff relations and equal opportunities and externally in terms of the provision of effective service to the public. Jordan (2004: 243) argued that police culture was a central factor underlying the failure of the service to effectively respond to victims of rape:

> **The beliefs of the police occupational subculture have been shaped by its origins as a male-dominated organisation enforcing laws designed to protect male property owners, with women being construed as part of men's property.**

Although minority ethnic officers have long been under-represented in the ranks of British police forces, they have not been subject to the same formal and overt barriers that have impacted upon female officers. While women had been employed as police officers in Britain and in the USA from early in the twentieth century, their employment was highly gendered and reflected stereotypes and prejudices about the role of women more generally. Their work was largely confined to dealing with other women or with children – tasks to which it was thought they were better suited than their male counterparts. During the First World War women were recruited, as volunteers, into the police service with the specific remit of protecting women and children, particularly women thought to be vulnerable due to their working in large numbers in war-related industries such as munitions production. After the War the employment of women was intended to help curb a perceived increase in prostitution (Carrier, 1988, cited in Heidensohn, 1992). Heidensohn (1992: 52) noted that the gendered nature of women's police work represented a curious victory for those who had campaigned for the rights of female police officers. While they achieved many of their goals relating to the provision of pay and pensions, the role they conceived of for women officers perpetuated patriarchal perspectives on the status of women:

> **Police work for women was still defined, and was to remain until well after the Second World War, as a specialist field, mainly confined to moral and sexual matters and inevitably making female officers complicit in their control of their own sex in ways in which men's behaviour was not controlled.**

It was not until the mid-1970s that female police officers achieved a degree of formal equality in policing as, in Britain, in 1975 the Sex Discrimination Act and the Equal Pay Act came into force. It was during this period that police services disbanded women's departments and integrated female officers into general police duties. Clearly the changing legal and organisational context did not wholly transform the position of women within the police service and they continue to be significantly under-represented in general terms in most police services around the world. In 2016 female officers constituted 28.6 per cent of police in England and Wales and 22.9 per cent of Chief Officers (Home Office, 2016b). This represented an increase: in 2005, for example, female officers were 21.1 per cent of the total and 9.7 per cent of senior ranks (Bibi et al., 2005). The status and position of women in police services have been promoted by the British Association of Women Police (BAWP), which has focused on a range of problems relating to recruitment and retention as well as cultural barriers. In 2016 the BAWP produced a third version of the *Gender Agenda* outlining its long terms aim (see Box 6.2). The representation of women in senior positions within policing was further advanced by the appointment in February 2017 of Cressida Dick as Metropolitan Police Commissioner. Since the head of the National Crime Agency and the President of the National Police Chiefs Council are both female, Dick's appointment meant that three of the most senior positions in British policing were held by women.

Box 6.2

The Gender Agenda: National Recommendations

- Explore and publicise the business case for diversity and support the importance of diversity within forces, with senior police leaders actively demonstrating their commitment to diversity.
- Police forces to have appropriate policies and structures to ensure the retention of the female workforce and to tackle existing barriers to progression, including the culture of the police service.
- Monitor the impact of changes to the job related fitness assessment.
- Define career pathways for police staff, part time officers, and staff on flexible working.
- Identify and further support forces without female officers at chief officer level, the superintending ranks, the chief inspector rank and in specialisms.
- To understand the implications of direct entry on women in policing.
- Work with providers of support programmes for female leaders.

(BAWP, 2016)

Just as sexism within police culture has explained the marginalisation of women within the police service, and the persistence of the 'glass ceiling' that has prevented them from progressing up the rank structure, so too it has detracted from the quality of service offered to female crime victims. As with the relationship between racism and the paucity of the police response to victims of racist crime, there is a symbiotic relationship between the lack of female officers and the failure of the service to understand the nature and impact of sexual offences and domestic violence (Jordan, 2004; Walklate, 1995). As with efforts to tackle racism and homophobia, a key response to problems of sexism in police subculture has been to seek to recruit more female staff, and it is clear that progress has been made in this area. However, it is not simply the absence of women officers that explains the failure of the service, police culture itself complicates the picture and makes the position more intractable. As with other minority groups within the service, evidence suggests that female officers have often sought to fit into their working environment by embracing the prevailing norms of the police working personality. In an effort to demonstrate that their primary working identity is as a police officer, not a *female* police officer, women in the service have tended to adopt the subcultural values predominant in the service. While this might prove an effective coping strategy for individual officers it suggests that simply recruiting more female officers is unlikely, in and of itself, to lead to a better provision for survivors of sexual assault or domestic violence (Walklate 1995: 112–14). However, it is much noted in the research literature that police culture is neither a unitary nor a fixed feature and the improved representation of women in policing is promoting change. McCarthy (2015), for example, argued that the female officers engaged in 'soft' alternative modes of policing (such as enforcing community penalties and work with young offenders) have created 'micro sites' of femininsed culture even within a dominant masculine environment. That these alternative modes are becoming more central to the overall police mission the possibilities for further cultural transformation are ripe.

Problems of sexism and policing also relate to police subculture in narrow terms of officer deviance. Denigrating female victims of sexual assault, for example, or making sexist comments about colleagues in the workplace have informally tended to be tolerated within the police service, but are clearly contrary to the official policies and public statements (Brown and Heidensohn, 2000). Officers found to engage in such activities are liable to be disciplined, dismissed or required to undertake training programmes. Additionally, problems of discrimination in the police workplace reflect a failure to introduce effective equal opportunities programmes that cater, for example, for the needs of part-time staff.

As with the problem of racism, however, there are wider dimensions of police culture, not related to specific misbehaviour among officers, which perpetuate stereotypes and disadvantage female staff. Although empirically misleading, it was noted in Chapter 1 that police work is often (mis)represented by officers who stress the action, danger and excitement of their role. One consequence of this is an emphasis on the corporal demands of police work and the centrality of a strong physical presence. As has been noted, recourse to the legitimate use of force is often offered as a defining characteristic of police work, and although sociological research clearly demonstrates that force is rarely used, is has contributed to the marginalisation of women, historically and contemporaneously (Westmarland, 2002). The machismo of police work is often foregrounded in news media and 'infotainment' representations of policing, which focus on tough crime-fighting, car chases, and physical confrontation. Equally, political rhetoric that surrounds competition between rivals as they lay claim to the most severe policies on law and order, often replete with language of 'cracking down on crime' and getting 'tough' on criminals, reinforces a particularly muscular police discourse. The culture of policing in these broad terms, as well as subcultural properties of the working norms and values of rank-and-file officers, clearly needs to be understood and addressed if women are to be treated equally, either within the police service or as victims of crime.

homophobia and police culture

In terms of research, publicity campaigns and pressure group activity the position of lesbian, gay, bisexual and transgender (LGBT) communities in relation to policing has been largely overlooked until recently (Jones, 2015). Unlike visible minority ethnic and female officers, LGBT officers can choose whether to be open about their sexual orientation, although the context of homophobia might mean that this is not a choice freely exercised. Partly for this reason there has been little systematic monitoring of the sexual orientation of police staff. Although statistical data on the status and rank of LGBT police staff is not available, there is considerable anecdotal information to suggest that homophobia has long been a central feature of police subculture.

Burke (1993) noted that gay and bisexual male officers have, until recently in Britain, been marginalised partly as a result of the potential criminality of their behaviour. Prior to 2000 – when the Sexual Offences (Amendment) Act equalised the age of consent for homosexual and heterosexual sexual relations – gay and bisexual men joining the force at the age of 18, the minimum starting age for police officers, faced a period of potential conflict, and risk of exposure, between their private activity and professional status as officers. In a number of the personal testimonies that Burke presents in his study officers recall that they were sometimes inhibited from challenging homophobia among their colleagues since to do so might risk their own status. Despite increasing equality in formal legal terms, studies of police culture continue to find that in the regulation of public space police officers continue to construe homosexuality as problematic deviant behaviour that requires a police response (Loftus, 2008). The association between police subculture and wider aspects of the police law-enforcement role has posed a particularly difficult environment for gay police officers:

> [M]embership of any highly regulated organization which has, as part of its own remit, the control of 'sexual deviance' is likely to result in the defamation of atypical sexualities at an organizational and thus, by extension, at a personal level. In addition, whilst crises of 'ambivalent identity' are suffered by many non-heterosexuals who are learning to accept their variation, proscriptions against their orientation are often subtle, implied, and indirect, whereas the explicitness of the collective police judgement on homosexuality, the machismo sub-culture, and the manifest discrepant status of homosexual activity in British law (with its related police activity) means that in trying to come to terms with a non-heterosexual orientation, many gay, lesbian, and bisexual police officers are liable to find themselves conducting multiple existences and many suffer profound psychological crises as a result.
>
> (Burke, 1994:199)

Praat and Tuffin (1996) also found that police subculture is partly antipathetic toward LGBT officers because of the perceived deviancy of the homosexual lifestyle, which exposed them to conflicts of interest that did not pertain to other officers. Officers argued that homosexuals were not marginalised because of their sexual orientation per se, since this would have a deleterious impact on their ability to discharge their duties impartially. Similar arguments have been used in respect of minority ethnic officers who, it was sometimes claimed, would act on the basis of cultural, religious or ethno-alliances (Whitfield, 2004). Even recently, in 2006, it was revealed that a Metropolitan Police internal report had suggested that Muslim officers might act corruptly in seeking to assist their extended family (Laville and Muir, 2006). Such claims about the risk of minorities acting partially fail to acknowledge evidence not only of the discriminatory discretion often associated with the operational activity of the mainstream of police work, but also that minority officers have been noted to over-identify with police sub-culture in order to ensure that they integrate with their colleagues.

The perceived homophobia of police subculture has created reluctance on the part of LGBT people to report homophobic incidents to the police. A study by the National Advisory Group/Policing Lesbian and Gay Communities (1999, cited in Williams and Robinson, 2000: 4) found that 80 per cent of homophobic incidents are not reported. Williams and Robinson (2000) argue that this reluctance to report stems from a number of factors related to a perception that police culture is antipathetic to sexual minorities, including the reputation that the police do not take reports of stranger and domestic violence aimed at the LGBT community as seriously as those experienced by heterosexual victims, concern that the victim of crime will be treated as though a perpetrator, a fear of 'coming out' to the police, and a fear of retaliation, isolation and not being believed.

Given the context of ongoing perceptions of homophobia within police subculture it is interesting to note that, in some respects, it appears that the status of sexuality has been transformed. Substantive evidence seems to suggest that the position of LGBT minorities in the police service is improving. In particular, in 2011, 15 of the top 100 'gay friendly' employers identified by the pressure group Stonewall were police services (Rumens and Broomfield, 2012: 284). That they were ranked highly on this index demonstrates that these police services could demonstrate good practice in terms of developing human resource policies, that they had support networks for staff, and that senior leaders championed sexual orientation diversity across the organisation (Stonewall, 2007: 3). Other research evidence also suggests that homophobia within police culture might be decreasing. Rumens and Broomfield's (2012) interviews with 20 gay police officers found that they had tended to anticipate a positive response to identifying as homosexual to their colleagues and that most of the sample reported that this had been their experience. This is reinforced by Colvin's (2009) study that found that officers reported some advantages associated with having a gay or lesbian identity in the workplace. A large survey of LGB officers conducted in 2010–11 found that 'the working environment for LGB police officers has been radically transformed' (Jones, 2015: 69). Three-quarters of officers reported that the police provided sufficient support for LGB officers, 74 per cent that they are 'satisfied' or 'very satisfied' with being an officer, and 82 per cent that they had never experienced discrimination in the workplace. None of these studies denies that homophobia is a continuing problem, but they provide further grounds for recognising that police culture is not fixed and universal but is contested and can be transformed.

THE ROOTS OF POLICE CULTURE

Key aspects of police occupational culture have been outlined in the above sections. The reasons why these features have tended to develop and to provide a working personality that is specific to police officers has often remained implicit within these discussions. In this part of the chapter, the roots of police culture are disentangled. Fielding (1988: 5) characterised these twin perspectives in the following terms, as he explained the emergence of studies that sought to explain police culture in terms of the working environment in which officers are situated:

> **Rather that the presumption that policing attracts malicious individuals of a punitive and reactionary bent, such work begins from the assumption that the work the police are given to do, and its institutional placing, largely accounts for the character of police practice.**

Put simply, the question to be addressed in the following paragraphs is: Are officers born or made? Explanations that suggest the police culture is best understood with reference to the pre-existing characteristics of those that enter the police service usually focus upon the relatively narrow socio-economic profile of entrants to the service, or on their psychological traits. Traditionally new entrants to the police service have tended to be males of school-leaving age and from a working-class background. The conservative and insular nature of police occupational culture has often been attributed to the profile of new recruits as it is held that the prejudices and preconceptions, such as those relating to minority ethnic communities, to women and to sexual minorities, reflects the prevailing cultural norms and values of the sections of society from which police officers are recruited. Claims that the norms and values associated with police culture reflect the prevailing disposition of officers as they enter the service draw upon the notion of the 'authoritarian personality', developed by Adorno et al. (1950) after the Second World War. Colman and Gorman (1982) measured the attitudes of new recruits to the police service on a range of controversial issues, such as the death penalty and migration, and compared the results to those obtained from a control group. They concluded that newly recruited police officers were significantly more illiberal and intolerant than the control group. Although criticised on methodological and other grounds (Waddington, 1982), the notion that police officers enter the service with regressive and insular values has remained a primary explanation of police culture. This is reflected in those efforts to change problematic dimensions of police culture by re-engineering the profile of police service personnel in order to include more minority ethnic and female officers (Rowe and Ross, 2015; Paoline et al., 2000). Some of these efforts have already been described in this chapter. Others include policies that seek to attract a broader age range of candidates for the police service by, for example, emphasising the importance of recruiting individuals who have experience of other occupations that might be valuable to the police service. Proposals to allow for officer-level entry into policing in England and Wales have been advanced in terms of promoting diversity and shifting cultural norms within the service. Additionally, reconfiguring initial police training programmes so that they are delivered in partnership with universities has had the goal of exposing new recruits to a broader spectrum of experience and learning than was available in the narrow confines of police training colleges.

At the other end of the spectrum of explanations of police culture are those who suggest that it is the nature of police work itself that engenders the cultural patterns identified in this chapter. Some of the characteristics of police work that perpetuate the culture common among officers relate to practical aspects of organisational policing. Shift-work, for example, might enhance group solidarity and insularity in that it makes it more difficult for officers to form social relations outside of 'the job' (Cain, 1973). Until recently probationer training was conducted almost exclusively in an extended period during which officers would be literally separated from the wider community as they resided in training college. Similarly, officers are required to observe certain regulations (relating to their political activity and the economic activities of their families, for example) that extend into the social and domestic spheres in ways not experienced by many other occupational groups. In addition to these institutional requirements it has been noted that the routine environment of police work also fosters a certain cultural framework. The uncertainty facing officers as they respond to incidents, for example, is often cited as a factor that explains group loyalty. Although officers rarely experience direct physical confrontation, the possibility of doing so shapes the nature of contacts with the public and provides strong instrumental reasons why officers place value on subscribing to the occupational subculture and team loyalty. These pressures might make it difficult for officers to challenge aspects of police culture to which they do not subscribe, since to do so might risk their isolation from colleagues, which may, in turn, have implications for their physical well-being.

Similarly, attributes of suspicion and cynicism might have important advantages in routine police work but have negative implications if practised on the basis of stereotyping and prejudice. The importance of understanding police subculture in the context of the broader operational nature of routine police work is reflected in the perspective of a gay police officer who left the policing after seven years' service:

> **I have faced the violent, the armed, the unstable, the drunk, the frightened, the battered, the injured. Having been part of this environment, I understand why policemen and women need to 'belong' – to identify with, and seek the support of, their own police companions. I understand the need for the canteen culture of cynicism, gossip, jokes and stereotyping. It all helps to let off the pressure of accumulated tension. But I have also seen how this often highly charged atmosphere, created by the enormous expectations laid on the individual police officer, particularly those on the front line, can lead to a peculiar bottling-up of emotion; a creation of the tendency to deny one's true feelings and beliefs on a number of issues in order to maintain the acceptance and affirmation given by the group which is so vital in fighting off the pressures both from the outside, and unfortunately, sometimes from the higher, managerial ranks inside the police.**
>
> **(Burke, 1993: 9)**

THE IMPLICATIONS OF POLICE CULTURE

In addition to debates about the roots of police culture are controversies about the implications that police culture has for the delivery of policing. As has been demonstrated inappropriate and unjust aspects of operational police work, related to the over-policing of some communities and the failure to provide an adequate response to the victims of some types of crime, have often been explained in terms of retrograde norms and values of frontline officers. A long sequence of media exposés of police work has contributed to a folkloric construction of police deviance that many have argued has undermined the legitimacy and authority of the police and lessened public esteem for a once-cherished symbol of national pride (Reiner, 2000).

Although such explanations have an intuitive 'common sense' appeal, and might be attractive to senior officers who are able to distance themselves from such portrayals, there are significant reasons why police culture might not offer a definitive basis to explain police behaviour. First, as Reiner (2000) noted, police culture is not 'monolithic, universal or unchanging' and it cannot be assumed that all officers share the values, attitudes and beliefs outlined above. Loftus (2008) showed that a focus on dominant aspects of police culture should not obscure other cultural forms that challenge and contest prevalent narratives of police work. Although she suggested that much of police work continues to be dominated by white, male, heterosexuality that provides the normative 'white space' of policing, alternative formations are also important and can shift the terrain. Indeed, she argued that the assertion of the dominant 'white space' can be understood in part as a defensive response to the development of a perceived 'politically correct' environment.

Clearly police culture does not provide any absolute guide to officer behaviour. The presence of different strains of police culture, for example between 'street cops' and 'management cops' (Reuss Ianni, 1982) or among those officers working in specialist departments (Innes, 2003), suggests that police culture is mediated by particular working environments. That police culture is not universally constant is illustrated by Moon's (2006) study of Korean police officers' attitudes towards community policing. In contrast to findings from research in other jurisdictions, Moon argued that Korean officers were not culturally resistant to key tenets of community policing, even though they appear to share other aspects of police culture such as machismo and sense of mission. Chan (1997) noted that police culture is not always resistant to change, and that police officers themselves are not passive dupes, unwittingly coaxed into a particular cultural domain. As she points out, 'while the culture may be powerful, it is nevertheless up to individuals to accommodate or resist its influence' (Chan, 1997: 66). Some more recent studies suggest that in relation to minority ethnic groups, LGBT and female officers there are signs that there has been cultural struggle and challenges to dominant cultural forms and that wider social and political changes have an impact on policing (Loftus, 2008; Colvin, 2009; Rumens and Broomfield, 2012). Moreover, Charman and Corcoran (2015) found that broader patterns of cultural change had been instigated in An Garda Síochána (the police force of the Republic of Ireland) as a programme of reforms had altered normative expectations of officers in the Irish police service.

In addition to recognising the heterogeneity of police subculture, a more fundamental question about the relation between officers' views and attitudes and their operational behaviour needs to be addressed. Waddington (1999b) argued that police culture needs to be understood as a means of interpreting and rationalising police work in a post-hoc sense, and does not necessarily play a strong causal role in terms of shaping their behaviour. He noted that police subculture is often discussed in highly pejorative terms, and implicitly or explicitly is portrayed as both inherently retrogressive and as determining officer action. On both these grounds Waddington argued the concept of police subculture needs to be fundamentally reassessed. Researchers have identified such a diversity of subcultures, relating to the specific contexts in which groups of officers work, that any notion of police culture as a common property shared among officers disappears 'into a near infinity of multiple sub-cultures' (Waddington, 1999b: 290). Moreover, Waddington challenges the notion that the cultural properties identified by researchers provide any explanation of their behaviour. On the contrary, he noted a range of studies that found considerable discrepancy between the canteen talk of officers 'off stage' and their professional behaviour. Even an early British study of routine police work in London conducted by the Policy Studies Institute (PSI) (Smith and Gray, 1983) which found considerable evidence of racism, for example, noted that this was not simply reflected in officers' behaviour. Waddington (1999b: 288–9) suggested that this discrepancy between attitudes and behaviours has been widely noted:

> **The PSI researchers frankly admitted that they were surprised at the discrepancy between canteen racism and actual treatment of black people, especially victims (Smith and Gray, 1983). I too found a gap between the identification of certain protest groups as 'the opposition' and the extensive steps routinely taken to facilitate their holding peaceful protests. Equally, the widespread republicanism amongst senior Metropolitan Police officers was not evident in their excessive responsiveness to royal sensibilities (Waddington 1994a, 1994b, 1993).**

Waddington does not suggest that consideration of police culture should be abandoned altogether. Instead, it should be 'appreciated' as a response to the 'structural contingencies' of police work, just as other forms of deviant subculture are interpreted (Waddington, 1999b: 295). The role of subculture is that it allows officers to make sense of their experience and to maintain professional self-esteem. The widely noted components of police culture, such as authoritarianism and machismo, directly reflect defining attributes of police work. The former relates to the authority that officers have over the territory that they patrol; since they are the symbolic representation of the state then this authority is real – uniquely they possess the legitimate recourse to the use of violence. For that reason, the machismo of officers is also best understood in terms of the routine features of police work. That the actual experience of violence is relatively rare is of marginal importance, the key point is that a defining characteristic of police work, shared by few other professions, is the potential for violent confrontation.

BROADENING THE HORIZON: CULTURE AND POLICING IN WIDER PERSPECTIVE

While Waddington's (1999b) critique of police culture provides an important reformulation that allows some of the simplistic assumptions of much of the literature to be critically reconsidered, it too needs to be critically reconsidered on the basis of the changing terrain of policing. As was argued in earlier chapters, and will be revisited in Chapter 10, discussion of 'policing' can no longer be confined to consideration of the monopolistic institution of the state police. As the nation state itself has been weakened by internal and external processes of privatisation and globalisation, policing has become as increasingly networked process of social control that engages a plethora of actors at a range of levels (Johnston and Shearing, 2003). Waddington's (1999b) analysis of police culture locates the concept in terms of the broader context of public police officers as the embodiment of state sovereignty with a monopoly on the use of legitimate violence. If the state, and the public police, is no longer the sole provider of policing several consequences arise for understanding police culture. First, the diffusion of state sovereignty among pluralised networks of private and public agencies at local, national and international levels means, among other things, that the police officer no longer has a monopoly on the legitimate use of force. The plethora of nodes within policing networks means that the range of agencies that have some coercive power has extended dramatically in recent years. While it might be that many of these agencies do not directly use force in the implementation of their powers and continue to rely upon the public police for enforcement, this is not the always the case. The recourse to the use of force might distinguish police work from that of many other occupations but this feature is increasingly fading as other agencies have become involved in policing. If Waddington (1999b) was right to suggest that the legitimate use of violence configured police subculture, then it seems likely that the influence of this property will extend to other professions who have a role in policing in its extended sense.

The research evidence relating to some members of the extended policing family, most notably private security guards and Police Community Support Officers, suggests that they do share some of the characteristics of police officers. For example, Johnston (2006) noted that Police Community Support Officers working for the Metropolitan Police Service shared some of the properties associated with police subculture, such as suspicion and racial prejudice. The extent to which other agencies enmeshed in policing networks develop occupational cultures similar to those found within the police service remains to be seen. Clearly, though, as the terrain of policing becomes more complex debates about the nature, foundations and impact of professional cultures will need to address the concepts outlined in this chapter in this broader context.

CONCLUSION

The concept of police culture has become a central feature of debates about the role of the police service in contemporary diverse societies. It has been used to explain the failure of the police service to provide an effective service to many victims of crime and the relative failure to recruit a workforce that represents the wider population. Many of these discussions afford too much weight to the notion, and associate it too closely with the negative characteristics of a minority of deviant police officers. Furthermore it is clear that the 'working personality' of police officers can largely be attributed to the organisational context and routine demands placed upon junior officers. Group loyalty might be a negative characteristic of police subculture in terms of covering-up to protect colleagues, but it is an understandable feature of a working environment when officers might rely upon their colleagues for support when faced with risky situations. Two fundamental conclusions can be drawn from this discussion. First, that while the concept of police culture is vital to understanding policing it provides a poor guide to police behaviour in particular circumstances. Second, if the defining characteristics of policing are increasingly shared with other agencies, then it seems likely that the cultural patterns that have emerged, partly in response to them, might themselves pervade networks of policing.

chapter summary

- Police organisational subculture has often been highlighted in media-driven exposés of scandals, and is a common theme in news-media and fictional representations of police work.

- The 'working personality' of police officers is held to influence the ways in which officers interpret the law and exercise the discretion that is a hallmark of routine police activity.

- Discretion is particularly significant because officers have to interpret how they will apply the law in particular circumstances, the power that they have over fellow citizens and the 'invisible' circumstances in which routine police work is carried out. Police culture has often been cited in explanations of the poor response the service has offered to victims of domestic and sexual violence and the apparent over-policing of minority ethnic communities.

- Successive studies have characterised police working culture in many societies in terms of insularity, cynicism, conservatism, machismo and prejudice.

- The failure of the police to respond to victims of domestic and sexual violence has often been attributed to a subculture dominated by male staff at all levels of the organisation. Women have always had a gendered role within the police service and until relatively recently have been formally barred from working in certain roles. As with other marginalised groups, evidence suggests that female officers have often over-subscribed to the machismo of police subculture as a way of demonstrating their affinity to the service.

- The position of lesbian, gay, bisexual and transgender (LGBT) communities within the police service has received less attention than that of other marginalised groups, and there is less statistical information relating to representation of these groups within police ranks. Some studies suggest that LGBT officers have reported a relatively positive response within police services to their sexual identity.

- Whatever its nature, the roots of police culture have been explained variously in terms of the profile of those who enter the service in the first instance, or the nature of police work itself.

- While few studies have presented alternative perspectives on the character of police subculture, the impact that it has on police work is more contentious. First, police culture is not singular or unchanging, and not all officers fit the description outlined. Individual police officers have agency and are not dupes influenced by an over-whelming regressive subculture. Second, police culture might be conceptualised as a response to police work, rather than something that determines operational practice.

- The broader terrain of policing in the contemporary period has meant that many features associated with the public police, such as the recourse to the use of force, power over fellow citizens and so on, are now increasingly shared with other agencies. If these characteristics of police work have, among other things, shaped the subculture of officers, then it might be expected that the dominant features might also become shared among diverse policing networks.

self-check questions (with answers at the back of the book)

1. How did Wilson famously characterise the particular character of police discretion?

2. What are the key features of police subculture?

3. What characterises the 'rotten apples' perspective on police racism?

4. What was the remit of early generations of female police officers?

5. What proportion of homophobic crime has it been estimated is *not* reported to the police?

6. In respect of what issues did Colman and Gorman (1982) measure the attitudes of police recruits?

7. What different 'strains' of police culture have been identified?

8. In what nation did Moon (2006) suggest police subculture is not resistant to community policing?

9. Who conducted an early study of routine police work in London?

10. Why might understanding of police culture need to be broadened?

study questions

1. Why might it be problematic to present undesirable aspects of police culture in terms of the characteristics of individual deviant officers?

2. Why might it be argued that police culture is not fixed or universal in character?

3. Does police culture determine police behaviour?

annotated further reading

Reiner (2000) outlines the sociological literature on cop culture, and how it came to be regarded as a central determinant of police behaviour as studies showed that the formal rules or law-enforcement codes were subject to the exercise of police discretion.

Waddington's (1999) article 'Police (Canteen) Sub-Culture: An Appreciation' provides an important reconceptualisation of subculture, and argues that it can be understood as a response to the demands of police work, rather than something that determines the way in which officers behave.

Cockroft's (2012) *Police Culture: Themes and Concepts* provides a concise analysis of contemporary approaches to many of the issues outlined in this chapter. Loftus's (2009) *Police Culture in a Changing World* examines the changing terrain of culture in policing in terms of results of a major ethnographic study conducted by the author.

annotated listings of links to relevant websites

The website of the National Black Police Association (www.nbpa.co.uk) provides an array of information on racism within the police service, and campaigns and policies introduced to tackle it. The site also provides links to many other police resources, including many of the associations linked to particular constabularies. Information about the Scottish Muslim Police Association can be found at www.spma.uk.com/. The Christian Police Association was established in 1883 and is part of an extended worldwide network; more information on the Northern Ireland branch can be found at www.cpani.com/.

The British Association of Women Police website (www.bawp.org/) contains more information relating to the 'gender agenda' and a host of other useful resources.

The website of the LGBT Police Network (www.lgbtpolice.uk/) contains useful updates on news items relating to homophobia, crime and policing.

Data on police workforce is published annually by the Home Office www.gov.uk/government/uploads/system/uploads/attachment_data/file/544849/hosb0516-police-workforce.pdf.

annotated links to journal articles

A useful early study examined the question of police working personality:

Balch, R.W. (1972) 'The Police Personality: Fact or Fiction?', *The Journal of Criminal Law, Criminology, and Police Science*, 63 (1): 106–119.

The status of a minority group among police ranks is reviewed in:

Jones, M. (2015) 'Who Forgot Lesbian, Gay, and Bisexual Police Officers? Findings from a National Survey', *Policing*, 9: 65–76.

The changing and dynamic nature of police culture is explored in Loftus' work:

Loftus, B. (2008) 'Dominant Culture Interrupted: Recognition, Resentment and the Politics of Change in an English Police Force', *British Journal of Criminology*, 48: 756–77.

An important re-appraisal of the nature and value of police subculture is offered by Waddington:

Waddington, P.A.J. (1999) 'Police (Canteen) Sub-Culture: An Appreciation', *British Journal of Criminology*, 39: 287–309.

7
POLICING DIVERSITY

CONTENTS

This chapter provides an overview of the recent development of the notion of 'policing diversity' in England and Wales. In addition to outlining why policing diversity has become a pre-eminent theme in current debates about policing, the chapter explores central conceptual issues and argues that increasing recognition of social diversity poses challenges to long-standing principles of 'policing by consent'. However, it argues that, taken to its logical conclusions, the concept might raise serious problems for the police service. The chapter aims to:

- outline the social and political context in which the concept of policing diversity has developed in recent times
- explore the widening understanding of 'diversity' issues
- consider why enhancing diversity is regarded as a priority for the police service
- reflect upon the limitations of the diversity agenda for contemporary policing.

KEY TERMS

disability; gender; hate crime; legitimacy and consent; religion; race and racism; sexuality and stop and search

INTRODUCTION

Although concern about police relations with sections of the community in the UK has been particularly salient since the urban unrest of the 1980s and became the defining issue of debate that followed the public inquiry into the murder of Stephen Lawrence, it is worth noting that police relations with Black and Minority Ethnic (BME) groups often have been fraught since the foundation of modern police forces in the mid-nineteenth century. Similar concerns have applied in many other societies and have been a major issue in the USA, Australia, Canada and elsewhere for many decades (Barlow and Barlow, 2001; Cunneen, 2001; Baker, 2006). Historians have demonstrated that various sections of the public in Britain have been understood as problematic for the police during particular periods (Emsley, 1996; Reiner, 2000). In the early decades of the modern policing era, the 'dangerous classes' located in urban slums were widely regarded as a threat to the police and to 'respectable society' more generally (Morris, 1994). In the century or so between the foundation of the modern police and the beginning of large-scale migration to Britain from the Commonwealth, Irish people, Jews from Eastern Europe, and Arabian and African seamen, among others, were in various ways understood as difficult groups for the police (Panayi, 1996; Rowe, 1998). That concern about police relations with minority communities is often regarded as a relatively recent phenomenon is perhaps because contemporary problems are understood against the background of the perceived 'golden era' of British policing that followed the Second World War (Reiner, 2000). If a longer-term perspective is taken, then a rather different picture of police–community relations emerges. Equally, analysis of actual – rather than mythical – police relations with minority communities during the halcyon period of the 1950s and 1960s reveals a reality of prejudice and stereotyping that belies the notion that such controversies are a recent development (Whitfield, 2004, 2007).

Contemporary concerns about police relations with BME communities in Britain can be traced back to the early 1970s. Detailed histories of such relations are available elsewhere (Fryer, 1984; Keith, 1993) and cannot be fully recounted here. The most significant occasion on which police relations with minority communities had a sustained impact on the national political agenda was the 1981 disorders in Brixton, South London and the subsequent Scarman Inquiry (see Box 7.1).

Box 7.1

The Scarman Report

The Scarman Inquiry into the 1981 Brixton disorders established an agenda for policing in Britain that continues to be influential decades later ... The Brixton disorders were not the first of the urban riots of the 1980s, others had taken place a year previously in Bristol, and they were not the most serious in terms of death, injury or destruction. They did, however, become iconic; epitomising urban crisis, decay and revolt, and a synonym for troubled police–community relations. The disorders occurred over the weekend of 10–12 April 1981 and followed a week-long police initiative (Operation Swamp) designed to tackle burglary and robbery. The operation entailed 'flooding' the streets with officers instructed to stop and search, on the basis of surveillance and suspicion, as many people as possible. Some 943 people were stopped, more than half of whom were black and two-thirds were aged under 21 ... Violence eventually erupted: although on a relatively minor level that evening, it reignited the following afternoon and the Saturday evening saw events that Scarman (1981: 1) described in the following terms:

[T]he British people watched with horror and incredulity ... scenes of violence and disorder in their capital city, the like of which had not previously been seen in this century in Britain. In the centre of Brixton, a few hundred young people – most, but not all of them, black – attacked the police on the streets with stones, bricks, iron bars and petrol bombs, demonstrating to their fellow citizens the fragile basis of the Queen's peace ... These young people, by their criminal behaviour – for such, whatever their grievances or frustrations, it was – brought about a temporary collapse of law and order in the centre of an inner suburb of London.

In the aftermath of the disorders Lord Scarman, a senior judge, was appointed to conduct an inquiry into the circumstances of the disorders and the police response ... Perhaps the central contribution of the report was its insistence that the disorders could only be understood against the particular context of social deprivation, political marginalisation, and economic disadvantage. An inflexible and militaristic style of policing, with poor public engagement, exacerbated the situation and made worse tensions and pressures but did not solely create them ... Many of Scarman's recommendations relating to policing, for example on training, the role of community policing, lay visitors to police stations, discipline, and stop and search, established an agenda for the following decade. That some of the problems he identified were reiterated almost twenty years later in the Lawrence Inquiry suggests both that the reforms Scarman advocated were crucial and that they had not been effectively implemented.

(Rowe, 2007b)

Scarman's restatement of the importance of policing by consent and community policing did not occur in a vacuum. As discussed in Chapter 4, other influential commentators, perhaps most notably the former Chief Constable John Alderson, were also arguing that post-Second World War British policing had become too isolated from the public and that officers had come to regard themselves as a group separate from society at large (Alderson, 1979). One high-profile report into police–community relations, published by Her Majesty's Inspectorate of Constabulary (HMIC, 1997: 7), notes that during the 1970s and 1980s

[p]olice force amalgamations created larger and sometimes impersonal service providers where policing strategies were decided upon, implemented and changed with a minimum of internal and external consultation. The traditional foot beat system had in many instances been replaced by unit-beat systems supported by 'panda' cars providing less continuity in personal contact between the police and the public. In many areas, particularly those within inner cities, reactive 'fire brigade' style policing had become more and more prevalent.

In addition to concerns that the style of policing as delivered to the public was serving to isolate officers from routine contact with members of the public, debates were also taking place about formal systems of accountability. The relative powerlessness of local police authorities vis-à-vis Chief Constables and the Home Secretary, within the tripartite framework laid down by the Police Act 1964, was causing some to argue that a democratic deficit existed in governance of the police (Jefferson and Grimshaw, 1984; Scraton, 1985). These issues are discussed at greater length in Chapter 4, where the introduction of Police and Crime Commissioners in 2012 is analysed. Relations with BME communities have formed an important strand in debates about policing but have been added to by concern about other aspects of diversity. Particularly these have related to police relations with religious and faith communities, the disabled, and those defined in terms of sexual orientation. The degree to which the 'diversity agenda' can be extended to include groups such as youth subcultures or sex workers has been debated in the recent past as many of the issues surrounding police relations with BME communities have widened to encompass other identity communities (Garland, 2012).

THE IMPACT OF THE LAWRENCE INQUIRY

Whereas the police had been subject to a series of criticisms with regard to interaction with BME communities in Britain for several decades, there can be little doubt that the enquiry by Sir William Macpherson (1999) into the murder of Stephen Lawrence marked a significant watershed and placed issues of race and racism at the heart of debates about policing (Rowe 2004; 2007c). Although the facts of the murder of 18-year-old Lawrence are relatively straightforward and incontrovertible, the impact that the case has had in terms of policing in Britain and society's attitudes toward racism has been wide ranging and fundamental. Because much of the discussion of particular developments in policing diversity are overtly rooted in the aftermath of the Lawrence murder and the subsequent report by Sir William Macpherson, it is important to provide an overview of the case and the developments that followed (see Box 7.2).

Box 7.2

The Stephen Lawrence Case

In April 1993, Stephen Lawrence, a black teenager with ambitions of becoming an architect, was waiting for a bus in Eltham, South London, accompanied by his friend, Duwyane Brooks, when a group of white youths shouted racist abuse and charged them from across the road. The group engulfed Lawrence, stabbing him repeatedly. Brooks fled, shouting for Lawrence to follow him, which he did. Bleeding heavily, though, Lawrence collapsed some 130 yards from the scene of attack and died soon after on the pavement. The jury at the subsequent inquest into Lawrence's death returned a verdict of unlawful killing in 'a completely unprovoked racist attack by five White youths'. In the years that followed the murder, two police investigations were conducted into the case by the Metropolitan Police and another, under the auspices of the Police Complaints Authority, by Kent Police. Subsequently, the Crown Prosecution Service decided against bringing a case against five suspects, which led the family of Stephen Lawrence to bring a private prosecution against the same men, a very unusual development with respect to a murder, and one that failed to bring any conviction in this case. Although the report of the official inquiry clearly rejected allegations that the failure to adequately investigate the murder was a result of police corruption or collusion, the conclusion that was arrived at offered scant comfort to the police:

> The conclusions to be drawn from all the evidence in connection with the investigation of Stephen Lawrence's racist murder are clear. There is no doubt but that there were fundamental errors. The investigation was marred by a combination of professional incompetence, institutional racism and a failure of leadership by senior officers. A flawed Metropolitan Police Service review failed to expose these inadequacies. The second investigation could not salvage the faults of the first investigation.
>
> (Macpherson, 1999)

In 2011, Gary Dobson and David Norris were jailed for the murder of Stephen Lawrence after the Court of Appeal had quashed their earlier acquittal in the light of new scientific evidence that linked them to the crime.

The Lawrence Report made 70 recommendations covering a wide range of police work, including improvements to training in first-aid, the management of murder investigations, police liaison with the victims of crime, and the use of stop and search powers. While the focus here – and more widely – is on the implications that the Macpherson Report had for police relations with BME communities, it is important to note that it also found that professional incompetence and a failure of leadership marred the investigation into the murder of Stephen Lawrence. Underpinning the specific recommendations was a more fundamental priority that the Home Secretary needed to improve the 'trust and confidence' that BME communities have in the police service. The Home Secretary responded by accepting the majority of the recommendations and establishing a steering group to oversee their implementation and report annually on progress made. Much of the initial political and media focus on the Report centred on the finding that the police service was institutionally racist. The Lawrence Report (Macpherson, 1999: 6.34) defined the concept in the following terms, which have become predominant:

> **The collective failure of an organisation to provide an appropriate and professional service to people because of their colour, culture or ethnic origin. It can be seen or detected in processes, attitudes and behaviour which amount to discrimination through unwitting prejudice, ignorance, thoughtlessness and racist stereotyping which disadvantages minority ethnic people.**

The concept of 'institutional racism' has long been controversial, not least because it has been used to mean many different things (Singh, 2000). While the Lawrence Report finding was accepted by many senior police officers, it has subsequently been criticised on various grounds. Some have argued that the term has hampered effective policing by undermining the public reputation of the service or that it has created a climate in which officers are reluctant to intervene because they are concerned that they will be labelled as racist by newly-emboldened minority communities (Hague, 2000). While there is anecdotal evidence that such concerns are expressed by officers it is not clear that they have had a significant impact in terms of routine police work. Although it is clear, to take one example, that the number of stop and searches did fall off in the period following publication of the Lawrence Report, it is equally apparent that the use of stop and search powers has remained a central feature of police work and that the number carried out has increased again in the wake of concerns about terrorism. Issues relating to the over-representation of minority ethnic groups in police stop search data are discussed at greater length later in this chapter.

Other criticism of the Report's use of the term 'institutional racism' suggest that, despite its apparent radical clarity, the term continues to be badly defined and contradictory. To that extent authors such as Lea (1999) and Solomos (1999) have argued that the definition does little more than reformulate forms of indirect racism that were prohibited by the Race Relations Act 1996. That legislation outlawed policies and procedures that had disproportionate impacts in terms of ethnicity, even where they did so unintentionally. Others have argued (Foster et al., 2005; Souhami, 2007) that police officer resistance to the charge of institutional racism and the difficulties that many have expressed in terms of responding to it, stem from a fundamental incoherence in the Report's analysis and cannot be reduced to a cultural or organisational sensitivity about racism. Souhami (2007) noted, for example, that the Report applied the term 'institutional racism' inconsistently, sometimes attributing errors to individual officers and other times to more general cultural or institutional processes. Among the arising incongruities not properly explained in the report was how institutional racism explained the failure of some officers to properly understand that the murder was a racist attack, while other officers – part of the same institution – recognised very quickly that it was a racist murder (Lea, 2003, cited in Souhami, 2007).

the development of anti-racist policing

One of the central features of the impact that the Lawrence Report (Macpherson, 1999) had has been in terms of the added impetus it has given to the development of policing diversity models. These might initially have focused on relations with BME communities but have now incorporated many other communities. Prior to the publication of the report, it might be argued, the predominant policing approach was one predicated on a 'race relations' or equal opportunities model – broadly based around the provision of a similar level and style of policing to all members of the wider public at large. The key focus was to ensure that BME communities received an equitable service to that delivered to all members of society. This perspective characterises the role of the police as essentially neutral, in which officers' proper concern is to enforce the law in a professional, even-handed and effective manner. Often the goal was to assure that officers refrained from behaving in certain ways considered to be illegal or morally and ethically undesirable. Post-Lawrence, conceptualisation of the police position in respect of minority groups has become one in which anti-racism is a central theme.

This has been enhanced by the legal provisions of the Equalities Act 2010, which prohibits discrimination on the grounds of race, age, gender, disability or sexual orientation, and that police have a duty to eliminate discrimination, harassment and victimisation and to foster good relations. This establishes a broader remit for individual police officers and the police service than a traditional requirement not to contravene legal or disciplinary codes. Not only does it reflect broader public policy shift in efforts to tackle racial discrimination, it also mirrors other efforts to reorientate the management of officers around positive goals and objectives rather than the negative avoidance of unacceptable practices. The principles of effective policing of a diverse society have formed part of a broader promotion of police professionalism and reflexive practice such that officers understand the impact that their actions have on the wider public. As is shown in Chapter 4, police services internationally have developed codes of ethical practice that supplement disciplinary regulations by producing statements about the standard of behaviour that officers ought to aspire to. The promotion of diversity within the police service places a greater onus on middle- and senior-ranking officers made responsible for 'delivering' on community and race relations targets, such as those relating to recruitment. Recognition that the active pursuit of good community and race relations is central to contemporary police leadership is evident in the remarks of the president of the Police Superintendents Association of England and Wales, who noted that 'if you are not delivering on this [policing diversity] you should not be a Basic Command Unit commander' (*Police Review*, 2001).

Efforts to develop a policing service that meets the needs of diverse communities have raised more profound questions about legitimacy and efficacy in complex and fragmented societies. Although it might be argued that the notion of policing by consent has never been wholly achieved in Britain, it has provided an important discourse and an apparent source of legitimacy. In an era in which many public agencies have consciously aped private sector consumer-focused approaches to service delivery, the provision of a one-dimensional standard has been replaced by an emphasis on meeting the diverse needs of heterogeneous clients.

Partly in response to increasing political and financial scrutiny from central government, senior police officers sought to 'reconfigure the working culture of the police so as to improve the 'quality' of the service it offers' (Loader and Mulcahy, 2003: 240).

In addition to adopting some of the financial rigours of the private sector, policing co-opted the language of service delivery and customer satisfaction. An early example of this was the launch in 1988 of the Metropolitan Police PLUS Programme, and ACPO's Statement of Common Purpose and Values, both of which sought to emphasise a role for the police beyond the narrow remit of crime-fighting (Reiner, 2000: 75). The party politics of law and order in the 1990s, among other factors, meant that issues relating to policing, race and racism were under particular scrutiny (McLaughlin, 2007a and b). Although the 'diversity agenda' of that period has somewhat waned, it has been suggested that the Big Society agenda of the coalition government provided some scope to continue the development of policing services that are more closely attuned to the needs of a diverse citizenry (Holdaway, 2013).

TWO DIMENSIONS OF POLICING DIVERSITY

As noted in the introduction, campaign groups, media exposés and political controversies relating to policing and race relations have centred around two tendencies that are superficially contradictory: the under-policing and the over-policing of minority ethnic communities. The latter refers to the police role in the criminalisation of minority ethnic youths and the former to the failure of the service to provide an adequate service to the victims of hate crime, as epitomised by the Lawrence case. Both failures have been attributed to factors including institutional racism, police culture and the under-representation of minority ethnic people in the police service. Chapter 6 included discussion of the recruitment, retention and the promotion of minority ethnic police officers, and female and gay staff. The discussion below focuses on long-standing concern about police use of stop and search powers, as the primary illustration of the over-policing of minority ethnic officers, and the under-policing of hate crime.

over-policing: stop and search

The over-representation of many BME communities in stop and search practices has been apparent in ethnic monitoring data that has been compiled since the early 1990s. The over-policing of black, and more recently Asian, communities – especially young males – in terms of their experience of stop and search is stark. In relation to searches conducted under the Police and Criminal Evidence Act 1984 (PACE), the largest category, Ministry of Justice (2015) data shows 14.6 in a 1,000 white people were stopped and searched in England and Wales in 2013/14. For black people the rate was more than four times higher (65.2 per 1,000). The discrepancy between white and Asian people was less marked but the latter still experienced a higher rate of 23.0 per 1,000 population. Interpreting this and similar data is made more difficult for a number of reasons – including concerns about the viability of ethnic classifications and the validity of using resident population statistics as a benchmark (Rowe, 2012). Despite these methodological concerns and the challenge of explaining disproportionality there can be little doubt that many BME communities are stopped and searched more frequently than other groups and that these disparities are widely cited as a major source of tension between BME (and other) groups and the police. Stop and search was a key aspect of police discrimination and disrespect, cited as a major cause of the 2011 riots (Guardian/LSE, 2011; Riots Communities and Victims Panel, 2012). In 2010 the Equalities and Human Rights Commission (EHRC) reported that disparities in the use of stop and search powers against different ethnic groups were rooted in police policies and practices that could not be justified in terms of offending rates or demographic trends.

Concerns about the over-representation of BME groups in stop and search has generally been expressed in terms of police powers under PACE, but extend to more recent anti-terrorism and public order legislation. Section 44 of the Terrorism Act 2002 gave police power in defined localities to stop and search vehicles, people in vehicles and pedestrians for articles that could be used for terrorism 'whether or not there are grounds for suspecting that such articles are present'. In this way the Act moved beyond PACE provisions that require officers have 'reasonable grounds' relating to individuals who are stopped and searched. In the last quarter of 2010, 19.7 per cent of those stopped and searched under s.44 powers were Asian (Home Office, 2010a: 17). As was discussed in Chapter 3, these powers were withdrawn after 2010 but concerns continue that other powers to stop and search at airports are disproportionally used against Asian people. Such evidence has led to arguments that Muslim people in Britain have become 'suspect communities' subject to surveillance by police and other agencies engaged in 'counter radicalisation' as part of the government's Prevent strategy against terrorism (Mythen et al., 2009).

Criticisms of police stop and search stem in part from the very small number of arrests that result from these practices. Figure 7.1 indicates that only 12.2 per cent of stop and searches conducted in England and Wales in 2013/14 resulted in arrest. This data suggests that stop and search is ineffective in terms of detecting crime. While other potential benefits relating to deterrence or intelligence gathering might be identified, these practices are beyond the legal basis of police stop and search powers that are clearly grounded in crime detection and investigation and not these other outcomes. Moreover, as Bowling and Weber (2011) have argued there is no reliable evidence that stop and search has a deterrent effect in terms of either individual or aggregate patterns of offending.

Explaining patterns of police stop and search practice on the basis of these recorded statistics requires caution. First, the ethnic classification itself is problematic, since

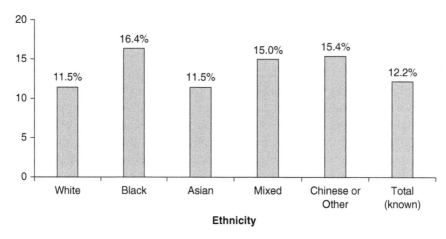

Figure 7.1 Proportion of stops and searches that resulted in arrest under section 1 PACE and other legislation by self-identified ethnicity, England and Wales, 2013/14 (Ministry of Justice, 2015)

'white' is an omnibus category that does not directly correspond to ethnicity, and 'Asian' conflates sub-groups that have sharply contrasting socio-economic profiles. Furthermore, problems with recording practices have been identified that might explain disparities in ways that do not relate simply to police racism. Fitzgerald and Sibbit (1997) found that officers were more likely to record stop and searches conducted on minority ethnic people than on whites, in part because they were more concerned to demonstrate that they had followed procedures when dealing with the latter than they were with the former. Clearly, this means it is more likely that encounters with minority ethnic people make their way into official records than are similar interactions with white people.

The tendency for minorities to be treated more formally has also been noted in the context of the response of senior officers to internal matters of complaints and discipline. One reason why concerns about the performance of minority ethnic officers are more likely to activate disciplinary processes and result in formal investigation is that middle-ranking officers, most of whom are white, lack the confidence needed to resolve issues informally as they would with white officers (Morris et al., 2004). More recent research by Smith et al. (2015) found that minority officers were disproportionally subject to internal complaints and that this was a result of efforts to disrupt their careers and was sometimes a result of stereotypes that black officers were 'trouble makers' and Asian officers 'dishonest'.

Returning to stop and search, research findings show that the use of alternative population benchmarks suggests a wholly different perspective in which minority ethnic communities are not over-represented. The data published annually by the Ministry of Justice is presented in terms of stop and searches per 1,000 of the resident population.

However, this benchmark is not the most appropriate since it is known that stop and searches tend to be conducted in particular times and particular places. The resident population comprises all those in the police area, many of whom are unlikely to be present when and where stop and searches are likely to be performed. In response to this limitation, efforts have been made to establish a more appropriate benchmark based on those available to be stopped and searched in the times and places where this is most likely to be done. MVA and Miller (2000) compiled a benchmark of the available population in five sites and used that to determine the ethnic proportionality of stop and search. Their report suggested that this measure led to a conclusion radically at odds with the predominant narrative based upon Home Office data outlined earlier:

> [T]he findings of this research did not suggest any general pattern of bias against those from minority ethnic backgrounds. This was true for minority ethnic groups as whole, as well as any particular minority ethnic group. Asian people tended to be under-represented in those stopped or searched, compared to their numbers in the available population, with some notable exceptions. The general picture for black people was mixed. For example, in Greenwich, and Chapeltown, they were mostly under-represented among those stopped or searched, yet in Hounslow and Ipswich, they were far more likely to be stopped or searched in vehicles than their available numbers would suggest. Perhaps surprisingly, the most consistent finding across sites was that white people tended to be stopped and searched at a higher rate than their numbers in the available population would predict.
>
> (MVA and Miller, 2000: 84)

Waddington et al. (2004) reproduced MVA and Miller's methodology in Reading and in Slough. They too found that this measure of police stop and search led to an important change in prevailing explanatory frameworks. They argued that

> it seems that a very different conclusion is reached from comparing stop and search figures with the composition of the 'available population' than with residential figures ... it is difficult to see how these figures could be interpreted as an outcome of officers' stereotyping: if anything, it is white people who are disproportionately stopped and searched.
>
> (Waddington et al., 2004: 900)

As these studies tend to note, these findings do not end concern about racism and police stop and search (Rowe, 2004). If officers are not discriminating against minority ethnic communities available in areas where stop and search is carried out, then it seems that explanations in terms of frontline officers exercising discretion on the basis of racist stereotypes need to be rethought. However, questions about racism and discrimination remain since stop and search practices are concentrated on deprived areas where some minority ethnic groups are more likely to reside. Moreover, socio-economic factors, coupled in some contexts with racism, shape the availability of populations to be stopped and searched. Poverty and exclusion determine availability; in some areas this impacts on visible minority ethnic communities and they might be over-represented in police stop and search data. In other districts, though, white communities, whether minority ethnic, such as the Irish, or otherwise, might be most affected and so have disproportionate contact with the police (Stenson and Waddington, 2007). Race and racism are crucial to understanding patterns of stop and search, but other issues, such as class and place, need to be incorporated into a convincing explanation. Bradford (2017: 77) illustrated the complex and multi-layered factors that underlie over-representation when he noted that

> [p]olice, even when operating with the best of (race-related) intentions, may produce distributively unfair, disproportinate outcomes … due to a confluence of factors revolving around the characterizations of places and individuals, which are driven in turn by the subjectivities of 'cop culture' as well as more widespread stereotypes and the 'objective' reality of the distributions of crime and populations in the areas that they patrol.

under-policing: hate crime

Concomitant concerns have recurred about the failure of the police service, and the criminal justice system more widely, to provide an effective response to hate crime. The inadequacy of the investigation into the murder of Stephen Lawrence resonated partly because it was a compelling illustration of a much more widespread problem about which minority ethnic communities, and others, had long campaigned. The racist murder of Kelso Cochrane in 1959 was a key factor in the Notting Hill riots and an early example of a police response that served to deny that the attack was racially motivated (BBC, 2006b). A common complaint has been that officers responding to incidents have tended to disregard suggestions of racist elements and instead to approach the victim's experience as an 'ordinary' offence. Similar concerns have been raised in the context of hate crimes against lesbian, gay, bisexual and transgender communities (Hall, 2005). The case of Fiona Pilkington – who took her own life and that of her disabled daughter after enduring years of abuse that was not taken seriously by police and other agencies – also illustrated how the cumulative impact of a catalogue of incidents is not recognised (Roulstone and Mason-Bish, 2012). Bowling (1999) showed that much racist violence and harassment tends to be relatively minor in character if the racist components of the offence are disregarded. His study of racist violence in the East End of London found that

> incidents were frequently described [by practitioners] as being 'low level' but 'persistent' and included such incidents as criminal damage, graffiti, spreading rubbish, abusive behaviour, egg throwing, stone throwing, threatening behaviour, and 'knock-down-ginger', often forming patterns of harassing behaviour. More serious incidents such as physical assaults and arson were believed to occur, though less frequently than mundane but persistent behaviour.
>
> (Bowling, 1999: 182)

Traditionally police officers have tended to seek relatively informal resolution of such disputes and have favoured an 'order maintenance' strategy over that of law-enforcement. While this might be an appropriate response in some circumstances it misunderstands the nature of racist victimisation, which is exacerbated by routine repetition such that it forms part of the fabric of everyday life for those who experience it. As Bowling (1999: 280) notes, however, this type of response – where 'normal' circumstances are restored without resort to legal sanction against perpetrators –

> **may simply serve to maintain the on-going process of … victimization. If the threat of violence and occasional use of actual violence is used to intimidate, exclude, or terrorize, the balance of power between victim and perpetrator remains.**

A further problem has been that police services have often not enjoyed strong relations with many minority communities that are affected by hate crime, and so encouraging initial reporting from victims has proved a challenge. Chakraborti and Garland (2009) have noted that police services have developed specialist units intended to provide expert police responses to hate crime victims and to promote more robust relationships that will encourage victims to come forward in the first instance. Along similar lines has been the introduction of various 'third-party' reporting mechanisms whereby community, educational, religious and other organisations can channel victim reports of hate crime incidents to the police service – a form of plural policing and Big Society policing of the type discussed in more detail in Chapter 10. Another mechanism to encourage victims to report to police has been the adoption of a victim-perception approach to police recording of hate crime incidents. Rather than the onus being on victims to demonstrate that their experience has been a 'crime' and has contained evidence of 'hate' in terms of motivation or commission, officers have been issued guidance such that any incident may be treated as a 'hate incident' if that is how it has been perceived by the person reporting. As Chakraborti and Garland (2009: 110) argued, the intention of such guidance is to prioritise the perception of victims and to ensure that this over-rides officer discretion. Figure 7.2 indicates the number and type of hate crimes recorded by police in England and Wales in 2011/12.

Additionally, the adoption of a broad definition of hate crime is intended to widen the range of incidents that are recorded and investigated under that category; again, this should prevent officers from disregarding reports of incidents they feel are of a minor character. The reactive, fire-brigade model of policing, where officers deal with single incidents as and when they arise, has meant that the sustained and repetitive nature of hate crimes has not been sufficiently recognised. Similar problems have applied more widely and much of the thrust of the 1998 Crime and Disorder Act, 'reassurance policing' projects, and the Neighbourhood Policing programme has been to focus attention on tackling antisocial behaviour which, while not necessarily serious criminal offences, undermines the quality of life of communities affected. Additionally, a key

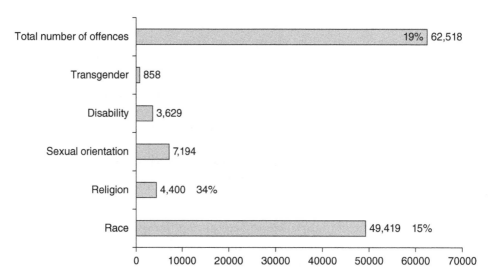

Figure 7.2 Hate crimes recorded by the police, by monitored strand, 2015/16, number and per cent increase from previous year (Home Office, 2016c)

dimension of the problem-oriented policing model is for officers to seek to resolve relatively minor issues before they escalate into more serious criminality (Goldstein, 1990; Leigh et al., 1996).

BROADENING THE DIVERSITY AGENDA: GENDER, SEXUALITY, AGE, DISABILITY ...

Developing a police service that meets the particular needs of minority ethnic communities clearly has implications for other groups that might have specific interests. While the initial impact of the 'diversity agenda' outlined above has been on race and ethnicity, it has latterly broadened to include other communities of interest, such as lesbian, gay, bisexual and transgender populations, people with mental or physical disabilities, elderly people, and myriad other groups. In 2003, an HMIC report outlined the importance of recognising the particular policing needs of a range of interest groups. While the report maintained that the police service ought to remain focused upon managing the issues relating to race and ethnicity that had been developed in the aftermath of the Lawrence Report, it suggested that other groups also had specific interests that needed to be addressed. The report highlighted 13 groups that ought to be brought into the diversity agenda, in addition to minority ethnic communities (HMIC, 2003: 62–3):

- Lesbian, gay or bisexual people

- The deaf or hard of hearing

- People with mental illness

- Gypsies/travellers

- People with disabilities

- Victims of domestic violence

- Asylum seekers

- Young people

- Older people

- Transgender people

- Those involved in child protection issues

- People from areas of poverty (the socially excluded)

It is clear that each of these groups might have particular policing needs and that different means of consultation might be necessary for an effective service delivery. However, the range of interests and needs that arise are broad, especially since any permeation of these is possible, that it is difficult to see how they could be operationalised. While the police service has invested significant resources into providing training on issues relating to 'community and race relations' it is difficult to imagine that officers or support staff could be trained in any meaningful way on the complex, unpredictable and changing patterns of diversity. One reason why the recruitment of minorities into policing is advanced is that a service which is itself more diverse will be more able to understand different needs, cultures and interests surrounding communities of identity.

Recent debates about hate crime victimisation illustrate something of the broader tension relating to the diversity agenda. While England and Wales has no generic 'hate crime' legislation (unlike, for example, many states in the USA), there are a range of groups identified in the Equalities Act 2010 that provides for particular sanctions in cases where offences are aggravated by hostility relating to their perceived identity. On this basis religion, disability, sexual orientation and gender have been added to race as key components of diversity. While this might demonstrate inclusivity and the extension of legal and policy protection to communities that have a history of victimisation and oppression, questions remain about the status of other identity groups. Subcultural groups such as emos and Goths might be included within hate crime and diversity agendas on the basis that they experiences victimisation that is related to perceptions of their 'difference' (Garland, 2010). Policy-makers have reported that the designation of offences against sex workers as hate crimes in Merseyside has enhanced the police and criminal justice response to such victims (Campbell, 2014).

WHY IS DIVERSITY IMPORTANT?

Although often not explicitly stated, a number of benefits are often alluded to by policy documents that seek to enhance the diversity of the contemporary police service. The recruitment of more minority ethnic, female and gay officers was discussed in relation to efforts to transform police culture that were reviewed in Chapter 6. Although the police service has not always been subject to employment law that governs other institutions it is subject to the Race Relations (Amendment) Act 2000, which requires the pursuit of policies that will promote antiracism. Avoiding legal sanction and high-profile employment tribunals provides a negative reason why police managers might seek to promote good practice in terms of diversity and equal opportunity policies. More positively, diversity is important to contemporary policing for pragmatic operational reasons and also to preserve, regain or promote legitimacy.

Practical advantages can be considered in two respects: those relating to operational effectiveness and those that emphasise human resource advantages. While Deputy Commissioner of the Metropolitan Police, Sir Ian Blair launched the Protect and Respect initiative, intended to promote diversity within the service, the programme was advanced because, Sir Ian insisted, there was a 'business case' to pursue recruitment of minority ethnic officers, and that concerns that the initiative represented a 'politically correct' agenda were misplaced. Instead he stated 'it is change for the most basic of business reasons. The future survival of this organisation ... which needs to recruit two-thirds of its police staff over the next ten years, depends on its ability to attract and retain the most talented employees from all our communities' (*Police Review*, 2001). Sometime later the operational advantages of recruiting minority ethnic officers were stressed by Peter Herbert, a member of the Metropolitan Police Authority, who argued that minority ethnic officers ought to be deployed with specialist operational units of the Met 'whether they like it or not'. This would, Herbert argued, bring operational benefits: 'how on earth are we supposed to have any insight into a terrorist group that is not from Northern Ireland without having anyone that, for example, speaks another language ... In the cause of common sense and good policing it has got to be imposed' (*Police Review*, 2002).

The development of the diversity agenda can be understood in terms of promoting and securing police legitimacy. As has been noted the development of public services that reflect the perceptions of citizens has been a core component of Big Society reforms advanced by the Conservative-led coalition government in recent years (Holdaway, 2013). Central to the discourse of policing by consent, which has surrounded the public police since the establishment of the Metropolitan Police in 1829, has been the notion that the police represents the 'citizen in uniform'. If legitimacy depends upon the police service being representative of the public, then clearly the long-term unrepresentative nature of police personnel undermines the principle of policing by consent. As Bradford (2014) argued, the police carry a 'heavy symbolic load' in that they communicate messages about social inclusion and exclusion. Internal dynamics around race, gender, religion, sexuality and so forth can be seen as a 'litmus test' of the organisational health of the police service more generally as well as its capacity to deliver effective services to vulnerable and marginalised communities.

THE COMPLEXITIES OF DIVERSITY

Once the principle of providing policing that meets the diverse needs of diverse communities is acknowledged, it is hard to identify where its consequences might end. Recent debates on the extent of and response to rural crime seem to indicate that rural communities have different policing needs than their urban counterparts. Other research suggests that minority ethnic communities living in rural areas experience different levels and forms of racism and discrimination compared to those in towns and cities (Garland and Chakraborti, 2004). Equally, the experience of the elderly, women, gays and lesbians suggests that still other sets of variables need to be factored into the equation when it comes to providing policing services that reflect the diversity of the community (Williams and Robinson, 2004). In addition, those who are unemployed, have mental health problems, sleep rough or have problems relating to addictions of various kinds are also likely to have certain specific requirements of the police. The types of 'communities at risk' (Johnston, 2000) are endless in their permutations, especially when the impact of intersectionality – cross-cutting complexities that can compound marginalisation – are taken into account. Clearly for policing to be both appropriate and effective, it is vital that the complex needs of various groups are met. However, organisational problems arise relating to the provision of training on the needs of diverse communities, the expectation that recruitment and retention issues will be adjusted to reflect diversity issues, the appointment of liaison officers and consultative groups, and that police performance will be monitored to ensure that service provision is appropriate.

Whether in the recruitment of staff or the development of service delivery, the identification of a particular trait as an organising principle around which policing or any other service can be delivered is a simplistic and limited approach. It is misleading to assume that the recruitment of minority ethnic staff, for example, will lead – in and of itself – to more effective communication with diverse communities. A police officer might be of the same ethnicity as the majority of the local community in which she serves but might have very little else in common with them. Certainly, if that community lives in a deprived area it is unlikely that a relatively well-paid public sector professional will live in the same vicinity. To assume that 'ethnic matching' of police staff and local communities will provide for more effective service delivery reveals a very shallow understanding of diversity issues. Although minority groups of different kinds are likely to have certain specific needs in relation to their disproportionate experience of certain types of crime, or because they need particular types of treatment from officers, it is not necessarily the case that this will extend into all aspects of the service that they might require from the police. Put simply, diverse groups are likely to have more in common than they do apart when it comes to the provision of police service in response to many incidents. Although minority groups, for example, might have specific cultural requirements in terms of the manner in which they are dealt with, the broad framework of their needs is likely to be fairly consistent with those of the mainstream.

Diversity needs to be recognised as increasingly significant – partly because social fragmentation, which should not be exaggerated, is increasingly salient and partly because policing has become more consciously located within the service industry and so must meet the particular needs of segmented markets. Clearly the models and frameworks outlined here will continue to develop and be applied to changing constellations of communities and interest groups. The police service needs to develop a more embedded and reflexive approach to diversity that recognises that race, ethnicity, gender, sexuality, age, mental health and so on can shape needs and expectations in important ways. They do so without guarantee though.

CONCLUSION

In the period since publication of the Lawrence Report (Macpherson, 1999) the police service has developed a wide range of policies, invested significant resources and reviewed operational practices in an effort to respond to the increasingly complex diversity agenda. With some justification, it might be argued that the scale of the response reflects the size of the problems identified. Measuring the impact that these efforts have had in terms of operational policing and the relatively intangible concept of legitimacy is difficult. Clearly, problems remain and controversies continue.

In many respects, the notion of policing diversity appears to encapsulate and further the principle of policing by consent that has informed the development of policing in Britain since the establishment of modern police forces in the first half of the nineteenth century. Although the need for some of the developments outlined above appears to indicate that policing by consent has not been achieved in practice, as an organising principle it has featured fairly consistently for many decades. In the past, consent was understood as a relatively straightforward concept: if the police acted in a way broadly consistent with the expectations of the public, if they used minimal force, tackled crime with reasonable effectiveness and efficiency, and treated noncriminal members of the public with courtesy and respect, it was held that consent would be forthcoming – it would be conferred upon the police for a job well done. Reiner (2000: 50–58) argues that securing public consent for the police in the nineteenth century was partly the result of a deliberate set of policy decisions focusing on bureaucratic organisation, the rule of law, minimal force, non-partisanship, accountability, the service role and effectiveness.

The emphasis on policing diversity might be understood as a subtle renegotiation of this traditional principle because it recognises that consent cannot be gleaned simply by treating all members of the public in the same manner. The public no longer has a consistent, or even a coherent, set of expectations for the police to fulfil. Given that society is increasingly diverse and culturally heterogeneous, the demands placed on the police are no longer straightforward and it may be increasingly recognised that the police cannot satisfy all of the expectations with which they are faced. It might be that the development of policing diversity is partly a response to the introduction of new managerialism, such that mission statements, targets and goals feature heavily in the commitments that police organisations make to their clients and customers. Recognition of the diverse requirements of the client base is a fairly fundamental principle of free-market provision, and in an age where the police service is increasingly understood as one provider of 'law and order' services among many, it is perhaps the case that retaining market share requires that the service attends more carefully to the varied needs of the community. Whereas these broader trends might provide an important context that has encouraged the development of the principle of policing diversity, it is also clear that there has been a significant political agenda which has driven the type of changes outlined in this chapter.

chapter summary

- Police relations with minority ethnic communities have been a matter of concern and controversy in Britain for many decades.

- The 1981 Scarman Inquiry into disorders in Brixton, South London, established an agenda for the development of community policing more widely. Scarman reiterated the principle of policing by consent that continues to underpin contemporary debates about policing in a diverse society.

- In 1999 the Macpherson Report found that the police investigation of the racist murder of Stephen Lawrence had been undermined by institutional racism, professional incompetence and a failure of leadership.

- The concept of institutional racism advanced by the Macpherson Report has been criticised as replicating existing models of indirect racial discrimination, and for being inconsistent.

- The Macpherson Report contributed to the development of a model of antiracist policing, which suggested that the police service ought to play a proactive and interventionist role to confront racism. The Equality Act 2010 requires public sector organisations, including the police service, to develop measures to confront prejudice and promote good community relations.

- The policing diversity agenda has been developed in concert with the promotion of a service-oriented, consumer-focused ethos. What began with a focus on relations with BME communities has extended to incorporate other communities and identity groups including lesbian, gay, bisexual and transgender people, disabled people and faith communities.

- Since the 1970s a key concern among debates about police relations with minority ethnic communities has been the disproportionate use of stop and search powers.

- Many communities have been under-policed in terms of the policing of hate crime. Under-pinning this has been the tendency for police officers not to recognise that the impact of incidents. Additionally has been a tendency for officers to follow an order maintenance strategy that restores 'normalcy' to relations between victims and perpetrators.

- The diversity agenda within policing has been developed for business reasons, to improve operational efficiency and effectiveness, and to enhance legitimacy and public consent. Nonetheless, important complexities remain, not least because of organisational challenges in terms of translating concepts and principles into routine police practices.

self-check questions (with answers at the back of the book)

1. Why has it been assumed, mistakenly, that concerns about police relations with minority ethnic communities have only developed in recent decades?

2. Which police service conducted the second investigation into the murder of Stephen Lawrence?

3. What police policy developments in the late 1980s were associated with developing a customer-focused service delivery model of policing?

4. What three factors did the Macpherson Report (1999) suggest had marred the investigation of the murder of Stephen Lawrence?

5. How was the traditional policing strategy used in response to hate crimes characterised?

6. How many hate crimes were recorded by the police in England and Wales in 2015/16?

7. What legislative change, relating to racist incidents, was introduced by the 1998 Crime and Disorder Act 1998?

8. What diverse populations were identified in a 2003 HMIC report?

9. On what basis did Sir Ian Blair defend efforts to recruit a more diverse police workforce?

10. What notion has been central to the concept of 'policing by consent'?

study questions

1. How are issues relating to policing diversity related to broader efforts to develop a 'consumer-focused' service delivery?

2. How do benchmarks of 'available' populations change explanations of the impact of stop and search on minority ethnic communities?

3. Will broadening the 'diversity agenda' result in more effective policing?

annotated further reading

A special edition of the journal *Policing* (2015, vol. 9, number 1) explored developments in policing and diversity over the period subsequent to the 1999 Macpherson Report. Articles explore developments around sexuality, race and ethnicity, comparative experiences in Britain, the USA and Norway, gender and diversity, and the role of the Special Constabulary.

Chakraborti and Garland have written and edited a number of pieces that analyse conceptual and operational issues relating to hate crime. Their 2009 book *Hate Crime: Impact, Causes, and Consequences* is the strongest overview of the development of debates relating to hate crime in Britain. They explored conceptual debates about broadening the scope of hate crime in their 2012 article in *Theoretical Criminology*.

Bradford's (2017) book *Stop and Search and Police Legitimacy* provides strong empirical evidence around a broad range of factors relating to debates outlined briefly in the discussion in this chapter. These are integrated into a wider discussion about the role of the police in contemporary society and how police practice links to questions about public legitimacy.

annotated listings of links to relevant websites

A host of Home Office reports and statistical information about policing, race and racism, are available at www.gov.uk/government/collections/race-and-the-criminal-justice-system.

Information about diversity issues in the police, including gender and race equalities schemes and diversity, is available at www.police.uk/metropolitan/E05000285/perform ance/diversity/.

A similar range of resources relating to hate crime can be found at www.gov.uk/govern ment/policies/reducing-and-preventing-crime--2/supporting-pages/hate-crime

annotated links to journal articles

An important insight into the views of minority officers on diversity in policing can be found in:

Cashmore, E. (2000) 'Behind the Window Dressing: Ethnic Minority Police Perspectives on Cultural Diversity', *Journal of Ethnic and Migration Studies*, 28: 327–41.

Holdaway explored police race relations in the context of recent developments in the diversity agenda and their prospects in the Big Society:

Holdaway, S. (2013) 'Police Race Relations in the Big Society: Continuity and Change', *Policing and Society*, 13: 215–30.

Understanding the nature of hate crime victimisation is a significant challenge in developing more effective responses, and this article provides excellent insight into the nature of the experience:

Chakraborti, N. and Garland, J. (2012) 'Reconceptualising Hate Crime Victimization through the Lens of Vulnerability and Difference', *Theoretical Criminology*, 16: 499–514.

8

GLOBAL AND TRANSNATIONAL POLICING

CONTENTS

LEARNING OBJECTIVES

The chapter considers how policing is undertaken beyond the territory of the nation state to deliver a range of services on transnational, international and global basis. Some of these activities are akin to the roles and functions that the police and other agencies deliver domestically. Cross-border crimes such as people trafficking or online fraud are perpetrated across national boundaries and require a transnational policing response. Other aspects of transnational policing, however, are inherently different from domestic functions as police services have become an important component of international development and capacity building in failed states. These entail policing adopting different strategies and modes of operation that engage with other sectors, including intelligence services, military and private security contractors. The chapter aims to:

- explore different dimensions of international, transnational and global policing against the context of wider social, political, economic and cultural trends in globalisation
- consider links between policing and international development, transnational policing within the European Union, and the emergence of private security companies within globalised policing networks
- reflect on key debates and challenges relating to governance and accountability, wider patterns of global inequality, and the emergence of a network of policing 'entrepreneurs' able to shape the development and direction of emerging forms of policing practice and organisation.

KEY TERMS

globalisation; governance and accountability; international development; militarisation; nation states; policy transfer; private policing and security

INTRODUCTION

Interest in transnational policing has developed since 1980s (Anderson, 1989) as interest in broader processes of globalisation have accelerated and there has been heightened awareness that economic, political, social and cultural worlds have come to transcend the boundaries of the nation state. Conceptual and theoretical concerns have been coupled with recognition that many aspects of police operational activity have also been reconfigured and new challenges have emerged. The globalisation of economic activities and the rise of transnational corporations, the increasing mobility of people and capital and the transformative capacity of communication technology have reduced the salience of time and space in human relationships. Pollitt's (2012) analysis of the impact of 'deterritorialisation' and technological changes indicates that police services face challenges in common with other public policy domains. Globalisation unsettles established modes and methods of policing and calls into question the organisation, delivery and conceptualisation of practices that evolved in the context of nation states. As Sheptycki (2000) outlined, consideration of the nature and impact of transnational policing followed in the wake of wider political concerns in the 1960s and 1970s about the increasing economic significance of multinational corporations that existed beyond the control of national governments. The extent to which nation states have diminished power in relation to transnational agencies and global corporations is an important question that underpins much of the discussion below but is not a matter that can be fully explored in general terms in this introduction. These wider debates apply in particular ways to policing systems which have been organised in territorial terms and under the authority of nation states. If the status of nation states themselves is undermined by globalisation then the mandate of police services is also brought into question. Moreover, the central position of the state in policing has also been eroded by processes of privatisation such that the delivery of core functions has been out-sourced to commercial companies. That many of those operating in the field of policing are themselves large transnational corporations indicates how aspects of global and international policing have been shaped in part by broader processes of pluralisation, as outlined in Chapter 10.

Beyond these important political and conceptual concerns, globalisation presents new operational challenges to police services. Although the nature and extent of transnational organised crime, relative to local crime problems, is debated it nonetheless poses more significant challenges to national police forces than in previous periods. Global communications and financial services mean that criminal opportunities exist beyond nation states, police forces and court jurisdictions. The development of transnational labour markets has increased problems of human trafficking and again posed new challenges to law-enforcement agencies seeking to develop common counter-strategies. The threat of terrorism is increasingly understood in transnational terms and responses have driven the expansion of international and global policing activities and been important factors in the incorporation of law-enforcement agencies, secret services, military and private sector companies into new policing arrangements.

Although the discussion below puts current developments in international and global policing in their contemporary context it should be recognised that policing has a long history of transnational activity. Interpol was established in 1923 to facilitate the exchange of information between police forces in different jurisdictions and the UN has been engaged in policing activity since the 1950s, as is outlined below. Moreover, operational strategy and tactics were developed by European colonial powers in the context of imperial policing (Brogden, 1987; Cole, 1999). Public order policing tactics, for example, and the use of fingerprint technology were developed by the British in the colonial periphery before being repatriated to the homeland (Anderson, 1989). More recently, though, the development of international, transnational and global policing has often been pursued on the basis that it underpins wider ambitions toward the expansion of democracy. As discussed below, the promotion of democratic government in various countries in transition has been a hallmark of the post-Cold War era. Before reviewing those developments the chapter considers the concepts of 'transnational', 'global' and international policing.

GLOBAL POLICING, INTERNATIONAL POLICING OR TRANSNATIONAL POLICING?

As many commentators have noted, policing is carried out beyond the boundaries of the nation state in a broad range of ways. Individual police officers might routinely cross state borders in pursuit of suspects and the exchange of information and intelligence between forces in different jurisdictions has long been a characteristic of policing. Imperial policing has clearly been of a transnational and international character throughout much modern European history. Since the end of the Cold War the USA has assumed a dominant role in policing around the world and has responded to emerging security threats by developing policing and legal systems that have had a wider impact beyond USA borders. This has been particularly felt in regions such as the Caribbean where nation states intent on preserving trade relations with the USA have had to comply with a range of measures designed to tackle drug trafficking (Bowling, 2010). More widely the USA has promoted legal measures to thwart the financing of terrorism, and these too have been forced upon other sovereign nation states in a form described as 'neo-colonialism' by McCulloch and Pickering (2005). These policing activities are structured and institutionalised through international law and a range of treaties and so represent a more formal and sustained aspect of transnational policing than that which might apply in the context of specific ad hoc criminal investigations. Although these are forms of cross-border activity, the nation state continues to be a central unit of analysis since it is the sovereign state that enters into agreements, authorises the deployment and funding of police. As in other dimensions of international relations, the nation state retains an important conceptual and legal status and is a key component even in policing activities that might be delivered at a considerable distance from its sovereign territory (Sheptycki, 2000).

The concept of 'global' policing, however, connotes a much reduced role for independent nations and suggests forms of networked regulation operating beyond the control and direction of sovereign states. Nation states might form important 'nodes' within these networks of pluralised policing and security but they are not necessarily of more significance or weight than other 'nodes' within the complex systems that govern global relations (Wood and Shearing, 2007). An important element of global policing relationships is the central role played by private corporations either directly in the delivery of law-enforcement services or as large-scale transnational companies whose business contributes indirectly to processes of regulation. Global corporations delivering banking or communication services might fall into this category. Rather than review each of these three forms as discreet types, the discussion below examines transnational, international and global policing in relation to specific contexts. This allows for recognition of the considerable similarities between the three forms and to review broader policy, economic and political factors that have shaped the emergence of contemporary forms of policing beyond the nation state. The chapter outlines the development of international policing in the context of European Union (EU) integration and trends in global pluralised policing that have emerged, in part, in response to terrorism and security threats. Before that, the chapter considers ways in which transnational policing has formed an important component of international development and efforts to promote democratic reform.

DEMOCRACY, TRANSNATIONAL POLICING AND INTERNATIONAL DEVELOPMENT: RULE OF LAW AND THE NURTURING OF CIVIL SOCIETY

The establishment of legitimate and accountable police services, in tandem with reform of criminal justice systems more widely, has become a central focus of democratic transition in many different social contexts in the last few decades. In post-Soviet societies in Eastern Europe, in post-apartheid South Africa, post-conflict Northern Ireland, and in East Timor – to cite only a few examples – the development of policing in accordance with the principles of the rule of law has come to be regarded as a crucial foundation for broader programmes of political, social and economic development. United Nations and many national government development agencies have placed increasing emphasis on police reform as a component of the development of rule of law programmes regarded as crucial to successful transition. Establishment of the rule of law and democratic policing has also been an important priority for international interventions in response to 'failed states' such as Bosnia or Haiti. Bayley (2001: 13) outlined the growth of American emphasis on police reform in transitional societies during the 1990s and concluded that, while there might be a relationship between democratic reform of the police and broader political developments, it is not clear that legitimate and accountable law-enforcement can instigate political democracy:

> **Police actions, however 'democratic,' are not determinative of democratic growth. Indeed, the causal connection runs strongly in the other direction: Democratic government is more important for police reform than police reform is for democratic government. Police reform is a necessary, but not a sufficient, condition for democratic government. The police tail cannot wag the government dog.**

A circular and interdependent relationship is identified whereby successful reform of law-enforcement is both a requirement of broader political and social democratisation, while at the same time such reform is also often regarded as an outcome that demonstrates broader transition has taken place. Taking up this point, Goldsmith (2009: 306) has argued that the development of legitimate and accountable policing is both a necessary (albeit insufficient) condition of democratic transition but also a litmus test by which citizens can judge the extent and impact of those reforms:

> **If police carry on under the new arrangements in similar ways to the old police, then many will be inclined to judge the wider political transitions process a failure. In order to render the new police more accountable and responsive to the community at large, there has often been a strong demand for democratic policing as part of a wider process of democratization, and for the police to be subject to the rule of law.**

Much of the policing work that is directed toward wider programmes of international development is carried out under the auspices of the United Nations (UN), which has developed a policing service that most closely resembles a 'world police force'. The UN first deployed police in 1960, when a small group of officers were sent to the Congo to help local police maintain civil order. For eight months in 1962–63 the UN Temporary Executive Authority administered West New Guinea, a process that included the deployment of a security force of local police under the direction of a British officer (Greener, 2009a: 10). Both of these early UN policing activities, and others that followed soon after, in Gaza and Sinai, for example, reflect the norm during the Cold War era that International Policing (IP) tasks were 'very restricted in scope and scale', amounting to 'a few police professionals who often had to work in a military-dominated environment' (Greener, 2009a: 8). An exception to this norm has been the deployment of the UN Force in Cyprus – which began in 1964 with the deployment of 134 police officers. The mission has continued in various phases and continues until the present day: at the end of 2012, 66 police officers were deployed from Australia, Bosnia and Herzegovina, Croatia, El Salvador, India, Ireland, Italy, Montenegro, Serbia and Ukraine (UNFICYP, undated).

As is noted at various points in this chapter, developments in transnational policing tend to reflect wider geopolitical, cultural and social dimensions of international relations and globalisation. The period following the end of the Cold War has seen an expansion in UN operations and the policing elements contained within them. Policing activity was an important component of UN missions in Namibia, El Salvador, Mozambique, Cambodia, South Africa and in several operations in the former Yugoslavia. UN statistics demonstrate the expansion in policing activity: in 1994 the UN deployed 1,677 officers in CIVPOL (Civilian Police) operations, by 2000 the number had risen to 5,840 and by 2010 the UN was authorised to deploy 17,500 officers (UN, undated). In 2005 CIVPOL was transformed into United Nations Police and member states provided staff for a standing force available for rapid deployment. Greener (2009a: 26) noted that policing activity within UN operations has also expanded in the sense that policing has become more embedded with UN decision making and has become relatively more equal with military in terms of the organisational status of senior staff. Furthermore, the role and mandate of police within UN activities has also expanded. Until the end of the 1990s, the CIVPOL role was focused on the SMART model (i.e. the provision of Support, Monitoring, Administering, Reporting and Training). Yet this has been challenged, and since the new millennium the role has tended to expand to include roles:

- Advisory
- Mentoring
- Law-enforcement
- Selection, recruitment, training, establishment of a credible local police force
- Human rights
- Humanitarian
- Elections
- Internally displaced persons and returnees.

Moreover, these roles have themselves become more complex: monitoring, for example, has moved from haphazard observation to systematic reviews in relation to international human rights standards and UN Criminal Justice Standards (Greener, 2009a: 24).

TRANSNATIONAL POLICING IN THE EUROPEAN UNION

The arrangements described in relation to the UN deployments outlined above illustrate the continued significance of the nation state within transnational policing. Although a supranational organisation, the UN directs and deploys officers in fields outside of their country of origin. This is done on the basis of authority delegated by nation states. On this basis the UN has no mandate of its own and acts as an agent of nation states, just as it does across the wider remit of its work. By contrast, the development of policing in the EU has developed along different lines as the political and bureaucratic governance of the union has assumed statist tendencies of its own and these have underpinned the direction of policing. Walker (2008) identified three tendencies in the development of the EU that have driven the development of policing arrangements. First has been the evolution of an internal security discourse 'that bears a family resemblance to the traditional security rationale linking policing to the state' (Walker, 2008: 130–31). Just as modern nation states have developed on the basis of providing physical security to citizens and police services represent the means by which state sovereignty is enacted, then so too has the EU developed a discourse that places security concerns near the centre of the union's mandate.

Second, Walker (2008) identified policing activities that have developed as a 'functional spillover' from other policy areas. Developments across various policy areas have given rise to a need for policing and security to be addressed. Walker (2008: 132) argued that 'competence in Justice and Home Affairs was justified, at least in some measure, by the need to ensure that the opening of borders did not have inordinate consequences in terms of the increase in security risks.' The need to provide common approaches in policing and security (and across criminal justice more widely) has been a by-product of the central EU mission to establish the free movement of goods and people. Particular examples of developments that have had secondary impact on the development of common approaches to policing might include the introduction of the euro currency in 2002 and the move to hold EU councils three times each year, which has created high-profile political occasions that have attracted protest movements. Neither examples were intended primarily to lead to developments in common approaches to police co-operation but both have driven these processes.

The third component that Walker (2008) identified relates to the role of policing within the symbolic apparatus of state-building. The wider political project of European integration entails furthering identity claims as well as claims over policy competence. The important role that police services occupy within the cultural and political fabric of nation states has extended to the EU as it has begun to develop along similar lines. Walker (2008: 132) argued that 'if the idea of the state is about the coincidence of territory, population and authority, then the prioritisation of an explicitly territorialised conception of security conveys a powerful message about the ambitions of the EU as a "state-*like*" entity, even if not a full-blown state.' Alongside adoption of constitutional treaties, flags, anthems and Europe Day, the EU has assumed some of the trappings of a state by developing its own policing capacity.

The development of policing within the EU, along the lines that Walker identified, represents an expansion of forms of 'high policing', as defined by Brodeur (1983). Whereas most analysis of policing, Brodeur (1983) argued, is focused on the prevention and detection of crime and the performance of a range of service roles (low policing), other important aspects of police work have always centred on protecting and nurturing the state itself (high policing). Much of the expansion of policing in the EU is best conceived of as high policing, although elements of low policing are also considered later in this section.

While the organisation and governance of law-enforcement remains the legal and constitutional responsibility of nation states, there has been a proliferation during recent decades of international treaties and various 'soft law' instruments that have established norms and standards in the field of policing and criminal justice. The role of the EU in terms of law-enforcement and police matters has not led to the development of community-wide police agencies with routine operational responsibilities (low policing) but has primarily focused on the promotion of co-operation between member state forces and the development of standards of practice and governance. The forms that police co-operation take within the EU are many and varied, and include informal co-operation between individual officers on a relatively ad hoc basis. More formal co-operation includes arrangements for mutual work around border areas. A long-standing example is the Cross Channel Intelligence Community (CCIC) established in 1968 by Belgian, British and French police to monitor migration of people and goods (Spapens, 2017). Other examples include TISPOL (established in 1999 to co-ordinate information relating to traffic policing), Aquapol (founded in 2002 between water police forces and inland navigation inspectors) and EnviCrimeNet (set up in 2010 in response to concerns about the illegal trade in environmental waste) (Spapens, 2017).

The different position of European countries in relation to the development of democratic policing continues to mean that a definitive statement of common policing arrangements is inappropriate. Instead there has been a focus on promulgating certain minimum standards. An important early set of principles is contained in the 1979 Council of Europe Declaration on the Police that establishes the principle of democratic policing under the rule of law and identifies a series of provisions relating to the status and independence of police officers. More recently the 2001 *European Code of Police Ethics* includes statements relating to the need for robust mechanisms of governance and accountability that reflect the principles of police accountability reviewed in Chapter 4. Article 59 of Section VI of the Code states that 'the police shall be accountable to the state, the citizens and their representatives. They shall be subject to efficient external control' (Council of Europe, 2001). Furthermore, article 60 of the Code specifies that 'state control of the police shall be divided between the legislative, the executive and the judicial powers'. The development of common EU approaches is driven by such documents that shape policing doctrine but do not provide a detailed blueprint of how police services ought to be organised in operational terms.

In addition to providing a framework for policy development of mechanism of police governance, European standards for accountability and regulation of law-enforcement are enhanced through the work of bodies designed to promote for commonality in terms of norms and strategy. Some of this work is developed through an EU focus on developing arrangements for police co-operation to tackle cross-border crime and security threats. Under the terms of the Schengen agreement, for example, which has been a cornerstone of EU police co-operation since the late 1990s, police services have been encouraged to work collectively in terms of sharing intelligence and joint operations in response to specific crime problems, some of which were outlined above. Inevitably such forms of police co-operation require a degree of commonality in terms of fundamental principles of governance and accountability. Such measures have not been pursued at an EU level in terms of particular programmes or policies for the governance of law-enforcement. This has continued to be the responsibility of individual member state governments.

However, police co-operation has been encouraged and facilitated through progress toward common approaches to tackling cross-border issues, which is deemed to be the proper responsibility of the EU. A 2011 American Bar Association/Rule of Law Initiative in Ukraine report noted a broad range of international and European standards relating to legal and operational regulation of police powers covering issues such as arrest, the use of firearms, and the detention of suspects (ABA/ROLI, 2011). While these do not relate directly to matters of democratic governance of law-enforcement, they can only be operationalised effectively in a context in which independence of police, accountability and scrutiny provide a fundamental set of arrangements such that the day-to-day exercise of police functions can be practised legitimately in accordance with established standards shared across the nation states of the EU. This demonstrates the links between high policing and low policing, since it illustrates how the security interests of the EU filter down to shape routine application of police work in its law-enforcement capacity. That EU directives influence policing arrangements at the local level also provide further support for Bowling and Sheptycki's (2012) argument that policing increasingly should be understood as a 'glocal' activity. They noted that the delivery of services at the neighbourhood level is undertaken within a policing architecture that extends upward to regional, transnational and global developments.

The influence of common approaches to the development of policing within the EU has a wider impact beyond member states to nations on the periphery that seek accession. Just as countries seeking membership have to converge towards EU standards in terms of economic and social policy, so too reforms to criminal justice and policing form part of the criteria against which accession states are evaluated. Levi (2008: 527) noted that prospective member states have been required to implement measures to tackle money laundering, organised crime and corruption, but that the EU has not developed effective mechanisms to ensure that such provisions are implemented effectively by existing member states. The work of bodies such as the Organization for Security and Co-operation in Europe (OSCE) has been focused on providing technical assistance in terms of police reform such that transitional states develop greater capacity in terms of responding to threats to security and public order. The development of such expertise, however, requires more than the establishment of applied technical provisions, and the work of OSCE has included a focus on enhancing democratic oversight and accountability and on developing stability in law-enforcement through strong arrangements for police governance (OSCE, 2008). Similarly, the work of the European Police College (CEPOL), since its inception in 2000, has been focused on developing pan-European training programmes for law-enforcement. While much, but not all, of CEPOL's work has focused on developing training to tackle cross-border crime and security threats, it is clear that the development of police co-operation in regard to training contributes towards the development of a stronger and more coherent EU police culture, which (as with the work of OSCE) also engenders common frameworks for accountability and governance (CEPOL, 2011).

The development such common frameworks for democratic police governance at the European level mirrors the emergence of a global discourse on policing which provides considerable initiative for police reform, even though it does not provide a legally enforceable series of proscriptions that states are obliged to enact. Nonetheless, forms of 'soft power' exerted through international declarations, as well as from civil society organisations such as Amnesty International and Human Rights Watch, have provided a framework for the development of democratic governance of law-enforcement that exerts considerable influence in terms of the development of policy and of political discourse. Reports from the UN and the Organisation for Economic Co-operation and Development (OECD) have both reflected and reinforced established principles for democratic oversight of policing and security services (for further details see ABA/ROLI, 2011). These have reiterated the importance of transparency and accountability in terms of individual conduct of police officers as well as the institutional arrangements for the governance of police institutions.

A conundrum is evident, though, in terms of the development of international standards for democratic oversight. While established principles for democratic policing within nation states are widely proclaimed by international agencies of various kinds, it remains acutely apparent that systems of accountability remain under-developed in terms of the regulation and oversight of transnational policing arrangements. As Wakefield and McLaughlin (2009) have noted, domestic arrangements for the governance of policing do not easily extend to transnational policing work which, by its very nature, is not conducted beneath the auspices of sovereign nation states. Moreover, transnational policing also tends to incorporate intelligence and security services, as well as commercial private security operations, which are usually not subject to domestic systems of accountability and governance to the same extent as police law-enforcement agencies (Goldsmith and Sheptycki, 2007).

GLOBAL PLURAL POLICING AND SECURITISATION

The role of private security companies, and the development of wider networks incorporating security services and the military, has been an important feature of global policing. Stenning and Shearing (2011) identified that the late recognition of the role of private security provision within processes of policing at the national level has recurred in terms of transnational and global policing. Just as scholars have tended to equate policing with the activities of the public police at the national level, so too analysis of transnational and global policing has tended to focus on the interactions of state public police as they are reconfigured to work collaboratively across national borders. This focus, Stenning and Shearing (2011) argued, means that the important role of the private sector in the development of truly global formations of policing has tended to be overlooked. They claimed that 'today it is private security organisations that are the pre-eminent global policing agencies' (Stenning and Shearing, 2011: 271). Ironically, studies of global and transnational policing has continued to be centred on the (inter)actions of nation states. Moving beyond this statist perspective entails recognising the importance of the international and transnational arrangements identified in the previous sections of this chapter but acknowledging that:

> **In addition to these various international policing organisations and activities, however, is a burgeoning range of private transnational policing. Most large multinational corporations (such as oil companies, mining companies, banks, shipping and airline companies, hotel chains, resort operators, etc.), for instance, have their own in-house security organisations, including investigative departments as well as guard forces, which are deployed to protect their assets and personnel in overseas locations. In addition, there is a growing array of transnational commercial security companies which provide a wide range of policing and security services to clients around the world.**
>
> **(Stenning and Shearing, 2011: 275–6)**

The rise of global security companies can be explained in relation to a number of inter-related and reinforcing trends. First, the global reach of security firms has partly followed in the wake of the broader expansion of global corporations that operate multinational sites, have operating systems and personnel that are mobile across different sectors. These multinational corporations rely on communication systems and technology that is itself based at key points around the world. In-house security departments working within large multinational corporations perform key business functions that are global because that is the terrain that the broader company operates within. Distinct from this is a second development in the emergence of a few large corporations that have a global reach in terms of their provision of local services to corporations and public sector organisations that might not themselves operate across national boundaries. Perhaps the prime example in Britain in the current period is G4S, which was founded in the early twentieth century and emerged through a long history of mergers and acquisitions to become a massive global presence by the twenty-first century. The company (motto: 'Securing Your World') had a turnover of £7.5 billion in 2011 and has operations in more than 125 countries and over 657,000 employees.

A third 'driver' of pluralised policing in a global transnational context has been the trend towards contractual relations between private security companies and nation states. Just as pluralisation domestically has been driven, in part, by the public sector jettisoning certain roles off to the private sector, so too such processes have been identified transnationally. Kempa et al. (1999) noted that private security companies were increasingly acting on behalf of nation states: 'international private security forces have been deployed by states in peacekeeping functions, bolstering regimes recognised as legitimate in times of insurrection.' In the context of responding to transnational organised crime in the form of drug trafficking and terrorism, for example, private corporations have been contracted by the USA to act as 'private military companies' or 'private security companies' in Iraq and Afghanistan (Newburn, 2007). In the former case private companies such as DynCorp and Blackwater were contracted to provide security services and policing and to contribute to the 'redevelopment' of the local criminal justice system: both corporations became embroiled in scandals relating to the brutal treatment of detainees and financial corruption (Greener, 2009a: 88).

These scandals, and the difficulty that the Iraqi government had in responding to them effectively, illustrate one of the most noted challenges relating to global private security, that of governance and accountability. As is discussed more fully in Chapters 4 and 10, private security remains difficult to govern in the public interest precisely because it is beholden to private interests. It is noted below that it is difficult for nation states to hold public transnational policing arrangements to account because it develops and operates in forms that are difficult for territorial authorities to 'capture'. These challenges are amplified since they apply doubly in the context of globalised private security companies which operate beyond the boundaries of the state since they are territorially extracted at the same time as being deployed and operated as private business, the largest of which are important elements of global capital.

Bowling and Sheptycki (2012) argued that just as the practices of private security companies within nation states tend to reflect and entrench social class differences, so too in the global context private police operate to the benefit of global corporations and capital accumulation. They argued that efforts to enhance human rights and human security at a global level will need to address the fundamental role of private security which tends to reflect inequalities between the global south and the global north. Encouraging such efforts, they maintained, requires that dominant ideological constructions of the 'war on terror' and the 'war on drugs' need to be challenged. Only by doing so can other geopolitical and economic problems that have a significant deleterious impact on the global population be recognised.

CONCLUSION

In his study of police co-operation in Europe, Benyon (1994) provided a useful framework for conceptualising policing activity that crosses over national boundaries. In order to capture the range and diversity of policing activity within the EU, he suggested a distinction between macro-, meso- and micro-level co-operation. Much of the discussion above has related to macro-level co-operation: the treaties, codes and formal aspects of Brodeur's high policing that has characterised the emerging state-craft of the EU and have underpinned UN transnational policing. The convergence of nation state legislation and development of EU institutions in the field of justice and security are further examples of macro-level international police co-operation. At the meso level are the various police agencies and personnel who are responsible for the development of collective strategy and activities in pursuits of their own professional goals and the political agenda passed on from the macro-level activity. The new cadre of liaison officers and advisors deployed to shape police reform on behalf of UN missions and EU programmes form an important professional class that help determine police doctrine at this meso level (Bigo, 2000). Micro-level co-operation refers to particular operations and investigations staged in response to particular criminal activities or on an ad hoc basis to tackle specific cross-border problems. One advantage of Benyon's typology of international and transnational co-operation is that it presents the range of activity on a continuum and so emphasises the links between local, national and international policing. This also serves as a reminder that for all that policing activity often takes place 'beyond the state', sovereign nations continue to form much of the bedrock for routine policing activity, even when that is delivered in an international or transnational context. Nonetheless the governance and accountability problem is significant in terms of policing across borders. Inherent challenges are made more difficult still by the role of global private security companies within such networks. The fundamental challenge, though, is that there is no global government and no global community that can provide democratic oversight, as Bowling and Sheptycki (2016: 216–17) noted:

> **Given that, the global system is a poly-centric power grid where there is no single sovereign to command, where a variety of competing power players vie for their own interests, our traditional modernist assumption about political and legal accountability – that 'the buck' needs to stop somewhere – simply does not apply.**

What the threefold vertical model does not capture, however, is the importance of 'soft' non-organisational dimensions of police work that have emerged from, and in turn have come to shape, police activity. Although the doctrine of democratic policing remains contested both in terms of what it contains and how it might be operationalised (Manning, 2010), discussion and debate about policing, reform and transitional societies is itself undertaken in a global context. Police reform in Northern Ireland in the wake of the Good Friday Agreement of 1996, for example, led to the Patten Report (ICPNI, 1999) and the establishment of the Police Service of Northern Ireland and was consciously influenced by earlier approaches to police reform in post-apartheid South Africa. More recently a review of police legislation in New Zealand was undertaken with reference to emerging analysis of developments in policing in other countries and with contributions from global experts. These examples illustrate the emergence of what Manning (2010) described as a global civil society informing the nature and direction of policing both in transitional societies and in developed countries. Hills (2009) noted that advocates of the development of a 'global police ethic' – a professional culture that reflects the principles of democratic policing – have to contend with fundamental challenges associated with the universalisation of liberal policing systems into countries and contexts that have different traditions. Moreover, the development of a civil society and professional culture of policing will be difficult in the context of differentials in power and political and economic status that characterise donor–host relationships (Grabosky, 2009). Against that background the development of international policing culture is disproportionally influenced by western police experts such as the International Liaison Officers (ILO) responsible for the formal and informal exchange of information within transnational policing networks. Bowling and Sheptycki (2012: 98) argued that in the absence of robust mechanisms for democratic governance of global policing arrangements, ILOs play a major role in shaping the agenda of transnational policing that is 'increasingly cut loose from … systems of legal sovereignty'.

The rise of the 'police entrepreneurs' who determine models and principles of policing that are applied broadly across vastly different societies has been noted in a number of contexts. Brogden (1999: 179) argued that the concept of 'community policing' that had been developed the USA and Britain was being exported by 'new missionaries' who had sold the model to 'all and sundry' and sought to apply its principles in societies and communities to which the approach was ill-suited. More recently other policing models – key among them problem-oriented policing and zero tolerance policing – have also been attractive products in the global trade in policing strategies. The growing role for private security companies within global policing networks has contributed to the scope for policing entrepreneurs to package and sell products, training and consultancy in an international marketplace. Bowling and Sheptycki (2012) argued that these actors distribute particular models of policing that might entrench rather than challenge global and regional inequalities and so might be problematic in terms of promoting human rights and security. This concern is significant in terms of the impact on the global south and in developing countries in which policing is in transition. However, the strength of global networks is such that the impact of emerging transnational policies and strategies can also be felt in developed stable democracies. As mentioned, police reform in Northern Ireland was influenced by the experiences of post-apartheid South Africa. Former New York Police Chief William Bratton – described by Bowling and Sheptycki (2012: 75) as the 'number one global policing celebrity' – 'sold' his model of zero tolerance policing to the UK, Germany, Italy, Japan, Norway, Brazil, China, Hungary, Switzerland, Portugal, the Netherlands and Israel. The scale of the reach of new policing strategies demonstrates that global communications and migration is contributing not only to new avenues for crime and threats to security, but also to an environment where global policy transfer becomes more routine. The impact that this has on policing arrangements that have developed in relation to the emergence of the modern nation state continues to unfold and will be a major dimension of future debates about governance and accountability and the basis of the relationship between police and citizen.

chapter summary

- Transnational and global policing have emerged alongside wider developments in terms of greater human mobility, global communications technology and an increase in the significance of transnational corporations. The growth in transnational policing mirrors shifts that have occurred in other policy areas. The relative decline of the nation state wrought by globalisation has been accompanied by privatisation of policing activities, and these have also developed transnationally.

- Although there has been a relative decline in the sovereign power of nation states, they continue to be centrally important to many elements of transnational policing. Even though many aspects of international policing activity are co-ordinated and delivered across national borders, nation states continue to be the building blocks in terms of treaties and the development of international law. The concept of global policing, in contrast, suggests a network of forms of regulation that exist beyond the control of the nation state.

- Transnational policing has become an important component of international development. Since the 1990s the USA has acted on the basis that the promotion of democratic policing and the rule of law are important components of wider political and economic transition. The United Nations first deployed police in Congo in 1960. Since that early period the scope and scale of UN operations have expanded. By 2010 the UN deployed 17,500 police and missions have taken on a wide range of functions.

- Police co-operation within the European Union has been shaped by the Union itself assuming a statist role in determining and shaping policing arrangements and making security a prime concern. Pursuing the principle of free movement of people in a Europe without internal borders has entailed establishing a strong external border and promoting common approaches to justice and home affairs.

- Although nation states retain control of policing within the EU, there has been a proliferation of treaties and various 'soft law' instruments that promote common frameworks and approaches. Many of these have had an impact beyond the EU and extended to countries at the borders, particularly those that seek accession to the Union.

- Just as within domestic arrangements, there has been a lack of recognition of the role of private security companies within global policing arrangements. In-house security departments within transnational corporations operate globally to enforce the private interests of the parent company in a range of territories. Distinct from those has been the emergence of large corporations that operate around the world to provide security services for local companies and public sector organisations.

- A third form of global policing is the increasing tendency for nation states to contract security firms to deliver services that once would have been delivered directly by the state, including some functions that are related to the military. In these ways, global private security companies further consolidate existing economic and political power inequalities between developed and developing nations.

- The range of activities performed globally and transnationally can usefully be considered in terms of 'low' and 'high' policing. 'Low' policing refers to the broad sweep of policing work that relates to core law-enforcement and service functions. 'High' policing, in contrast, relates to dimensions of police work that are directed at protecting and security nation states. Aspects of police work in the EU and in terms of peace-keeping and state-building in the context of international development can be understood in these terms.

- The growing network of transnational policing has created a class of global 'police entrepreneurs' who develop policy and strategy across a broad sweep of countries. The promotion of certain models and strategies has been apparent in relation to police reform in emerging democracies. Moreover, it is also clear that global policy transfer in policing extends back into developed countries where trends and innovations are imported and exported among a network of transnational agencies and actors.

self-check questions (with answers at the back of the book)

1. What operational challenges has globalisation posed for police services?

2. How did McCulloch and Pickering (2005) characterise American promotion of measures to tackle terrorist financing?

3. Which country was administered by a UN Temporary Executive Authority in 1962–63, and in which country has a UN force been active since 1964?

4. Identify four networks of police co-operation in the EU.

5. What has been the cornerstone agreement of EU police co-operation since the late 1990s?

6. Which civil society agencies were identified in relation to the development of 'soft power' influences on the development of transnational policing norms?

7. What three forms of global private security provision were identified by Stenning and Shearing (2011)?

8. Who argued that private security companies service the interests of global corporations and capital accumulation?

9. Who operates at the 'meso' level of EU police co-operation, in Benyon's (1994) typology?

10. Why did Hills (2009) suggest that it would be difficult to develop a 'global police ethic'?

study questions

1. Does it matter if policing is increasingly 'deterritorialised'?

2. Critically assess the three factors that Walker (2008) suggested have shaped the development of transnational policing in the EU.

3. Can global policing arrangements be made accountable in the absence of a global government?

annotated further reading

Two books provide authoritative reviews of the development of global and transnational policing. Greener (2009a) reviews international policing using several case studies and the arising theoretical debates. Bowling and Sheptycki (2012) examine global policing in terms of security and terror and the implications for global inequalities and democracy. A collection edited by Hufnagel and McCartney (2017) offers a comprehensive overview of many debates relating to a wide range of transnational policing activities.

annotated listings of links to relevant websites

A wealth of information relating to the development of transnational policing operations and the historical development of missions can be found at:

UNFICYP (undated) *United Nations Peacekeeping Force in Cyprus – Facts and Figures*, www.un.org/en/peacekeeping/missions/unficyp/facts.shtml.

UN (undated) details of peacekeeping programmes, www.un.org/en/peacekeeping/operations/.

annotated links to journal articles

The development of policing in the EU at different levels is catalogued in:

Benyon, J. (1994) 'Policing the European Union: The Changing Basis of Cooperation on Law Enforcement', *International Affairs*, 70: 497–517.

A special edition of the journal *Policing and Society* contained a broad range of articles examining topics explored in this chapter. Those below explore the development of policing and international development and the evolution of policing within the UN:

Grabosky, P. (2009) 'Police as International Peacekeepers', *Policing and Society: An International Journal of Research and Policy*, 19: 101–105.

Greener, B.K. (2009) 'UNPOL: UN Police as Peacekeepers', *Policing and Society: An International Journal of Research and Policy*, 19: 106–118.

Hills considers the conceptual basis of transnational policing:

Hills, A. (2009) 'The Possibility of Transnational Policing', *Policing and Society: An International Journal of Research and Policy*, 19: 300–317.

9

CRIMINAL INVESTIGATION AND POLICING

CONTENTS

LEARNING OBJECTIVES

This chapter provides an overview of the principles and practices of police crime investigations, arguing that social, organisational and managerial aspects of police work have a considerable influence, alongside technical and scientific considerations. The discussion begins with foundational matters of the purpose of investigations – which are shown to be more diverse than simply identifying an offender – before considering organisation and deliver, and how criminal investigations mesh with the work of other agencies within criminal justice. The chapter aims to:

- outline the breadth and diversity of criminal investigation in terms of the various purposes of investigations, and the range of personnel and organisations that are involved

- review practices of police crime investigations and the various stages at which they are conducted in relation to wider practices within criminal justice

- provide a critical sociological perspective on the organisational, situational, cultural and legal factors that shape contemporary investigations in the context of pluralised and transnational policing.

KEY TERMS

fraud; media detectives; private detectives; prosecutions; social and cultural factors and technology

INTRODUCTION

Investigating human behaviour has been a ubiquitous feature of society throughout history. From the earliest recorded human history investigation has been a feature of the social world that is carried on by a broad range of agencies and individuals in a host of formal, informal, institutional and private contexts. As with other dimensions of the policing task, some of which are discussed in Chapter 2, in early pre-modern societies the responsibility for identifying culprits fell directly upon local communities. In various societies the investigation of apparent criminal offending rested with religious or feudal authorities and has only tended to be specifically delegated to identify law-enforcement authorities in the relatively recent past (Palmiotto, 2013). Although the public police service perhaps has the primary role in terms of criminal investigation, this remains an area of policing that epitomises wider trends in pluralisation. The diversity of agencies engaged in investigative work is striking. Many government departments and public agencies conduct investigations of activities within their specific domain – including local authority food safety inspectors, the Financial Services Authority regulation of transnational commerce, trading standards officials, and the Health and Safety Inspectorate. Private corporations, such as insurance companies, conduct investigations into potential civil or criminal wrong-doing and many institutions may carry out forms of investigation against employees, customers or clients. Companies conduct pre-employment investigations in an effort to screen out undesirable job-seekers and monitor the activities of those who are already employed in order to protect their commercial opportunities and reputation. Diverse though the practices of investigation are, they tend to be focused upon establishing the veracity of claims about past practices or incidents, to determine culpability and to identify responsibility. Innes's (2003) study of homicide detectives, which is discussed in more detail later in this chapter, led him to the view that crime investigation is best understood as a social process that produces 'the legally and socially sanctioned record of the past'.

While recognising the breadth and diversity of investigation activities, this chapter is focused on the role of the police in relation to the investigation of crime, rather than violations of the civil law or private matters. It examines the organisation and conduct of criminal investigations and identifies key principles and purposes, as well as common pitfalls, that emerge from the research and policy literature. As with many other aspects of police work, a useful starting point in the examination of criminal investigations is the recognition that the reality of this dimension of policing bears little resemblance to popular cultural, media and political representation. Much fictional presentation of criminal investigation – from nineteenth-century novelists such as Wilkie Collins or Sir Arthur Conan Doyle to contemporary writers such as Ian Rankin and James Lee Burke – suggests that serious criminal activity is thwarted by inspired detectives operating on the basis of a combination of inspiration, cunning, intuition and hard work. Since their inception, television and cinema have presented their own versions on the theme of the detective, often bitter and cynical and able to out-smart criminals in part because they share elements of the same mindset.

The realities of the criminal investigation of homicide are briefly explored at various points later in this chapter. Although it is useful to consider the principles and practices of police investigation into this type of crime it is important to recognise that it is an atypical offence that is distinctive in the extent to which it is subject to police attention. Furthermore, as criminological research attests, homicide is an unusual offence in the sense that it is rare but also because it is subject to high rates of reporting (i.e. relative to other crimes homicide is likely to be reported to and recorded by the police) and has a high clear-up rate (i.e. relative to other crimes, a perpetrator is likely to be identified and/or apprehended). An HMIC (2000, cited in Innes, 2003) review suggested that around 90 per cent of homicides in England and Wales each year are cleared up.

Homicide is also an unusual class of offending in that it is subject to a high degree of investigation. When taken as a whole, most criminal offending is not investigated.

In part this is because many crimes do not become known to the police, or are subject to only a relatively cursory investigation. Some forms of offending, such as white-collar and corporate crime, are considerably under-investigated and certain categories of offender are not subject to the same level of police investigation as others. In the USA, for example, white middle-class cocaine users are less likely to be subject to police attention than African-American lower-class crack smokers (Mustard, 2001).

As with other aspects of police work the conduct of police investigation is an area where popular, media-generated conceptions can be misleading. Perhaps the prime misconception is that the primary purpose of criminal investigations is to establish the identity of the culprit. The classic focus of the 'whodunnit' is unrealistic in as much as investigation often is not about establishing the identity of the probable offender. Instead investigations might be concerned with determining whether a criminal offence occurred at all and, if it did, identifying the circumstances of the events and gathering evidence that can be used for prosecutorial purposes. The period of investigation – relative to the offence and the wider processes of criminal justice – also shapes its purpose. While police investigations occur in the immediate aftermath of incidents – and so can be directed at identifying perpetrators and understanding the circumstances of a crime – they are also conducted post-arrest in order to gain information needed to establish if criminal charges should be laid. If a prosecution does ensue, investigations continue before the trial in order to gather evidence to present before the court. In cases that result in a conviction and subsequently an appeal, it is likely that investigations may continue even beyond the initial court hearing. These various stages indicate that the conduct of police investigations into criminal offences does not continue in isolation from the wider criminal justice process. In Britain, the police service is not responsible for charging offenders or for conducting prosecutions in court, and so decisions about the extent and nature of criminal investigations are made in relation to the demands of other elements of the system. The influence of some of these relations is considered in further detail later in this chapter, but prior to that the discussion seeks to establish some basic ground in terms of the purpose and conduct of police crime investigation.

WHY INVESTIGATE OFFENCES?

The following section focuses upon the different combinations of agencies and staff who are engaged in various forms of investigation. As will be demonstrated, investigations operate across a range of public, private and third-sector organisations. Given that they are deployed on behalf of members of the public, and private companies of all sizes and interests, it is unsurprising that there might be a variety of reasons why investigations are carried out. As Gill and Hart (1997, cited in Johnson, 2007: 277) noted, the word 'investigator' has a Latin root (*vestigium*) that has a literal meaning – 'footprint' – as well as a figurative one – 'something lost or that has passed before'. Clearly both meanings convey central aspects of investigations but when applied across diverse operational environments the purpose of investigation becomes more difficult to identify. An obvious starting point is that investigations often have a forensic purpose in that they seek information to be presented to a court. Maguire (2007) argued that a recurring myth of investigations is that a key purpose is to establish the truth of an alleged criminal incident. In criminal law terms, however, it is the role of the jury and the trial process to determine the truth of an event and investigation is a creative and interpretative activity that requires judgements, perception and representation of information that is often partial, incomplete and does not 'speak for itself' in the way that a television detective show might suggest. Along similar lines, Stelfox (2009: 6–7) characterised 'the main problem of criminal investigation is … one of matching the dry certainty of the law to the messy, unpredictable and complex reality of the human behaviour called crime.' Stelfox identified seven key reasons why an offence might be investigated, as outlined in Box 9.1.

Box 9.1

Seven Key Reasons for Investigations

- To bring offenders to justice (and to exonerate the innocent).
- To serve victims and witnesses (originally 'serving victims' was the key purpose, indeed wronged parties were responsible for private prosecutions before the development of modern policing systems). This is about providing for some recompense and justice to victims and witnesses.
- To reassure the community by demonstrating that the police are responding to their concerns and taking offences seriously.
- To recover assets from offenders.
- To gather intelligence about offences and offenders that might inform future crime prevention.
- To disrupt criminal activity.
- To reduce crime, including the prospect that offenders will be deterred.

(Stelfox, 2009: 6–7)

Some of these reasons apply more widely to other forms of investigation, not all of which is criminal justice and offence-related. However, a frequent criticism relating to private investigations is that they are often conducted in the interests of private rather than public justice such that decisions over the outcome of prosecutions might vary significantly from case-to-case and in ways that are difficult to reconcile with the seven attributes identified above. The investigation of a fraud against a private corporation, for example, might result in a settlement based upon that corporation maintaining secrecy over its victimisation. This might avoid unsettling investor confidence, though this might be achieved at the expense of bringing the offender to justice. Many of these concerns reflect more general concerns about justice, equity and ethics that relate to private policing, as outlined in Chapter 10.

WHO INVESTIGATES OFFENCES?

A broad range of police officers and civilian staff conduct criminal investigations. The latter include staff employed by police services, those working for private investigation companies, as well as security specialists working in house for major corporations and organisations. Included in this latter category are Counter Fraud Specialists (CFS) employed by public sector agencies to investigate various forms of fraud that are estimated to cost public sector agencies £16 billion per annum (Button et al., 2007). A government review of fraud investigations suggested that the three biggest employers of counter fraud specialists (CSF) were the Department for Work and Pensions (3,300 staff investigating social security fraud), local authorities (over 2,000 staff investigating housing benefit fraud) and the NHS (over 500 staff investigating fraud) (Fraud Review Team, 2006, cited in Button et al., 2007). The size of the staff group working as CFS in the public sector, combined with their common training and operating standards, led Button et al. (2007: 193) to describe this role as 'an embryonic profession in the broader policing family'. Moreover, Walsh and Milne (2007) found that the techniques used by such investigators (in terms of interviewing techniques, for example) have become similar to those used by the police in general crime investigations and that this has reflected an increasing emphasis on prosecuting benefit fraud rather than primarily seeking to halt fraudulent claims. However, Button (2011) noted that although investigators in some public sector agencies had the capacity to conduct surveillance and computer forensic analysis, others were subject to organisational and financial pressures that inhibited effective responses to fraud. For these reasons he argued that 'differential justice' as agencies had different policies and thresholds for instigating prosecutions in fraud cases (Button, 2011: 263–4).

Similar concerns have been expressed about standards of justice that apply in the context of wholly private investigations, conducted by private security companies or by in-house security divisions of corporations. Private investigators have a lengthy history that pre-dates the establishment of the modern public police service. In the eighteenth century, for example, victims who could afford their services might employ 'thief takers' to recover property stolen from them. The private investigators who performed such tasks were often corrupt in that they were complicit in the theft of the property in the first instance and operated in consort with the thieves. Emsley (1996: 18) recorded that the most notorious thief taker of his day was Jonathan Wild, who recovered stolen property while operating as a receiver and controller of criminal gangs. Wild was executed in 1725, although similar notoriety surrounded the activities of thief taker Stephen Macdonald in the 1750s (Emsley, 1996: 18). Emsley cautioned against simplistic portrayals of all private investigations in this period as corrupt or ineffective. Equally, though, he noted that while the Bow Street Runners (see Chapter 2) may have been relatively professional compared to previous arrangements, they too were subject to some contemporary suspicion (Emsley, 1996: 19). Private investigation arrangements endured the establishment of the modern police in the early decades of the nineteenth century and were boosted by the Matrimonial Causes Act 1857, which created trade in the investigation of adultery (Johnston, 2007). In both the UK and the USA private investigation companies were also widely employed to investigate trade union activity and potential strikes. In the USA the Pinkerton Detective Agency was widely employed on the rail network to protect cargo but also to investigate workers suspected of being labour organisers (Monkkonen, 1992). While problems of abuse of power and corruption might have been reduced in relation to investigative services provided by the private security sector, it remains the case that they are predominantly concerned with pursuing the instrumental ends of their clients rather than any wider publicly-oriented social justice. Johnston (2007: 280) argued that:

> **Unlike police detectives, who collect evidence for constructing cases within a system of public justice, private investigators aim only to minimize the economic, social or personal losses of their clients. Instrumentalism is driven by a proactive, risk-based mentality, the object of which is to anticipate, recognize and appraise risks and, having done so, to initiate actions that will help to minimize their impact on clients.**

For a range of reasons, the international research literature presents a strong consensus that there has been a rise in private investigation over the last few decades. To a large extent the factors that have underpinned this expansion are the same as those that have inflated the size and scope of private policing more generally, and which are discussed in Chapter 10 of this book. Bradley and Sedgwick's (2009) study of the growth of private security in New Zealand indicates a massive rise in the number of registered private investigators (PI), which increased from 94 in 1976 to 1,536 by 2007. This rise might be in part an artefact of increasing official registration rather than an absolute rise in the number of PIs at work. Nonetheless, Bradley and Sedgwick's study (2009: 477) led them to argue that PIs have come to occupy the central role in many sectors in New Zealand:

In one particular area, the detection and investigation of fraud and other 'economic' crime, contract and in-house investigators clearly dominate. Interviewees typically point out that within the corporate sector especially, and due to their ability to supply tailored products and services and avoid unwanted publicity ... PIs have largely replaced the police as the principal fraud investigation resource. It was further noted that when police do become involved it is typically at the end of the investigative process where, having taken receipt of case files compiled by a third party, police sometimes initiate prosecutions.

The function of PIs in terms of investigating fraud in New Zealand mirrors the earlier point about the use of non-police investigators in tackling public sector fraud in the UK. While that is an important component of private sector investigations, studies have suggested other dimensions of private sector investigations:

- *Legal work*: including serving summons and writs; asset recovery and debt collection; conducting background work or finding information for lawyers in civil or criminal cases.

- *Domestic work*: including missing person searches; gathering information for divorce and child custody hearings.

- *Commercial work*: including liability investigations; employee screening; copyright investigations; workplace theft; assessment of risk and security; road traffic accident enquiries.

(Jones and Newburn, 1998: 65–6; Johnston, 2007: 284–5)

THE ORGANISATION OF POLICE CRIMINAL INVESTIGATION

As was noted in the introduction to this chapter, criminal investigations are conducted at various stages in the progress from offence, to arrest, to charge, and up to and beyond the conduct of a trial. The timescale of criminal investigations is made further challenging by recent increases in reporting of historical sexual abuse cases in which physical evidence is likely to be lost and witness testimony affected by the elapsed time. Even in terms of the immediate conduct of an investigation that follows on from an initial report of a criminal offence, several different elements of investigation can be identified. As Palmiotto (2013) noted, three stages may apply in a criminal investigation, although it is by no means necessarily the case that each incident will proceed through each of them – in fact many reported incidents will not move beyond the first base. Following the initial report of an incident to the police a preliminary investigation is conducted, often by the routine patrol police officer who receives the report from a member of the public, witness, or victim. The preliminary investigation is primarily concerned, Palmiotto (2013: 14–15) argued, with establishing the 'solvability' of the case. To this end, once assured that a criminal offence has transpired, the preliminary investigator's responsibility is to gather information from witnesses, from CCTV cameras and other sources that might provide evidence about the nature of the event and, crucially, the likely identity and whereabouts of the suspect. The extent and quality of this information are vital factors in terms of providing reassurance to the victim and to the public more generally as well as shaping the conduct of any subsequent investigation. Stelfox (2009) noted that research findings suggest that routine patrol officers spend approximately one-fifth of their working time on preliminary investigations of this kind and are overseen in this work by sergeants and inspectors. Burrows' (1986) study of police investigations found that the average residential burglary was subject to less than four hours' of police attention. On the other hand, missing persons' investigations, which might not be related to criminal activity, are a significant demand on police resources: Fyfe et al. (2015) reported that 300,000 cases occur each year, meaning that someone is recorded missing by the police every two minutes. An important aspect of the training and induction of new officers is ensuring that they understand the legal and policy requirements relating to the gathering of evidence and presentation of information in reporting systems that are passed to prosecuting authorities. If little substantial information emerges from the preliminary stage, and the 'solvability factor' remains low, then no further resources might be dedicated to subsequent investigation. Palmiotto (2013) and Stelfox (2009) report that many cases do not proceed beyond this stage since preliminary investigations suggest there is little prospect that a successful prosecution could ensue.

In serious incidents and in cases where the 'solvability factor' is relatively strong, criminal incidents may become subject to 'follow-up' investigation by a specialist detective. In the British context this role is performed by officers from Criminal Investigation Departments (CID). Burrows and Tarling (1987) reported that detectives spend between 40–50 per cent of their working time on criminal investigations. Stelfox (2009) suggested that around 10 per cent of operational police staff have received specialist training and are deployed in CID. The detective generally has the responsibility of determining the viability of potential leads in a case and the likelihood that an offence might form part of a wider pattern of crimes that might be committed by the same perpetrator. On this basis, detectives might use crime analysis and mapping techniques of the sort identified in Chapter 11. Detectives might also make use of offender profiling techniques, described more extensively below. In cases where a preliminary investigation quickly leads to the identification and apprehension of an offender, the follow-up investigation might occur in the context of preparation of charges by prosecution authorities.

The third form of criminal investigations identified by Palmiotto (2013) are the 'special-subject' enquiries conducted by dedicated detective teams. The organisation and specialist responsibilities of special squads of this kind varies between police services and develops over time as criminal offending patterns and social priorities change. Although many police services have long-established vice squads or fraud squads, the development of specialist investigators focused on child protection work or hate crime cases reflects more recent recognition that such types of offending merit expert investigation. In addition to providing specialist investigation in response to particular cases that are referred via generalist investigators, the special subject squads are often tasked with monitoring and surveillance of known offenders and undertaking proactive work to tackle such crimes (Burrows and Tarling, 1987). Although many specialist squads are organised at police service level, some of them act collaboratively across constabulary boundaries and co-operate regionally, nationally and transnationally. Much of this collaborative work is co-ordinated by the National Crime Agency (NCA), under Home Office control. The NCA includes specialist investigators operating in four 'commands': international cases, organised crime, economic crime, and the Child Exploitation and Online Protection Centre (CEOP).

RELATION OF POLICE INVESTIGATIONS TO THE WIDER CRIMINAL JUSTICE SYSTEM

In some jurisdictions prosecutors might play a significant role in the conduct and direction of police investigations, and in many European countries public prosecution services have some role in shaping the conduct of police investigations. In France and Spain, for example, examining magistrates have a formal role in overseeing the conduct of police crime investigations, especially in relation to more serious incidents (Elsner et al., 2008). In England and Wales the Crown Prosecution Service (CPS) took over the prosecution of offences from the police in 1986. Although the CPS continues to function independently of the police services there has been an emphasis in the relatively recent past on collaboration between CPS and police in investigations. To this end, for example, many larger police stations will house CPS staff who routinely become accessible to police officers who might need advice in terms of ensuring that investigations are conducted in such a way that they are consistent with legal and police frameworks for prosecutions. This has been intended to improve police investigations in terms of the quality of evidence that emerges for the conduct of successful prosecutions (Elsner et al., 2008). In Scotland the Procurator Fiscal is the public prosecutor and also plays a role in the direction of police crime investigations (Scott, 2011).

THE CONDUCT OF POLICE CRIME INVESTIGATIONS

Clearly the practice of police crime investigations is likely to differ, to a greater or lesser extent, depending on the nature and complexity of the incident. Various common approaches apply, nonetheless, in relation to the range of purposes for which investigations are carried out. As Stelfox (2009) argued, the investigation of any type of crime is fundamentally focused on gathering, collating and processing data, and this tends to be sourced from individual witnesses, victims, offenders or bystanders, or from material evidence taken from crime scenes, or secured from information captured electronically from CCTV, mobile phone, computer records and similar sources. Knowledge is gathered from human beings using a range of investigative techniques, as outlined in Table 9.1.

Table 9.1 Knowledge-gathering for criminal investigations

Technique	Subject	Material
Investigative interviewing	Victims and witnesses	Witness statements and notes, officers' notes, audio and video tapes
	Suspects	Recorded interviews, written statements
	Community informants	Officers' notes, intelligence reports
	Covert human intelligence sources	Intelligence reports
Surveillance	Human surveillance	Surveillance logs, officers' notes and statements
	Technical surveillance	Recorded video and audio images
Witness canvassing	Media appeals	Media reports, records of calls from public, details of potential witnesses
	House-to-house enquiries	
	Anniversary and road-checks	
Intelligence and knowledge management and analysis		Database information

Source: adapted from Stelfox, 2009: 108

The conduct of the knowledge and information-gathering investigative techniques outlined in Table 9.1 is largely regulated by statutes including the Police and Criminal Evidence Act 1984 and the Regulation of Investigatory Powers Act 2000, aspects of which are further discussed in Chapter 3. As Stelfox (2009) highlighted, some of these investigation techniques are directed at individuals who might have direct knowledge of an incident while others might have only indirect information. Sources of information that are included in police investigations become known by police in various ways; some might emerge to volunteer information directly, others need to be canvassed (e.g. via house-to-house enquiries), while others are courted through media coverage (such as 'anniversary appeals' conducted at key milestones after an incident). The diversity of information sources highlights the need for strong investigative management and organisation and for the effective processing and analysis of the extensive and complex data results, especially in large-scale cases. This aspect of criminal investigation is considered further in discussion of homicide investigations later in this chapter.

Research studies strongly indicate that investigative efforts focused on gathering knowledge and information from victims and witnesses (and other members of the public) are the most significant means of resolving cases, as Burrows and Tarling (1987) attested. Bottomley and Coleman (1981) found that information obtained during interview was the most important source of detections; similarly, Mawby (1979) found that this accounted for 40 per cent of detections. Burrows' (1986) study found that direct assistance from the public was crucial to nearly half of the arrests of burglars, and Mawby (1979) suggested that direct victims of crime, rather than bystanders or witnesses, were the most common source of 'citizen information'. In around 10 per cent of cases, Mawby (1979) found, 'special agents' such as shop security guards provided crucial information that led to the detection of an incident. It seems likely that the importance of information provided by victims is a reflection of the frequent finding that victims of crime often have a prior relationship with the offender.

Forensic evidence is also gained from crime scene investigations. As with other forms of identification, scientific crime scene analysis is only partially focused on identifying suspects but can play an important role in terms of case-building and establishing forensic evidence. Technological developments in the power and range of DNA identification techniques have meant that the collection of blood, tissue and other human samples has become a more important aspect of routine criminal investigations but represents only a recent addition to scientific techniques that have advanced considerably since the mid-nineteenth century. It was during that period that fingerprinting techniques were refined, crucially through Alphonse Bertillon's innovation anthromorphic methods, which were adapted by Sir Edward Henry, a civil servant working in Bengal, and subsequently introduced into British policing in the early twentieth century (Pepper, 2005). Scientific developments in terms of the evidence that could be gained from post-mortem examinations (e.g. to establish the presence of poison) had significant impact on criminal investigations in the nineteenth century.

However, as Morris (2007) argued, the capacity of science to enhance investigation is not only a matter of technical capacity but also depends upon the social context in which it is applied in routine police work and communicated within the legal system. An important watershed in criminal investigations followed Locard's development of the 'exchange principle' in the early twentieth century (Pepper, 2005; Stelfox, 2009): this established that any contact between two materials leads to the transfer of trace elements between them. It has only been through the development and application of professional crime scene investigation procedures, though, that scientific innovations have contributed to criminal enquiries. Analysis of the Ripper murders of sex workers in London in the late nineteenth century, which famously remain unsolved, indicates that opportunities to gather evidence from crime scenes were missed because investigations were conducted in ways that came to be understood as seriously flawed. The removals of corpses from crime scenes, and the washing of bodies before they were examined, are examples of practice that remained common in the period but which clearly hindered effective investigation (Camps and Barber, 1966).

The array of sophisticated scientific techniques available to the contemporary investigator clearly enhance the potential to collect powerful forensic evidence from crime scenes. A full review of scientific techniques is beyond the scope of the discussion in this chapter, which is focused instead on understanding the broader role of investigation within policing and the criminal justice system itself. Whatever scientific practices are available to crime scene investigators it remains the case that, as with other forms of criminal investigation, the procedures that apply need to be understood in relation to the wider demands of the justice system. It is for this reason that crime scene investigators need to ensure that protocols are observed to ensure that forensic evidence does not become contaminated, that secondary transfer does not occur, and that continuity of evidence can be demonstrated such that the court can be satisfied of the integrity of material that comes before it. Following the closure of the Forensic Science Service in 2012 police have contracted forensic science services to private contractors, whose work is subject to standards and inspection by the national Forensic Science Regulator (FSR). In 2017, the FSR noted a series of concerns about the quality and consistency of services provided to police and argued that under-funding posed potential risks to justice. Concerns were identified relating to high risks of DNA contamination in police custody and at Sexual Assault Referral Centres, and that few forces were compliant with required standards for digital forensics. As noted earlier, the impact of austerity measures on police budgets has led to considerable debate about the protection of 'frontline' police services, which are usually defined as those that involve routine interaction with members of the public. If the preservation of those roles is regarded as a policing priority then it is conceivable that the status of scene of crime officers – who tend to be relatively poorly paid civilian staff in any case – could be further threatened by financial cutbacks. In the current environment, it seems unlikely that the police organisational infrastructure is well placed to better support the effective use of scientific crime scene investigation.

THE MANAGEMENT OF CRIME INVESTIGATION

The current financial pressures on police work raise important concerns about the effective and efficient conduct of crime investigation as well as other services and functions. They also illustrate a broader and more fundamental point about the institutional and social context in which crime investigation is undertaken. While there is a tendency to discuss investigation in techno-centric terms that focus upon the deployment of scientific methods or psychological approaches to interviewing, it is important to recognise that evidence gathering is conducted in institutional and managerial contexts. Almost fifty years ago, Camps and Barber (1966) wrote an account of murder investigation that reviewed high-profile cases between the Ripper murders of the 1880s and the crimes of Crippen in the 1940s. They demonstrated various ways in which the development of scientific methods relating to finger printing, the identification of poison and photographic techniques evolved over this period and the manner in which police deployed contemporary breakthroughs in their work. The study also demonstrated not only that innovative techniques were not always applied in ways that might have benefitted the criminal justice process, but also that even standard procedures of each period were not always followed. In relation to some of the victims in the Ripper case, for example, bodies were removed from crime scenes to mortuaries were they were washed clean before any forensic investigation was conducted. It might be highly unlikely that this would occur in the twenty-first century, but even in the nineteeth century the management and training of police and medical staff was insufficient to prevent what was already known to be poor practice. Indeed, much of Camps and Barber's (1966) account is directed towards establishing a stronger institutional structure for murder investigation that could ensure that scientific innovation is properly harnessed and deployed. Twenty-first-century debates about evidence-based policing similarly focus not just on the development of scientific knowledge, but also how good practice can be deployed operationally (Telep and Lum, 2014).

Other more recent studies of homicide investigations have also shown how management can contribute to successful innovation or can hamper effective work. The murders committed by Colin Pitchfork in Leicestershire in the mid-1980s are often held to be significant because they represented the first time in which genetic fingerprinting techniques were applied. Clearly the scientific innovation that this represented was significant, but the application of this new method required senior officers to have the confidence to invest considerable police resources into that investigative route (Wambaugh, 1989). Equally, in the opposite direction, the Macpherson Inquiry (1999) into the racist murder of Stephen Lawrence in London in 1993 found that senior investigating officers did not know how to properly use the Home Office Large Major Enquiry System (HOLMES) that provided the means to collate and analyse the significant amount of data generated by the investigation. As Roycroft et al. (2007) have shown, this represented a management failure to respond to problems identified following an earlier review of the conduct of the investigation into the serial murderer Peter Sutcliffe.

CONCLUSION

Police investigations, it follows from the above discussion, comprise a complex and diverse set of practices conducted by a range of individuals at different periods relative to an incident and for a variety of purposes. Although the investigation of homicide cases does not represent a typical body of investigative practice – nothing could – Innes's

(2003) study of this form of detective work provides a useful perspective on a wider range of investigations. Innes argued that crime investigation is best understood in terms of a frame that comprises three key elements:

- The particular qualities and circumstances of the incident.
- The social organisation of the police response.
- The law as a system of labels, a model of rationality and a set of constraining and enabling resources.

It has been seen in the brief review throughout this chapter that the qualities and circumstances of incidents themselves only partly determine the nature and extent of police investigation. Many incidents are subject to no investigation whatsoever simply because they do not pass the preliminary stages necessary to be reported to, or recorded as crimes by the police. Some incidents that are recorded are subject to little investigation because they are considered too trivial to warrant more than preliminary enquiries. A low-gravity offence, one that has little chance of being resolved, or one that officers do not prioritise, might receive little investigation. Recent policies have sought to force officers to prioritise the investigation of crimes that have tended to be treated as marginal and so to improve the investigation of hate crimes, domestic violence and sexual offences (see, e.g. Chakraborti, 2010; Roulstone and Mason-Bish, 2013). The nature and extent of an investigation does not develop exponentially in relation to the properties of the event or the gravity of an incident as determined by the criminal law: the 'qualities and circumstances' that Innes (2003) referred to are also shaped by the wider social context in which it unfolds.

Emphasis on the social organisation of crime investigation directs attention to the institutional frameworks that surround this aspect of police work. As has been shown, police services organise crime investigation in very different ways in terms of the range of routine patrol officers, specialist units, civilian and support staff that might be engaged in this part of police work. The management and policy environment is clearly significant. One of the reasons why sexual violence cases might not have been adequately investigated, for example, has been linked to the poor quality of training and operational guidance offered by police service investigation manuals issued to detectives (Rowe, 2009). Equally other studies have noted similar failings in the conduct of a host of investigations into serious crimes, including homicide cases (Roycroft et al., 2007). Although training, resources and management are important dimensions of the social organisation of police investigations, it is also widely noted in the literature that 'cop culture' is as influential in this aspect of policing as others. Bacon's (2016) study of detectives investigating drug crime argued that understanding this aspect of police work needs to recognise that it was shaped by informal as well as formal practices. The law, for example, clearly shaped what officers did or did not choose to do. So too, though, did a range of other considerations derived from officers' informal understanding of the context in which they operated.

As was noted earlier in this chapter, the legal framework in which investigations take place enable the police to conduct certain practices and also constrains work in terms of procedures and practices that must be observed. Innes (2003) went further than this, though, and argued that the law develops as a mechanism which determines what facts and data reach the necessary standard to be counted as evidence for presentation in court. In that sense police investigations can be understood as efforts to create narrative accounts – not objective scientific truth – that are supported by a body of evidence sufficient to establish a version of events considered by the court to be the most authoritative among competing claims and counter-perspectives. Along similar lines, Bacon (2016) found that detectives regarded paperwork and the generation of robust accounts of investigations as a core part of their task. He also noted that prosecutors themselves had different requirements in terms of the form and extent of evidence they demanded from detectives. Just as police investigations are socially and culturally determined in particular organisational contexts, so too the demands that the legal system exerts on these aspects of police work are themselves socially constructed. The influence of legal systems and practices is mirrored by other extrinsic relationships which help to shape police investigations. In their study of the development of risk models of policing in Canada, for example, Ericson and Haggerty (1997: 224) argued that police became 'reactive servants' of insurance companies with which they conducted joint investigations. Other investigations – perhaps including those conducted in international development and post-conflict situations – also require police working under the direction of external agencies that will, quite properly, shape the conduct of their operations.

The breadth and diversity of police investigations defies easy categorisation. They range from taking witness statements through to complex investigative interviews, the management and interrogation of large quantities of information through to elaborate and specialist scientific analysis of crime scene data, including that collated in the relatively distant past. Generalist and specialist police officers as well as a broad range of other public, private and third-party agencies undertake these tasks in a pluralised policing environment. The focus of investigations is also complex and can be contradictory and tends only rarely to be about discovering the identity of an offender. Police investigations are often driven by demands developed by the legal system in terms of the quality and processing of evidence for forensic purposes. In a period when policing increasingly tends to be understood as pluralised, networked and transnational it is important to recognise that investigations are shaped by different modes of regulation including national legal codes, policies, transnational treaties and international laws.

chapter summary

- In pre-modern European societies the responsibility for identifying offenders, as with other aspects of policing, fell directly upon the population. Contemporaneously, the range of agencies engaged in investigative work is striking.

- Diverse though the practices of investigation are, they tend to be focused upon establishing the veracity of claims about past practices or incidents, to determine culpability and to identify responsibility.

- As with other aspects of police work the conduct of police investigation is an area where popular, media-generated conceptions can be misleading. Perhaps the prime misconception is that the primary purpose of criminal investigations is to establish the identity of the culprit.

- Reasons for investigation include bringing offenders to justice, to serve the interests of victims and witnesses, reassuring the community, recovering assets, gathering intelligence, disrupting criminal activity and reducing crime.

- Concerns about differential standards of justice applying in the conduct of private and public investigations have been noted in relation to fraud investigation and private security companies. Historically private investigators have been associated with corruption and abuse of power.

- Police investigations occur in the immediate aftermath of an incident; this primary investigation is largely concerned with establishing the 'solvability' of the crime. A secondary investigation might follow, primarily to gather material for the preparation of criminal charges. A third form of investigation is that of specialist detectives, including those carried out proactively to monitor known offenders.

- The supervision of investigation is conducted along different lines across different jurisdictions. In England and Wales the Crown Prosecution Service functions independently of police but does not formally supervise police investigations. In Scotland the Procurator Fiscal is the public prosecutor and also plays a role in directing police investigations.

- Police investigative interviews are directed at victims and witnesses, suspects, the public and covert sources of intelligence. Surveillance targets human subjects and technical sources such as phone and video data. Witnesses are sought via media appeals, house-to-house enquiries, anniversary appeals and road-checks. All of these can be supplemented through interrogation of intelligence and databases.

- The funding, organisation and management of detective work have the potential to influence the conduct and success of investigations as much as technological capacity. Many of the failings associated with high-profile investigations – from the Ripper murders of Victorian London to the racist killing of Stephen Lawrence – have been caused by management failings rather than incapacity to gather or process forensic evidence.

- Investigations are best understood as dynamic social activity, dependent on the qualities and circumstances of the incident, the social organisation of the police response and the extent to which the system of law constrains or enables resources.

- As in other aspects of policing, institutional practices, cultural dynamics, training and resources, and the relation of police to other agencies in the criminal justice sector, combine to influence the investigation of crime.

self-check questions (with answers at the back of the book)

1. What proportion of criminal homicides in England and Wales are 'cleared-up'?

2. What did Maguire (2007) argue was a recurring myth relating to criminal investigations?

3. Which were the three biggest public sector employees of fraud investigators?

4. Which nineteenth-century piece of legislation boosted trade for private detectives?

5. According to Stelfox (2009), how much time did routine police patrol officers spend on preliminary investigations?

6. What four 'commands' form the core of work co-ordinated by the National Crime Agency?

7. What does research suggest is the aspect of investigation most significant to resolving cases?

8. Who developed the 'exchange principle' that any contact between two materials leads to the transfer of trace elements between them?

9. In response to which crimes were genetic fingerprinting techniques first applied?

10. Whose study of investigations of drug crime found that detectives regarded the completion of robust paperwork as central to the preparation of evidence?

study questions

1. Consider an example of a fictional detective you are familiar with. How does the presentation of their work differ from the practices of criminal investigation outlined in this chapter?

2. Why might it matter if private investigations operate 'differential' standards of justice?

3. Why should crime investigation be understood as a dynamic and social process?

annotated further reading

Studies by Innes (2003) and Bacon (2016) provide excellent insight into the practice of criminal investigation in their real-world context. Although they focus on types of crime (homicide and drug crime respectively) that are not necessarily representative of more general investigations, they illustrate very effectively that detective work is socially and culturally determined to a significant extent.

Pepper (2005) and Stelfox (2009) offer accessible and authoritative guides to practices and principles of crime investigation.

Button (2011) and Walsh and Milne (2007) are good sources to develop understanding of the investigation of fraud by a host of public and private sector agencies. In addition to establishing the extent and historical development of these practices, these sources also consider the implications that such investigations have in terms of legitimacy, principles of justice and accountability.

annotated listings of links to relevant websites

The National Crime Agency plays an important role in terms of developing and professionalising police investigative practice; more information can be found at www.nationalcrimeagency.gov.uk/.

Information about efforts to investigate fraud within the National Health Service can be found at www.nhsbsa.nhs.uk/Protect.aspx.

Details of guidelines and practice relating to the use of forensic science in police investigations is available from the Forensic Science Regulator at www.gov.uk/government/organisations/forensic-science-regulator.

annotated links to journal articles

An overview of key strategies and the development of police investigations can be found in:

Burrows, J. and Tarling, R. (1987) 'The Investigation of Crime in England and Wales', *British Journal of Criminology*, 27: 229–51.

Button examines strategies and limitations in the investigation of fraud:

Button, M. (2011) 'Fraud Investigation and the "Flawed Architecture" of Counter Fraud Entities in the United Kingdom', *International Journal of Law, Crime and Justice*, 39: 249–65.

The changing context of forensic science in criminal investigations is reviewed in:

Lawless, C.J. (2011) 'Policing Markets: The Contested Shaping of Neo-Liberal Forensic Science', *British Journal of Criminology*, 51: 671–89.

The use of CCTV and its impact on crime and the conduct of investigations is reviewed by Waples et al., who conclude that spatial displacement does occur but only infrequently:

Waples, S., Gill, M. and Fisher, S. (2009) 'Does CCTV Displace Crime?', *Criminology and Criminal Justice*, 9: 207–224.

10

PLURAL POLICING

CONTENTS

The implications of the pluralisation of policing have been referred to at various stages of the discussion so far. This chapter explores the growing importance of the private sector to current debates about policing and police work and the development of complex networks of agencies involved in crime prevention, patrol work, investigation and reassurance policing in the UK and beyond. The chapter aims to:

- explain why academic and policy debates have focused on the role of the private sector in policing
- examine the development of a mixed economy of policing and the idea of the 'extended police family'
- consider the implications of pluralisation for the conceptualisation and governance of policing.

KEY TERMS

antisocial behaviour; extended police family; multi-agency partnerships; networks; new public management; pluralisation; private policing and visible patrols

INTRODUCTION

Most of the discussion of policing in this book has focused upon the organisation and delivery of the service provided by the public police; in the context of England and Wales, analysis has centred upon the 43 constabularies directed by the Home Office and local police authorities. Chapter 1 noted that, historically, the concept of policing has been applied much more broadly in reference to a range of regulatory activities provided formally and informally by diverse providers. Although popular and political discussion of policing tends to concentrate narrowly on the powers and practices of the public police, academic interest in policing in Australasia, North America, Britain and elsewhere has become increasingly concerned with the pluralisation of policing. Bayley and Shearing's (2001: 1) review of contemporary policing developments led them to suggest that the processes of pluralisation outlined in this chapter fundamentally transform policing:

This involves much more than reforming the institution regarded as the police, although that is occurring as well. The key to the transformation is that policing, meaning the activity of making societies safe, is no longer carried out exclusively by governments. Indeed, it is an open question as to whether governments are even the primary providers. Gradually, almost imperceptibly, policing has been 'multilateralized': a host of nongovernmental groups have

assumed responsibility for their own protection, and a host of nongovernmental agencies have undertaken to provide security services. Policing has entered a new era, an era characterized by a transformation in the governance of security.

Initially, from the early 1970s onward, debates about private policing questioned the role and the extent of those engaged in 'policing for profit' (South, 1988), the proper regulation of the private security companies and what relation they should have with the public police. As the discussion below illustrates, these continue to be key questions for those interested in policing in the twenty-first century but they have been supplemented by discussion of more recent forms of 'hybrid' policing that engages a range of private, public and voluntary agencies at the local, national and international level. The austerity measures applied to public police services in the 2010 comprehensive Spending Review have led to debate about the nature of 'frontline' policing, which the government claimed would not be affected by spending cuts, and other policing activities (HMIC, 2011a and 2011b). The possibility of further privatising functions has been a key element of these debates. Two police service areas (Surrey and West Midlands) announced plans to put all aspects of their activity out to tender, raising the prospect that even crime investigation and arrest functions could be delivered by the private sector, although the plans were withdrawn in autumn of 2012.

While the private security sector continues to demand legitimate attention of policy-makers and researchers it seems clear that conceiving of policing in terms of a straightforward dichotomy between public and private providers fails to account for the emergence of more complex arrangements. This chapter examines the development of private policing and other aspects of the pluralisation debate relating to third-party policing and 'multi-agency' partnerships. In particular, analysis of the diverse 'nodes' engaged in policing indicates that 'policing' is an emergent property of the complex network of relations that exists between agencies. The implications that this has for the ways in which policing is conceptualised are considered toward the end of the chapter.

DIMENSIONS OF PLURALISATION

The first chapter outlined the distinction between the police, the public institution established in Britain in the early nineteenth century, and policing, a broader process of social regulation (Reiner, 2000). Traditionally, discussion of policing has referred to governance in general terms and the distinction between that and 'the police' continues to be useful in distinguishing between functions performed by different agencies. As this chapter indicates, contemporary academic and policy debate increasingly focuses upon policing in terms that include but go beyond the traditional public police forces epitomised in the 'Dixon of Dock Green' image at its height in the decades after the Second World War (Reiner, 2000; McLaughlin, 2007a). Loader (2000) charted the new policing terrain explored in this chapter, and argued that 'we inhabit a world of networked, plural policing'. Figure 10.1 indicates the five dimensions of the emerging plural policing identified by Loader (2000), who noted that the categories are porous and interconnected:

- *Policing by government*: the traditional publicly-funded police.
- *Policing through government*: activities co-ordinated and funded by the government but delivered by agencies other than the police service.
- *Policing above government*: transnational policing activities co-ordinated by international agencies.
- *Policing beyond government*: activities funded and delivered privately by citizens and corporations.
- *Policing below government*: voluntary and community activities, self-policing and vigilantism.

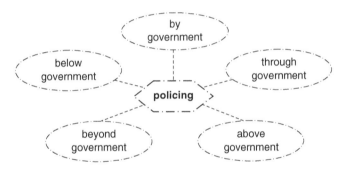

Figure 10.1   Five dimensions of plural policing (Loader, 2000)

PRIVATE POLICING

the nature and extent of private policing

Much of the discussion of private policing has focused upon size and the range of functions fulfilled by the security industry. As Prenzler (2005) noted in his study of Australia, a particular focus for many researchers has been to establish the strength of the private sector in relation to the number of public police officers, suggesting that it is particularly significant that there might be more private security personnel than constables. Similar research in New Zealand came to the conclusion that private security was as common place as public police and that this process had been driven by a range of factors:

> The creeping withdrawal of the police and their pre-occupation with serious forms of offending, fear of crime and a greater degree of security consciousness have combined to create a 'reassurance deficit' and consequently an increased public reliance on private security. The point has now been reached where ... citizens in their everyday lives are more likely to encounter private security personnel rather than public police officers
>
> **(Bradley and Sedgwick, 2009: 485)**

In Britain various estimates of the strength of private policing have grappled with definitional and methodological problems associated with measuring a complex, fragmented and, until recently, relatively unregulated industry. One indication of the size and scope of private policing is the membership of the British Security Industry Association (SIA), the main professional body that regulates private security companies. The BSIA has a dual role in terms of regulating and certifying individuals licenced to perform specific roles and companies as approved contractors. Figure 10.2 indicates that a total of 368,839 individual licences were in place in 2016, around 55 per cent of which were for door supervisors. In February 2017, 828 companies were registered under the Approved Contractor Scheme. The Private Security Industry Act 2001 that established the BSIA created a range of offences that the regulator is responsible for investigating and bringing prosecutions. In the year to February 2017, 37 prosecutions brought by the SIA were completed, mostly in cases where individuals had acted as unlicensed security operatives or company directors had been convicted of supplying unlicensed staff. In this element of its role,

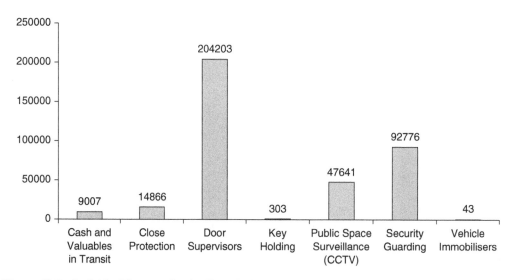

Figure 10.2 Individual licenses by the Security Industry Association, by role, 2016 (source: SIA, Licensing Statistics, www.sia.homeoffice.gov.uk)

the BSIA itself becomes part of the wider network of policing agencies, having a clear responsibility in terms of investigating crime.

The BSIA data does not include staff employed as in-house security by companies. Other sources, reflecting a wider definition of the private security industry, suggest a greater number of staff. Button (2002) reviewed various estimates of the size and scope of the sector and suggested that, in the early years of the twenty-first century, there were around 317,500 staff and a turnover of £5.5 billion. Many employees are engaged in the manufacture, retail and installation of security products and so not fulfilling traditional policing functions. Eliminating such staff from the calculation led George and Button (2000) to estimate that there were around 217,000 private sector staff employed in policing activities in 2000, which was more than the number of police staff.

explaining the growth of private security

Although estimates of the size and scope of the private security industry vary, most research suggests that it has grown during recent years. A number of factors have contributed to this expansion. In a period of austerity private sector provision in criminal justice have been promoted in terms of efficiency and effectiveness that might deliver services at a reduced cost to the public purse. Although the outsourcing of police work to the private sector has developed more slowly than has been the case with other aspects of criminal justice, such as probation and prisons, it seems likely that the privatisation of some elements of policing will continue. The demand for private security industry services has been fuelled by public insecurity about levels of crime and disorder, as public perceptions have not recognised falling crime rates since the mid-1990s. The 'reassurance gap' between realities and perceptions of crime trends, coupled with a responsibilisation strategy that has sought to encourage the public to take steps to secure property, have encouraged private companies to undertake tasks once considered the responsibility of the state. The public police service has been 'dethroned' and is no longer a monopoly provider (McLaughlin, 2007a). Further, wider societal trends have meant that the individuals spend considerable proportions of their working and social lives in private venues rather than public spaces. As the high street has been eclipsed by the shopping mall, individuals increasingly inhabit privately owned locations that deploy private security guards in order to prevent crime and disorder, but also to provide a sanitised environment conducive to a profitable retail experience (Davis, 1990; Beck and Willis, 1995; Wakefield, 2004). Shearing and Stenning (1983) argued that the public police traditionally have not, for resource and cultural reasons, engaged in the policing of 'mass private property', and that those who own these spaces have tended to prefer to retain control over regulation.

Not only may the growth of private property be symbolically important in terms of the declining state of civic and communal interaction, it has also had an important impact in terms of creating environments in which our behaviour is overseen and controlled by private security guards using the range of technologies analysed in Chapter 11. Putnam (2000) and Young (1999) have argued that the privatisation and atomisation of contemporary life has undermined collective identities that underpin the public provision of some goods and services. The erosion of community might be crimi-nogenic, it also creates an environment in which private security is increasingly important as individuals seek to provide for themselves what might once have been considered the collective responsibility of the community, derogated to the public police. Similarly, the rise of 'gated communities', whereby security and reassurance can be provided – for those who can afford them – domestically by guards and patrols raise questions about social exclusion and social justice. Not only has consumerism generated the space (in some cases, literally the physical space) in which private security can flourish, it has also allowed for the commodification of security. As mentioned, public agencies have encouraged a process of responsibilisation, whereby private citizens are reminded of the importance of looking out for their own, and this has been encouraged by manufacturers and retailers intent on catering to the existential need for security.

The increasing role of the private sector in the provision of policing mirrors devel-opments in other areas of the public sector, as role of the state has been 'hollowed out' as governments have retreated from direct provision in a host of sectors. Johnston (1992) argued that the fiscal constraints that enveloped liberal democratic states from the 1970s onwards was an important factor in promoting the role of the private sector in criminal justice, although Jones and Newburn (1998) noted that state spending on the police increased during the 1980s and that the service was not subjected to the 'rigours of the market' to anything like the same extent as other aspects of the public sector. State sovereignty has also been undermined by globalisation and the fact that there are now many private corporations with more power and resources than those available to some countries. To the same end global technologies render national boundaries more porous and less meaningful, as is discussed at greater length in Chapter 8. The develop-ment of global policing networks in response to emerging transnational problems of crime and terrorism have required national police services to move beyond borders, as has growing emphasis on security and law and order in the context of international development. In this context the position of the nation state has become precarious. Since the development of the public police service in the nineteenth century was closely related to the concomitant expansion of the nation state itself, it is inevitable that con-temporary shifts in the scope and function of the state impacts upon patterns of policing (Stenning, 1989).

Garland (2001) argued that the process of 'responsibilisation', whereby the onus to provide for personal security is transferred from state to citizen, is a direct conse-quence of the changing role of the state itself. While governments might continue to play a fundamental role in terms of regulation of services, and controls the framework, funding and manages performance, it is no longer directly responsible for provision. In the much-cited phrase of Osborne and Gaebler (1992), the state continues to be responsible for 'steering' public services but has become disengaged from the business of 'rowing'. A host of private, voluntary and hybrid providers have assumed responsibility for the delivery of security. Garland (2001: 17) puts it thus:

> [F]or most of the last two centuries the state's specialist institutions of criminal justice have dominated the field, and have treated crime as a problem to be governed through the policing, prosecution and punishment of individual law-breakers. Today we see developments that enlist the activity of citizens, communities and companies ... At the same time we have seen the remarkable expansion of a private security industry that originally grew up in the shadow of the state but which is increasingly recognized by government as a partner.

Considering the expansion of the private security industry in terms of a market model, whereby public insecurity about crime and disorder increases demand and restructuring of the public sector provides new opportunities to suppliers, is a convenient characterisation of recent patterns, but in practice the two may often be related. Loader (1997, cited in Jones and Newburn 1998: 104) noted that private companies have 'first to generate a demand for their products by stimulating and channelling people's anxieties and desires in particular ways'. Lee (2007) described a 'feedback loop' whereby the private security sector, and others, fuel demand for its products and services by highlighting both the extent of crime risks and the ability of security companies to offer protection from them. Gated communities, for example, claim to offer a refuge from crime and insecurity by physically excluding risky people and providing an environment in which private provisions protect the comfortably off from a range of inconveniences associated with the routine interaction with the public at large. Caldeira's (2000: 234, cited in Landman and Schönteich, 2002) study of gated communities in São Paulo led him to argue that social relations in such environments are characterised by

> suspicion and danger. Residents of all social groups have a sense of exclusion and restriction. For some, the feeling of exclusion is obvious, as they are denied access to various areas and are restricted to others. Affluent people who inhabit exclusive enclaves also feel restricted; their feelings of fear keep them away from regions and people that their mental maps of the city identify as dangerous.

The implications that discourses of private security have on civic and public relations are subject to much debate. Stenson (2002) has argued that the very concept of 'private security' is oxymoronic since it establishes individuals in relation to potential danger and, by atomising the public, undermines the basis for collective reassurance. Similarly, Hughes (2007) has argued that policy innovation in the field of community safety is fundamentally antisocial, since strategies of risk management and crime prevention – the organising principles of plural policing partnerships – cast citizens as potential offenders, representing a threat that must be diverted by one of a wide range of interventions. It might be wondered why, in an era in which threat, risk and danger can all, apparently, be eliminated by the purchase of the correct equipment, public concern about crime seems higher than ever.

regulating the private security industry

Stenning (2000) has noted that private policing, internationally, has been subject to 'regulatory pluralism' embracing voluntary, statutory and market-based forms of control. More recently White (2017) outlined a mixture of regulatory regimes relating to private security and suggested that original market self-regulation continues but has been supplemented by more formal regulation as well as a form of 'soft power' critical public discourse. The latter, White argued, was applied to G4S after it failed to deliver security for the 2012 London Olympics and was subject to considerable public criticism from parliamentary committees (and other public commentators). In relation to the EU, Button and Stiernstedt (2016) suggested that private security has expanded in scope since the Second World War and has become officially expressed in the official agenda of the union. Over this time they suggest that regulation was initially laissez-faire since it was largely left to industry groups to make their own arrangements. Following from this was a period of 'centrifugal' regulation from the mid-1970s to mid-1990s when some member states began to develop stronger regulation but with little common EU-wide framework and considerable differences between nation states. Since the mid-1990s, as free movement of labour and the single European market developed, the need for harmonisation in private security legislation has seen a 'centripetal' model whereby common standards and arrangements are brought forward. It is interesting to note that this echoes similar developments identified in relation to the public police by Walker (2008), as outlined in Chapter 8. Through the propagation of EU frameworks, Button and Stiernstedt (2016) noted that the purpose of regulation has expanded from initial efforts aimed at 'cleansing the market of deviant providers, to efforts to communalise by equalising access to the security market'.

In the British context, the sector has been subject to relatively little legal regulation. Before the introduction of the Private Security Industry Act 2001 the regulation of private policing in Britain was left to the market mechanism and the requirements imposed by voluntary membership of bodies such as the BSIA and the International Professional Security Association (IPSA). The BSIA and IPSA require that member companies comply with British Standards codes of practice relating to guarding and the installation of equipment. Other sectors, such as private investigations, remained largely unregulated. George and Button (1997) reviewed international approaches to the regulation of the private security sector and identified five models, moving from the least to the most intrusive. At the lower end of scale is a 'non-interventionist' approach, with no statutory requirements, followed by a 'minimum narrow' approach that requires limited checks on personnel working in specific roles. Further along the spectrum is a wider approach that requires minimum regulation of the whole sector, followed by a model that requires the comprehensive regulation of a narrow range of personnel, to the broadest category in which a wide range of regulations are applied across the sector. As Chapter 4 noted, the Private Security Industry Act 2001 introduced statutory licensing to Britain. The Security Industry Authority is empowered to inspect companies and ensure that personnel are vetted and licensed, a system that equates with George and Button's mid-range level, comprising minimal regulation of the whole sector. As part of the government's deregulation agenda the role of the BSIA is reviewed on a triennial basis. The most recent review in 2016 was focused on the contribution that authority makes to core government business, its efficiency and effectiveness, the degree to which its role is proportionate and necessary, and the extent to which it meets 'customers' priorities (Home Office, 2016d). The last of these suggests that the regulation of private security continues to be considered in terms of the narrow interests of the sector rather than the broader public.

Critics have argued that this light-touch regulation does not provide for meaningful accountability of an increasingly important part of the policing sector. While it might ensure that those with criminal records are not employed by security companies, it does not provide for the control and direction of the industry in more general terms (White, 2010). Johnston and Shearing (2003) and Loader (2000) have argued that the growth of private security reinforces social inequalities since the poor are not able to buy the same level of protection as more affluent communities. This raises the possibility that existing public police might become a provision of last resort, offering an inferior service to those unable to afford private provisions. They suggest that such an outcome is not inevitable, and that the principles of social justice and public interest can be retained via public funding being allocated to policing authorities that can act as local buyers in the marketplace of security.

private sector discipline in the public police

In addition to considering the extent and nature of the private security sector, the growing 'marketisation' of policing is also evident in terms of the internal organisation of the public police service which, in keeping with many other public services, has become increasing organised along quasi-market lines. Private sector discipline in the police service has been apparent in efforts to promote resource efficiency, by employing lower-cost civilian staff to perform tasks previously assigned to officers or by 'contracting out' services such as cleaning or catering. Some aspects of police services have been commercialised in recent decades; for example, revenues have been raised through encouraging local businesses to sponsor vehicles and the police has sought to recover costs through charging for certain services, such as the policing of football matches. One implication of the latter development has been to set the police service in competition with private sector stewarding companies well-placed to offer services at a lower price (Garland and Rowe, 1999). Guidelines to police services suggests that there are types of police activity that can be considered as above and beyond routine duties and so might be subject to charge. A distinction is made between 'special police services' delivered on behalf of another organisation that is seeking to make profit, for which police can charge, and non-commercial activity or statutory services where police services can or should be delivered without additional charge (ACPO/APA, 2011). Box 10.1 illustrates the range of activities and how charging might apply in some circumstances.

Box 10.1

Paying the Bill?

Policing events now has an enormous range of scale to consider. From local festivals to Grand Prix; from lower league football to the FA Cup final – all are events which need consideration. In general, the police service exists to police local communities and its resources are structured to achieve this. Few would argue that part of this involves policing small scale events, as part of the role of visibility and public reassurance. But, this is far removed from policing 70,000 supporters in Manchester converging on a small locality to watch a football match, or over 100,000 people attending a 3–5 day pop festival.

(ACPO, 2012: 10)

Chapter 4 examined arguments that the scrutiny of officer behaviour and force performance has been an important method by which central government control over the police service has been enhanced. In Chapter 11 the reach of information technology in the management of the police service is considered in terms of the impact that this has on routine police work. Clearly, as in the public sector more generally, the micro-management of police performance through setting targets has enabled league tables of Basic Command Unit (BCU) performance to be complied, in imitation of private sector balance sheets that measure performance in terms of profit and loss. The Conservative government developed new public management into the police service during the early 1990s, by devising a results-based and 'customer-focused' approach to policing that set targets, reviewed performance indicators, market tested services, and a host of reviews intended to modernise the workforce (McLaughlin, 2007). From 2010 the Conservative-led coalition government sought to reduce the bureaucratic and management burden associated with this form of managerial accountability. The use of targets and performance indicators was scaled back and replaced with the 'democratic accountability' of the Police and Crime Commissioners (PCCs) – as analysed in Chapter 4. Part of the remit of PCCs is to commission services (e.g. for victims) and promote greater diversity in terms of local providers. In other parts of the criminal justice system this has been supplemented with the free-market discipline apparently offered by the policy of 'contestability'. Under this strategy all aspects of public provision have the potential to be subject outsourced to private providers, a process that it is claimed will improve standards and efficiency. Although this has yet to be applied to core police services it has been reflected in prison privatisation and the Transforming Rehabilitation reforms that have brought private- and third-sector providers into the delivery of offender management services (Alonso and Andrews, 2016; Robinson et al., 2016).

THIRD-PARTY AND MULTI-AGENCY POLICING

Not only have policing activities seeped into the private sector, they have also come to be shared by a broad range of agencies within the public sector that have not traditionally been conceived of in terms of policing. The development of multi-agency community safety partnerships have drawn a host of local authority and voluntary sector organisations into networks engaged in crime prevention and public reassurance work. An early example of third-party policing, in the British context, were efforts developed in the early 1980s to tackle racist harassment in public housing by the inclusion of clauses in tenancy agreements that made such behaviour grounds for eviction. In a period during which the police often failed to effectively intervene to tackle racist harassment, local authority housing departments and charitable housing associations were thus enabled to take action through the civil courts to evict tenants who breached their contracts by engaging in racist behaviour against their neighbours (Forbes, 1988). Such provisions were greatly extended by the Housing Act 1996, which not only enhanced the power of social landlords to evict those engaging in antisocial or nuisance behaviour, it also allowed for them to be excluded from future housing waiting lists. Those identified as perpetrators of antisocial behaviour then are subject to sanctions drawn from an increased portfolio of interventions comprising diverse civil measures as well as traditional criminal justice. More recently landlords have become required to check on the immigration status of their tenants, further enhancing their regulatory role.

Critics have pointed out that civil law procedures require a lower standard of proof than those conducted through the criminal courts and that this might lead to punishments being imposed unfairly. Additionally, as the potential loss of housing illustrates, it might be that those who engage in problematic behaviour are not the only ones who suffer the consequences since their family members are also likely to be adversely affected. Other injustices arise since the provision of the Housing Act 1996 does not extend to private landlords, and so those engaging in nuisance behaviour who rent outside of the public sector will not be liable to such sanctions (Crawford, 2003: 145). Hughes (2007: 128) noted that antisocial behaviour orders (ASBOs) have tended to be applied to young people, since the average age of recipients is 16 years old, and that 'put brutally, these are the children with no chance, having been failed by their families and the care and control system'.

While these developments have raised important ethical concerns, it is clear that efforts to tackle low-level offending and incivilities through civil actions in the form of ASBOs and voluntary agreements have greatly accelerated multi-agency policing in Britain. Central to the Crime and Disorder Act 1998, the 'flagship' criminal justice legislation of the New Labour government elected in 1997, was the creation of ASBOs and the establishment of a legal responsibility for crime prevention and community safety upon local authorities. Multi-agency community safety partnerships have incorporated a wide range of agencies in policing-related activities, even though their primary responsibilities lie elsewhere. That community safety partnerships are often able to allocate resources for crime prevention and other projects might provide financial incentives for community groups to seek closer relations with their 'partners' from the statutory sector. Crawford (2003) noted that the increasing emphasis on crime prevention and community safety has been an important factor driving the development of plural policing, since it is clear that a range of services need to be engaged if preventative work is to be effective.

Patrol work has been a totemic policing activity in Britain and elsewhere and the 'bobby on the beat' has been central to discourses of policing and national identity for decades. Third parties have contributed to the provision of high-visibility policing in the form of Police Community Support Officers and local authority neighbourhood wardens. Wakefield (2006) argued that long-standing policing dilemmas surrounding the provision of patrols have moved to the forefront of contemporary debates and that the identification of new providers raises the prospect of satisfying increasing public demands without placing untenable strain on police resources. Crawford et al. (2005) and Crawford and Lister (2006) have detailed the emergence of the 'mixed economy' of policing provisions and argue that patrol work has been one of the roles most clearly opened up to diverse providers, including local authority 'neighbourhood' and 'street crime' wardens.

While these numbers are relatively small, compared to those employed as police officers and in the private security, Crawford and Lister (2006) reported that the funding supplied to employ them had led local authorities to seek other resources; coupled with rising local demands for patrol services, it seems likely that plural policing patrols will expand further. As Crawford and Lister have noted elsewhere, though, it is not clear that the greater patrol capacity of the 'extended police family' can satisfy public demands since the pluralisation process has served to raise expectations to higher levels. Furthermore it is also clear that multi-agency patrols do not provide for reassurance to all sections of the community. Those who have negative experiences and perceptions of the police are unlikely to welcome additional patrols, and those living in high crime areas favour other policing methods that target known offenders. For these reasons Wakefield (2006: 24) suggested that 'the activity of visible patrolling could … be seen as the policing activity of choice for the citizen least troubled by crime.'

Plural policing entails not only a proliferation in terms of the range of providers, but also an expansion of legal and regulatory technologies used to deliver security and reassurance, beyond crime control or law-enforcement in traditional terms. These combinations of agencies, strategies and tactics have not been restricted to efforts to tackle incivilities and antisocial behaviour, as was discussed above. The Proceeds of Crime Act 2002 requires that businesses submit Suspicious Activity Reports (SARs) to police agencies if they have indications that individuals might be engaging in money laundering or financial crime (Levi, 2002). Similarly, Universities are required to police the citizenship of students and to report to the UK Border Agency (UKBA). The *Guardian* (2012b) newspaper described the 'policing' powers that the agency has over universities in the following terms:

> **The UKBA police the system through announced and unannounced visits. Failure to comply can lead to the suspension or revocation of a sponsor's licence or a reduction in the number of international students that the institution is allowed to recruit.**
>
> **If a licence is revoked the institution will no longer be able to recruit international students. Existing students will have their permission to stay curtailed. There is no right of appeal against the revocation of a licence which has led to a huge upsurge in judicial review cases.**

Bosworth (2008) argued that the expansion of monitoring border controls to agencies beyond government, including private sector employers, further represented declining state sovereignty that has underpinned wider dimensions of the pluralisation of policing. All of these developments reflect the core characteristics of third-party policing, conceived by Mazerolle and Ransley (2005: 2–3) as

> **police efforts to persuade or coerce organizations or non-offending persons, such as public housing agencies, property owners, parents, health and building inspectors, and business owners to take some responsibility for preventing crime or reducing crime problems … Central … to third party policing is the use of a range of civil, criminal and regulatory rules and laws, to engage (or force) third parties into taking some crime control responsibility.**

NETWORKS OF POLICING

Most discussion of pluralisation of policing focuses, as this chapter has done, on the growing size and scope of the extended police family. Clearly these developments raise important questions about funding, effectiveness and regulation. More fundamentally, the proliferation of family members has transformed the character of policing itself, which increasingly needs to be understood as an emergent property of relations between nodal points within a policing network. Drawing on political science analysis of the transition from government to governance and Foucauldian perspectives on the diffusion of power, analysis suggests that policing has traditionally been conceptualised as the product of a particular institution ('the police'). Increasingly policing is better conceived of as a process arising from developing relations between the host of public, private and 'hybrid' agencies integrated in partnership arrangements of the kind described earlier. Wood and Shearing (2006) go so far as to argue that attention should no longer rest on policing, but on the wider network of agencies transversing national boundaries and transcending the state sphere as they seek to provide security in more general terms. They noted that the impact of pluralisation extends beyond just extending the range of service providers and affects the ways in which security is 'imagined':

> Governance is not performed simply by institutions of the state, nor shaped solely by thinking originating from the state sphere. Today, ways of imagining and realizing security governance in the business sector as well as the 'third sector' (e.g. community groupings, non-governmental organizations) shape and influence the thinking of state institutions and vice versa. This is the essence of nodal governance.
>
> (Wood and Shearing, 2006: 13)

Johnston and Shearing (2003) have argued that policing ought to be reconceptualised in terms of the governance of security. Policing, whether in narrow pursuit of law-enforcement or a wider provision of services, they argue, has to be understood as part of a more general process of avoiding risk and meeting the subjective and objective security needs of private citizens. They highlighted that the networks of agencies responsible for co-producing security are

> increasingly complex. On the one hand, states continue to have a major role in security governance, the state sector of criminal justice being more extensive than other. On the other hand, a growing pluralisation of security governance is evident, estimates suggesting that commercial police outnumber public police by ratio of almost two to one in Britain, two to one in India, between two and three to one in North America, five to one in Hong Kong, and between five and seven to one in South Africa.

Johnston and Shearing (2003) argued that networked security in Britain has developed along five key paths. First, the state is no longer definitive in the face of private sector activity and a growing influence of the EU in shaping external border control, for example. At the subnational level, they argued, local partnerships of the kind outlined above have also shifted focus away from the nation state. The second area that Johnston and Shearing have noted is the continuing debate over the relation between private and public interests. Controversies relating to the balance between intrusion into personal privacy and seeking to secure private interests are multiple in relation to CCTV and other technological innovations, as Chapter 11 explores. Third, the focus of policing networks is increasingly future-oriented, seeking to limit and reduce opportunities for crimes to be committed and/or identify those individuals who might be particularly criminogenic. Fourth, security governance is increasingly conducted at a distance by lay people and commercial operators, as has been demonstrated in this chapter and in discussion of community policing. Fifth, security is increasingly 'distanciated' and 'embedded'; in other words, responsibility for the provision of security is transferred from the professionals working in the public sector, to communities. 'Security' becomes embedded into the routine responsibilities of a wide range of actors working in various capacities that have not traditionally had crime-control or law-enforcement dimensions.

Of course, many of the dimensions of 'networked' security identified by Johnston and Shearing (2003) have been noted by others who have analysed the pluralisation of policing. Community involvement in multi-agency partnerships and the distanciation of security such that it comes to be embedded in the work of 'third-party' actors have all been widely discussed in this chapter. What arguments about networked policing highlight, above and beyond the proliferation of policing activities, is that these processes have not only led to a broader range of players, but that fundamental conceptualisation of the way in which the game is conducted needs to be rethought. As Crawford (2003: 136–7) argued that these developments provide us with a 'new set of things to look at' as well as a 'new way of looking at things'. Zedner (2006) has noted that debates about pluralisation have tended to focus upon charting emerging patterns and players and has paid relatively little attention to normative questions about social justice, equity, democracy and accountability. The extent to which these debates increasingly unfold on a transnational or global basis is considered further in Chapter 8.

REBIRTH OR NEW PARADIGM?

Concerns about measuring the extent of the private security industry were outlined earlier in this chapter. Some have argued that while academic and policy interest in the sector has grown over recent decades, the plural policing arrangements identified are not of recent vintage but have been a consistent feature of British policing for centuries. In recognition of this debate Johnston's important study was entitled *The Rebirth of Private Policing* (1992), suggesting that the developments he was analysing mirrored earlier arrangements. Jones and Newburn (2002) argued that those who proclaimed a new paradigm of policing emerged in the last decades of the twentieth century over-state the impact and extent of the pluralisation process. They based their argument on three important factors that suggest that the pluralisation thesis has been over-played. First, the long history of private policing activity demonstrates that the state has never been a monopoly provider. Policing arrangements have always been plural. Similarly Crawford (2003) noted that the role of social landlords in the governance of the behaviour of tenants is not a new development, and it has often been argued that contemporary interventions to discipline those regarded as problematic seem to recreate distinctions between the 'deserving' and the 'undeserving' poor that informed welfare and charitable efforts in Victorian times.

Second, Jones and Newburn (2002) also argued that the evidence of pluralisation is over-stated, since many agencies are only lightly engaged in networks of policing and community safety, and that these continue to be dominated by the public police. The police might increasingly work in 'partnership' with other agencies, but these are often not equal partners, not least because the public police continue to have relatively privileged access to information and other resources relating to local crime and disorder-related issues. As was noted in Chapter 3, an important dimension of police powers is derived from their ability to identify and define local priorities and to provide an authoritative discourse outlining the most appropriate solutions. Those partners who suggest alternative measures might be marginalised. Edwards and Hughes (2002) and Hughes (2007) have noted how social crime prevention approaches have tended to be sidelined by community safety partnerships focused instead on enforcement measures.

Third, while Jones and Newburn (2002) acknowledged that new managerialism has transformed the conduct of police work, private sector discipline has not debunked entirely a public sector ethos. The continuing importance of public policing is also apparent in numerical terms since, in Britain, the number of officers employed in the public sector has risen in the recent past. Although financial restrictions mean that numbers fell from 2010, police numbers have fallen back to where they were in the relatively recent past. In September 2016 there were 122,859 police officers, only marginally lower than the 2001 total of 125,600.

Nonetheless considerable evidence suggests that current developments in the pluralisation of policing herald a new era of policing beyond 'the police'. New agencies and new partnerships are made and remade in pursuit of priorities of reassurance and community safety that have not been part of the traditional police service mandate. On the other hand, it seems that this patchwork of policing arrangements – conducted through, alongside, above and below the state, as Loader's (2000) model in Figure 10.1 suggested, closely mirrors earlier, premodern arrangements. Zedner (2006) argued that some of this confusion can be attributed to analysts' tendency to too readily cast developments in fundamental terms of epochal transformation. She explored a series of historical juxtapositions between premodern eighteenth-century criminal justice and contemporary features. Key among these were the transformation of the eighteenth-century ancestors of the contemporary extended police family, incorporating 'thief takers' – rewarded and incentivised as they were by performance-related pay – turnpike keepers, pawnbrokers and inn-keepers into the global security market of the twenty-first century. Additionally, social reformers and policy-makers of the eighteenth century saw crime prevention as a central function of the old police. While modern techniques of risk management and avoidance are transformed by the technological sophistication they employ, they are not fundamentally distinct from their earlier counterparts. Zedner (2006) also drew parallels between the eighteenth-century emphasis on self-help and community-based measures to apprehend offenders and more recent trends at 'responsibilisation', understood in the twenty-first century in terms of the Big Society. Contemporary trends for private citizens to club together to contract private security services, perhaps under the auspices of gated communities, are also reminiscent of premodern 'prosecution associations' that would offer rewards and pay for private prosecutions connected with those who had committed offences against members.

As Zedner (2006) argued, in the light of such evidence it is tempting to dismiss current claims about the new pluralisation of policing on the grounds that it is historically ignorant. To conclude, though, that since not all is new, nothing is, misses some important points of difference between the pre-police era and the contemporary period. In particular, technological advances, some of which are outlined in Chapter 11, and globalisation, discussed in Chapter 8, have significantly altered the scope of private security providers. Moreover, the continued role of the nation state provides for a distinctive context that simply did not exist in earlier periods. While the twenty-first-century nation state, in many countries, has withdrawn somewhat from its role as primary provider of law and order, and has thus contributed to the pluralisation process by vacating a series of roles now filled by voluntary, private or hybrid organisations, it continues to play an important role in terms of regulation that its eighteenth-century counterpart did not. The 'regulatory state' might have a more narrow role than it once enjoyed, but it should not be assumed that it has lost power as it has relinquished various functions, since it has often assumed a central role in regulating those providers who have entered the spaces it has recently vacated. The state might have ceded certain roles to the private security industry in Britain, for example, but it continues to exert influence over it via regulation, albeit relatively 'light touch', and through contractual arrangements that underpin public–private relations.

CONCLUSION

Each chapter of this book has noted that the pluralisation of policing means that concerns and debates that have surrounded the public police service need to be extended to consider a broader range of players. Early approaches to the study of private security industry tended to regard it as the 'junior partner' to the public police, providing marginal services that supplemented the more significant business of law-enforcement. In the early twenty-first century the private sector plays a direct role in the provision of a range of policing activities and is increasingly responsible for the regulation of fellow citizens, who conduct their lives on private property under the gaze of surveillance technologies that monitor their movement, shopping habits and financial practices. Furthermore, the principles of private sector market discipline have been extended into the public sector such that police managers, like their counterparts across the public sector, are engaged in managing the performance of their junior staff, budgeting and preparing business cases to justify innovative projects that they develop. While the work of the police service might be coming to imitate the business sector, other sections of the public sector have come to share police concerns with crime prevention and community safety. Like other kinship groups, the 'extended police family' of the twenty-first century might at times be dysfunctional or marriages of convenience. The various partners are, for better or worse, bound together by common interests, if nothing else.

Although it is clear that the public police service never enjoyed a true monopoly position, contemporary networks are more complex than previous arrangements and consideration of policing as a social process is eclipsing analysis of the police as one agency among many. This does not necessarily mean that a fundamentally new epoch of policing is underway: such a claim might over-exaggerate the role of the state in both modern and late- or post-modern periods. However striking the historical parallels between policing in the eighteenth and twenty-first centuries, it should not be assumed that current developments represent a straightforward reversion to plural policing arrangements from earlier times. With this caveat in mind, a useful perspective is found in Zedner's (2006: 81) observation that the system of policing dominated by the public police service, which has come to be seen as synonymous with 'policing' in general terms, 'may come to be seen as a historical blip in a more enduring schema of policing as an array of activities undertaken by multiple private and public agencies, and individual and communal endeavours'.

chapter summary

- Academic and policy interest in policing during the last few decades has come increasingly to notice the role played by the private security industry. Initially much of this focus was upon charting the size of the sector, the functions that it performed and its relation to the public police service.

- Pluralisation of policing has increasingly been conceived in more complex ways than a private security/public police dichotomy. Loader suggested that it occurs by government, through government, above government, beyond government and below government.

- Although reliable estimates are hard to find, it seems that in many countries the private security industry out-numbers the public police to a significant degree. The notion of the private sector as a junior partner, providing minor services that complement the public police, is increasingly outmoded as the private sector has proliferated and diversified.

- The declining role of the state in the provision of goods and services to the public, partly due to fiscal constraints, has encouraged the private sector to develop. The growing importance of mass private property has created a context in which private policing arrangements have been preferred. Additionally, there has been a growing demand for private security.

- In Britain the private security industry continues to be subject to only 'light touch' regulation. Until 2001 there was no statutory framework to license the sector. The Private Security Industry Act 2001 requires that individuals are vetted and allows for companies to be inspected.

- The increasing importance of private sector 'discipline' within public sector policing has been noted. This has had an effect on budgets and management and seen some commercialisation of police work, as sponsors have been sought and police services have been 'hired out'.

- Pluralisation has meant also that a host of other agencies that have not traditionally had law-enforcement or crime-control responsibilities have come to be included in policing partnerships.

- Describing these emerging patterns in terms of networks of policing, or networks for the governance of security, focuses attention on the changing character of police work, and not just that a broader variety of actors are involved in delivery.

- While few doubt that private sector policing, and plural policing more generally, has become increasingly salient in policy and academic debate during recent years, there is less agreement about the extent to which this represents a fundamental epochal shift in policing arrangements or something of a return to earlier patterns.

- The association of pluralisation of policing with the growth in mass private property has led some to argue that modern policing arrangements have declined alongside the nation state that developed with them in the early decades of the nineteenth century. The emerging networks of plural agencies that deliver policing in broad terms amount to a qualitatively new environment.

- Alternatively, others have noted that the plural policing identified in recent years is actually of long pedigree. Equally, the monopoly that the public police are held to have lost during this period was never as strong as is often suggested. Policing has always engaged diverse agencies, mixtures of public, private and voluntary providers, organised and less organised, and using a host of strategies.

self-check questions (with answers at the back of the book)

1. What five dimensions of policing were outlined by Loader (2000)?

2. How many firms were registered as Approved Contractors by the British Security Industry Association (BSIA) in 2017?

3. How did Shearing and Stenning (2003) explain the growth of the private security sector?

4. How might the notion of 'responsibilisation' be defined in the context of private security?

5. What body was established by the Private Security Industry Act 2001 to regulate the sector?

6. Which piece of legislation introduced Suspicious Activity Reports (SARs) as a response to money laundering?

7. What is the name of civil orders introduced by the Crime and Disorder Act 1998 to quell low-level nuisance behaviour?

8. How did Wakefield (2006) characterise police patrol work?

9. For what reasons did Jones and Newburn (2002) argue that the pluralisation thesis exaggerates the transition from the public policing model?

10. Which occupations did Zedner (2006) suggest were eighteenth-century forerunners of the 'extended police family'?

study questions

1. Does the reputed growth in private security in recent decades reinforce social, political and economic inequality?

2. What role should agencies other than the police play in the regulation of crime and antisocial behaviour?

3. Are the public police strengthened or weakened by the pluralisation of policing?

annotated further reading

Button and Stiernstedt's (2016) article 'The Evolution of Security Industry Regulation in the European Union' provides an excellent overview of the development of private security in Europe and the evolution of modes of regulation. These are linked to broader political and legal developments within the EU. White's (2016) chapter examines accountability of the security industry in terms of different forms, arguing that market self-regulation has been supplemented by formal legal mechanisms as well as 'critical public discourse'.

Crawford and Lister's (2006) article 'Additional Security Patrols in Residential Areas: Notes from the Marketplace' also explores the development of pluralised residential patrol services. They argue that competition between different agencies hinder effective security provision, that they can raise unrealistic public expectations, and exacerbate local competition for limited resources.

Zedner's (2006) article in the *British Journal of Criminology* compares and contrasts elements of plural policing in the era before the establishment of the Metropolitan Police and contemporary debates. Unlike some commentators she does not argue either that all is new in the contemporary period or that current developments amount to a straightforward reversion to premodern patterns of policing. Instead Zedner examines specific aspects of current developments in their particular context and so provides a nuanced analysis of changes and continuities.

annotated listings of links to relevant websites

The British Security Industry Authority (BSIA), established by the Private Security Industry Act 2001, provides a relatively light-touch regulation of the sector. The SIA website outlines its role (www.sia.homeoffice.gov.uk/Pages/home.aspx) and the process by which it licenses the industry. The site addresses the nature of the licensing process that it oversees and responds to some criticisms of the system.

The extent and long-standing of the security industry is demonstrated by the breadth of topics covered by the American Society of Industrial Security (ASIS International), which was established in 1955 and has approximately 35,000 members organised into more than 200 'chapters' worldwide. The ASIS website, www.asisonline.org, provides details of its work and the security industry more generally.

The Scottish Community Safety Network is a charity that aims to promote good practice in community safety, to represent the interests of agencies working in the sector, and to encourage collaboration among members. More can be found at www.safercommunities scotland.org/.

annotated links to journal articles

The impact of security patrols on public perceptions and expectations are analysed in:

Crawford, A. and Lister, S. (2006) 'Additional Security Patrols in Residential Areas: Notes from the Marketplace', *Policing and Society*, 16 (4): 164–88.

The development of 'user-pays' policing – where public police charge for services – is analysed in:

Ayling, J. and Shearing, C. (2008) 'Taking Care of Business – Public Police as Commercial Security Vendors', *Criminology and Criminal Justice*, 8: 27–50.

The regulation of private policing across Europe is reviewed in:

Button, M. (2007) 'Assessing the Regulation of Private Security across Europe', *European Journal of Criminology*, 4: 109–128.

Theoretical debates relating to the development of plural policing and the changing nature of the state are identified and reviewed in:

Crawford, A. (2006) 'Networked Governance and the Post-Regulatory State? Steering, Rowing and Anchoring the Provision of Policing and Security', *Theoretical Criminology*, 10: 449–79.

11

SURVEILLANCE, IT AND THE FUTURE OF POLICING

CONTENTS

LEARNING OBJECTIVES

This chapter explores the changing role of technology in contemporary policing. The impact of surveillance technology on crime and social relations is outlined and the implications that it has for policing in broader terms of social regulation are critically assessed. In particular, the chapter aims to:

- consider the extent to which technological developments transform police work, with particular reference to CCTV and road traffic policing

- explore the implications that crime mapping has for intelligence-led policing and the communication of crime risks

- examine the impact of surveillance technology and information systems on the character of police work and the extent to which this curtails individual officer discretion.

KEY TERMS

'hot spots' policing; CCTV; communication systems; discretion; information and intelligence; police culture; surveillance; supervision and traffic policing

INTRODUCTION

Glossy visions of high-tech law-enforcement officers have long been a staple of fictional representations of police work. Perhaps the most prominent example of this genre is the CBS television show *CSI: Crime Scene Investigation* in which homicide detectives, assisted by technical support staff, use state-of-the-art technology and powerful databases to analyse crime scenes and conclusively identify the killer. If kids' television cartoons of a certain vintage often ended with the villain ruefully lamenting that 'I'd have gotten away with it if it wasn't for those meddlesome kids', it now seems as though science and the scientist are the bête noir of the over-confident murderer. The CSI genre, which includes a number of factional or infotainment-style programmes that blur the reality/fiction boundary, can be criticised on a number of grounds. As with much cinematic or television crime and policing shows, it is an easy criticism to point out that 'real' cases are rarely resolved within the timeframe of a one-hour show. Moreover, guilt, or innocence, often cannot be established as a certain verifiable fact, and even scientific evidence requires interpretation and explanation rarely conveyed in television programmes. The role of technology in policing and its impact upon routine police work is considered critically in the discussion below. In the concluding section it is argued that the fictional representations reflect a more general tendency toward technological determinism, which assumes that policing is fundamentally transformed by expanded technological capacity. Instead, enhanced information and communications technology needs to be considered in the context in which it is deployed and that police culture, for example, is able to resist and transform some of the potential implications of new technology.

TECHNOLOGY IN CONTEXT

The ubiquity of information and communication technology in media representations of policing also marks them out from 'real' police work, which often continues to be a relatively low-tech business, even when it comes to investigations of serious criminal incidents. Innes's (2003) study of murder investigations found that the collection of forensic evidence was regarded as important to police officers, not least because of the 'symbolic' capital it brought in terms of persuading the Crown Prosecution Service to press charges. However, the value of scientific tests, DNA profiling and so on was limited and officers regarded it as important to also seek other forms of evidence in order to build a successful case. One limit on the value of scientific scene-of-crime analysis was that it took three months to get conclusive results to some of the tests used, which meant that investigating officers treated them tentatively (Innes, 2003). The need to understand scientific procedures in the context of real-life investigations demonstrates the need to avoid technological determinism, as was pointed out in Chapter 9.

That investigations do not proceed solely along the lines of the technical capacity of scientific analysis or ICT processing was further demonstrated by the Macpherson Inquiry (1999) into the police investigation of the racist murder of Stephen Lawrence in London in 1993. Although attention has focused on Macpherson's findings about institutional racism, failures in many aspects of the police investigation were also identified. Technological developments and the experience of previous investigations had led to the creation of the HOLMES (Home Office Large Major Enquiry System) computer system, which allowed for information to be cross-referenced and data to be retrieved. However, it was not used in the early stages of the investigation because the Deputy Investigating Officer was not trained to use it (Macpherson, 1999: 14.5). The frailty of human operatives of surveillance and IT systems is noted at various stages in the discussion that follows.

Although the current reality of policing does not mirror the technological wonders of many 'cop shows', politicians and policy-makers have long sought to improve the technological capacity of the police service. More effective communication systems have been regarded as an important prerequisite of improved police performance. The introduction of Unit Beat Policing in Britain in the 1960s, for example, depended on the technology of two-way radios which allowed patrolling officers to communicate more freely and meant that the beats no longer had to be drawn around the location of police telephone boxes as they has previously done (Rawlings, 2002: 200). More recently efforts to reduce the impact of administrative duties have focused upon developing secure laptop computers that would allow officers to complete crime reports and the like without returning to police stations and disappearing from public view. Not only would this lessen the time officers take to complete routine administrative tasks, it was claimed, it would also mean that officers could complete more procedures from their patrol cars and thus promote a visible police presence on the streets. Handheld computer technology, social media and new techniques to harness web-based information offer the capacity to transform the nature of police work (Innes and Roberts, 2011).

As with IT projects more generally, it should be remembered that the promise offered by such developments has often been greater than the impact in reality, although this impact continues to unfold. Nonetheless, the potential of hi-tech solutions to routine problems of police work and crime investigation continues to be emphasised. The following discussion reviews some of the main features of emerging technologies and considers their impact on the nature of police work and the broader dimensions of policing as a process of social regulation. Particular attention is paid to continuing debates about the role of surveillance technology, such as closed-circuit television (CCTV) and automatic number plate recognition (ANPR) and traffic monitoring systems. The use of crime mapping as a tool in intelligence-led policing is then considered before the chapter concludes by reflecting upon the impact of these technological developments upon police work.

CCTV, ANPR AND TRAFFIC MONITORING: BENEVOLENT GAZE OR BIG BROTHER?

In 2009 a House of Lords select committee reported a widely-held view that the UK was the world leader in the use of CCTV. The report noted that during the 1990s, 78 per cent of the Home Office crime prevention budget was spent on CCTV and that in the decade up to 2006, £500 million of public money was spent on this form of surveillance – the amount spent by private corporations and individuals was not recorded (House of Lords, 2009). Several years earlier, the British Information Commissioner warned of the danger of 'sleepwalking into a surveillance society' and that the exponential growth of CCTV capacity raised serious concerns about civil liberties (Evans and Mostrous, 2006). The Commissioner noted that private companies monitored individuals' online shopping patterns in order to develop consumer profiles and enable highly-targeted advertising, that radio frequency identification (RDIF) tags are increasingly inserted into products allowing them to be monitored when in transit, and that an increasing range of private and public agencies were developing profiles of their customers and clients. Parents, for example, were being required to pay for their children's school meals via electronic cards, which would, among other things, allow the local education authority to monitor the eating patterns and habits of pupils. At the forefront of this panoply of monitoring and surveillance infrastructure is CCTV, a field in which Britain has become a global leader, with an estimated 20 per cent of all the world's cameras. In 1999, Norris and Armstrong suggested that an individual living in urban Britain going about their routine working and social life might be captured by up to 300 cameras in 30 different systems during the course of a single day. CCTV was employed at that time on residential estates, transport networks, retail outlets, football stadia, by police and town-centre managers, in schools and hospitals, in telephone boxes, and at cash machines, petrol stations and in car parks. The ubiquity of CCTV was such that, Norris and Armstrong (1999: 42) argued, it was unlikely that an individual could avoid its electronic gaze.

Since then the suppliers of CCTV have developed new inroads into the domestic security industry such that relatively cheap systems can be bought to protect private property, which suggests that the public are prone to be captured by them. The development of 'dash cam' recorders has meant that similar systems are now operated and controlled by private citizens on the roads; the impact of such systems on policing is considered later in this chapter. One major limitation of CCTV is that it has tended to be a passive presence, able to record or monitor events but not necessarily an effective means to intervene. Indeed, Norris and Armstrong (1999: 166) observed CCTV operations for 600 hours, during which time police or other personnel were deployed to intervene in a situation on just 45 occasions. While their study suggested a largely passive role for CCTV, it seems that the development of interactive systems might change the way in which cameras are used. Although the coalition government continued to acknowledge the crime prevention and detection possibilities of CCTV (and ANPR) technology it has also emphasised the importance of civil liberties and individual privacy. To these ends the Protection of Freedom Act 2012 requires the development of a regulatory code of practice and the appointment of a Surveillance Camera Commissioner to oversee implementation. The Home Office (2013: 7) published a consultation document and described its central ethos in the following terms:

> **Public confidence that a surveillance camera system is being used appropriately, without disproportionate interference with the right to private and family life, is seen as being largely dependent upon the transparency, integrity and accountability of the system operator. In the draft code of practice, the government has drawn a parallel with the well-established concept of policing by consent and described the purpose of the code as helping to establish surveillance by consent.**

assessing the impact of CCTV

Debates about the impact of CCTV have focused on a range of issues, most notably its effectiveness in terms of crime prevention and deterrence (see Box 11.1). Although it seems that there is little definitive evidence that CCTV is effective in preventing crimes in general terms, studies have shown that it can be useful when used in bounded or limited terms, such as the monitoring of crime in car parks (Gill and Spriggs, 2005). Other debates have concentrated on civil liberties issues or the release of deviant sexual behaviour or footage of dangerous reckless driving that have been broadcast by the entertainment media. As Jewkes (2015) has noted, CCTV images have become a staple of a genre of reality television crime programmes that have often relied upon the thinnest of public interest grounds to defend the broadcast of salacious or gratuitous footage.

Box 11.1

Deterrence

The notion that crime prevention initiatives such as CCTV have a deterrence effect is widely claimed, and often a matter of 'common sense'. Just as with the deployment of officers or members of the extended police family on high-visibility patrol is valued since it dissuades people from taking advantage of opportunities to commit crime, so too crime prevention is often predicated on signalling the risks of offending. The counterpart to the deterrence effect is the notion of displacement, the notion that crime is not wholly prevented but is redeployed to other places, other times, or other victims or that offenders turn their attention to other forms of crime. Although there is evidence that displacement can limit the impact of situational crime prevention, such as CCTV, most of the research evidence suggests that deterrence reduces the overall level of crime and that only a proportion is displaced.

The impact of CCTV on policing can be considered in terms of the relatively narrow work of the public police and, more broadly, in relation to policing as a process of social regulation. First, the effectiveness of CCTV as an aid to crime detection is considered. Photographic records of offenders have been used by detectives since the late-nineteenth century and efforts to develop effective databases of these images began with card indexes during the same period (Norris and Armstrong, 1999). Since the 1960s, British television shows have used photofits, video stills and e-fits of suspects in an effort to gather information about suspects from the general public, and CCTV footage has become a staple ingredient of such programmes. The overall impact of CCTV as an aid to crime detection is difficult to gauge. Footage captured by cameras has been pivotal in some high-profile cases, although the actual identification and arrest of offenders has often arisen from traditional low-tech policing, even where hi-tech developments might have contributed to the process. A good example of this followed a series of bombings in London in 1999, aimed at gay and minority ethnic communities. During April of that year three nail bombs exploded, the first in Brixton, followed by a second attack in Brick Lane at the heart of the Asian community in the East End of London, and a third on the Admiral Duncan, a pub in Soho associated with the gay community. During the last of these attacks, three people were killed. The extent of CCTV in the capital city was evident in the investigation of these attacks, as the Metropolitan Police analysed thousands of hours of footage. Facial recognition software meant that detectives could interrogate millions of images and identify a person caught on camera in the vicinity of each incident prior to the explosions. To that extent CCTV and the computer software that supported the investigation added capacity to the police investigation that would not otherwise have been possible. Subsequently, however, the perpetrator, David Copeland, was identified following a tip-off in response to publication of photograph enhanced from the CCTV images. Surveillance and information technology enabled and accelerated the course of the investigation, but it continued to rely upon information supplied by observant members of the public.

Home Office sponsored research has shown that police officers regard CCTV images as a major source of intelligence in the investigation and routinely seize footage from public and private systems in the vicinity of a criminal incident (Levesley and Martin 2005). In addition to enhancing the capacity of the police to identify offenders, CCTV also expedites custody procedures since suspects are more likely to admit offences once presented with CCTV-derived evidence, although presumably the time spent collecting and sifting CCTV evidence needs to be offset against that saved once in the custody suite.

CCTV and the electronic gaze

In addition to evidential benefits, CCTV is also heralded as an effective means to deploy officers in the pursuit of offenders or to tackle particular crime and disorder problems. In this context, the power of CCTV to observe and monitor public space and to register problem behaviour has been enhanced by computer software that can identify incongruous activity that might warrant closer police attention. The observational capacity of CCTV was, in its early incarnations, limited by the ability of operatives, who often tended to be poorly paid and under-motivated, to physically watch over the images presented to them on screens in the control room (Wakefield, 2004). Subsequently, however, the development of algorithmic systems that can automatically sense movement that might be a cause of concern offers a significantly more enhanced capacity for CCTV to direct the deployment of resources to scenes of crime, disorder, traffic congestion or one of the myriad scenarios anticipated by cameras (Norris and Armstrong, 1999). Nonetheless, studies of police work do not suggest that officers are often deployed to situations identified by CCTV cameras. While the police control room plays an important role in determining the work that officers do, it seems likely that this continues to be shaped predominantly by telephone calls received from members of the public (Bayley, 1994). The benefits of CCTV in terms of the operational deployment of officers appear to be stronger in specific instances than they are in general terms. CCTV seems to play little overall role in identifying general crime problems as they occur. Many CCTV cameras are not operated directly by police staff, or by operators who have dedicated means to communicate with police services (beyond the normal phone system). Many CCTV cameras are not deployed for general reasons to detect crime problems in broad terms. It was for these reasons that Norris and Armstrong (1999) found so few deployments arising from the many hours spent observing the operation of CCTV systems.

While CCTV does not play a significant role in determining the deployment of officers on routine duties, it clearly is important to the conduct of particular policing operations. In the policing of football matches, for example, CCTV is widely used to direct officers to particular pressure points where crowds have congregated or to monitor for those individuals banned from grounds following incidents of hooliganism (Garland and Rowe, 1999). Police officers suggested to Levesley and Martin (2005: 4–5) that CCTV was most useful in dealing with public order incidents, cases of assault and theft, and was typically used in town centres on Friday and Saturday nights as pubs and clubs closed and large numbers of people spilled onto the streets. As with claims about the crime prevention properties of CCTV, it seems that the potential benefits for the police service also need to be treated with some caution. It seems that there are some evidential benefits to be gained, but these depend upon the police being able to recognise the images of offenders and the quality and forensic value of images captured on systems that vary in quality enormously. In terms of the ability of CCTV to assist in operational terms it also seems that caution is required; research into the demands on police time rarely suggest that much crime or disorder is spotted on CCTV and then 'passed' to the police.

traffic policing and technology

A more recent technological development has been ANPR systems, whereby digital cameras record vehicle registration plates and trawl databases such as the Police National Computer in an effort to identify vehicles that are reported stolen or are otherwise 'of interest' to the police. ANPR was first used in Britain as part of the development of a 'ring of steel' around the City of London, whereby technological and physical interventions were installed in an effort to safeguard London's financial centre from terrorist attack (Goold, 2004). ANPR has not been subjected to the same degree of public debate as CCTV, as described above, or the use of traffic monitoring (speed cameras) systems, discussed below, which may be because it has widely been presented as a straightforward law-enforcement tool that has no broader implications for the population at large. Box 11.2 demonstrates the way in which Thames Valley Police explains the use of APNR.

Box 11.2

Automatic Number Plate Recognition – an Effective Policing Tool to 'Deny Criminals the Use of the Roads'

Most criminals rely on vehicles to commit crime. Automatic Number Plate Recognition (ANPR) is a tool designed to make it far more difficult for them to use vehicles without being detected.

As a vehicle passes through an ANPR camera, it takes an image of the number plate. Those details are then fed into a system which checks them against sources such as the Police National Computer (PNC), Driver and Vehicle Licensing Agency (DVLA), Local Force Intelligence systems and motor insurers databases. If the number plate is matched to one of the sources, the ANPR equipment will sound an alert.

Vehicles which have sounded an alert will then be stopped by intercept team officers for further investigation. Only vehicles that are highlighted by enforcement agency data-bases will be stopped, so no law-abiding citizen has anything to fear from ANPR operations. Unlicensed or uninsured vehicles are likely to be seized on the spot by ANPR equipped officers.

ANPR can be used to gather intelligence on known criminals or for post-incident crime investigation as well as for running pro-active operations using dedicated intercept teams.

ANPR cameras are located in mobile units (vans), in Roads Policing patrol cars, at dedicated fixed sites and via Closed Circuit Television (CCTV) schemes in urban areas.

ANPR cameras are NOT 'safety' cameras, so are not used in Thames Valley to catch speeding or otherwise law-abiding motorists. Nor are they used to generate revenue for the government or other agency.

The use of ANPR by Thames Valley Police fully complies with the Data Protection Act 1998 and the Human Rights Act 1998.'

www.thamesvalley.police.uk/news_info/departments/anpr/index.htm
(accessed 27 April 2007)

While APNR might be presented as a neutral technology, it has raised concern about civil liberties issues and the privacy of individuals. Although the recording of vehicle registration details might not, in itself, amount to the collection of personal information concerns have been raised that the systems can also capture images of people present in vehicles, which might bring ANPR within the remit of data protection legislation. Moreover, while ANPR cameras are often deployed in identified static positions, in other circumstances cameras might be used covertly, which means that they would require permission under the terms of the Regulation of Investigatory Powers Act (RIPA) 2000, which was discussed in Chapter 3. The Scottish Chief Surveillance Commissioner (Office of Surveillance Commissioners, 2006) suggested that the capacity of ANPR systems to capture information indiscriminately means that they would not meet the tests of proportionality required by RIPA. The use of ANPR represents another context in which police act as knowledge or information brokers in regulatory networks that span the public and private sector (see example in Box 11.2) by trawling motor insurers' databases for information. In 2013 the pressure group Big Brother Watch (2013) published a report detailing the widespread use of surveillance technology by private investigators contracted to the public sector but not subject to RIPA provisions. Clearly proposals for a code of practice might address this legal blind spot, which also further demonstrates the plurality of policing as a network of social regulation.

Traffic monitoring systems, particularly speed cameras, have featured in much media debate about the proper focus of policing and law-enforcement in Britain in recent years and reveal much about the ways in which crime is socially constructed. Speed enforcement cameras were introduced to British roadsides from the early 1990s, although it was often found that cameras were not operative since forces either did not put film into them or did not monitor the pictures (Corbett, 2000). Debates about speed cameras have become a media staple in recent years, with concerns focusing upon the effectiveness of cameras in reducing speed, arguments about the revenue-raising role of cameras, and the impact that cameras have upon law-abiding members of the public. Corbett and Caramlau (2006) suggested that, media campaigns notwithstanding, around 75 per cent of people support the use of cameras, although concerns persist about the 'stealthy' use of cameras (i.e. those deployed in 'hidden' ways or when not adequately signposted) and the notion that cameras are used to raise revenue rather than to target speeding motorists in high-risk areas. These latter concerns suggest that the use of speed cameras have the potential to undermine police legitimacy, especially when co-joined with perceptions that the use of cameras has accompanied a reduction in the deployment of 'real' police officers. The House of Commons Transport Committee (2006) noted that technological innovation ought to enhance, rather than usurp, the role of the police officer. The Committee suggested that continuing technological developments would see a range of new measures, including 'time-distance' cameras (which record the time at which vehicles enter and exit a stretch of road and so calculate average speed),

Constable (to Motorist who has exceeded the speed limit). " AND I HAVE MY DOUBTS ABOUT THIS BEING YOUR FIRST OFFENCE. YOUR FACE SEEMS FAMILIAR TO ME."

Figure 11.1   Policing the motorist, circa. 1905 (Doran, 1990: 36, cited in Clapton, 2004)

'intelligent road studs' (planted into the road surface to gather information about road and weather conditions, traffic flow and speed) and 'intelligent speed adaptation' (which uses GPS and digital mapping to control the speed of vehicles and ensure compliance with speed limits).

The tone of media coverage reveals much about the cultural status of private cars, crime and policing in contemporary Britain. Although car 'accidents' (itself a loaded term) are usually associated with excessive speed and result in far more deaths than homicide, speeding continues to be socially constructed as a non-serious offence (Corbett, 2000). Legal sanctions against the use of mobile phones while driving were strengthened in 2017, and efforts to make the use of mobile devices normatively unacceptable have been a feature of campaigns against this significant cause of harm. The prospects of extending the technological enforcement of traffic law runs the risk of criminalising sections of society that would not otherwise have negative contact with the police. Concern about the impact of traffic policing on relations with the public is one factor that explains the low priority police officers have often given to traffic policing (Waddington, 1999a). The deleterious impact of road policing on the legitimacy and authority afforded to the police by 'respectable' middle-class society has been noted since the expansion of car ownership in the middle of the twentieth century (Loader and Mulcahy, 2003: 114). Figure 11.1 shows that media concern about these developments is also long-standing. As early as the 1920s, Emsley (1996: 147) noted that

[t]he development of the motor car, and its increasing availability to middle-class families, was, even by this date, bringing members of a social group, who hitherto had had virtually no contact with the police, into regular conflict with them. In the summer of 1928 the Home Secretary made a 'pressing personal appeal' to all chief constables that they should urge caution on their men in the way they behaved towards the public on the roads. Stressing the Bobby's unique qualities, his good humour and impartiality was an additional way to seek to check the new and damaging confrontations between policemen and members of the middle class on the roads.

While pleas for impartiality in the 1920s seem to be thinly-veiled requests for officers to exercise their discretion to the benefit of middle-class motorists, a key concern about the use of technology to enforce traffic legislation is that that it is not possible to turn a blind eye when the observer is an automated electronic system. The impact of technology on the exercise of police discretion is discussed more fully in the penultimate section of the chapter.

EYES IN THE SKY: POLICE DRONES

The military have used drones – lightweight 'unmanned aerial vehicles' (UAVs) – in various operational contexts in the recent past, including in Iraq and Afghanistan. The extension of this technology to civilian use, by police and other agencies, has been noted in the USA and to a limited extent in Britain. Drones represent an extended capacity for surveillance that is rapidly mobile and can be used covertly at a greater distance from subjects than can CCTV cameras. The campaign group Privacy International reported in 2012 that four police services had tested UAVs but had reported mixed results (Ardizzone, 2012). A European Commission (2012) report suggested that the use of UAVs was likely to expand in a range of public and commercial activities and could be of use in circumstances where safety concerns precluded the deployment of people, such as into volcanic ash clouds or in the aftermath of chemical or nuclear accident. In law-enforcement, UAVs could be used in crowd and traffic control, detection of offenders or the more generally in the prevention of crime. Concerns about the use of 'drones' has tended to focus on safety issues – a trial by Merseyside ended with a UAV crashing into the river Mersey in 2012 – and on civil liberties implications. Studies have suggested that they have disproportionately been used against minority and marginalised communities and raise fundamental concerns about regulation and the right to privacy (Finn and Wright, 2012).

CRIME MAPPING, INTELLIGENCE AND THE REGULATION OF POLICING

The technological developments described in the previous section have related to various innovations intended to regulate and survey behaviour in a range of public and private contexts. By various means they are intended to exert a deterrent effect on those who might otherwise commit crime or antisocial behaviour. As has been noted, they have significant impacts on policing and police work, but these are not their primary aims. In the following discussion the focus shifts to technological regimes that have been introduced within the police environment in an effort to improve the efficiency of the police organisation, to make the service more accountable, and to develop the capability to tackle crime more effectively.

crime-mapping and policing

Criminological research has long shown that crime is not randomly distributed, but tends to impact disproportionately on certain populations and in specific places. A plethora of victimisation surveys have demonstrated that just as a minority of offenders commit a disproportionate number of offences, so too a minority of people and locations experience relatively high levels of crime. In very narrow terms this criminological canard has formed the basis for the development of focused and targeted policing that uses computer software and other technology in an effort to map patterns of crime and so to enable a more effective deployment of police resources (see Figure 11.2). As with other technological developments described in this chapter this does not amount to a qualitatively new form of policing, since officers have tended to rely upon conceptual maps of local areas informed by knowledge of crime problems and offenders (Keith, 1993). While collating information on the characteristics and habits of 'nominals' (i.e. known offenders) has always been central to police work, developments in ICT have transformed the capacity to develop intelligence about local problems and to more effectively respond to them. Much of the recent impetus to develop policing along these lines developed from a growing realisation in Britain and elsewhere in the 1970s and 1980s that traditional police patrol work appeared to have little impact upon crime rates. An assessment of traditional policing strategies of that era led Bayley (1994: 3) to the withering – and much cited – conclusion that:

> **The police do not prevent crime. This is one of the best-kept secrets of modern life. Experts know it, the police know it, but the public does not know it. Yet the police pretend that they are society's best defence against crime … This is a myth. First, repeated analysis has consistently failed to find any connection between the number of police officers and crime rates. Secondly, the primary strategies adopted by modern police have been shown to have little or no effect on crime.**

One response to this counsel of despair was to use information technology such that police could collate data about criminal offences and use geographical information systems to pinpoint locations and so produce local maps that enabled the identification of particular 'hot spots' (areas that were particularly criminogenic). Particularly high-profile applications of such approaches were developed in many American cities in the 1990s; the development of the Compstat system in New York in the 1990s proved particularly influential as it was widely imitated by other police departments in the USA and was lauded by politicians, policy-makers and academics alike (Silverman, 2006) (see Box 11.3).

Box 11.3

The Panopticon

Derived from the prison designs developed in the eighteenth century by Jeremy Bentham, the term 'panopticon' refers to a system whereby the maximum degree of surveillance is derived from the minimum deployment of resources. In the context of Bentham's plans for the ideal prison, this related to a system whereby prison cells were organised in tiers around the circumference of a circular prison, in the middle of which stood a tower. Each cell was open to surveillance by only a few guards who were located out of sight at the top of the central tower. In this way prisoners knew that they could be observed at any time, but were unable to know precisely when, or if, they were actually watched. One result of this efficient system of control was that prisoners internalised the disciplinary regime such that they regulated their own behaviour in the expectation that the prison guards were keeping them under observation.

The development of 'high definition' policing (McLaughlin, 2007a: 124) that Compstat and other forms of crime mapping enable has a number of implications. First, there is some evidence that it is an effective strategy in law-enforcement terms. While some have argued that other factors also played a significant role in reducing crime levels in New York City in the 1990s (Bowling, 1999; Stenson, 2001), a more general analysis of hot spots policing programmes in the USA concluded that there was a positive impact in reducing crime, and that this was not at the expense of displacing crime problems to other areas (Weisburd and Braga, 2006: 232–4). However, concerns about other aspects of this form of targeted policing suggest that such success comes at a price when accompanied by aggressive tactics, such as those associated with zero tolerance policing. In the American context, Rosenbaum (2006) cautioned that 'hot spots' policing is often associated with aggressive enforcement and that this can weaken police–community relations and undermine legitimacy. Furthermore, Rosenbaum (2006) argued that these technological approaches redefine crime problems in relatively narrow terms and that a geographical perspective of crime problems risks ignoring the broader dimensions of, for example, illegal drug dealing.

intelligence-led 'hot spots' policing

The same technology used to map crime for the purposes of intelligence-led policing operations has been extended, in the USA, to develop information for the public about criminal incidents and patterns in particular neighbourhoods. Since 2011 the Home Office has provided online crime maps that allow the public to obtain information about incidents and trends in their local area. A host of incidents are displayed and, in some cases, extended details are provided including the outcomes of police investigations, where these are known. Other initiatives include police using smartphone apps to communicate with victims and the public and the use of social media to report local issues to the public. Enabling the public to access authoritative data about crime promises to empower citizens to effectively assess the performance of local police and Police and Crime Commissioners through the 'democratisation' of knowledge.

In practice, of course, the project is more difficult. The local crime maps provide no contextual information and fail to convey the ways in which categories and types of crime are open to interpretation and do not represent natural or objective categories. The crime data presented does not speak for itself. As Ratcliffe (2002) has outlined, such representation raises serious ethical concerns about privacy, the risk of vigilante activity and the broader impact that such representation of crime problems can have on communities in terms of perpetuating negative perceptions that can impact upon their economic development. Moreover, they suggest a level of scientific and technological authority that might be unwarranted. Ratcliffe (2002) identified reasons why the apparent certainty of locating an incident using geographical information systems technology might be misleading. Most of these relate to the real world context in which information about criminal incidents is (mis)understood by victims and witnesses and subsequently recorded inaccurately by the police. Increasingly significant forms of crime – technologically driven forms of fraud, for example – transcend traditional geographies of territory and community. Against these developments it seems likely that crime mapping might not capture these emerging patterns.

technology and the routines of police work

While crime mapping technology provides a platform for the strategic direction of police services, albeit one that might be imperfect, other technological innovations have shaped the routines of police work, just as they have transformed working life more generally. As was noted above, technological developments played a significant role in the development of Unit Beat Policing in Britain during the 1960s, when the introduction of computer-aided dispatch (CAD) systems offered the promise a more efficient response to demands from the public. CAD systems use a terminal in patrol cars via which a

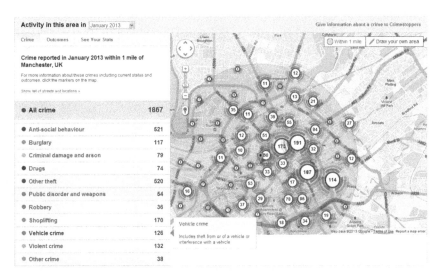

Figure 11.2 Mapping crime (www.police.uk/)

central control room directs officers to respond to incidents reported by the public. Details of the incident, such as the address, names of those involved, previous history of the address and the caller, and the degree of priority attached to the report, are transmitted to a screen in the patrol car. Manning (1992, cited in Chan, 2001) commented that the promises of increased efficiency offered by CAD, and other technological innovations, have often not been met and that they have had less impact on police practices than were forecast. However, Ericson and Haggerty (1997) found that officers regarded CAD as a positive innovation that allowed them to perform vehicle and other checks relatively quickly and securely (unlike older police radios, CAD systems are not susceptible to being monitored by illicit scanners).

An addition to technological innovations that assign officers to cases has been the development of computerised crime reporting systems into which details of incidents are entered. Although police officers have always been concerned to gather and process information about criminal and other incidents, the development of databases that store, sort and communicate such policing outputs has transformed traditional practices. In an era when the deployment of police officers and PCSOs on 'high visibility' patrol has become an imperative, the impact of computerised reporting systems on officer's time is an important concern. A Home Office study (PA Consulting Group, 2001) found that officers spent 43.1 per cent of their time engaged in 'backroom' activity, in police stations and custody suites out of public sight. Not all of this time was spent completing incident reports, but the study identified problems with IT systems that were out of date, non-intuitive and so difficult to use, did not have sufficient terminals and access points, and were prone to system failures. Chan's (2001) study of the impact of IT on an Australian police service found similar concerns about the time that officers had to devote to computerised recording and reporting systems, and the negative consequences that this had in terms of patrol work. However, she also found that officers valued the communicative and intelligence capacity of systems and the advantages offered in terms of generating knowledge of offenders and broader crime patterns.

Enhancing the role of IT within the routines of police work has also impacted upon the dynamics of power relations within police services. Not only is the status of technical support staff, such as data analysts, enhanced relative to other specialist and general police staff, but so too the nature and reach of supervision is affected and the command and control capacity of central police management is enhanced. The ability of line managers to oversee the work of their officers is greatly enhanced by the easy availability of accessible information on the status of enquiries that an officer is assigned to. Not only does this allow for the 'performance' of officers to be inspected, and compared with that of colleagues, it can also impact upon the ways in which officers approach incidents. One consequence of this might be that the officers become relatively deskilled as they perform routine duties according to prescribed procedures and policies, secure in the knowledge that any deviation from these can quickly be identified by supervisory officers. In recent years officers have been required to identify, when inputting incident details, cases that might be hate crimes of some kind, the 'flagging' of which then prompts senior officers to ensure that they have been investigated according to established guidelines. Additionally the better identification of such cases provides for more effective communication of problems to other agencies involved in policing partnerships (Hall, 2005: 203–40).

THE IMPACT OF TECHNOLOGY ON POLICING AND POLICE WORK

As the proceeding discussion demonstrates, technological developments have impacted upon the police service in diverse ways. Some of these have enhanced traditional features of police work, on occasion transforming them to such an extent that they significantly affect the capacity and capability of the police service. DNA-fingerprinting, for example, might be regarded as a more sophisticated version of long-established efforts to capture and collate the unique properties of individual victims or offenders. Technology in this context enhances and transforms the cultural attribute of suspicion that has been widely regarded as central to police work. Where once officers structured their suspicion of vehicles in terms of the age, make and state of repair or the ascribed character of those within it, or the speed or driver's response to the presence of a patrol car, they now have recourse to technological verification of the status of all vehicles.

Ericson and Haggerty (1997) suggested that the apparent scientific and objective certainty of such data both empowers officers, since it elevates their perceptions beyond 'suspicion' towards 'knowledge', and, conversely, threatens to deskill police work by removing the traditional craft aspect of patrol.

Technological innovations might have reshaped police work for some years but emerging new forms of technology, coupled with other shifts in terms of reducing officer numbers and an emphasis on professional practice, have the potential to act as a progressive platform for reform. Innes (2013) argued that new web and social media technologies mean that the ownership and use of intelligence and information can be devolved away from central police databases and instead can be operationalised more effectively by response officers during routine police activities. He noted that automated systems and algorithms mean that intelligence no longer needs to be reviewed and processed by central experts within police services but can be used via apps by officers directly in real-time work. Innes proposed a form of community intelligence-led policing whereby technology combines with forms of Neighbourhood Policing (as outlined in Chapter 5) and enhanced public consultation so that policing can be delivered more effectively on the basis of community expectations. This model of policing, Innes suggested (2013: xx),

> imagines a police constable who is plugged into a variety of community intelligence 'feeds', using policing informatics to make sense of these data to steer their decisions about how and when to intervene. A critical point being that the informatics technologies decenter the knowledge-work involved, moving it out from central units to locations far closer to the point of delivery.

the surveillance society?

A central debate in academic discussion of the use of CCTV, ANPR and other technological innovations relates to the supposed panoptical effects of such forms of surveillance and the development of a disciplinary society. Foucault (1977) argued that systems of dispersed social control had spread beyond the penitentiary such that society itself, and the governance thereof, could be considered in panoptical terms (see Box 11.4). Along these lines, one of the key concerns about the power and reach of police surveillance technology has been that it extends the capacity of the state to monitor the previously private realm of the citizen. An early forecast of these developments was offered by Marx, who couched concerns about police surveillance in the USA in the following terms (1988: 206–7):

> Powerful new information-gathering technologies are extending ever deeper into the social fabric and to more features of the environment. Like the discovery of the atom or the unconscious, new control techniques surface bits of reality that were previously hidden or didn't contain informational clues. People are in a sense turned inside out, and what was previously invisible or meaningless is made visible and meaningful. This may involve

space-age detection devices that give meaning to physical emanations based on the analysis of heat, light, pressure, motion, odour, chemicals, or psychological process, as well as the new meaning given to visible individual characteristics and behaviour when they re-judged relative to a predictive profile based on aggregate data.

Box 11.4

Compstat

Essentially Compstat is a police management tool that co-ordinates 'up-to-date computerized crime data, crime analysis, and advanced crime mapping as the bases for regularized, inter-active crime strategy meetings which hold managers accountable for specific crime strategies and solutions in their areas' (Silverman, 2006: 268). It is often used as part of a strategy whereby senior officers meet regularly to review crime patterns in their districts and are held to account on a daily or weekly basis.

The watchful gaze of CCTV has been regarded as one means of extending the 'maximum surveillance society', in which the disciplinary powers of governance are at their zenith (Cohen, 1985). The implications of these debates for policing are complex: in broad terms, if the net of social control is widened and the mesh thinned, then the extension of surveillance systems will mean that the focus of the police service expands onto individuals, groups and activities that would not previously have been considered the business of the police. As was noted above, this argument has been made by sections of the media in relation to road traffic policing criminalising 'ordinary' motorists not construed as offenders. In addition, as has already been suggested, the growth of CCTV in British society has been in many and diverse directions and the technology has spread in ways such that many agencies, and individuals, have become part of a policing network. The pluralisation of policing has been discussed in Chapter 10, but technology and surveillance systems, such as those that encourage citizens to remotely monitor the security of their property or to consult websites that map local crime patterns, enlist private citizens into policing networks. Hudson (2003) argued that technological developments transform policing and security into matters of private responsibility that are related to the broader expansion of consumer culture into public services (Loader, 1999).

watching the police

Another implication of the growth of CCTV technology, CAD systems and crime reporting regimes relates to their potential to regulate and survey police officers.

In some circumstances, the power of CCTV to discipline officer behaviour is explicitly utilised, such as the use of cameras to monitor behaviour in custody suites (Newburn, 2002). Increasingly, though, researchers are identifying the capacity of citizens to use mobile phones and social media to monitor police behaviour, creating an 'ambient surveillance through which graphic violence is now routinely captured and circulated' (Stalcup and Hahn, 2016: 483). Sandhu and Haggerty (2017) found that officers subjected to perpetual surveillance adopted three broad orientations. Some were 'camera shy' on the basis that footage failed to capture a complete account of interactions, that the presence of cameras had a negative impact on routine encounters, and made it more difficult for officers to do their job in a safe manner. Other officers were 'habituated' to cameras, seeing their presence as part of the working environment that was highly unlikely to record anything remarkable or controversial. The third perspective identified by Sandhu and Haggerty (2017) was that of 'strategic advantage', emphasising the evidentiary benefits that recording offered the police and that they could help prevent false complaints about officers' behaviour. These findings mirrored the study by Ariel et al. (2017), which argued that body-worn cameras (BWCs) influenced the behaviour of both police officers and citizens such that complaints against police 'virtually vanished' when BWCs were deployed. On this basis they argued that 'the use of BWCs … signals a profound sea change in modern policing' (Ariel et al., 2017: 303).

micro-managing police performance

Technological surveillance might inhibit officers otherwise liable to behave inappropriately but information systems also enhance the micro-management of police performance, which impacts upon routine police work. As Ericson and Haggerty (1997) suggested the enhanced reach of line managers, technologically enabled to review officer performance, can shape and limit the exercise of discretion. By requiring an officer to complete certain procedures, and being able to determine whether this has been done, supervisory officers can limit discretion in ways not previously possible. While this is ostensibly a retrospective review it has anticipatory powers since officers are aware that their actions might be subject to scrutiny. As with Bentham's panoptical prison, the disciplinary capacity of surveillance affects the ways in which officers conceive of their role and exercise their powers. This is illustrated by Rowe's (2007a) finding that officers' response to incidents of domestic violence adopted the principles of risk avoidance. Partly this was based around their understanding that there was a strong likelihood of repeat victimisation, which meant they ought to proactively intervene in what otherwise they might have regarded as a 'trivial' private dispute. Moreover, though, the risk of non-intervention was also understood in terms of consequences for themselves, since they anticipated that their judgement and interventions would be scrutinised by senior officers. In some cases, this meant that officers decide to intervene and arrest a perpetrator on the grounds that to do otherwise would risk their being sanctioned by senior officers. At times this was done even though the officer felt that affecting an arrest was not the most suitable way of solving the particular problem. The often-noted tendency of officers to take a non-interventionist stance in response to 'domestics' was being transformed by regulatory regimes which held officers open to scrutiny. Given that most of the routine calls that officers deal with are routed through the CAD system, much of the work that they do is subject to such inspection. The impact on routine police work is not all-encompassing, however, since officers still have considerable discretion in dealing with cases brought directly to their attention while on patrol and it is more difficult to review officer response to incidents that are not first 'captured' by information systems.

changing police culture

Curtailing police decision making through the use of technology and information systems has clear implications for police subcultures, which has often, even if simplistically, been associated with the inappropriate exercise of discretion. Chapter 5 provides a fuller discussion of police culture. Extending the capacity of senior officers to supervise the behaviour and actions of frontline staff might make it easier, for example, to identify officers who over-police minority communities. The 'reach' of technology in this sense, though, is easily over-stated since officers inevitably retain some control over the information that is entered into computer systems in the first instance. Equally, in practice, police officers usually retain control over when BWCs are activated: not everything can be recorded and stored for logistical and legal reasons. Moreover, problems of stereotyping and discrimination cannot be solely ascribed to negative characteristics of canteen culture shared by junior ranking officers. The broader institutional framework of policing, the role and influence of the plural policing beyond the public police, and the social context in which crime and policing are conceptualised must all be addressed. Micro-managing the decisions of officers on patrol will not, in isolation, prevent the inappropriate exercise of police discretion. While not providing a technological fix in terms of regulating or deterring police deviance, the changing environment in which officers' work will be influenced, but not determined, by increasing use of computer-based information and communication systems. As noted above, the role of intelligence systems changes relations within police services and alters the nature and status of police knowledge (Ericson and Haggerty, 1997). Police culture, though, has never been a fixed monolithic entity that can be moulded by external technological or management regimes. Elements of police work will be transformed by the developments outlined in this chapter, just as they were in the face of technological innovations such as the police radio and the patrol car, but the direction and extent of these transformations are difficult to predict.

CONCLUSION

Technological innovation has transformed late-modern society in complex ways that continue to unfold. Many have argued that they have contributed to processes of cultural, political and economic globalisation, promoted the knowledge economy, and transformed time and space. As Williams (2006) has noted, new forms of technological communication have the potential to fundamentally restructure the means by which individuals form communities and construct notions of deviance and the means to regulate human behaviour. While online virtual communities offer insight into possible futures that are in equal part horrifying and alluring, it is also apparent that information and communication technology has already had a significant impact on police work and crime. As with other debates about change and innovation in policing, however, there is a tendency to assume that such developments represent a fundamental epochal transformation (Jones and Newburn, 2002). The technological capacity of electronic surveillance and intelligence systems does not determine the manner in which they are used or the impact that they have in broader social terms.

There are two main reasons for resisting technologically-determinist views of the developments outlined in this chapter. First, police leaders and politicians have sought technological solutions to crime problems and as a means to achieve efficiency in police work since modern police services were established in the nineteenth century. The pace of technological change might have increased, with significant implications in terms of the power and reach of intelligence systems, but earlier innovations have tended to lead to evolutions in policing, rather than revolutions. The second reason for a cautious reading of these trends is that the impact of technological innovation has often been shown to be dependent upon the fallible human beings responsible for their operationalisation. As has been shown in the context of CCTV, for example, the employment of poorly-paid and under-motivated staff has often meant that technological capacity has not been reached in practice (Norris and Armstrong, 1999). Moreover, just as technological change presents new opportunities for crime and deviance, innovations also create avenues for 'counter appropriation' whereby officers can find means to use, for example, mobile phones to communicate with one another beyond the sight of inspection or surveillance systems (Manning, 1996, cited in Chan, 2003). Policing will continue to be shaped by technological developments that broaden and transform networks of regulation in the global information age; the direction and nature of this impact will be determined by the context in which it is deployed. For this reason predicting technological configurations of policing in the twenty-first century remains a risky pursuit.

chapter summary

- Academic and policy research tend to suggest that science and technology are important components of contemporary policing but that they play only a partial role in most criminal investigations.

- In addition to enhancing the investigation of crime, technology has transformed the nature of police communication and information management. This has not been a wholly recent phenomenon, however, and again it has been limited by 'real-world' considerations relating to funding, training and police subculture.

- In Britain, CCTV has been at the forefront of new technologies that monitor a host of human interactions in residential, education, retail, business and leisure environments. In 2006, the Information Commissioner (Evans and Mostrous, 2006) warned that Britain was 'sleepwalking into a surveillance society', and it is estimated that the country is monitored by 20 per cent of the world's cameras.

- The research evidence on the impact of CCTV on crime rates is not extensive, but tends to suggest that it can reduce rates of crime without significant problems of displacement, but that this is only the case when it is applied in certain environments and in respect of certain types of crime. Although CCTV-generated images have proved very useful in the investigation of some high-profile criminal cases, like other forms of technology, there is little definitive evidence of the impact it has on detection more generally.

- ANPR technology was developed in response to threats of terrorism, and provides the police with the capacity to identify large numbers of vehicles and to retrieve information about those that might be stolen, uninsured or associated with known offenders.

- Arguments that the police criminalise law-abiding motorists have been appeared periodically since the expansion of car ownership in Britain in the 1920s and 1930s.

- Although not used routinely, unmanned aerial vehicles (drones) offer financial savings to police and the capacity to operate in circumstances that otherwise would be inaccessible. As with other aspects of police surveillance, concerns have arisen about the privacy and civil liberties implications of the use of drones, as well as their impact on communities already over-policed.

- Technological change has transformed the ways in which police work is conducted. That crime is not evenly distributed, either in terms of offenders or patterns of victimisation, has led to the development of crime mapping techniques that promise to identify locales, times and circumstances in which criminal acts occur.

- While there is some evidence that crime mapping has enabled the effective targeting of specific crime problems, concerns are also identified about the impact of aggressive police tactics on police–community relations.

- Technology has been used to develop 'hot spots' policing, whereby information about criminal incidents is used to provide maps of local crime problems. This can then underpin operational policing strategy. In some cases such maps are available directly to the public via the web.

- Beyond the identification and investigation of crime, technology has impact upon routines of police work, particularly in terms of communication and information management. CAD systems play a central role in shaping the work that officers do, and limit the exercise of officer discretion.

- Social media and web technology offer the potential to integrate intelligence-led strategies with community policing. Officers can access and analyse information and data within routine police work through the use of apps, for example, that can enhance public consultation and the delivery of police services.

- These developments have a range of implications for society. Many have argued that the expansion of surveillance technology pushes society into the realms of the panopticon, whereby individual behaviour is disciplined by anticipated processes of regulation. This has various implications for the police, not least that an increasing range of agencies and individuals come to be engaged in processes of social control. It also extends surveillance of police behaviour itself, and conditions the nature in which officers exercise their discretion.

- There is a strong imperative to avoid technological determinism in considering the influence that these developments will have on crime, policing and social relations more widely. Technology is deployed into particular institutional and cultural contexts, which means that its capacity and possibilities can be resisted, deflected or transformed in practice.

self-check questions (with answers at the back of the book)

1. What does the acronym HOLMES stand for?

2. What percentage of the world's CCTV cameras was it estimated are deployed in Britain?

3. In relation to what three types of crime did police officers suggest CCTV was particularly effective?

4. Against what sources of information does Thames Valley police check information gathered via ANPR?

5. What percentage of the British population support, in general terms, the use of cameras to police speeding drivers?

6. What is Compstat?

7. In Britain in the 1960s computer-aided dispatch systems were introduced in the development of what model of policing?

8. Who developed a model prison that enshrined the concept of the panopticon?

9. To what broader social and political processes do Hudson (2003) and Loader (1999) relate the development of technology in policing?

10. Which three perspectives on video recording of police behaviour did Sandhu and Haggerty (2017) identify?

study questions

1. What should be the balance between civil liberty concerns about the 'right to privacy' and the security dividends associated with surveillance technology?

2. Does crime mapping provide information useful to the general public?

3. What might be the implications of technological limitations on police officer discretion?

annotated further reading

Erison and Haggerty's (1997) *Policing the Risk Society* is probably the key recent study of policing and technology, not least because it argues that the development of new information and intelligence systems has importance far beyond discussion of efficiency and effectiveness. The book's central theme is that technological innovation transforms routine police work into a form of knowledge work, whereby officers are increasingly responsible for transmitting information about risk across networks of agencies engaged in policing.

Gill and Spriggs' (2006) *Assessing the Impact of CCTV* is a Home Office research study based upon an extensive study of the effectiveness of surveillance cameras in 14 sites, including town centres, residential areas, hospitals and car parks. The study used control group areas to assess the impact that CCTV had on local crime rates and examined public attitudes to the systems. The findings show a very mixed picture. CCTV proved reasonably effective in certain areas (particularly those with controlled and fixed entry and exit points, such as car parks) and in relation to certain types of crime. In other areas, such as residential locations, and in relation to crimes such as violent assault, the study suggested that CCTV had little impact.

Innes's (2013) book chapter provided a fascinating case for integrating information technology more centrally within community policing. He argued that technological innovations, coupled with parallel developments in financing, professionalism and globalisation, mean that frontline officers can make decisions based upon intelligence and professional analysis.

This will contribute to more effective policing that is more closely aligned to community expectations.

annotated listings of links to relevant websites

The College of Policing (www.college.police.uk) was established in 2012 and provides professional development, training and expertise intended to spread 'best practice', encourage innovation and to raise the standard and quality of police services.

The National Institute of Justice is a subdivision of the US Department of Justice and its website (www.nij.gov/topics/technology/maps/pages/welcome.aspx) provides a wide range of material on crime mapping and hot spots policing. The principles and practices of crime mapping are outlined in detail and supporting research is analysed. The site includes software programmes used by crime analysts.

Privacy International is a pressure group campaigning on surveillance issues such as data protection, communication surveillance, border technology, ID cards and others. The group's website (www.privacyinternational.org) contains a wide range of resources, including country profiles.

annotated links to journal articles

Chan identified the impact on technology on police work, both in organisational terms and in relation to the culture of policing:

Chan, J. (2001) 'The Technological Game: How Information Technology is Transforming Police Practice', *Criminal Justice*, 1: 139–59.

Barnard-Wills and Wells provide a useful overview of contemporary debates about surveillance in policing in their introduction to a special edition of a journal containing a range of useful articles:

Barnard-Wills, G. and Wells, H. (2012) 'Surveillance, Technology and the Everyday', *Criminology and Criminal Justice*, 12: 227–37.

A fascinating insight into ways in which officers respond to being filmed on duty by members of the public:

Sandhu, A. and Haggerty, K. (2017) 'Policing on Camera', *Theoretical Criminology*, 21: 78–95.

The practical and political implications of crime mapping are explored in:

Ratcliffe, J. (2002) 'Damned if You Don't, Damned if You Do: Crime Mapping and its Implications in the Real World', *Policing and Society*, 12: 211–25.

12
THE FUTURE OF POLICING

CONTENTS

LEARNING OBJECTIVES

It would be historically inaccurate to suggest that policing has been a stable and settled matter that only recently has been subject to pressure to reform. Nonetheless, it remains the case that policing in the second decade of the twenty-first century has faced a 'perfect storm' in terms of the potential cumulative impact of financial restructuring, workforce modernisation, the impact of technology and the changing demands that police continue to face. A policing system which continues to bear more than a passing resemblance to the Metropolitan Police established in 1829 seems to be on the cusp of a series of changes that have the potential to fundamentally reshape this key social institution. There is a danger in suggesting that all that is solid might melt into air, and while what follows is largely focused on areas of potential reform and innovation it is highly likely that policing futures will be characterised by much continuity as well as significant change. With this caveat in mind, the chapter aims to:

- review emerging trends that might transform future internal organisation, culture and operational practices of policing

- review challenges external to policing – in relation to financial austerity and a range of social changes – that seem likely to radically alter the context against which policing is delivered

- consider the impact that the changing landscape of policing might have in terms of the role and mandate of police.

KEY TERMS

culture; evidence-based policing; financial austerity; leadership; pluralisation; police reform; police role and mandate; professionalisation; social transformation and technology

---

INTRODUCTION

Recent proposals for police reform suggest that the Conservative government regard the service as the last bastion of an unreformed public sector, stuck to insular practices and policies that have not been subjected to the modernisation that neo-liberalism has wrought on other public institutions. As much of the discussion in the preceding chapters of this book testifies, this narrative justification for austerity drives, workforce modernisation and pluralisation does not sit comfortably with the contemporary historical evidence. The police service has been subject to close political attention and successive waves of reform that can be traced back at least as far as the early 1990s.

Neo-liberal reforms might have been applied earlier to the heath service, to local government and to education so the police service might be a 'late-adopter' but it has not been excluded from new public management, marketisation, and pressures to deliver in terms of efficiency and effectiveness.

This chapter reviews some of the key themes that emerge from the preceding discussion. These are explored in the context of current trends that are likely to shape the future of police and policing in the near future. Reiner (2013: 176) noted that 'criminologists are not gifted with Mystic Meg powers of prophesying the future' and it is apposite to also admit that the discipline finds it difficult enough to reach a consensus on past events without also seeking expert insight into the future. With this in mind the discussion that follows claims no more than to be a tentative foreshadowing of patterns, problems and possibilities that seem likely to be of continuing influence as the service approaches the 200th anniversary of the 'new police'. To this end the discussion is organised around three key topics related to the internal organisation of policing: professionalisation, the potential of 'scientific policing' and technology, and pluralisation. This is followed by a review of broader trends that might influence not only the institutional character of policing but also the role of policing in society more widely. This is focused on the potential impact of economic austerity and social transformation on policing. The conclusion reconsiders the role and mandate of the police service in the light of these future propsects. All of these topics are interrelated and there is no suggestion that this is an exhaustive catalogue of future directions.

PROFESSIONALISATION

Chan (2003) argued that the promotion of professionalism has been an important logic of police reform alongside bureaucratic measures and quasi-market approaches encompassing targets and league tables. More recently, Neyroud's (2011) report into police training and leadership argued that the service needs to develop a more professional approach in order to deliver outcomes that meet public expectations and complement a new framework of democratic accountability. Neyroud (2011) argued that the police service needs to be transformed from one that acts professionally to a service that is professional. This distinction is widely made in much of the recent literature on professionalism (see Sklansky, 2011, 2013; Fleming, 2013) and is based on an understanding that a wide range of occupations might act professionally in terms of providing a high level of service and meeting customer standards but that this is somewhat less than conditions which make for a more ideal type of professionalism. In order to meet the latter, the police service would need to implement professional hallmarks associated with doctors, lawyers, architects and so on. These include requirements for high-level pre-entry qualification (perhaps a tertiary-level qualification), professional licensing and a degree of self-regulation and autonomy, perhaps such as is offered by the Law Society or the General Medical Council. Following Neyroud's report, the College of Policing was established in 2011 to act as professional body for policing. The College delivers a range of services in terms of training, education, scientific support and dissemination of best practice in order to fulfil five outcomes:

- Understand needs in policing.
- Identify 'what works' in policing.
- Share knowledge and enable its use.
- Develop, maintain and test standards.
- Enable professional development.

Some of these functions were previously delivered by other agencies that have been subsumed within the College, and so are not distinctly new elements. An innovative aspect of the College's role is to licence and regulate training delivered to police forces by external providers, including universities. Establishing policing as a profession will require new officers to complete a Certificate of Knowledge in Policing prior to joining the service, the intention being to provide for a common framework for all officers and to improve standards and expertise. In the longer term the government intends transforming the College into a statutory body, independent of government, and with regulatory powers. These developments indicate that police professionalism will continue to be a significant element of the reform agenda reviewed more widely in this chapter. Other aspects of the professionalism debate that will impact on the police service in the coming years include workforce modernisation and efforts to enhance leadership, possibly through the introduction of direct entry of staff into senior ranks from outside of the service. Workforce modernisation is currently primarily associated with the Winsor (2011) review of police pay and terms and conditions. Winsor, who subsequently became Her Majesty's Inspector of Constabulary, recommended fundamental changes to the structure of the workforce in an effort to allow for greater flexibility in relation to roles and remuneration. This would, the report argued, allow for greater professional specialism. Debates about the quality and effectiveness of police leadership have continued for many decades in Britain, certainly as long ago as the 1930s (Reiner, 2000). In 2010 the Home Office published proposals to allow for talented individuals to be appointed directly into leadership ranks, rather than the established policy that all officers join at the lowest rank and then 'work their way up' to senior positions (Home Office, 2010b). The traditional model, it has been argued, deters talented leaders from a career in policing. In 2013 the government launched a further consultation process and ministers have signalled a commitment to ensuring that direct entry is introduced (Home Office, 2013).

Fleming (2013) noted that, as much as the components of the professionalisation agenda might be laudable, they reiterate aspirations that have been pursued in different countries for many decades. Early in the twentieth century, for example, Augustus Vollmer, Chief of Police in Chicago – often identified as the 'father' of modern American policing – proposed that all police recruits be required to complete a degree programme in order to develop the professional status of the service (Polk and Armstrong, 2001). In recognising the historical antecedents of current commitments Fleming (2013) draws attention to the considerable barriers that have thwarted previous ambitions to develop police professional status. These barriers have included resistance from police labour organisations and aspects of police working culture, but are also related to fundamental issues in respect of the role and mandate of police services. Judging the impact that elements of professionalisation might have on police work is made more difficult in the absence of a clear consensus about the mandate of the police service. A crime-control model of policing might emphasise that professional investigations deliver better outcomes in terms of detection and prosecution but the broad range of service roles and symbolic functions fulfilled by police are more difficult to evaluate. The impact of enhanced police officer education – a key element of professionalism – is difficult to assess because it is not clear which criteria should be used to measure officer performance. Wimshurst and Ransley (2007: 107) noted 'there remains widespread uncertainty in the research literature about what a university education means in terms of doing a "better" job of policing' and that this uncertainty is rooted in the ambiguity surrounding how 'doing a "better" job' is defined.

Other ambiguities relate to established notions of police work that emphasis craft aspects of the role. This model emphasises that policing constitutes a diverse range of practices that are learnt through direct experience and based on understanding gleaned from colleagues that is communicated through informal as well as formal routes. Craft models of policing reflect principles that the police officer is a 'citizen in uniform' and that many aspects of police work do not require specialist professional knowledge but are relatively routine and prosaic. A number of studies of police work have suggested that many aspects of the job are unskilled and based upon custom and practice more than professional knowledge (Reiner, 1978; Holdaway, 1983), and policing does not tend to be ranked as a profession in classifications of occupational status. Critics of programmes to professionalise policing have often argued that they risk detaching policing from the public and of elevating expertise over responding to the demands of the community. Sklansky (2013) noted that professionalism in policing has been resisted on the basis that self-regulation and the development of an internal discourse about what constitutes appropriate responses to crime and social problems might be problematic. He characterised the tension about the ambiguity of police professionalism in the following terms: 'if professionalism means arrogance and a lack of accountability, no one favors it; if it means thoughtful, reflective, ethical policing, no one is against it' (Sklansky, 2013).

EVIDENCE-BASED POLICING AND TECHNOLOGY

Debates about professionalisation are closely related to the potential to improve policing services through the more systematic use of scientific methods and principles. Better understanding of crime hot spots or more sophisticated knowledge of the potential for perpetrators of domestic violence to reoffend can be obtained through robust evaluation and analysis that applies scientific principles used in other sectors to the policing environment. Transforming evidence into intelligence that is useful in operation terms is possible because IT systems and software have the capacity to provide real-time analysis. The National Police Chiefs' Council (undated) acknowledge that 'digital policing' using social media as a means of communication with the public will provide new opportunities, but that the growth of online crime will pose significant challenges. Studies of crime and social media have tended to focus on the capacity of the latter to help police in responding to major incidents (such as the London Riots; see Lewis et al., 2011) or on public reaction to terrorist or significant crime issues (such as the murder of Lee Rigby; see Innes, 2015), but relatively little attention has been paid to the use of social media in more routine police practices (although Schneider's 2016 work adds useful perspective). Bullock (2016) argues that these contemporary online forms of police–public communication strategies amount to a strategic aim to 'manage impressions' of the police – in pursuit of representing police 'order' in a controlled way.

The potential contribution of science to policing has been advocated alongside the promotion of experimental criminology more broadly. Both endorse the application of scientific advances, for example relating to collection and analysis of DNA samples collected at crime scenes, and the use of evaluative methodologies to assess the effectiveness of policing techniques and innovations. In a recent paper advocating that scientific approaches ought to have a central role in policing, Weisburd and Neyroud (2011) noted that law-enforcement contrasts very poorly with sectors such as agriculture and medicine when it comes to investment in technological innovation and evaluation. In the UK, they argued, government investment in medical research amounts to £600 million per year, whereas the annual Home Office budget for crime research amounted to just £2 million. If police services are to be delivered more effectively to meet public expectations in a period of financial austerity, and the professional reputation of policing is to be enhanced, Weisburd and Neyroud (2011: 12) proposed that:

> Police science must 'make the scene' and become part of the policing world. Police involvement in science must become more generally valued and rewarded. For that to happen, the policing industry must take ownership of police science. Police science is often irrelevant to the policing world today because it is not part of the policing enterprise but something external to it. To take ownership the police will have to take science seriously, and accept

that they cannot continue to justify their activities on the basis of simplistic statistics, often presented in ways that bias findings to whatever is advantageous to the police. We accept that this is not a straightforward challenge.

Weisburd and Neyroud (2011) argued that it is the political, institutional and cultural contexts of policing that make the development of a new paradigm of police science challenging. Sherman (2013) argued, perhaps more optimistically, that the 2012 establishment of the College of Policing, which has as a primary function the promotion of evidence-based policing, means that British policing is now well placed to build upon positive approaches that have developed in only a piecemeal way over recent years. He suggested that the three 'R's of traditional policing (Random patrol, Rapid response, Reactive investigations) are being replaced by a triple-T (Targeting, Testing, Tracking) model that makes use of scientific principles and practices.

It might be that the contested and ambivalent mandate of policing makes a scientific evidence-based model difficult. If the role and function of the police service cannot easily be identified, then it is difficult to imagine how it can be scientifically evaluated in overall terms. Clearly scientific innovations can contribute to the investigation of crime, enhance police communications and provide for better health and safety of officers, but not all aspects of policing can easily be subjected to scientific evaluation or the rigours of the randomised control trial. Not only are there significant methodological challenges to be overcome in the development of scientific evaluation of police interventions (Hope, 2009), but many key functions of policing are inherently subjective, open to interpretation and fundamentally contested. A classic police function – routine foot patrol – illustrates these conundrums very clearly. It might be that rigorous analysis could measure the impact of routine foot patrol in relation to crime rates, deterrence and public reassurance, three of the primary reasons often advanced for this iconic element of police work, but the performance of officers on the beat remains a matter of subjective interpretation. The value of patrol work in one respect cannot be easily assessed against the impact that it might have in another domain. If patrol work has no impact in terms of deterrence but is positively correlated to public reassurance, for example, then the overall value of patrol work remains a matter for discussion and debate.

Closely coupled to debates about the role of scientific evidence in policing are questions about the capacity of technology to transform traditional practices. Innes (2013) explored the possibility that new generations of web-based technology mean that officers might be able to process and access data more directly than in the past and that this might enable them to make better use of scientific evidence. A limitation of crime analysis has been the difficulty of translating robust evidence about crime problems and patterns into operational practice in an environment where much police work has been continued on a craft basis of custom and practice. Smart phone technology, for example, offers the potential for officers to directly access apps that could enable them to effectively utilise information in a way that can make evidence-based policing a meaningful part of routine police activity. Innes and Roberts (2011) suggested that the increased scope to apply situational intelligence via new technology to frontline police work could form part of a fundamental transformation in police practice and organisation. More recent work by Chan and Bennett Moses (2017), however, cautions that the capacity of big data to transform police work might be limited since organisational frameworks mean that technological developments continue to be focused on enhancing existing strategies around crime investigation. Wider possibilities to transform policing through using data were recognised by staff engaged in technological work, but their conception often was not shared by those in operational roles. Chan and Bennett Moses' (2017: 315) study of big data and law-enforcement in Australia led them to comment that

> [w]hile data was considered useful for past-focused activities (e.g. detection and investigation), future-oriented exercises (e.g. prevention, disruption or risk-reduction), as well as 'real time' operations (e.g. situational awareness, monitoring of events), the focus was almost always on identifying and learning about individuals rather than understanding broader trends.

PLURALISATION

As was outlined in Chapter 10, debates about the pluralisation of policing have tended to focus on the role of the private sector in relation to public police. Internationally, researchers have sought to establish trends in terms of the relative number of private security personnel to public police officers and the range of policing tasks that have passed from public to private hands. Concerns have been raised about the quality and efficiency and about the 'legitimacy deficit' that stems from a lack of democratic oversight of the private security industry. All of these debates continue to be important but the central notion of pluralisation needs to be understood as more than a binary distinction between public and private. Loader (2000) identified five key domains in which policing as a process of social regulation is delivered, as outlined in Figure 10.1. Useful though this conceptualisation of policing is, the future direction of pluralisation might mean that there is increasing co-production and diversification within sectors as well as between sectors. In terms of public policing, for example, it is clear that financial and other pressures to reform the delivery of policing will mean that a blended approach incorporating traditional police and other agencies is likely to become the norm. Some of the change instigated by the professionalism agenda and an enhanced role for science and technology will mean that private companies are likely to become more closely embroiled in the design and delivery of policing services. If policing incorporates social media and web-based technology, then those engaged in the development of software and hardware will have an enhanced role as the nature of police patrol is transformed

(Innes and Roberts, 2011). Scientific analysis to underpin evidence-based policing will mean that technical staff will contribute to the development of strategy and operational deployment, and the evidential basis might be co-produced using universities or private companies with specialist skills. Pluralisation will impact on internal culture and workforce arrangements in an environment where the police technologist and analyst are as significant as the detective or the custody sergeant.

Predicting the future scope or direction of plural policing is difficult, partly due to the clear residual significance of the public police within the cultural and symbolic dimension of civil society. For all that police services and politicians have argued that all aspects of police work could be 'contested' by the private sector, the experiences of Surrey and West Midlands police, as discussed in Chapter 10, suggests that public and political problems remain. While the government remains committed to exploring new frontiers for the private sector within criminal justice – and this has led to the privatisation of prisons and the contracting of private companies to deliver probation – these developments continue to be subject to political contingencies.

Alongside concerns about cost and efficacy of moving policing functions into the private sector are debates over the extent to which democratic oversight can be applied to bodies outside the public sector. Many of these issues have been reviewed in Chapters 4 and 10, but it is important to underline that, coupled with some of the other future trends identified in this chapter, these raise important concerns about legitimacy and public consent. Antipathy towards 'policing for profit' raises significant ethical and political debates that have operational implications given that much of the research evidence suggests that public support for police and belief in the rule of law depends on perceptions of procedural justice (Hough et al., 2010). While private security might behave professionally and with integrity – and on occasion the public police might not – they might remain beyond the democratic oversight that is embodied in established legal and political frameworks.

Although private security has faced some reversal in recent years, as Crawford (2013) noted, the private security industry continues to see policing as an area of potential growth. Their optimism might be well-founded given that financial pressures on the public sector, coupled with increasing public demand for security and the significance of private space all look likely to create increasing opportunities that will see the policing sector becoming further pluralised. The increasing centrality of cyberspace in human interaction and transaction also will mean an enhanced role for private corporations who regulate the virtual world more easily than territorially-based police services. Even when professional specialists from the public police, such as the Child Exploitation Online Protection Service, are engaged in policing the web they will operate in close collaboration with software agencies, internet service providers and other commercial groups. Furthermore, Police and Crime Commissioners play an important role in terms of procuring a range of crime-related services from local providers, including private and third-sector providers. Their joint oversight of policing and wider community safety partners also encourages the police service to work more closely with a plurality of agencies.

For these reasons, Crawford (2013) advised that policing will continue to become increasingly pluralised in the future. He suggested that we need to focus on the broad definition of policing as social regulation that was outlined in Chapter 1:

> [I]t is inappropriate and misleading to think about the future of policing solely, or even pre-dominantly, in terms of the activities carried out by the state agency we refer to as 'the police' … the future of policing is likely to be increasingly pluralised and multifaceted. This process of pluralisation is to be found occurring both inside the police organisation – in terms of changes to the workforce, the fracturing of the notion of the omnicompetent police constable and the essential role played by civilians, not least PCSOs and 'designated officers' – and outside the police among the diverse providers of specialist policing functions, private security and novel kinds of formalised secondary social control.

The three trends that will shape the future of policing that have been discussed above broadly relate to the internal development of police services. The final two reviewed below will certainly impact upon the interior organisation and delivery of policing but they extend more widely across a host of institutions. General patterns of social transformation and their impact on policing are discussed further below, but the discussion now turns to the impact that financial austerity might have on British policing.

FINANCIAL AUSTERITY

The trajectory of the economy, fiscal policy and government spending plans are beyond the scope of this text and very difficult to forecast, especially given wider uncertainty arising from Brexit. What seems relatively certain is that public expenditure will continue to be subject to downward pressures for the medium term as the economic shock caused by the banking crisis that developed from 2007 continues to be felt in many leading economies. The appropriate political and economic response to that crisis inevitably is a matter of debate but for the purpose of discussion it is assumed that the police service will face ongoing budget restrictions for the foreseeable future. The 2010 government spending review implemented a programme of expenditure cuts that reduced police funding by 20 per cent over the period to 2015. This period of austerity forced police to reconfigure provisions with fewer officers and support staff. This has promoted debate about the most appropriate way to organise and deliver policing functions; as has been discussed, this has driven much of the recent efforts to promote pluralism. Police leaders and politicians have tended to claim that achieving greater efficiency through pluralisation, better procurement practices and collaboration between police services in terms of the provision of some support services means that public spending on policing can be reduced without cutting 'frontline' services. Inevitably this has led to prolonged discussion of what aspects of the diverse functions the police fulfil should be considered 'frontline' and which might be categorised as 'middle' or 'back office'. Frontline police activities have been defined as those that involve routine interaction with the public, a definition that serves to value some aspects of police work over others. In terms of the internal organisation of public policing, financial austerity looks likely to continue to shape other trends reviewed in this chapter. The professionalisation agenda and further pluralisation are responses, in part, to the impact of financial restrictions on the public sector. In some respects, though, austerity will be in tension with these other trends. A reduction of police salaries, for example, has seen the starting salary for a new recruit fall by £4,000 to £19,000 from 2013 and many forces have imposed recruitment freezes in response to funding cuts. In the 2015 public spending review the government announced that police budgets would not be further reduced and that inflationary rises would be in place until 2019.

Financial austerity clearly has an impact on society as a whole and there are two distinct ways in which the effects of wider reductions in public expenditure might impact on the police. First, public sector spending cuts will see significant reductions in funding for a host of community safety, youth, education and social services that have become increasingly integrated into policing and crime prevention over the last 15 years or so. The development of Crime and Disorder Reduction Partnerships has been a core feature of community safety strategy since the late 1990s. A problem identified by research examining the effectiveness of these partnerships has been the tendency for them to be dominated by police services such that other agencies that might have different perspectives on priorities and approaches to local problems have been marginalised (Hughes, 2007). Funding cuts across all partner agencies might reduce their scope to engage in partnership activities, which might mean that a police-centric approach becomes further embedded. Demands on police resources look likely to increase if other agencies are forced to withdraw their services. Closure of youth service provisions might lead to increasing use of public spaces, which might increase problems of crime and antisocial behaviour. Reductions in funding for emergency and social housing are likely to exacerbate the chaotic lifestyles of prolific offenders and extend their criminal activities. While cuts to public sector provision will be implemented differently between local authorities and will not be uniform either in extent or in terms of the focus of budget restrictions, it seems highly likely that they will have a disproportionate impact upon disadvantaged communities that do not have the social or other capital to withstand a withdrawal in services. The service role of police officers in responding to the needs of vulnerable and marginalised communities – which led Bayley (1994) to describe patrol officers as 'tour guides in the museum of human frailty' – will be greatly extended in a recessionary period as other social and welfare services are diminished. In addition, demand on the police to intervene might rise from a public more anxious about perceived threats to their safety and security.

Related to cuts in public expenditure is the possibility that the recession will have an impact on crime rates. Previous attempts to research the extent and nature of the relationship between crime trends and the economic environment have been fraught with difficulty and there is little consensus on whether there is any relationship between, for example, unemployment and property crime (see Finklea, 2010, for a recent overview of the literature). As Box's (1987) influential study noted, the evidence linking unemployment to crime is relatively weak, and different conclusions might be reached in relation to different types of offending. While there might be a weak link between unemployment and property crime, such that a rise in the former leads to a much smaller increase in the latter, it might be that a rising unemployment leads to a reduction in other types of offending that might be linked to consumption, such as violence associated with the night-time economy. A reduction in personal income that might prevent individuals socialising, and committing crime, in bars and city streets might, on the other hand, increase domestic violence if the consumption of alcohol is more likely to take place in the home. This echoes Field's (1990) analysis of long-term trends in the relationship between crime and the economy, which suggested that patterns and trends in consumption have a greater influence on offending than does unemployment. What the results of such analysis means in terms of future demands on the police service is uncertain: while it might not be the case that a period of austerity will necessarily increase crime, it might mean that the type and nature of offending will change if the pattern and extent of consumption is altered by the worsening economic climate.

As well as operating in a different environment in terms of crime, policing will be affected by heightened challenges in terms of maintaining public order. While the causes and consequences of the urban unrest of summer 2011 remain contested, if there are associations with social inequality then it seems likely that the police service will face a growing demand in terms of responding to relatively spontaneous incidents of public disorder as well as those associated with more organised political protests. The recent experiences of policing protest groups such as UK Uncut and Occupy London (and equivalent) seem likely to loom larger on the horizon in a period of financial austerity.

SOCIAL TRANSFORMATION

It is likely that every aspect of the discussion in previous chapters illustrates the relationship between policing and social transformation. The historical development of policing over time – whichever interpretation is preferred – and changes to the legal and institutional powers available to the police reflect developments in wider social and political history. The expansion of constabularies in the nineteenth century reflected wider trends in the development of the infrastructure of the nation state. These in turn influenced frameworks of police governance that have been remodelled and reshaped under new circumstances. More recently nineteenth-century models of policing have come under increased pressure as the sovereignty of the nation state has been transformed by globalisation and by new technological possibilities that make global communications and transactions a central component in the lives of citizens. The impact of social media on the policing of public disorder in the context of the 2011 London riots has been subject of considerable interest as participants were seen to be able to communicate and plan strategies and tactics in ways that were not possible in previous periods (*Guardian*/LSE, 2011; Riots Communities and Victims Panel, 2012). A few years earlier, similar technology was seen to offer democratic potential in the various uprisings that became known as the Arab Spring, during which citizens were able to communicate and campaign outside of the confines of control of repressive regimes (Skinner, 2011). In terms of police accountability, information technology has proved powerful in many cases: from the video recording of the police assault on Ian Tomlinson at the G20 protests in London (Greer and McLaughlin, 2010) to the cases where mobile phones have been used to record officers making incriminating comments to members of the public (as was discussed in Chapter 11).

Intimately related to technological developments are processes of globalisation that also unsettled the policing landscape. Modern policing systems – that is, as established in the nineteenth century – are organised territorially around individual beats, divisional command units, police service areas and the boundaries of nation states. Increasing mobility – in terms of individuals, capital, technology and security threats such as environmental degradation – mean that social regulation becomes increasingly detached from territory. The security problems posed by climate change that causes flooding and drives human migration mean that challenges police forces in one territory face originate externally, and might ultimately be global in origin. As Stenning and Shearing (2011) noted, the chief of the Australian Federal Police claimed that global warming was a major challenge to law-enforcement agencies in that country, which not only suggests a broadening of the police mandate but also that the geography of policing is being transformed.

Social transformation will also continue to impact on policing in terms of public demand for responsive services that meet heightened expectations. As Innes (2011) and Holdaway (2013) have noted, the 2010–15 coalition government's commitment to the Big Society represents something of a continuum of established ideas of Neighbourhood Policing such that active citizens be encouraged to participate in the design and delivery of the services that they receive. Innes (2011) noted that a key element of this strategy has been that police ought to 'see like citizens' such that they come to understand, and respond to, the interest and demands of the public. The introduction of local crime maps and the establishment of Police and Crime Commissioners are intended to complement these strategies such that police become more closely enmeshed in local communities and democratic oversight is strengthened at a local level. As has been discussed at various stages in this book, these are bold ambitions and questions remain in relation to cultural barriers within policing that might be resistant to greater involvement in community policing. Additionally the means by which principles of democracy and consent that underpin Neighbourhood Policing can be extended to other agencies within plural policing networks are not clear. It also remains to be seen to what extent multiple and competing community priorities can be reconciled within a coherent operational police strategy. If aspects of current models of community policing, transparency and democratic accountability represent something of a continuation of principles of policing by consent, then it seems likely that wider social transformations in terms of political individualism and the relations of citizens to the state seem likely to create an environment in which policing is increasingly subject to public examination and increasingly tested. In a neo-liberal environment were citizens are 'consumers' of public services it seems likely that the demands placed on policing agencies will increase and become more complex.

CONCLUSION

Each of the previous issues identified as likely to shape the future direction of policing raises, implicitly or explicitly, the fundamental question that was discussed in the first chapter of this book: What is policing? Given that this concluding chapter is an exercise in future-gazing, perhaps that question can be reworked to 'What should policing be?' It was been widely noted in this discussion that the role and mandate of the police is complex and potentially very broad. While there has rarely been a straightforward answer to the question that could bear much scrutiny, it is certainly the case that the various pressures that will shape policing in the future have led to a series of effort to reconsider the underlying mandate of the police. Millie (2013) argued that the expansion of policing from the mid-1990s until 2010 was about increasing resources and officer numbers but was also reflected in a widening brief for the service. As public police services became enmeshed in networks delivering community safety, offender management provisions and a host of social policy functions, then the mandate of the service became increasingly broad and blurred. A period of contraction, caused by austerity measures, might provide useful, Millie argued, as it provides cause to reconsider the remit of police and to develop a more focused and narrow set of responsibilities. To some extent this is what the coalition government sought to do. In a speech to the Association of Chief Police Officers in 2011, the Home Secretary announced plans to abolish the plethora of targets that had been introduced to measure performance. In their place, the Home Secretary announced that the police would be subject to only one measure: crime reduction (May, 2011). Loader (2013) argued that this pledge was part of a fundamental government strategy that was intended to 'release the police's inner crime-fighter'. More recently, though, the National Police Chiefs' Council (NPCC) (undated, 4) vision for policing to 2025 provided a wider interpretation of the role of the police, rediscovering a broader mandate:

[The mission is] to make communities safer by upholding the law fairly and firmly; preventing crime and antisocial behaviour; keeping the peace; protecting and reassuring communities; investigating crime and bringing offenders to justice.

The difference between the Home Secretary and NPCC might seem narrow but in that gap lays a host of potential functions that could hugely expand the horizons of policing. Expectations that the public police might retreat into a relatively narrow crime-fighting role and leave other agencies to take over tasks extraneous to this core mandate might be consistent with political and popular cultural assumptions that police officers are primarily concerned with law-enforcement. As soon as the mandate is expanded, as the HMIC suggests, then the scope of police work broadens considerably. That wider definition is consistent with the historical functions of the police and is inevitable if it is accepted that prevention of crime and disorder could entail a very broad range of tasks. Conceptually this does not provide for a clear or tidy view of the public police mandate. Nonetheless, a broad definition is preferable for other reasons, not the least of which is that the continued provision of a wide public service ethos means that there is at least the opportunity to pursue policing that is legitimate, democratic and accountable.

chapter summary

- Although policing has experienced many waves of reform, current pressures to change are of a far-reaching character and might mean that key principles and organisation will be fundamentally reshaped in the years leading up to the 200th anniversary of the 'new' Metropolitan Police.

- The development of police professionalism has led to a host of changes to internal training and recruitment practices, to leadership and the conduct of police work. The professionalisation agenda focuses on creating police services that are self-regulating and operate high levels of internal regulation and develop a core body of expertise and knowledge. The College of Policing has been established to promote professional policing and it is intended that the College will be become a statutory body with regulatory powers.

- Ambiguities relating to professionalisation stem from the difficulties of defining how 'best practice' in policing can be defined. There are also concerns that some elements of professionalisation might mean that the service becomes more insular and less accountable to the general public.

- Evidence-based policing and more effective use of technology form another dimension of police development. The application of scientific principles and practices offer the possibility for more effective practice in terms of officer deployment and crime investigation and prevention. More embedded technology (through smart phones and social media, for example) would provide the means to effectively integrate such evidence into routine police activity.

- Although science and technology can contribute to specific aspects of policing it might be more difficult to see how they can be extended across the broad remit. The value of community policing, for example, is difficult to quantify and measure since much of what it intends to achieve relates to subjective concepts such as 'public reassurance'.

- Pluralisation of policing has usually been examined in terms of the different sectors that contribute to broad processes of policing. It seems likely that delivery of a blended approach within sectors will become increasingly common as public police employ private contractors and volunteers and external agencies provide services to the public sector.

- Concerns about the quality of private provisions have emerged and challenges in relation to accountability and governance will be exacerbated given the transnational operation of many private police agencies. Nonetheless, it seems inconceivable that pluralisation will not continue to develop.

- Financial austerity might impact on policing in three key ways. First, in terms of the pressures wrought by reductions in public spending on police services. These will mean reductions in personnel. Second, concurrent reductions in expenditure on other agencies that also fulfil roles that reduce crime and disorder might mean that the police – the service of last resort – faces an increased workload. Third, demands on police services might also be increased if cuts in welfare spending, rising unemployment and associated social problems fuel a rise in crime or public disorder.

- Social changes in terms of globalisation, environmental change, technology and communications will combine to transform the context in which policing is delivered. They will create new challenges for governments and many agencies but these will be particularly significant for the police since they are difficult to reconcile with the territorial basis of modern policing.

- Other social transitions related to the nature of citizenship will have implications for policing. The principles of community and Neighbourhood Policing might represent early forms of Big Society activity, incorporating inclusiveness, voluntarism and grass-roots engagement in delivery of services.

- It might be difficult to extend democratic accountability to a pluralised policing environment, though, and the development of a more individualistic consumer-based society will mean that increasingly complex demands are made on police services.

- Many of these dimensions that will shape the future direction of policing raise important questions about the role and mandate of policing. Recent statements by the Home Secretary have envisioned a future in which police have crime-fighting as their core mandate. This narrow perspective may be politically appealing and consistent with popular media and cultural representations. It does not bear much scrutiny, however, in terms of the wide range of functions police have performed historically.

- A wider perspective on the police mandate, which incorporates crime prevention and service roles, is less tidy but at least provides a framework to develop forms of policing that secure public consent an can be legitimate, democratic and accountable.

self-check questions (with answers at the back of the book)

1. Alongside what other factors did Chan (2003) suggest that professionalism had been an important component of police reform?

2. What did Vollmer suggest ought to be required of all Chicago police recruits in order to enhance professionalism?

3. How much did Weisburd and Neyroud suggest the UK government spent on medical research and on crime research?

4. What are the triple-Ts that might underpin scientific models of policing?

5. Which police services withdrew plans to consider privatising police services in the aftermath of problems relating to policing the London 2012 Olympics?

6. What role might Police and Crime Commissioners play in the development of pluralism?

7. What proportion of police funding was cut in the 2010 government spending review?

8. What did Field (1990) suggest had a stronger impact on offending – unemployment rates or patterns of consumption?

9. The chief of which service suggested that global warming would be a major challenge for police?

10. How did Loader (2013) characterise government strategy to refocus police work?

study questions

1. What might be reasons to argue that policing ought not to be understood as a profession?

2. In relation to different police functions consider whether policing can be delivered on the basis of scientific evidence.

3. What would be the consequences of the wholesale privatisation of policing?

annotated further reading

A collection of essays edited by Jennifer Brown (*The Future of Policing*, 2013) provides an excellent overview of contemporary challenges and debates, and includes perspectives from around the world.

Issues relating to the potential for scientific and evidence-based criminology are debated in a series of articles published in volume 9 of *Criminology and Criminal Justice*. In his article in that journal Sherman makes a case for evidence-based criminology, which is critiqued in articles by Hope and Tilley.

The National Police Chiefs' Council website contains useful documentation on current and future developments, including Policing Vision 2025, available at www.npcc. police.uk/.

annotated listings of links to relevant websites

The Police Executive Research Forum was established in the USA in the 1970s and provides a wide range of publications and research reports related to debates addressed throughout this book. The Forum's website is www.policeforum.org/.

The College of Policing website provides a similar range of material and is particularly useful for those interested in learning more about the professionalisation debate: www. college.police.uk. The Society for Evidence-Based Policing website also contains useful information on this strategy: www.sebp.police.uk/

There are a number of useful blogs and websites offering debate and opinion on contemporary policing. Among these are the Police Oracle site www.policeoracle.com/; the British Society of Criminology Policing Network blog http://bscpolicingnetwork.wordpress.com/pn-blog/; and the police chiefs' blog www.npcc.police.uk/ThePoliceChiefsBlog/.

annotated links to journal articles

A special edition of *Criminology and Criminal Justice* examined the impact of financial austerity on contemporary policing and the articles below develop many of the debates explored in this chapter:

Millie, A. (2013) 'The Policing Task and the Expansion (and Contraction) of British Policing', *Criminology and Criminal Justice*, 13: 143–60.

Reiner, R. (2013) 'Who Governs? Democracy, Plutocracy, Science and Prophecy in Policing', *Criminology and Criminal Justice*, 13: 161–80.

Hough, M. (2013) 'Procedural Justice and Professional Policing in Times of Austerity', *Criminology and Criminal Justice*, 13: 181–97.

The consequences of insecurity in the urban environment generates demands on policing, and the context of these trends is outlined in:

Sparks, R., Girling, E., and Loader, I. (2001) 'Fear and Everyday Urban Lives', *Urban Studies*, 38 (5–6): 885–98.

Glossary

Accountability: the legal and regulatory systems that govern the police service. While the principle of operational independence means that the police service enforces the law without political interference, the priority and general direction of policing in Britain has been overseen by arrangements that combine local and central governance. More specifically, management and auditing procedures seek to hold individual police officers to account by scrutinising their work in an effort to promote efficiency and effectiveness. Police officers are also held to account by complaints and disciplinary systems. The prospects of accountability in an era when the role of private security and plural policing is increasingly salient are much debated.

Antisocial behaviour: low-level persistent nuisance behaviour, not all of which is criminal, traditionally has not been a high priority for police services, even though it has been a significant problem in many communities. The Crime and Disorder Act 1998 introduced Antisocial Behaviour Orders (ASBO) that seek to regulate future conduct. Police or local authorities can apply for an ASBO in the magistrates' court. Although ASBOs are civil-law provisions, breaching them is a criminal offence. Antisocial Behaviour Contracts (ABCs) are a lower-level intervention that seek provide a framework whereby individuals or families are offered support in return for their commitment to improved conduct. The number of ASBOs issued has declined steeply in recent years. From 2014, ASBOs have been replaced by Criminal Behaviour Orders.

Arrest: there are various common law and statute provisions determining the circumstances in which a person can be arrested. Essentially these fall into two categories: those conducted under the terms of a court warrant and those carried out without warrant. The former applies to circumstances in which it is necessary to enforce an individual to be brought to court in connection with a suspected offence that has already been committed. Arrests without warrant can be implemented in a wide variety of circumstances, some of which rely upon specific legal measures that give police officers particular powers in identified circumstances. For example, public order legislation gives constables power to arrest those wearing political uniforms. Other powers are more generally defined, such that an officer can arrest in relation to 'serious arrestable offences'. More generally yet, citizens and police officers can arrest in the case of an actual or anticipated breach of the peace. Upon arrest an individual is told the grounds on which they are detained and cautioned. They must be taken to a designated police station as soon as is practicable.

Association of Policing and Crime Commissioners: the collective body for Policing and Crime Commissioners that is intended to help PCCs formulate policy and to exchange good practice and mutual support.

Association of Chief Police Officers (ACPO): representative body of senior police officers, all of or above the rank of Assistant Chief Constable or their equivalent in the Metropolitan Police. Originally established as a social network, ACPO came to play an important role as a corporate voice for the police service. It was replaced by the National Police Chiefs' Council in 2015.

Basic Command Unit (BCU): BCUs are responsible for tackling local crime and disorder problems, for working with local partners and for delivering Neighbourhood Policing. Previously BCUs would have been known as divisions or sub-divisions and each is headed by a Chief Superintendent. There are more than 200 across England and Wales.

Black Police Association (BPA): staff association and pressure group that seeks to represent the interests of black and Asian officers and staff. The first BPA was established as a relatively informal support network in the Metropolitan Police in the mid-1990s, since then BPAs have been established in man police service areas and a National Black Police Association acts as an umbrella group and is an important voice in public debate about policing issues. The relation of the BPA and the Police Federation, the established staff association, have sometimes been fraught. The work of BPAs has been supplemented by many other groups representing particular ethnic, cultural and religious minorities within police.

British Association for Women in Policing (BAWP): the Association was established in 1987 and represents women officers and police civilian staff of all ranks and all police services, including the eight Scottish forces, the Police Service of Northern Ireland, the British Transport Police and others. In 2001 the BAWP launched the 'gender agenda', which details aims relating to the service and conditions facing female staff and the broader cultural landscape that has marginalised the position of women in police.

Chief Constable: the senior officer of each of the 43 police services in England and Wales, the eight in Scotland, and the Police Service of Northern Ireland. In terms of governance and accountability, Chief Constables have operational independence in law-enforcement. Chief Constables are appointed by, and accountable to, local police authorities although both matters have been subject to increased scrutiny by the Home Office.

Civilianisation: in an effort to dedicate police officers to operational roles, services have sought to employ civilian staff to perform duties previously allocated to constables. Initially civilian staff were used to perform 'backroom' administrative and support duties but the range of activities have extended to include, for example, scene of crime investigations, prisoner transport, and a host of training and human resource activities.

Closed-Circuit Television (CCTV): surveillance and monitoring systems that provide remote visual, and occasionally audio, images of public and private spaces. As technology has advanced, facial recognition and other software have enhanced the power of CCTV systems. A central component of situational crime prevention strategies the impact on the detection and deterrence of criminal and disorderly behaviour are widely heralded, even though the research evidence on the effects of CCTV often tends to be equivocal. It is frequently claimed that Britain has the highest ratio of CCTV cameras to population of any country in the world.

College of Policing: the College provides information and training on leadership and the development of professional practice to police in England and wales.

Commissioner: the senior officer of the Metropolitan Police, with broadly similar powers and responsibilities as Chief Constables in other police services.

Consent: the doctrine of 'policing by consent' has been influential, even though the police service has always had difficult relations with significant sections of society. The need for the police service to maintain public legitimacy has been a central ethical and democratic principle, and important in terms of effectiveness since the police service require the support and co-operation of the public.

Constable: the office of constable originated during Norman times. All officers enter the police service at the level of constable and, although some statutes give specialist powers to more senior ranks, most legislation confers powers generically to those who hold the office of constable, whatever their rank. These powers are also extended to special constables.

Consultation: the principle that the police ought to consult with local communities has been central to the notion of policing by consent. The legislative requirement for the police to consult has been enhanced by the Crime and Disorder Act 1998 and has been a core principle of Neighbourhood Policing.

Crime control model: the principle that the primary aim of the police service ought to be to prevent and detect crime. Originally outlined by Packer, this model of the criminal justice system prioritises the police role in arresting offenders, gathering evidence and contributing to a quick and efficient conviction. The main purpose of the police is to suppress criminal behaviour, even if this means that officers might occasionally act outside of the law or disregard the rights of suspects; see also **Due process model**.

Crown Prosecution Service (CPS): independent of the police, the CPS is responsible for the prosecution of offenders. Until the CPS was established in 1986, the police prosecuted offenders.

Discretion: the translation of the 'law in books' to the 'law on the street' requires police officers to interpret complex circumstances and make judgements about the most appropriate response, all of which entails the exercise of discretion. While it is inevitable and desirable that officers exercise discretion, considerable and sustained controversies surround the extent to which this is done so inappropriately on the basis of sexist, racist, homophobic or other forms of prejudice, stereotyping and bias. Measures to influence and limit officer discretion also stem from managerial imperatives to effectively deploy resources in an effort to achieve performance targets.

Due process model: emphasises the importance of police officers following rules and procedures to ensure that principles of justice and equity are fulfilled. Outlined by Packer (1964), this model applies to the criminal justice system more generally. In terms of policing, it holds that the police need to ensure that suspects' rights and interests are guaranteed in order that the courts can determine innocence or guilt; see also **Crime control model**.

Ethics: in policing terms references to 'ethics' usually indicates that the service needs to recognise its broader social responsibilities. Officers are encouraged to consider the implications of their actions beyond their responsibilities in terms of law-enforcement and the wider social and cultural context in which they exercise their powers. Codes of ethical behaviour differ from more traditional disciplinary frameworks in that they rarely proscribe behaviour considered unacceptable but instead outline normative ideals to which officers ought to aspire.

Evidence-based policing (EBP): an approach advocating that policing be delivered on the basis of scientifically developed evidence, as other expert professions operate. EBP emphasises that police need to conduct experiments, to develop scientific approaches and to evaluate practice.

'Extended police family': a phrase developed with the police reform agenda in England and Wales in the last decade or so, it recognises that traditional policing activities are increasingly provided by a mixture of sworn constables, special constables, Police Community Support Officers, Neighbourhood Wardens, traffic wardens and other public and private sector agencies.

Frontline policing: much of the debate about the impact of financial austerity on policing has related to the consequences for the 'frontline' of policing. In contrast to 'back office' or 'middle office' functions, HMIC (2011b) defined the term as 'the police front line comprises those who are in everyday contact with the public and who directly intervene to keep people safe and enforce the law'.

Gay Police Association (GPA): formed as the Lesbian and Gay Police Association in 1990, the GPA represents the interests of officers and staff from all sectors of the British police service. The GPA provides specific advice and support to individual members as well as acting as a pressure group within public and policy debates about general policing matters as well as more specific issues such as hate crime.

Her Majesty's Inspectorate of Constabulary (HMIC): the first Inspectors of Constabulary were appointed following the 1856 County and Borough Police Act. The HMIC is a crown agency, although in practice it reports to the Home Office. The HMIC conducts inspections of the performance of all Basic Command Units as well as 'thematic' inspections that review generic matters of importance to the police service.

'Hot spots' policing: a method of organising the deployment of police resources that recognises that crime and disorder tend to be concentrated into certain places and occur at certain times. By using computer-aided mapping systems police managers can make more effective use of resources, although this might mean that less-directed patrol work, popular with the public, is marginalised.

Human rights: issues relating to human rights apply to policing in two broad ways. Specifically human rights legislation that define relations between state and citizens have significant implications on the police service, variously described as the 'state in uniform' and the 'citizen in uniform'. For example, the human right to personal privacy shapes the circumstances in which police officers can conduct surveillance operations. More generally, domestically and internationally policing has been increasingly connected with promoting and securing human rights through ensuring the rule of law and good governance.

'Intelligence-led' policing: a model of policing that promotes effectiveness and efficiency through collecting, collating and analysing information relating to crime. Patterns and trends are examined such that police can intervene in ways that will have the most impact on offenders. Intelligence-led approaches are relatively proactive and interventionist in contrast to more traditional reactive or 'fire-brigade' styles whereby the service responds to demands from the public.

Macpherson Report: published in 1999 the Report into the racist murder of Stephen Lawrence continues to exercise a huge influence on debates about British policing. The Report found that the police service was 'institutionally racist', and had demonstrated weaknesses in the management of the investigation, the preservation of the scene, the gathering of evidence and other shortcomings.

Multi-agency partnerships: a broader range of public sector agencies have assumed a role in crime prevention and community safety in recent years. A locally co-ordinated multi-agency approach to crime prevention had been advocated for many years before the Crime and Disorder Act 1998 placed Crime and Disorder Reduction Partnerships on a statutory footing. The inclusion of housing, education, health, fire service and other agencies from the public, private and voluntary sectors has removed the police's former pre-eminence in crime prevention, although it is often suggested they remain dominant partners amid these networks.

National Police Chiefs' Council: in 2015 ACPO was replaced by the Council. The NPCC describes itself as 'a body bringing together chief officers to share ideas and drive improvements in policing'.

National Policing Improvement Agency (NPIA): established by the Police and Justice Act 2006, the NPIA became operational from 1 April 2007. It has subsequently been subsumed within the College of Policing.

Neighbourhood Policing: the devolution of policing to the level of particular neighbourhoods (coterminous with political wards) has been an important contemporary political priority. It is intended that the establishment of Neighbourhood Policing will reinvigorate contacts between local people and police officers, enhance accountability and improve public confidence in the police service.

Organisational subculture: studies suggest that police work is characterised by a particular organisational subculture and that this can exercise a negative influence on routine policing. The disproportionate exercise of police powers are among the problems often ascribed to the nature of police subculture – sometimes referred to as 'canteen culture' in reference to the unofficial and informal context in which it develops. The concept has been criticised for being overly determinist and for failing to recognise the institutional context in which police officers operate.

Plural policing: while policing has never been the sole preserve of the public police service, increasing attention is paid to the proliferation and range of those who regulate social behaviour. The private security industry pre-dates the public police but the concept of plural policing reflects the wider development of 'third-party' policing whereby agencies such as banks, schools and insurance companies are made responsible for regulating and reporting on aspects of their clients' behaviour. Not only does plural policing mean new constellations of agencies, it also changes principles of policing, raising questions of legitimacy, justice and equity. Pluralisation also means that policing is a property that emerges from relations and networks, rather than being the output of a particular institution; see also **Private security**.

Police and Criminal Evidence Act (PACE) 1984: the central piece of legislation that governs the powers of the police in relation to citizens. PACE outlines the circumstances in which officers can stop and search people, search premises, seize evidence, enter premises, effect arrests and detain suspects. PACE also governs the rights of suspects, including the circumstances in which they are remanded or bailed, and the interview process.

Police and policing: the distinction between police and policing differentiates between the relatively narrow range of activities conducted by the police service and broader processes of social regulation performed more widely by a diverse range of agencies and actors. As an increasing range of public, private and civil sector organisations become involved in law-enforcement, crime prevention and community safety, policing in these broader terms has become more salient.

Police Community Support Officers (PCSOs): auxiliary police staff who do not hold the full powers of constables but provide for a visible police patrol presence. The role of PCSO was created by the Police Reform Act 2001 and has been a major feature of the 'extended police family'.

Police Federation: the organisation that represents all officers up to and including the rank of Chief Inspector. In addition to making it illegal for police officers to strike, the Police Act 1920 created the Federation to represent the interests of frontline staff in respect of welfare and the terms and conditions of employment. In more general terms the Police Federation continues to be a powerful influence on the development of policing.

Police service: a wide variety of police services operate in Britain. Much discussion of policing refers to 'Home Office' police services: the 43 English and Welsh services, Policing Scotland, and the Police Service of Northern Ireland. These constabularies are supplemented by many other specialist services that are governed and operated under other arrangements, including the British Transport Police that works on railways and transport networks, the Ministry of Defence Police that operates on UK military bases domestically and abroad, and the Royal Parks Police that patrols a small number of parks owned by the Crown.

Police Superintendents' Association: as policing has become devolved to local BCUs the role of Superintendent has become increasingly important. The Superintendents' Association was formed in the 1950s and incorporates officers from each of the 43 services in England and Wales as well as the British Transport Police. The Association has some 1,500 members.

Private security: although analysis of policing has tended to concentrate upon the role of the public sector police, private companies have played an important role in crime prevention and control work for very many decades. Reliable estimates of the size and scope of the private security industry are difficult to come by but studies tend to suggest that it is comparable, in terms of the number of staff employed in the sector, with the public police service. In an era when the development of plural policing and the 'extended police family' are high on political and policy agendas the role of the private sector has come under increasing scrutiny; see also **Plural policing**.

Problem-oriented Policing (POP): a model of policing that encourages officers to address underlying dynamics of crime and antisocial behaviour rather than simply respond to incidents as they arise. A creative approach to resolving problems in partnership with other agencies is required by POP, which relies, partly, on mapping and analysing local crime patterns. Research suggests there are often tensions between the principles of POP and the need for police services to respond to demands for assistance from the public.

Rank structure: all police officers begin their careers at the lowest rank of constable, which means that all senior officers have served some time on the 'frontline'. Ascending the hierarchy are ranks of Sergeant, Inspector (and sometimes Chief Inspector), Superintendent (and sometimes Chief Superintendent), Assistant Chief Constable, Deputy Chief Constable, and Chief Constable. Above the rank of Superintendent the position is somewhat different in the Metropolitan Police, where the senior ranks are Commander, Deputy Assistant Commissioner, Assistant Commissioner, Deputy Commissioner and Commissioner.

Service role: although less high profile than crime-fighting and law-enforcement, much police work is characterised in more diffuse terms of service provision. Dealing with missing persons, directing traffic and assisting other emergency services do not directly relate to law-enforcement or crime control, but account for a significant proportion of police work. The first Commissioners of the Metropolitan Police emphasised the 'service' role of the New Police in an effort to court public support, and it has continued to be regarded as an important source of legitimacy.

Special constables: volunteer officers who contribute to a wide range of policing activities on a part-time basis. The role of special constable pre-dates modern professional policing; the current framework governing their work was established by the 1831 Special Constables Act. Special constables have the same legal powers as other constables. As of March 2012 there were 20,343, a significant rise on the 11,598 'Specials' in England and Wales in 2002.

Use of force: while police officers are allowed, in general terms, to use a reasonable degree of force in the exercise of their duties, it is often held that the doctrine of the 'minimal use of force' has been central to securing the legitimacy of the British police. While frequently thought of as an unarmed police force, specialist units providing firearms support are commonly on patrol, and the range of 'less-than-lethal' weapons available to officers has increased as CS-spray and 'tasers' have been deployed.

Visible patrols: as police work became professionalised and reorganised from the late 1960s onward, routine foot patrol became marginalised within police work. Although crime levels have fallen, in broad terms, since the mid-1990s, public concern about crime and disorder has not abated. Increasing the visible presence of officers on patrol has become central to efforts to provide reassurance.

Zero-tolerance Policing (ZTP): usually associated with a proactive and aggressive policing strategy that prioritises intervention against relatively minor offences in order that more serious criminal activity is pre-empted. As well as preventing small problems escalating, ZTP claims to reassure the public by providing a substantial police presence on the streets. While proponents have often claimed that ZTP successfully reduced the crime problem in New York City in the 1990s, critics maintain it has a deleterious effect on relations with marginalised communities.

Answers to Self-check Questions

CHAPTER 1: WHAT IS POLICING?

1. How can narrow and broader definitions of policing be characterised? [narrow set of functions performed by the institution of the police service and the broader processes of social regulation and reproduction that govern everyday lives]

2. What agencies, apart from the police service, play a role in regulating social life? [among others, schools, religious groups, health providers, business sector, and the media]

3. Why did Mawby (2003) argue that media images of policing are important? [media accounts provide the authoritative narrative of policing for large sections of the public]

4. Who provided a 'classic' definition of state sovereignty? [Max Weber: state sovereignty as the possession of a legitimate use of force over a given territory]

5. Why might the 'use of force' offer only a limited understanding of the police function? [among others, the police tend to under-utilise their potential to use force, and other agencies have coercive powers over citizens]

6. In what, very broad, terms did Bittner (1974) define the police task? ['no human problem exists, or is imaginable, about which it could be said with finality that this certainly could not become the proper business of the police.']

7. What proportion of public calls to the police did Bayley (1994) find were related to crime? [seven to ten per cent]

8. How did Ericson and Haggerty (1997) characterise police officers? ['knowledge workers' whose primary role was to communicate risk]

9. What two factors explain, according to research published in 2001, the significant amount of time officers spend within the police station? [processing prisoners in custody and 'other paperwork', such as completing crime and intelligence reports, dealing with missing property and persons]

10. What relation does the police service have to the criminal justice system more generally? [it acts as a 'gateway agency']

CHAPTER 2: HISTORICAL ORIGINS AND DEVELOPMENT OF THE POLICE IN ENGLAND AND WALES

1. What features characterised policing in England between the 1740s and 1850s? [self-policing, community engagement in street patrols, and private sector provision of many policing services]

2. Name the constitutional arrangement that enshrined the key features of policing from the thirteenth century until the establishment of the 'new police' in the nineteenth century [Statute of Winchester]

3. To what did Sir John Fielding attribute the crime problems of the 1740s? [illegal drinking establishments]

4. Who addressed the Chartist rally at St Peter's Field, Manchester 1819 that fuelled concern about using the military to control crowds? [Henry Hunt]

5. How did Storch characterise the role of the police in the mid-nineteenth century? ['domestic missionaries']

6. What measures were introduced in an effort to overcome public suspicion of the 'new police' in the early nineteenth century? [emphasising the service role of the police, deploying police in uniforms distinct from the military, the appearance of the police as unarmed]

7. What proportion of the 3,000 officers recruited to the Metropolitan Police when it was established in 1829 is it estimated were still in post four years later? [Bailey suggested the figure was one-sixth]

8. What legislation required counties to establish a police force? [the 1856 County and Borough Police Act]

9. How do orthodox perspectives explain dissatisfaction with the use of the military to respond to political and social unrest? [practical difficulties compounded by fears that soldiers might side with protestors and 'the mob' rather than the authorities]

10. How do revisionist accounts tend to explain the development of the 'new police'? [in terms of the changing demands of early industrial capitalism, which required the suppression of political disorder and the greater regulation of the urban working class]

CHAPTER 3: POLICE POWERS: THE LEGAL FRAMEWORK

1. How did Sir Robert Mark characterise the power of the police over the citizen? [he suggested that the key feature was that police officers had the power to inconvenience citizens]

2. What was introduced in 1912 to govern the treatment of those held in custody? [the Judges' Rules]

3. What is the general condition for the police powers to stop and search an individual under section 1 of PACE? [that the officer has 'reasonable suspicion' that the individual is in possession of stolen or prohibited items]

4. How does PACE define a 'public place'? [those places to which the public have access, whether upon payment or otherwise, but is not a dwelling]

5. What legislation prohibits police officers from discriminating on grounds such as race, gender, or disability? [the 2010 Equality Act]

6. What documents cannot be searched under the terms of general search warrant? [items identified as legally privileged, for example communication between a client and professional legal advisor, including journalistic documents, medical records and items held in confidence for business purposes]

7. Under what circumstances can magistrates issue a warrant for arrest? [when the identity of an offender is known but the person cannot be located or when an individual has failed to attend court in response to a summons]

8. What conditions does PACE stipulate justify detaining an individual in custody prior to their being charged with an offence? [the detention of a person is only legal if it is necessary to allow further enquiries to be made, for example, to prevent that person from destroying evidence or interfering with witnesses]

9. Why does a concentration on the legal powers granted to the police provide only a partial understanding of police work? [because a focus on the legal framework of police powers reflects a jurisprudential approach to policing that fails to address the cultural and sociological determinants of police practice]

10. How did Loader and Mulcahy characterise the power of senior police officers to identify and define crime problems? [the 'power of legitimate naming']

CHAPTER 4: WHO GUARDS THE GUARDS?

1. Prior to the Police Reform Act 2002, which agencies and groups had advocated the establishment of an independent system to investigate complaints against the police? [the consultancy firm KPMG, the civil rights group Liberty, and the Lawrence Inquiry Report, a report of the Home Affairs Committee of the House of Commons, and the European Committee for the Prevention of Torture and Inhuman or Degrading Treatment or Punishment]

2. What does the 'local resolution' of a complaint against the police entail? ['local resolution' involves the complaint being settled via mediation between the local police service and the complainant, and may involve a local officer investigating the circumstances surrounding the complaint]

3. When was the Code of Ethics of the Police Service of Northern Ireland first established? [2003].

4. Under the terms of the European Convention on Human Rights, what conditions need to be met if individual rights are to be set aside? [in the broader public interest, but only if the breach is necessary and proportionate]

5. What did the Patten Commission into policing in Northern Ireland suggest was the main purpose of the police? [it is a central proposition of this report that the fundamental purpose of policing should be ... the protection and vindication of the human rights of all]

6. What piece of legislation established the office of Police and Crime Commissioner? [2011 Police Reform and Social Responsibility Act]

7. What form of accountability did the government claim was introduced via the establishment of PCCs? [democratic accountability]

8. Why did Shearing and Stenning (1983) suggest that concern about the role of private security had been marginalised in the USA, prior to the 1980s? [questions about social justice and accountability had been marginalised by a conceptualisation of the private sector as the junior partner to the public police]

9. What is the primary requirement of the 2001 Private Security Industry Act? [the primary requirement introduced by the Act is that all personnel – officers, managers and directors of companies – be licensed]

10. What concerns did Loader (2000) suggest are made more salient by the changing environment of international policing? [questions about social justice, accountability, governance and legitimacy]

CHAPTER 5: COMMUNITY POLICING

1. What three elements did Skolnick (2006) suggest characterise community policing initiatives in the USA? [citizen involvement, problem-solving and decentralisation]

2. How did Weatheritt (1987) suggest the term 'community policing' had been used in Britain? ['to denote projects of which authors' approved']

3. Identify four aspects of Alderson's (1979) model of community policing. [to contribute to liberty, equality and fraternity; to help reconcile freedom with security and to uphold the law; to uphold and protect human rights and thus help achieve human dignity; to dispel criminogenic social conditions, through co-operative social action; to help create trust in communities; to strengthen security and feelings of security; to investigate, detect and activate the prosecution of crimes; to facilitate free movement along public thoroughfares; to curb public disorder; to deal with crises and help those in distress involving other agencies where needed]

4. What was the name of the policing model introduced alongside panda cars, two-way radios and other innovations in the late 1960s? [Unit Beat Policing]

5. What legislation required that the police, in partnership with other agencies, conduct audits to establish the community safety needs of local communities? [Crime and Disorder Act 1998]

6. How many people was it estimated lived in areas covered by Neighbourhood Watch schemes? [3.3 million]

7. What did a 2001 HMIC report establish as the three core features of reassurance policing? [visibility, familiarity and accessibility]

8. What features of police work explain the tendency for officers to be culturally isolated from the wider community? [according to Reiner (1978): the boredom, unsociable hours, occasional periods of danger, and the routine exposure to shocking and traumatic events]

9. Why might local residents' perceptions of crime risks not be reliable? [they might not correspond to objective risks facing them]

10. What trend appears to contradict moves to devolve policing closer to local communities? [the apparent increase in central control over the direction of policing]

CHAPTER 6: POLICE CULTURE

1. How did Wilson famously characterise the particular character of police discretion? ['the police department has the special property … that within it discretion increases as one moves down the hierarchy' (Wilson, 1968: 7)]

2. What are the key features of police subculture? [a range of features are often identified: cynicism, suspicion, conservatism, sense of mission, isolation/solidarity, machismo, pragmatism, racial prejudice, orientation to action, 'covering-your-ass']

3. What characterises the 'rotten apples' perspective on police racism? [the 'rotten apples' perspective associates the problem with the negative prejudices and stereotyping of a small minority of officers that has a disproportionate impact on the organisation as a whole]

4. What was the remit of early generations of female police officers? [protecting women and children, dealing with prostitution]

5. What proportion of homophobic crime has it been estimated is not reported to the police? [the National Advisory Group/Policing Lesbian and Gay Communities (1999) found that 80 per cent of homophobic incidents are not reported]

6. In respect of what issues did Colman and Gorman (1982) measure the attitudes of police recruits? [the death penalty and migration]

7. What different 'strains' of police culture have been identified? [between 'street cops' and 'management cops', between different specialist departments, between different nations]

8. In what nation did Moon (2006) suggest police subculture is not resistant to community policing? [South Korea]

9. Who conducted an early study of routine police work in London? [the Policy Studies Institute/ Smith and Gray (1983)]

10. Why might understanding of police culture need to be broadened? [the 'changing terrain of policing', for example, the expansion at local, national and international levels of agencies involved in the process of policing]

CHAPTER 7: POLICING DIVERSITY

1. Why has it been assumed, mistakenly, that concerns about police relations with minority ethnic communities have only developed in recent decades? [because of a mythical view of the golden age of policing in the 1950s and 1960s; in fact, during that period there were problems of police racism, and these can be traced back much further]

2. Which police service conducted the second investigation into the murder of Stephen Lawrence? [Kent Police]

3. What police policy developments in the late 1980s were associated with developing a customer-focused service delivery model of policing? [the Metropolitan Police PLUS Programme and ACPOs Statement of Common Purpose and Values]

4. What three factors did the Macpherson Report (1999) suggest had marred the investigation of the murder of Stephen Lawrence? [professional incompetence, institutional racism, and a failure of leadership]

5. How was the traditional policing strategy used in response to racist incidents characterised? [order-maintenance]

6. How many hate crimes were recorded by the police in England and Wales in 2015/16? [62,518]

7. What legislative change, relating to racist incidents, was introduced by the Crime and Disorder Act 1998? [racially-aggravated offences]

8. What diverse populations were identified in a 2003 HMIC report? [lesbian, gay or bisexual people; the deaf or hard of hearing; people with mental illness; gypsies/travellers; people with disabilities; victims of domestic violence; asylum seekers; young people; older people; transgender people; those involved in child protection issues; people from areas of poverty (the socially excluded)]

9. On what basis did Sir Ian Blair defend efforts to recruit a more diverse police workforce? [that there was a 'business case' to do so, not that it was a matter of 'political correctness']

10. What notion has been central to the concept of 'policing by consent'? [that the police officer is a 'citizen in uniform']

CHAPTER 8: GLOBAL AND TRANSNATIONAL POLICING

1. What operational challenges has globalisation posed for police services? [transnational organised crime, human trafficking, online crimes and terrorism are among the key challenges mentioned in the discussion]

2. How did McCulloch and Pickering (2005) characterise American promotion of measures to tackle terrorist financing? [neo-colonialism]

3. Which country was administered by a UN Temporary Executive Authority in 1962–3 and in which country has a UN force been active since 1964? [West New Guinea and Cyprus]

4. Identify four networks of police co-operation in the EU. [Cross Channel Intelligence Co-operation, Tispo, Aquapol, EnviCrimeNet]

5. What has been the cornerstone agreement of EU police co-operation since the late 1990s? [the Schengen agreement]

6. Which civil society agencies were identified in relation to the development of 'soft power' influences on the development of transnational policing norms? [Amnesty International and Human Rights Watch]

7. What three forms of global private security provision were identified by Stenning and Shearing (2011)? [in-house security divisions within transnational companies, large transnational security companies contracted locally, and global corporations contracted by nation states]

8. Who argued that private security companies service the interests of global corporations and capital accumulation? [Bowling and Sheptycki]

9. Who operates at the 'meso' level of EU police co-operation, in Benyon's (1994) typology? [the various police agencies and personnel who are responsible for the development of collective strategy and activities]

10. Why did Hills (2009) suggest that it would be difficult to develop a 'global police ethic'? [due to the fundamental challenges associated with the universalisation of liberal policing systems into countries and contexts that have different traditions]

CHAPTER 9: CRIMINAL INVESTIGATION AND POLICING

1. How many criminal homicides are recorded in England and Wales each year? What proportion is 'cleared-up'? [around 90 per cent]

2. What did Maguire (2007) argue was a recurring myth relating to criminal investigations? [Maguire (2007) argued that a recurring myth of investigations is that a key purpose is to establish the truth of an alleged criminal incident]

3. Which were the three biggest public sector employees of fraud investigators? [Department for Work and Pensions (3,300 staff investigating social security fraud), local authorities (over 2,000 staff investigating housing benefit fraud) and the NHS (over 500 staff investigating fraud)]

4. Which nineteenth-century piece of legislation boosted trade for private detectives? [1857 Matrimonial Causes Act]

5. According to Stelfox (2009), how much time did routine police patrol officers spend on preliminary investigations? [Stelfox (2009) noted that research findings suggest that routine patrol officers spend approximately one-fifth of their working time on preliminary investigations]

6. What four 'commands' form the core of work co-ordinated by the National Crime Agency? [organised crime; border policing; economic crime; child exploitation and online protection]

7. What does research suggest is the aspect of investigation most significant to resolving cases? [research studies strongly indicate that gathering knowledge and information from victims and witnesses (and other members of the public) are the most significant means of resolving cases]

8. Who developed the 'Exchange Principle' that any contact between two materials leads to the transfer of trace elements between them? [Locard]

9. In response to which crimes were genetic fingerprinting techniques first applied? [the murders committed by Colin Pitchfork in Leicestershire in the mid-1980s]

10. Whose study of investigations of drug crime found that detectives regarded the completion of robust paperwork as central to the preparation of evidence? [Bacon, 2013]

CHAPTER 10: PLURAL POLICING

1. What five dimensions of policing were outlined by Loader (2000)? [policing by government; policing through government; policing above government; policing beyond government; policing below government]

2. How many firms were registered as Approved Contractors by the British Security Industry Association (BSIA) in 2017? [828]

3. How did Shearing and Stenning (2003) explain the growth of the private security sector? [in terms of the expansion of 'mass private property']

4. How might the notion of 'responsibilisation' be defined in the context of private security? [whereby the onus to provide for personal security is transferred from state to citizen]

5. What body was established by the Private Security Industry Act 2001 to regulate the sector? [Security Industry Authority]

6. Which piece of legislation introduced Suspicious Activity Reports (SARs) as a response to money laundering? [Proceeds of Crime Act 2000]

7. What is the name of civil orders introduced by the Crime and Disorder Act 1998 to quell low-level nuisance behaviour? [Antisocial Behaviour Order (ASBO)]

8. How did Wakefield (2006) characterise police patrol work? ['the activity of visible patrolling could … be seen as the policing activity of choice for the citizen least troubled by crime']

9. For what reasons did Jones and Newburn (2002) argue that the pluralisation thesis exaggerates the transition from the public policing model? [the state was never a monopoly provider; many agencies are only loosely engaged in 'multiagency partnerships'; private sector discipline has not debunked the public sector ethos in public policing]

10. Which occupations did Zedner (2006) suggest were eighteenth-century forerunners of the 'extended police family'? ['thief takers', turnpike keepers, pawnbrokers and inn-keepers]

CHAPTER 11: SURVEILLANCE, IT AND THE FUTURE OF POLICING

1. What does the acronym HOLMES stand for? [Home Office Large Major Enquiry System; used to cross-reference and retrieve data collated in crime investigations]

2. What percentage of the world's CCTV cameras was it estimated are deployed in Britain? [20 per cent]

3. In relation to what three types of crime did police officers suggest CCTV was particularly effective? [public order offences, assault and theft]

4. Against what sources of information do Thames Valley police check information gathered via ANPR? [Police National Computer (PNC), Driver and Vehicle Licensing Agency (DVLA), Local Force Intelligence systems and motor insurers databases]

5. What percentage of the British population support, in general terms, the use of cameras to police speeding drivers? [75 per cent]

6. What is Compstat? [Compstat is a police management tool that co-ordinates 'up-to-date computerized crime data, crime analysis, and advanced crime mapping as the bases for regularized, interactive crime strategy meetings which hold managers accountable for specific crime strategies and solutions in their areas' (Silverman, 2006: 268)]

7. In Britain in the 1960s Computer-Aided Dispatch systems were introduced in the development of what model of policing? [Unit Beat Policing]

8. Who developed a model prison that enshrined the concept of the panopticon? [Jeremy Bentham]

9. To what broader social and political processes do Hudson (2003) and Loader (1999) relate the development of technology in policing? [private prudentialism, consumer culture and neo-liberalism]

10. Which three perspectives on video recording of police behaviour did Sandhu and Haggerty (2017) identify? [camera shy; habituated; strategic advantages]

CHAPTER 12: THE FUTURE OF POLICING

1. Alongside what other factors did Chan (2003) suggest that professionalism had been an important component of police reform? [alongside bureaucratic measures and quasi-market approaches]

2. What did Vollmer suggest ought to be required of all Chicago police recruits in order to enhance professionalism? [that they be required to complete a degree]

3. How much did Weisburd and Neyroud suggest the UK government spent on medical research and on crime research? [£600 million and £2 million]

4. What are the triple-Ts that might underpin scientific models of policing? [Targeting, Testing and Tracking]

5. Which police services withdrew plans to consider privatising police services in the aftermath of problems relating to policing the London 2012 Olympics? [Surrey and West Midlands Police]

6. What role might Police and Crime Commissioners play in the development of pluralism? [through procuring services from a range of providers and encouraging police services to engage with a plurality of agencies]

7. What proportion of police funding was cut in the 2010 government spending review? [20 per cent]

8. What did Field (1990) suggest had a stronger impact on offending: unemployment rates of patterns of consumption? [patterns of consumption]

9. The chief of which service suggested that global warming would be a major challenge for police? [the Australian Federal Police]

10. How did Loader (2013) characterise government strategy to refocus police work? [as an effort to 'release the police's inner crime-fighter']

References

Adorno, T. (1950) *The Authoritarian Personality*, New York: Harper Row.

Alderson, J. (1979) *Policing Freedom*, Plymouth: Macdonald and Evans.

Alderson, J. (1984) *Law and Disorder*, London: Hamish Hamilton.

Alonso, J.M. and Andrews, R. (2016) 'How Privatization Affects Public Service Quality: An Empirical Analysis of Prisons in England and Wales', *International Public Management Journal*, 19 (2): 235–63.

American Bar Association/Rule of Law Initiative in Ukraine (ABA/ROLI) (2011) *Guidelines to Effective Law Enforcement Reform in Line with European Standards*, Kyiv: ABA/ROLI.

Anderson, M. (1989) *Policing the World*, Oxford: Oxford University Press.

Ardizzone, G. (2012) 'Police Drones in the UK? Watch this Airspace...', *Privacy International*, 7 August. Available at www.privacyinternational.org/node/144 (accessed 1/8/17).

Ariel, B., Sutherland, A., Henstock, D., Young, J., Drover, P., Sykes, J., Megicks, S. and Henderson, R. (2017) '"Contagious Accountability": A Global Multisite Randomized Controlled Trial on the Effect of Police Body-Worn Cameras on Citizens' Complaints against the Police', *Criminal Justice and Behaviour*, 44: 293–316.

Ascoli, D. (1979) *The Queen's Peace: The Origins and Development of the Metropolitan Police 1829–1979*, London: Hamish Hamilton.

Association of Chief Police Officers (ACPO) (2003) *Police Membership of the British National Party*, press release ref: 56/03, London: ACPO.

Association of Chief Police Officers (ACPO) (2011) *Paying the Bill 2: ACPO/APA Guidance on Charging for Police Services*, London: ACPO.

Ayling, J. and Shearing, C. (2008) 'Taking Care of Business – Public Police as Commercial Security Vendors', *Criminology and Criminal Justice*, 8: 27–50.

Bacon, M. (2016) *Taking Care of Business: Police Detectives, Drug Law Enforcement and Proactive Investigation*, Oxford: Oxford University Press.

Bailey, V. (ed.) (1981) *Policing and Punishment in Nineteenth Century Britain*, London: Croom Helm.

Baker, D. (2006) *Forms of Exclusion: Racism and Community Policing in Canada*, Oshawa: De Sitter.

Balch, R.W. (1972) 'The Police Personality: Fact or Fiction?', *The Journal of Criminal Law, Criminology, and Police Science*, 63 (1): 106–119.

Banton, M. (1964) *The Policeman in the Community*, London: Tavistock.

Barlow, D. and Barlow, M. (2001) *Police in a Multicultural Community: An American Story*, Long Grove, IL: Waveland Press.

Barnard-Wills, G. and Wells, H. (2012) 'Surveillance, Technology and the Everyday', *Criminology and Criminal Justice*, 12: 227–37.

Barry, N.P. (1981) *An Introduction to Modern Political Theory*, London: Macmillan.

Bayley, D. (1985) *Patterns of Policing*, Princeton, NJ: Princeton University Press.

Bayley, D. (1994) *Police for the Future*, New York: Oxford University Press.

Bayley, D. (2001) *Democratizing the Police Abroad: What to do and How not to do it*, Washington DC: National Institute of Justice, US Justice Department.

Bayley, D. (2015) 'Human Rights in Policing: A Global Assessment', *Policing and Society*, 25 (5): 540–47.

Bayley, D. and Shearing, C. (2001) *The New Structure of Policing: Description, Conceptualization, and Research Agenda*, Washington DC: National Institute of Justice.

BBC (2006a) 'Feeling Whose Collars', *Analysis*, BBC Radio 4, 2 March, London: BBC.

BBC (2006b) *Who Killed My Brother?*, BBC 2, 12 May.

Beck, A. and Chistyakova, J. (2004) 'Closing the Gap Between the Police and the Public in Post-Soviet Ukraine: A Bridge Too Far?', *Police Practice and Research*, 5 (1): 43–65.

Beck, A. and Willis, A. (1995) *Crime and Security – Managing the Risk to Safe Shopping*, Leicester: Perpetuity Press.

Bennett, T. (1990) *Evaluating Neighbourhood Watch*. Aldershot: Gower.

Bennett, T.H. (1994) 'Community Policing on the Ground: Developments in Britain', in Rosenbaum, D. (ed.) *The Challenge of Community Policing: Testing the Promises*. London: Sage, pp. 224–240.

Benyon, J. (1994) 'Policing the European Union: The Changing Basis of Cooperation on Law Enforcement', *International Affairs*, 70: 497–517.

Bibi, N., Clegg, M. and Pinto, R. (2005) *Police Service Strength: England and Wales, 31 March 2005*, London: Home Office.

Big Brother Watch (2013) *Private Investigators – The Use of Private Investigators by Councils, Public Authorities and Government Departments in the United Kingdom*, London: Big Brother Watch.

Bigo, D. (2000) 'Liaison Officers in Europe: New Officers in the European Security Field', in Sheptycki, J.E.W. (ed.) *Issues in Transnational Policing*, London: Routledge, pp. 67–99.

Bittner, E. (1974) 'Florence Nightingale in Pursuit of Willie Sutton: A Theory of the Police', in Jacob, H. (ed.) *The Potential for Reform of Criminal Justice*, Beverly Hills: Sage, pp.17–40.

Blackwood, L., Hopkins, N. and Reicher, S. (2013) '"I know Who I am, but Who do They Think I Am?" Muslim Perspectives on Encounters with Airport Authorities', *Ethnic and Racial Studies*, 36: 1090–1108.

Blair, I. (2005) 'What Kind of Police Service do We Want?', *The Dimbleby Lecture*, BBC 1, 16 November.

Bosworth, M. (2008) 'Border Control and the Limits of the Sovereign State', *Social Legal Studies* 17: 199–215.

Bottomley, A. and Coleman, C. (1981) *Understanding Crime Rates*. London: Saxon House.

Bourdieu, P. (1991) *Language and Symbolic Power*, Cambridge: Polity.

Bowling, B. (1999) 'The Rise and Fall of New York Murder: Zero Tolerance or Crack's Decline?', *British Journal of Criminology*, 39 (4): 531–55.

Bowling, B. (2010) *Policing the Caribbean*, Oxford: Oxford University Press.

Bowling, B. and Phillips, C. (2007) 'Disproportionate and Discriminatory: Reviewing the Evidence on Police Stop and Search', *Modern Law Review*, 70: 236–961.

Bowling, B. and Foster, J. (2002) 'Policing and the Police', in Morgan, R., Maguire, M. and Reiner, R. (eds) *The Oxford Handbook of Criminology*, Oxford: Oxford University Press.

Bowling, B. and Sheptycki, J. (2012) *Global Policing*, London: Sage.

Bowling, B. and Sheptycki, J. (2016) 'Reflections on Legal and Political Accountability for Global Policing', in Lister, S. and Rowe, M. (eds) *Accountability of Policing*, London: Routledge, pp. 214–229.

Bowling, B. and Weber, L. (2011) 'Stop and Search in Global Context: An Overview', *Policing and Society*, 21 (4): 480–88.

Box, S. (1987) *Recession, Crime and Punishment*, London: Macmillan.

Bradford, B. (2014) 'Policing and Social Identity: Procedural Justice, Inclusion and Cooperation between Police and Public', *Policing and Society*, 24: 22–43.

Bradford, B. (2017) *Stop and Search and Police Legitimacy*, London: Routledge.

Bradley, T. and Sedgwick, C. (2009) 'Policing Beyond the Police: A "First Cut" Study of Private Security in New Zealand', *Policing and Society: An International Journal of Research and Policy*, 19: 468–92.

Brain, T. (2010) *A History of Policing in England and Wales from 1974: A Turbulent Journey*, Oxford: Oxford University Press.

British Association of Women Police (BAWP) (2016) *Gender Agenda 3*, London: BAWP. Available at www.bawp.org/Resources/Documents/BAWP%20Gender%20Agenda%203%20final%20%20 16-oct-2014.pdf (accessed 1/8/17).

Brodeur, J.P. (1983) 'High and Low Policing: Remarks about the Policing of Political Activities', *Social Problems*, 3: 507–520.

Brogden, M. (1982) *The Police: Autonomy and Consent*, London: Academic Press.

Brogden, M. (1987) 'The Emergence of the Police: The Colonial Dimension', *British Journal of Criminology*, 27: 4–14.

Brogden, M. (1999) 'Community Policing as Cherry Pie', in Mawby, R.I. (ed.) *Policing Across the World: Issues for the Twenty-First Century*, London: UCL Press, pp. 167–86.

Brogden, M. and Nijhar, P. (2005) *Community Policing: National and International Models and Approaches*, Cullompton: Willan Publishing.

Brown, J.M. (ed.) (2014) *The Future of Policing*, London: Routledge.

Brown, J. and Heidensohn, F. (2000) *Gender and Policing – Comparative Perspectives*, London: Macmillan.

Bullock, K. (2016) 'Representing "Order" Online: The Construction of Police Presentational Strategies on Social Media', *Policing and Society*, 12 August. Available at www.tandfonline.com/doi/full/10.10 80/10439463.2016.1177529 (accessed 1/8/17).

Burke, M. (1993) *Coming Out of the Blue*, London: Cassell.

Burke, M. (1994) 'Homosexuality as Deviance: The Case of the Gay Police Officer', *British Journal of Criminology*, 34 (2): 192–203.

Burrows, J. (1986) *Burglary: Police Actions and Victims' Views*, Research and Planning Unit Paper 37, London: Home Office.

Burrows, J. and Tarling, R. (1987) 'The Investigation of Crime in England and Wales', *British Journal of Criminology*, 27: 229–51.

Butt, R. (2006) 'Police Officers Disciplined for Email Showing Decapitation', *Guardian*, 29 November.

Button, M. (2002) *Private Policing*, Cullompton: Willan.

Button, M. (2007) 'Assessing the Regulation of Private Security across Europe', *European Journal of Criminology*, 4: 109–128.

Button, M. (2011) 'Fraud Investigation and the "Flawed Architecture" of Counter Fraud Entities in the United Kingdom', *International Journal of Law, Crime and Justice*, 39: 249–65.

Button, M. and Stiernstedt, P. (2016) 'The Evolution of Security Industry Regulation in the European Union', *International Journal of Comparative and Applied Criminal Justice*, 26 December. Available at www.tandfonline.com/doi/abs/10.1080/01924036.2016.1270842 (accessed 1/8/17).

Button, M., Johnston, L., Frimpong, K. and Smith, G. (2007) 'New Directions in Policing Fraud: The Emergence of the Counter Fraud Specialist in the United Kingdom', *International Journal of Law, Crime and Justice*, 39: 192–208.

Cain, M. (1973) *Society and the Policeman's Role*, London: Routledge and Kegan Paul.

Caldeira, P.R. (2000) *City of Walls: Crime, Segregation and Citizenship in São Paulo*, Berkeley, CA: University of California Press.

Campbell, R. (2014) 'Not Getting Away With It: Linking Sex Work and Hate Crime in Merseyside', in Chakraborti, N. and Garland, J. (eds) *Responding to Hate Crime: The Case for Connecting Policy and Research*, Bristol: Policy Press.

Camps, F.E. and Barber, R. (1966) *The Investigation of Murder*, London: Michael Joseph.

Carrier, J. (1988) *The Campaign for the Employment of Women as Police Officers*. Aldershot: Ashgate.

Carswell, S. (2006) *Family Violence and the Pro-arrest Policy: A Literature Review*, Wellington: Ministry of Justice.

Cashmore, E. (2000) 'Behind the Window Dressing: Ethnic Minority Police Perspectives on Cultural Diversity', *Journal of Ethnic and Migration Studies*, 28 (2): 327–41.

CEPOL (2011) *European Police College – Five Year Report*, Bramshill: CEPOL.

Chakraborti, N. (ed.) (2010) *Hate Crime: Concepts, Policy, Future Directions*, Cullompton: Willan.

Chakraborti, N. and Garland, J. (eds) (2004) *Rural Racism: Contemporary Debates and Perspectives*, Cullompton: Willan.

Chakraborti, N. and Garland, J. (2009) *Hate Crime: Impact, Causes, and Consequences*, London: Sage.

Chakraborti, N. and Garland, J. (2012) 'Reconceptualising Hate Crime Victimization through the Lens of Vulnerability and Difference', *Theoretical Criminology*, 16: 499–514.

Chan, J. (1997) *Changing Police Culture: Policing in a Multiracial Society*, Cambridge: Cambridge University Press.

Chan, J. (1999) 'Governing Police Practice: Limits of the New Accountability', *British Journal of Sociology*, 50 (2): 251–70.

Chan, J. (2001) 'The Technological Game: How Information Technology is Transforming Police Practice', *Criminal Justice*, 1 (2): 139–59.

Chan, J. (2003) 'Policing and New Technologies', in Newburn, T. (ed.) *Handbook of Policing*, Cullompton: Willan, pp. 655–79.

Chan, J. and Bennett Moses, L. (2017) 'Making Sense of Big Data for Security', *British Journal of Criminology*, 57: 299–319.

Channel 4 (2006) 'Undercover Copper', *Dispatches*, 27 April.

Charman, S. and Corcoran, D. (2015) 'Adjusting the Police Occupational Cultural Landscape: The Case of An Garda Síochána', *Policing and Society*, 25: 484–503.

Clapton, R. (2004) 'Keeping Order: Motor-Car Regulation and the Defeat of Victoria's 1905 Motor-Car Bill', *Provenance: The Journal of Public Record Office Victoria*, no. 3.

Cockroft, T. (2012) *Police Culture: Themes and Concepts*, London: Routledge.

Cohen, P. (1979) 'Policing the Working Class City', in Fine, B., Kinsey, R., Lea, J. Picciotto, S. and Young, J. (eds) *Capitalism and the Rule of Law*, London: Hutchinson.

Cohen, S. (1985) *Visions of Social Control – Crime, Punishment, and Classification*, Cambridge: Polity Press.

Cole, B. (1999) 'Post-Colonial Systems', in Mawby, R. (ed.) *Policing Across the World: Issues for the Twenty-First Century*, London: UCL Press, pp. 88–108.

Coleman, R., Tombs, S. and Whyte, D. (2005) 'Capital, Crime Control and Statecraft in the Entrepreneurial City', *Urban Studies*, 42 (13): 2511–30.

Colls, R. (2002) *Identity of England*, Oxford: Oxford University Press.

Colman, A. and Gorman, P. (1982) 'Conservatism, Dogmatism and Authoritarianism in British Police Officers', *Sociology*, 16 (1): 1–26.

Colvin, R. (2009) 'Shared Perceptions Among Lesbian and Gay Police Officers Barriers and Opportunities in the Law Enforcement Work Environment', *Police Quarterly*, 12: 86–101.

Corbett, C. (2000) 'The Social Construction of Speeding as Not "Real" Crime', *Crime Prevention and Community Safety – an International Journal*, 2 (4): 33–46.

Corbett, C. and Caramlau, L. (2006) 'Gender Differences in Responses to Speed Cameras: Typology Findings and Implications for Road Safety', *Criminology and Criminal Justice*, 6 (4): 411–33.

Council of Europe (2001) *The European Code of Police Ethics*, Strasbourg: Publishing Division, Communication & Research Directorate. Available at http://www.bak.gv.at/cms/BAK_en/service/downloads/files/European_Code_of_Police_Ethics.pdf (accessed 1/8/17).

Crawford, A. (2003) 'The Pattern of Policing in the UK: Policing Beyond the Police', in Newburn, T. (ed.) *Handbook of Policing*, Cullompton: Willan, pp. 136–68.

Crawford, A. (2006) 'Networked Governance and the Post-Regulatory State? Steering, Rowing and Anchoring the Provision of Policing and Security', *Theoretical Criminology*, 10: 449–79.

Crawford, A. (2012) 'The Advent of Police and Crime Commissioners (PCCs): The Politicisation of Crime and Policing or the Dawn of Democratic Oversight?', *Building Sustainable Societies*, 9 October. Available at www.bss.leeds.ac.uk/2012/10/09/the-advent-of-police-and-crime-commissioners-pccs-the-politicisation-of-crime-and-policing-or-the-dawn-of-democratic-oversight/ (accessed 1/8/17).

Crawford, A. (2013) 'The Police, Policing and the Future of the "Extended Policing Family"', in Brown, J. (ed.) *The Future of Policing*, London: Routledge.

Crawford, A. and Lister, S. (2004) *The Extended Policing Family: Visible Patrols in Residential Areas*, York: Joseph Rowntree Foundation.

Crawford, A. and Lister, S. (2006) 'Additional Security Patrols in Residential Areas: Notes from the Marketplace', *Policing and Society*, 16 (4): 164–88.

Crawford, A., Lister, S., Blackburn, S. and Burnett, J. (2005) *Plural Policing: The Mixed Economy of Visible Patrols in England and Wales*, London: Policy Press.

Crawshaw, R., Devlin, B. and Wiliamson, T. (1998) *Human Rights and Policing: Standards for Good Behaviour and a Strategy for Change*, The Hague: Kluwer Law International.

Critchley, T.A. (1978) *A History of Police in England and Wales* (2nd edn), London: Constable.

Cunneen, C. (2001) *Conflict, Politics and Crime: Aboriginal Communities and the Police in Australia*, Crows Nest: Allen and Unwin.

Daily Telegraph (2005) 'We Want Answers, Not Questions', 19 November, p. 24.

Davis, M. (2006) *City of Quartz: Excavating the Future in Los Angeles* (2nd edn), London: Verso.

Dixon, B. and Smith, G. (1998) 'Laying Down the Law: The Police, the Courts and Legal Accountability', *International Journal of the Sociology of Law*, 26: 419–35.

Dixon, D. (1997) *Law in Policing*, Oxford: Oxford University Press.

Doran, A.J. (ed.) (1990) *The Punch Cartoon Album: 150 Years of Classic Cartoons*, London: Grafton.

Dunning, E., Murphy, P., Newburn, T. and Waddington, I. (1987) 'Violent Disorders in Twentieth Century Britain', in Gaskell, G. and Benewick, R. (eds) *The Crowd in Contemporary Britain*, London: Sage, pp. 19–75.

Eck, J.E. and Rosenbaum, D.P. (1994/2000) 'The New Police Order: Effectiveness, Equity and Efficiency in Community Policing', in Glensor, R.W., Correia, M.E. and Peak, K.J. (eds) *Policing Communities: Understanding Crime and Solving Problems – an Anthology*, Los Angeles: Roxbury, pp. 30–45.

Edwards, A. and Hughes, G. (eds) (2002) *Crime Control – The New Politics of Public Safety*, Cullompton: Willan.

Ekblom, P. (1986) 'Community Policing: Obstacles and Issues', in Walker, A., Ekblom, P. and Deakin, N. (eds) *The Debate about Community: Papers from a Seminar on Community in Social Policy*, PSI Discussion paper 13, London: Policy Studies Institute, pp. 27–39.

Elsner, B., Lewis, C. and Zila, J. (2008) 'Police Prosecution Service Relationship within Criminal Investigation', *European Journal on Criminal Policy and Research*, 14: 203–224.

Emsley, C. (1996) *The English Police – A Political and Social History* (2nd edn), Longman: Harlow.

Emsley, C. (2003) 'The Birth and Development of the Police', in Newburn, T. (ed.) *Handbook of Policing*, Cullompton: Willan, pp. 66–83.

Emsely, C. and Clapson, R. (1994) 'Recruiting the English Policeman C. 1840–1940', *Policing and Society*, 3: 269–8.5

English, J. and Card, R. (2015) *Police Law* (14th edn), Oxford: Oxford University Press.

Equalities and Human Rights Commission (2010) *Stop and Think – A Critical Review of the Use of Stop and Search Powers in England and Wales*, London: EHRC.

Ericson, R. and Haggerty, K. (1997) *Policing the Risk Society*, Oxford: Clarendon.

European Commission (2012) *Towards a European Strategy for the Development of Civil Applications of Remotely Piloted Aircraft Systems*, Brussels: EU.

Evans, R. and Mostrous, A. (2006) 'Spy Planes, Clothes Scanners and Secret Cameras: Britain's Surveillance Future', *Guardian*, 2 November.

Field, S. (1990) *Trends in Crime and their Interpretation*, Home Office Research Study 119, London: Home Office.

Fielding, N. (1988) *Joining Forces – Police Training, Socialization and Occupational Competence*, London: Routledge.

Fielding, N. (2005) *The Police and Social Conflict*, London: Portland.

Finklea, K.M. (2010) *Economic Downturns and Crime*, Washington DC: Congressional Research Service.

Finn, R.L. and Wright, D. (2012) 'Unmanned Aircraft Systems: Surveillance, Ethics and Privacy in Civil Applications', *Computer Law and Security Review*, 28: 184–94.

Fitzgerald, M. and Sibbit, R. (1997) *Ethnic Monitoring in Police Forces: A Beginning*, Home Office Research Study 173, London: Home Office.

Flanagan, R. (2007) *The Review of Policing: Interim Report*, London: Home Office.

Flanagan, R. (2008) *The Review of Policing*, London: Home Office.

Fleming, J. (2005) *'Working Together': Neighbourhood Watch, Reassurance Policing and the Potential of Partnerships*, Canberra: Australian Institute of Criminology.

Fleming, J. (2013) 'The Pursuit of Professionalism: Lessons from Australasia', in Brown, J. (ed.) *The Future of Policing*, London: Routledge.

Forbes, D. (1988) *Action on Racial Harassment: Legal Remedies and Local Authorities*, London: Legal Action Unit and London Housing Group.

Forensic Science Regulator (2017) *Annual Report November 2015 – November 2016*, Birmingham: Forensic Science Regulator.

Foster, J., Newburn, T. and Souhami, A. (2005) *Assessing the Impact of the Stephen Lawrence Inquiry*, Home Office Research Study 294, London: Home Office.

Foucault, M. (1977) *Discipline and Punish: The Birth of the Prison*, New York: Pantheon.

Foucault, M. (1981) *The History of Sexuality*, Harmondsworth: Penguin.

Fraud Review Team (2006) Final Report, London: HMSO.

Friedman, R. (1992) *Community Policing: Comparative Perspectives and Prospects*, London: Palgrave Macmillan.

Fryer, P. (1984) *Staying Power: The History of Black People in Britain*, London: Pluto Press.

Fyfe, N.R., Stevenson, O. and Woolnough, P. (2015) 'Missing Persons: The Processes and Challenges of Police Investigation', *Policing and Society*, 25: 409–25.

Garland, D. (2001) *The Culture of Control: Crime and Social Order in Contemporary Society*, Oxford: Oxford University Press.

Garland, J. and Chakraborti, N. (2007) '"Protean Times?": Exploring the Relationships between Policing, Community and "Race" in Rural England', *Criminology and Criminal Justice*, 7: 347–65.

Garland, J. (2010) 'Victimization of Goths and the Boundaries of Hate Crime', in Chakraborti, N. (ed.) *Hate Crime: Concepts, Policy, Future Directions*, Cullompton: Willan, pp. 40–57.

Garland, J. (2012) 'Difficulties in Defining Hate Crime Victimization', *International Review of Victimology*, 18: 25–37.

Garland, J. and Rowe, M. (1999) 'Policing Racism at Football Matches – An Assessment of Recent Developments', *International Journal of the Sociology of Law*, 27: 251–66.

George, B. and Button, M. (1997) 'Private Security Industry Regulation: Lessons from Abroad for the United Kingdom', *International Journal of Risk, Security and Crime Prevention*, 2: 187–200.

George, B. and Button, M. (2000) *Private Security*, London: Palgrave Macmillan.

Gill, M. and Hart, J. (1997) 'Private Investigators in Britain and America: Perspectives on the Impact of Popular Culture', *Policing: An International Journal of Police Strategies & Management*, 20: 631–640.

Gill, M. and Spriggs, A. (2005) *Assessing the Impact of CCTV*, Home Office Research Study 292, London: Home Office.

Goldsmith, A. (2009) 'Transitional Policing', in Wakefield, A. and Fleming, J. (eds) *The Sage Dictionary of Policing*, London: Sage, pp. 305–308.

Goldsmith, A. and Harris, V. (2017) 'International Policing Missions', in Hufnagel, S. and McCartney, C. (eds) *Trust in International Police and Justice Cooperation*, Oxford: Hart, pp. 51–73.

Goldsmith, A. and Sheptycki, J. (2007) *Crafting Transnational Policing: Police Capacity-Building and Global Policing*, Oxford: Hart.

Goldstein, H. (1990) *Problem-Oriented Policing*, Philadelphia: PA: Temple University Press.

Goold, B. (2004) *CCTV and Policing – Public Area Surveillance and Police Practices in Britain*, Oxford: Oxford University Press.

Grabosky, P. (2009) 'Police as International Peacekeepers', *Policing and Society: An International Journal of Research and Policy*, 19: 101–105.

Grant, S. and Rowe, M. (2011) 'Running the Risk: Police Officer Discretion and Family Violence in New Zealand', *Policing and Society*, 21: 1–18.

Greener, B.K. (2009a) *The New International Policing*, London: Palgrave Macmillan.

Greener, B.K. (2009b) 'UNPOL: UN Police as Peacekeepers', *Policing and Society: An International Journal of Research and Policy*, 19: 106–118.

Guardian (2012a) 'Judge Clears Police Officer who was Recorded Calling a Man Under Arrest "a Nigger" after Jury Fails to Reach Decision', 25 October.

Guardian (2012b) 'Universities Need to be Ready when a UK Border Agency Inspector Calls', 16 July.

Guardian/LSE (2011) 'Reading the Riots: Investigating England's Summer of Disorder', 14 December.

Hague, W. (2000) 'Where was Jack Straw when Damilola Died?', *Sunday Telegraph*, 17 December.

Hall, N. (2005) *Hate Crime*, Cullompton: Willan.

Hay, D. (1975) 'Property, Authority and the Criminal Law', in Hay, D., Linebaugh, P., Winslow, C., Rule, J. and Thompson, E.P. (eds) *Albion's Fatal Tree: Crime and Society in Eighteenth Century England*, London: Penguin, pp. 17–63.

Heidenshon, F. (1992) *Women in Control? The Role of Women in Law Enforcement*, Oxford: Clarendon Press.

Her Majesty's Inspectorate of Constabulary (HMIC) (1997) *Winning the Race: Embracing Diversity*, London: Home Office.

Her Majesty's Inspectorate of Constabulary (HMIC) (2000) *Policing London, Winning Consent*, London: HMSO.

Her Majesty's Inspectorate of Constabulary HMIC (2001) *Open All Hours: A Thematic Inspection Report on the Role of Police Visibility and Accessibility in Public Reassurance*, London: HMIC.

Her Majesty's Inspectorate of Constabulary (HMIC) (2003) *Diversity Matters*, London: Home Office.

Her Majesty's Inspectorate of Constabulary (HMIC) (2011a) *Adapting to Austerity: A Review of Police Force and Authority Preparedness for the 2011/12–14/15 CSR Period*, London: HMIC.

Her Majesty's Inspectorate of Constabulary (HMIC) (2011b) *Demanding Times – The Front Line and Police Visibility*, London: HMIC.

Hills, A. (2000) *Policing Africa: Internal Security and the Limits of Liberalization*, Boulder, CO: Lynne Rienner.

Hills, A. (2009) 'The Possibility of Transnational Policing', *Policing and Society: An International Journal of Research and Policy*, 19: 300–317.

Holdaway, S. (1983) *Inside the British Police: A Force at Work*, Oxford: Basil Blackwell.

Holdaway, S. (2013) 'Police Race Relations in the Big Society: Continuity and Change', *Policing and Society*, 13: 215–30.

Home Office (1991) *Safer Communities: The Local Delivery of Crime Prevention through the Partnership Approach*, London: Home Office.

Home Office (2005a) *Guidance on the Handling of Complaints Relating to the Direction and Control of a Police Force by a Chief Officer*, Home Office Circular 19/2005, London: Home Office.

Home Office (2005b) *Neighbourhood Policing – Your Police; Your Community; Our Commitment*, London: Home Office.

Home Office (2006a) *Neighbourhood Policing: Progress Report*, London: Home Office.

Home Office (2006c) *Statistics on Race and the Criminal Justice System 2005*, London: Home Office.

Home Office (2006e) *The National Police Improvement Agency: Regulatory Assessment Impact*, London: Home Office.

Home Office (2010a) *Operation of Police Powers under the Terrorism Act 2000 and Subsequent Legislation: Arrests, Outcomes and Stops and Searches, Quarterly Update to September 2009*, Statistical Bulletin 0410, London: Home Office.

Home Office (2010b) *Policing in the 21st Century: Reconnecting Police and the People*, London: Home Office.

Home Office (2013) *Protection of Freedoms Act 2012 – Statutory Consultation over the Surveillance Camera Code of Practice*, London: Home Office.

Home Office (2013) *Direct Entry to the Police: Consultation*, London: Home Office.

Home Office (2014) *Code A Revised Code of Practice*, London: The Stationery Office. Available at www.gov.uk/government/uploads/system/uploads/attachment_data/file/414195/2015_Code_A_web-19-03-15.pdf (accessed 1/8/17).

Home Office (2016a) *Police Powers and Procedures, England and Wales, Year Ending 31 March 2016*, Statistical Bulletin 15/16, London: Home Office.

Home Office (2016b) *Police Workforce, England and Wales, 31 March 2016*, Statistical Bulletin 05/16, London: Home Office. Available at www.gov.uk/government/uploads/system/uploads/attachment_data/file/544849/hosb0516-police-workforce.pdf (accessed 1/8/17).

Home Office (2016d) *Review of the Security Industry Authority – Terms of Reference*, London: Home Office.

Home Office (2017) *Police and Criminal Evidence Act 1984 (PACE) Codes of Practice*, London: Home Office. Available at www.gov.uk/guidance/police-and-criminal-evidence-act-1984-pace-codes-of-practice (accessed 1/8/17).

Hope, T. (2009) 'The Illusion of Control: A Response to Professor Sherman', *Criminology and Criminal Justice*, 9: 125–34.

Hough, M. (2013) 'Procedural Justice and Professional Policing in Times of Austerity', *Criminology and Criminal Justice*, 13: 181–97.

Hough, M., Jackson, J., Bradford, B. (2013) 'The Drivers of Police Legitimacy: Some European Research', *Journal of Policing, Intelligence and Counter Terrorism*, 8: 144–65.

Hough, M., Jackson, J., Bradford, B., Myhill, A. and Quinton, P. (2010) 'Procedural Justice, Trust, and Institutional Legitimacy', *Policing*, 4: 203–210.

House of Commons (2013) *Extradition and the European Arrest Warrant – Recent Developments*, London: House of Commons Library.

House of Commons Transport Committee (2006) *Roads Policing and Technology: Getting the Right Balance, Tenth Report of Session 2005–06*, London: House of Commons.

House of Lords (2009) *Surveillance: Citizens and the State: Vol 1*, London: House of Lords.

Hudson, B. (2003) *Justice in the Risk Society: Challenging and Re-affirming Justice in Late Modernity*, London: Sage.

Hufnagel, S. and McCartney, C. (eds) (2017) *Trust in International Police and Justice Cooperation*, Oxford: Hart.

Hughes, G. (2007) *The Politics of Crime and Community*, London: Palgrave.

Hughes, G. and Rowe, M. (2007) 'Neighbourhood Policing and Community Safety: Researching the Instabilities of the Local Governance of Crime, Disorder and Security in Contemporary UK', *Criminology and Criminal Justice*, 7 (4): 317–46.

Independent Commission on Policing for Northern Ireland (ICPNI) (1999) *A New Beginning: Policing in Northern Ireland*, Belfast: Northern Ireland Office.

Independent Police Complaints Commission (IPCC) (2007) *Public Perceptions of the Police Complaints System*, London: IPCC.

Independent Police Complaints Commission (IPCC) (2013) *Policing for a Better Britain: Report of the Independent Police Commission*, London: IPC. Available at www.lse.ac.uk/socialPolicy/Researchcentresandgroups/mannheim/pdf/PolicingforabetterBritain.pdf (accessed 1/8/17).

Independent Police Complaints Commission (IPCC) (2014) *Public Confidence Survey*, London: IPC.

Independent Police Complaints Commission (IPCC) (2015) *Police Complaints: Statistics for England and Wales 2014/15*, London: IPCC.

Independent Police Complaints Commission (IPCC) (2016) *Police Complaints: Statistics for England and Wales 2015/16*, London: IPCC.

Innes, H. and Innes, M. (2011) *Police Presence and Public Confidence in Local Policing: An Analysis of the British Crime Survey*, Cardiff: Cardiff Universities' Police Science Institute.

Innes, M. (2003) *Investigating Murder: Detective Work and the Police Response to Criminal Homicide*, Oxford: Clarendon Press.

Innes, M. (2004) 'Reinventing Tradition? Reassurance, Neighbourhood Security and Policing', *Criminal Justice*, 4 (2): 151–71.

Innes, M. (2011) 'Doing Less With More: The 'New' Politics of Policing', *Public Policy Research*, 18: 73–80.

Innes, M. (2013) 'Reinventing the Office of Constable: Progressive Policing in an Age of Austerity', in Brown, J. (ed.) *Policing Futures*, London: Routledge.

Innes, M. (2015) *After Woolwich: Social Reactions on Social Media*, ESRC Research Grant, ES/L008181/1, Swindon, ESRC.

Innes, M. and C. Roberts (2011) *Policing, Situational Intelligence and the Information Environment*, London: HMIC.

Jason-Lloyd, L. (2005) *An Introduction to Policing and Police Powers* (2nd edn), London: Cavendish.

Jefferson, T. and Grimshaw, R. (1984) *Controlling the Constable: Police Accountability in England and Wales*, London: Methuen.

Jewkes, Y. (2015) *Media and Crime*, London: Sage.

Johnston, L. (1992) *The Rebirth of Private Policing*, London: Routledge.

Johnston, L. (2000) *Policing Britain: Risk, Security and Governance*, London: Longman.

Johnston, L. (2006) 'Diversifying Police Recruitment? The Deployment of Police Community Support Officers in London', *The Howard Journal*, 45 (4): 388–402.

Johnston, L. (2007) 'Private Investigation', in Newburn, T., Williamson, T. and Wright, A. (eds) *Handbook of Criminal Investigation*, Cullompton: Willan Publishing, pp.277–98.

Johnston, L. and Shearing, C. (2003) *Governing Security – Explorations in Policing and Justice*, London: Routledge.

Jones, M. (2015) 'Who Forgot Lesbian, Gay, and Bisexual Police Officers? Findings from a National Survey', *Policing*, 9: 65–76.

Jones, T. and Newburn, T. (1998) *Private Security and Public Policing*, Oxford: Clarendon Press.

Jones, T. and Newburn, T. (2001) *Widening Access: Improving Police Relations with Hard to Reach Groups*, Police Research Series Paper 138, London: Home Office.

Jones, T. and Newburn, T. (2002) 'The Transformation of Policing?', *British Journal of Criminology*, 42 (1): 129–46.

Jordan, J. (2004) *The Word of a Woman? Police, Rape and Belief*, London: Palgrave.

Judge, A. (1986) 'The Provisions in Practice', in Benyon, J. and Bourn, C. (eds) *Police: Powers, Proprieties and Procedures*, Oxford: Pergamon, pp. 175–82.

Keith, M. (1988) 'Squaring Circles? Consultation and "Inner City" Policing', in *New Community*, 15 (1): 63–77.

Keith, M. (1993) *Race, Riots, and Policing: Lore and Disorder in a Multiracial Society*, London: Macmillan.

Kempa, M. and Johnston, L. (2005) 'Inclusive Plural Policing in Britain', *Australian and New Zealand Journal of Criminology*, 38: 181–91.

Kempa, M., Carrier, R., Wood, J. and Shearing, C. (1999) 'Reflections of the Evolving Concept of "Private Policing"', *European Journal on Criminal Policy and Research*, 7: 197–223.

Klockars, C. (1985) *The Idea of Police*, Beverly Hills, CA: Sage.

Koffman, L. (1985) 'Safeguarding the Rights of the Citizen', in Baxter, J. and Koffman, L. (eds) *Police: the Constitution and the Community: A Collection of Original Essays on Issues Raised by the Police and Criminal Evidence Act 1984*, London: Professional Books, pp. –37.

Landman, K. and Schönteich, M. (2002) 'Urban Fortresses: Gated Communities as a Reaction to Crime', *African Security Review*, 11: 71–85.

Laville, S. and Muir, H. (2006) 'Secret Report Brands Muslim Police Corrupt', *Guardian*, 10 June.

Lawless, C.J. (2011) 'Policing Markets: The Contested Shaping of Neo-Liberal Forensic Science', *British Journal of Criminology*, 51: 671–89.

Lea, J. (2000) 'The Macpherson Report and the Question of Institutional Racism', *The Howard Journal of Criminal Justice*, 39: 219–233.

Lea, J. (2003) 'Institutional Racism in Policing: The Macpherson Report and its Consequences', in Matthews, R. and Young, J. (eds) *The New Politics of Crime and Punishment*, Cullompton: Willan.

Lee, M. (2007) *Inventing Fear of Crime*, Cullompton: Willan.

Lee, W.L. Melville (1901) *A History of Police in England*, London: Methuen.

Leigh, A., Read, T. and Tilley, N. (1996) *Problem Oriented Policing: Brit Pop*, Crime Detection and Prevention Series Paper 75, London: Home Office.

Leigh, L.H. (1985) *Police Powers in England and Wales*, London: Butterworth.

Levesley, T. and Martin, A. (2005) *Police Attitudes to and Use of CCTV*, Home Office On-line Report 09/05, London: Home Office.

Levi, M. (2002) 'Money Laundering and its Regulation', *The Annals of the American Academy of Political and Social Science*, 582: 181–94.

Levi, M. (2008) 'Policing Fraud and Organised Crime', in Newburn, T. (ed.) *Handbook of Policing* (2nd edn), Cullompton: Willan, pp. 522–52.

Lewis P., Newburn T., Ball J., Procter R., Vis F. and Voss A. (2011) *Reading the Riots: Investigating England's Summer of Disorder*, London: *Guardian*/LSE.

Lister, S. (2013) 'The New Politics of the Police: Police and Crime Commissioners and the "Operational Independence" of the Police', *Policing*, 7 (3): 239–47.

Lister, S. and Rowe, M. (2015) 'Electing Police and Crime Commissioners in England and Wales: Prospecting for the Democratisation of Policing', *Policing and Society*, 25: 358–77.

Loader, I. (1997) 'Policing and the Social: Questions of Symbolic Power', *British Journal of Sociology*, 48 (1): 1–18.

Loader, I. (1999) 'Consumer Culture and the Commodification of Policing and Security', *Sociology*, 33: 373–92.

Loader, I. (2000) 'Plural Policing and Democratic Governance', *Socio-Legal Studies*, 9: 323–45.

Loader, I. (2013) 'Why Do the Police Matter?', in Brown, J. (ed.) *The Future of Policing*, London: Routledge.

Loader, I. (2016) 'Changing Climates of Control: The Rise and Fall of Police Authority in England and Wales', in Bosworth, M., Hoyle, C. and Zedner, L. (eds) *Changing Contours of Criminal Justice*, Oxford: Oxford University Press, pp. 3–14.

Loader, I. and Mulcahy, A. (2001a) 'The Power of Legitimate Naming: Part I—Chief Constables as Social Commentators in Post-War England', *British Journal of Criminology*, 41: 41–55.

Loader, I. and Mulcahy, A. (2001b) 'The Power of Legitimate Naming: Part II—Making Sense of the Elite Police Voice', *British Journal of Criminology*, 41: 252–65.

Loader, I. and Mulcahy, A. (2003) *Policing and the Condition of England: Memory, Politics and Culture*, Oxford: Oxford University Press.

Loader, I. and Walker, N. (2007) *Civilising Security*, Cambridge: Cambridge University Press.

Loftus, B. (2008) 'Dominant Culture Interrupted: Recognition, Resentment and the Politics of Change in an English Police Force', *British Journal of Criminology*, 48: 756–77.

Loftus, B. (2009) *Police Culture in a Changing World*, Oxford: Oxford University Press.

Lukes, S. (1974) *Power: A Radical View*, London: Macmillan.

Lukes, S. (2005) *Power: A Radical View* (2nd edn), London: Palgrave Macmillan.

Macpherson, Sir W. (1999) *The Stephen Lawrence Inquiry – Report of an Inquiry by Sir William Macpherson of Cluny*, London: HMSO.

Maguire, M. (2012) 'Criminal Investigation and Crime Control', in Newburn, T. (ed.) *Handbook of Policing*, (2nd edn), Cullompton: Willan Publishing, pp. 430–64.

Mann, S., Nolan, J. and Wellman, B. (2003) 'Sousveillance: Inventing and Using Wearable Computing Devices for Data Collection in Surveillance Environments', *Surveillance and Society*, 1/3: 331–55.

Manning, P.K. (1992) 'Information Technologies and the Police', in Tonry, M. and Morris, N. (eds) *Modern Policing – Crime and Justice, A Review of the Research, Vol. 15*, Chicago, IL: University of Chicago Press, pp. 349–98.

Manning, P.K. (1996) 'Information Technology in the Police Context: The "Sailor" Phone', *Information Systems Research*, 7: 52–62.

Manning, P.K. (2010) *Democratic Policing in a Changing World*, Boulder, CO: Paradigm.

Marlow, J. (1971) *The Peterloo Massacre*, London: Panther.

Marx, G.T. (1988) *Undercover: Police Surveillance in America*, Berkley, CA: University of California Press.

Mawby, R. (1979) *Policing the City*, Farnborough: Saxon House.

Mawby, R.I. (1999) *Policing Across the World: Issues for the Twenty-First Century*, London: UCL Press.

Mawby, R.I. (2003a) 'Competing the "Half-Formed Picture"? Media Images of Policing', in Mason, P. (ed.) *Criminal Visions: Media Representations of Crime and Justice*, Cullompton: Willan, pp. 214–37.

Mawby, R.I. (2003b) 'Models of Policing', in Newburn, T. (ed.) *Handbook of Policing*, Cullompton: Willan, pp. 15–40.

May, T. (2011) *Police Reform: Home Secretary's Speech to ACPO Summer Conference*, London: Home Office. Available at www.homeoffice.gov.uk/media-centre/speeches/acpo-summer (accessed 1/8/17).

Mazerolle, L. and Ransley, J. (2005) *Third Party Policing*, Cambridge: Cambridge University Press.

McCarthy, D.J. (2015) 'Gendering "Soft" Policing: Multi-Agency Working, Female Cops, and the Fluidities of Police Culture/s', *Policing and Society*, 23: 261–78.

McCulloch, J. and Pickering, S. (2005) 'Suppressing the Financing of Terrorism: Proliferating State Crime, Eroding Censure and Extending Neo-Colonialism', *British Journal of Criminology*, 45: 470–86.

McEvoy, K. and Mika, H. (2002) 'Restorative Justice and the Critique of Informalism in Northern Ireland', *British Journal of Criminology*, 42: 534–62.

McLaughlin, E. (1991) 'Police Accountability and Black People: Into the 1990s', in Cashmore, E. and McLaughlin, E. (eds) *Out of Order? Policing Black People*, London: Routledge, pp: 109–33.

McLaughlin, E. (2005) 'From Reel to Ideal: The Blue Lamp and the Popular Cultural Construction of the English Bobby', *Crime, Media, Culture*, 1 (1): 11–30.

McLaughlin, E. (2007a) *The New Policing*, London: Sage.

McLaughlin, E. (2007b) 'Diversity or Anarchy? The Post-Macpherson Blues', in Rowe, M. (ed.) *Policing Beyond Macpherson*, Cullompton: Willan.

Millie, A. (2013) 'The Policing Task and the Expansion (and Contraction) of British Policing', *Criminology and Criminal Justice*, 13: 143–60.

Ministry of Justice (2015) *Race in the Criminal Justice System*, London: Ministry of Justice.

Monkkonen, E. (1992) 'History of Urban Police', in Tonry, M. and Morris, N. (eds) *Modern Policing, Vol. 15*, Chicago, IL: University of Chicago Press, pp. 547–80.

Moon, B. (2006) 'The Influence of Organizational Socialization on Police Officers' Acceptance of Community Policing', *Policing: An International Journal of Police Strategies and Management*, 29: 704–722.

Moore, M.H. (1992) 'Problem-Solving and Community Policing', in Tonry, M. and Morris, N. (eds) *Modern Policing*, Chicago, IL: University of Chicago Press, pp. 99–158.

Moran, L. (2007) '"Invisible Minorities": Challenging Community and Neighbourhood Models of Policing', *Criminology and Criminal Justice*, 7: 417–41.

Morgan, R. and Newburn, T. (1997) *The Future of Policing*, Oxford: Clarendon.

Morris, B. (2007) 'History of Criminal Investigation', in Newburn, T., Williamson, T. and Wright, A. (eds) *Handbook of Criminal Investigation*, Cullompton: Willan, pp.15–40.

Morris, L. (1994) *Dangerous Classes: The Underclass and Social Citizenship*, London: Routledge.

Morris, Sir W., Burden, Sir A. and Weekes, A. (2004) *The Case for Change: People in the Metropolitan Police Service, the Report of the Morris Inquiry*, London: Metropolitan Police Authority.

Murphy, P., Eckersley, P. and Ferry, L. (2016) 'Accountability and Transparency: Police Forces in England and Wales', *Public Policy and Administration*, 32 (3).

Mustard, D. (2001) 'Racial, Ethnic and Gender Disparities in Sentencing: Evidence from the US Federal Courts', *The Journal of Law and Economics*, 19: 285–314.

MVA and Miller, J. (2000) *Profiling Populations Available for Stop and Search*, Police Research Series Paper 131, London: Home Office.

Mythen, G., Walklate, S. and Khan, F. (2009) '"I'm a Muslim, but I'm not a Terrorist": Victimization, Risky Identities and the Performance of Safety', *British Journal of Criminology*, 49: 736–54.

National Advisory Group/Policing Lesbian and Gay Communities (1999), *Breaking the Chains of Hate*, Manchester: NAGS.

National Police Chiefs' Council (undated) *Policing Vision 2025*, London: National Police Chiefs' Council.

Newburn, T. (2002) 'The Introduction of CCTV into a Custody Suite – Some Reflections on Risk, Surveillance and Policing', in Crawford, A. (ed.) *Crime and Insecurity: The Governance of Safety in Europe*, Cullompton: Willan, pp. 260–73.

Newburn, T. (2003) 'Policing Since 1945', in Newburn, T. (ed.) *Handbook of Policing*, Cullompton: Willan, pp. 84–105.

Newburn, T. (2007) 'Governing Security: The Rise of the Privatized Military', in Downes, D., Rock, P., Chinkin, C. and Gearty, C. (eds) *Crime, Social Control and Human Rights: From Moral Panics to States of Denial: Essays in honour of Stanley Cohen*, Cullompton: Willan, pp. 195–210.

Newburn, T. and Sparks, R. (2004) *Criminal Justice and Political Cultures – National and International Dimensions of Crime Control*, Cullompton: Willan.

Neyroud, P. (2003) 'Police and Ethics', in Newburn, T. (ed.) *Handbook of Policing*, Cullompton, Willan.

Neyroud, P. (2011) *Review of Police Leadership and Training*, London: Home Office.

Neyroud, P. and Beckley, A. (2001) *Policing, Ethics and Human Rights*, Cullompton: Willan.

Niederhoffer, A. (1969) *Behind the Shield: The Police in Urban Society*, New York: Anchor.

Norris, C. and Armstrong, G. (1999) *The Maximum Surveillance Society – The Rise of CCTV*, Oxford: Berg.

Northern Ireland Policing Board (2003) *Code of Ethics for the Police Service of Northern Ireland*, Belfast: Northern Ireland Policing Board.

Office for National Statistics (ONS) (2017) *Crime in England and Wales: Year Ending Sept 2016*. Available at www.ons.gov.uk/peoplepopulationandcommunity/crimeandjustice/bulletins/crimeinenglandandwales/yearendingsept2016 (accessed 1/8/17).

Office of Surveillance Commissioner (2006) *Annual Report of the Chief Surveillance Commissioner to the Prime Minister and to Scottish Ministers for 2005–2006*, Edinburgh: Office of Surveillance Commissioner.

Organization for Security and Co-operation in Europe (2008) *Guidebook on Democratic Policing*, Vienna: OSCE.

Osborne, D. and Gaebler, T. (1992) *Reinventing Government: How the Entrepreneurial Spirit is Transforming the Public Sector*, New York: Plume.

Oxford, K. (1986) 'The Power to Police Effectively', in Benyon, J. and Bourn, C. (eds) *Police: Powers, Proprieties and Procedures*, Oxford: Pergamon, pp. 61–74.

PA Consulting Group (2001) *Diary of a Police Officer*, Police Research Series Paper 149, London: Home Office.

Packer, H. (1964) *Two Models of the Criminal Process*, University of Pennsylvania Law Review, 113: 1–68.

Palmer, S.H. (1988) *Police and Protest in England and Ireland 1780–1950*, Cambridge: Cambridge University Press.

Palmiotto, M. (2013) *Criminal Investigations*, (4th edn), Boca Raton, FL: CRC Press.

Panayi, P. (1996) *Racial Violence in Britain in the Nineteenth and Twentieth Centuries*, Leicester: Leicester University Press.

Paoline, E.A., Myers, S.M. and Worden, R.E. (2000) 'Police Culture, Individualism and Community Policing: Evidence from Two Police Departments', *Justice Quarterly*, 17: 575–605.

Pepper, I.K. (2005) *Crime Scene Investigation: Methods and Procedures*, Maidenhead: Open University Press.

Police Review (2001) 'President Delivers Race Relations Warning to BCU Commanders', 16 February, 109 (5609): 6.

Police Review (2002) 'Plan to Increase Ethnic Officers in Specialisms', 17 May, p. 13.

Polk, O.E. and Armstrong, D.A. (2001) 'Higher Education and Law Enforcement Career Paths: Is the Road to Success Paved by Degree?', *Journal of Criminal Justice Education*, 12: 77–99.

Pollitt, C. (2012) *New Perspectives on Public Services: Place and Technology*, Oxford: Oxford University Press.

Praat, A.C. and Tuffin, K.F. (1996) 'Police Discourses of Homosexual Men in New Zealand', *Journal of Homosexuality*, 31: 57–73.

Prenzler, T. (2000) 'Civilian Oversight of the Police – A Test of Capture Theory', *British Journal of Criminology*, 40: 659–74.

Prenzler, T (2005) 'Mapping the Australian Security Industry', *Security Journal*, 18: 51–64.

Prenzler, T. and Porter, L. (2016) 'Improving Police Behaviour and Police-Community Relations through Innovative Responses to Complaints', in Lister, S. and Rowe, M. (eds) *Accountability of Policing*, London: Routledge, pp. 49–68.

Punch, M. (1979) *Policing the Inner City: A Study of Amsterdam's Warmoesstraal*, London: Macmillan.

Putnam, R.D. (2000) *Bowling Alone – the Collapse and Revival of American Community*, New York: Simon and Schuster.

Ratcliffe, J. (2002) 'Damned if You Don't, Damned if You Do: Crime Mapping and its Implications in the Real World', *Policing and Society*, 12: 211–25.

Rawlings, P. (2002) *Policing – A Short History*, Cullompton: Willan.

Reiner, R. (1978) *The Blue Coated Worker: A Sociological Study of Police Unionism*, Cambridge: Cambridge University Press.

Reiner, R. (2000) *The Politics of the Police* (3rd edn), Oxford: Oxford University Press.

Reiner, R. (2003) 'Policing and the Media', in Newburn, T. (ed.) *Handbook of Policing*, Cullompton: Willan, pp. 259–81.

Reiner, R. (2013) 'Who Governs? Democracy, Plutocracy, Science and Prophecy in Policing', *Criminology and Criminal Justice*, 13: 161–80.

Reiner, R. (2016) 'Power to the People: A Social Democratic Critique of the Coalition Government's Police Reforms', in Lister, S. and Rowe, M. (eds) *Accountability of Policing*, London: Routledge, pp. 132–49.

Reiss, A.J. (1971) *The Police and the Public*, New Haven, CT: Yale University Press.

Reith, C. (1948) *A Short History of the British Police*, Oxford: Oxford University Press.

Reuss Ianni, E. (1982) *Two Cultures of Policing: Street Cops and Management Cops*, Piscataway, NJ: Transaction.

Reynolds, E. (1998) *Before the Bobbies: The Night Watch and Police Reform in Metropolitan London, 1720–1830*, London: Macmillan.

Riots Communities and Victims Panel (RCVP) (2012) *After the Riots – The Final Report of the RCVP*, London: RCVP.

Roberg, R., Novak, K. and Cordner, G. (2005) *Police and Society* (3rd edn), Los Angeles, CA: Roxbury.

Robertson, A. (2005) 'Criminal Justice Policy Transfer to Post-Soviet States: Two Case Studies of Police Reform in Russia and Ukraine', *European Journal on Criminal Policy and Research*, 11: 1–28.

Robilliard, St. J. and McEwan, J. (1986) *Police Powers and the Individual*, Oxford: Basil Blackwell.

Robinson, G., Burke, L. and Millings, M. (2016) 'Criminal Justice Identities in Transition: The Case of Devolved Probation Services in England and Wales', *British Journal of Criminology*, 56: 161–78.

Rosenbaum, D.P. (2006) 'The Limits of Hot Spots Policing', in Weisburd, D. and Braga, A. (eds) *Police Innovation – Contrasting Perspectives*, Cambridge: Cambridge University Press, pp. 245–63.

Roulstone, A. and Mason-Bish, H. (eds) (2012) *Disability, Hate Crime and Violence*, London: Routledge.

Rowe, M. (1998) *The Racialisation of Disorder in Twentieth Century Britain*, Aldershot: Ashgate.

Rowe, M. (2004) *Policing, Race and Racism*, Cullompton: Willan.

Rowe, M. (2007a) 'Rendering Visible the Invisible: Police Discretion, Professionalism and Ethics', *Policing and Society*, 17: 279–94.

Rowe, M. (2007b) 'The Scarman Inquiry', in Newburn, T. (ed.) *Dictionary of Policing*, Cullompton: Willan.

Rowe, M. (2007c) (ed.) *Policing Beyond Macpherson*, Cullompton: Willan.

Rowe, M. (2009) 'Notes on a Scandal: The Official Enquiry into Police Deviance and Corruption in New Zealand', *Australian and New Zealand Journal of Criminology*, 42: 123–38.

Rowe, M. (2012) *Race and Crime: A Critical Engagement*, London: Sage.

Rowe, M. and Ross, J. (2015) 'Comparing the Recruitment of Ethnic and Racial Minorities in Police Departments in England and Wales with the United States', *Policing: A Journal of Policy and Practice*, 9: 26–35.

Roycroft, M., Brown, J. and Innes, M. (2007) 'Reform by Crisis: The Murder of Stephen Lawrence and a Socio-Historical Analysis of Developments in the Conduct of Major Crime Investigations' in Rowe, M. (ed.) *Policing Beyond Macpherson*, Cullompton: Willan, pp. 148–64.

Rumens, N. and Broomfield J. (2012) 'Gay Men in the Police: Identity Disclosure and Management Issues', *Human Resource Management Journal*, 22: 283–98.

Russo, F. (2007) 'Who Should Read Your Mind?', *Time*, 29 January, pp. 76–9.

Sampson, F. (2012) 'Hail to the Chief?—How far does the Introduction of Elected Police Commissioners Herald a US-Style Politicization of Policing for the UK?', *Policing*, 6(1): 4–15.

Sandhu, A. and Haggerty, K. (2017) 'Policing on Camera', *Theoretical Criminology*, 21: 78–95.

Scarman, Lord (1981) *The Brixton Disorders*, London: HMSO.

Schneider, C.J. (2016) 'Police Presentational Strategies on Twitter in Canada', *Policing and Society*, 26: 129–47.

Scott, K. (2011) 'Policing and Criminal Justice in Scotland', in Donnelly, D. and Scott, K. (eds) *Policing Scotland* (2nd edn), Abingdon: Routledge, pp. 355–74.

Scraton, P. (1985) *The State of the Police*, London: Pluto.

Sharpe, J.A. (1984) *Crime in Early Modern England, 1550–1750*, London: Longman.

Sharpe, J.A. (1995) *The History of Crime in England, 1550–1914*, Chichester: Economic History Society. Available at www.ehs.org.uk/the-society/assets/sharpe20b.pdf (accessed 1/8/17).

Shearing, C. and Stenning, P. (1983) 'Private Security: Implications for Social Control', *Social Problems*, 30: 493–506.

Sheptycki, J.W.E. (ed.) (2000) *Issues in Transnational Policing*, London: Routledge.

Sherman, I. (2013) 'The Rise of Evidence-Based Policing: Targeting, Testing, and Tracking', *Crime and Justice*, 42: 377–451.

Silke, A. and Taylor, M. (2000) 'War Without End: Comparing IRA and Loyalist Vigilantism in Northern Ireland', *Howard Journal of Criminal Justice*, 39: 249–66.

Silver, A. (1967) 'The Demand for Order in Civil Society: A Review of Some Themes', in Bordua D.J. (ed.), *The Police: Six Sociological Essays*, New York: John Wiley and Sons, pp. 1–24.

Silverman, E.B. (2006) 'Compstat's Innovation', in Weisburd, D. and Braga, A. (eds) *Police Innovation – Contrasting Perspectives*, Cambridge: Cambridge University Press, pp. 267–83.

Singh, G. (2000) 'The Concept and Context of Institutional Racism', in Marlow, A. and Loveday, B. (eds) *After Macpherson: Policing After the Stephen Lawrence Inquiry*, Lyme Regis: Russell House.

Skinns, L. (2010) 'Stop the Clock? Predictors of Detention without Charge in Police Custody Areas', *Criminology and Criminal Justice*, 10: 303–320.

Sklansky, D.A. (2011) *The Persistent Pull of Police Professionalism – New Perspectives in Policing*, Washington DC: National Institute of Justice/Harvard Kennedy School.

Sklansky, D.A. (2013) 'The Promise and the Perils of Police Professionalism', in Brown, J. (ed.) *The Future of Policing*, London: Routledge.

Skogan, W. (2006a) 'The Promise of Community Policing', in Weisburd, D. and Braga, A.A. (eds) *Police Innovation: Contrasting Perspectives*, Cambridge: Cambridge University Press, pp. 27–43.

Skogan, W. (2006b) *Police and Community in Chicago: A Tale of Three Cities*, Oxford: Oxford University Press.

Skolnick, J. (1966) *Justice without Trial: Law Enforcement in Democratic Society*, New York: John Wiley & Sons.

Smith, D.J. (1987) 'The Police and the Idea of the Community', in Wilmott, P. (ed.) *Policing and the Community*, London: Policy Studies Institute.

Smith, D.J. and Gray, J. (1983) *Police and People in London, Vol. 4, The Police in Action*, London: Policy Studies Institute.

Smith, G., Hagger Johnson, H. and Roberts, C. (2015) 'Ethnic Minority Police Officers and Disproportionality in Misconduct Proceedings', *Policing and Society*, 25: 561–78.

Solomos, J. (1999) 'Social Research and the Stephen Lawrence Inquiry', *Sociological Research Online*, 4 (1).

Souhami, A. (2007) 'Understanding Institutional Racism', in Rowe, M. (ed.) *Policing Beyond Macpherson – Issues in Policing, Race, and Society*, Cullompton: Willan, pp. 66–87.

South, N. (1988) *Policing for Profit: the Private Security Sector*, London: Sage.

Spapens, T. (2017) 'Building Trust and More – The Importance of Police Cooperation Networks in the European Union', in Hufnagel, S. and McCartney, C. (eds) *Trust in International Police and Justice Cooperation*, Oxford: Hart, pp. 149–68.

Sparks, R., Girling, E. and Loader, I. (2001) 'Fear and Everyday Urban Lives', *Urban Studies*, 38: 885–98.

Stalcup, M. and Hahn, C. (2016) 'Cops, Cameras, and the Policing of Ethics', *Theoretical Criminology*, 20: 482–501.

Stelfox, P. (2009) *Criminal Investigation: An Introduction to Principles and Practice*, Cullompton: Willan.

Stenning, P. (1989) 'Private Police and Public Police: Toward a Redefinition of the Police Role', in Loree, D. (ed.) *Future Issues in Policing: Symposium Proceedings*, Ottawa: Minister of Supply and Services, pp. 169–92.

Stenning, P. (2000) 'Powers and Accountability of Private Police', *European Journal on Criminal Policy and Research*, 8: 325–52.

Stenning, P. and Shearing, C. (2005) 'Reforming Police: Opportunities, Drivers and Challenges', *Australian and New Zealand Journal of Criminology*, 38: 167–80.

Stenning, P. and Shearing, C. (2011) 'The Shifting Boundaries of Policing: Globalisation and its Possibilities', in Newburn, T. and Peay, J. (eds) *Policing: Politics, Culture and Control*, Oxford: Hart, pp. 265–84.

Stenson, K. (2001) 'The New Politics of Crime Control', in Stenson, K. and Sullivan, R.K. (eds) *Crime, Risk and Justice – The Politics of Crime Control in Liberal Democracies*, Cullompton: Willan, pp. 15–28.

Stenson, K. (2002) 'Community Safety in Middle England', in Edwards, A. and Hughes, G. (eds) *Crime Control and Community*, Cullompton: Willan.

Stenson, K. and Waddington, P.A.J. (2007) 'Macpherson, Police Stops and Institutional Racism', in Rowe, M. (ed.) *Policing Beyond Macpherson – Issues in Policing, Race, and Society*, Cullompton: Willan, pp. 128–47.

Stephens, J.F. (1964) *A History of the Criminal Law of England*, New York: Burt Franklin.

Stone, V. and Pettigrew, N. (2000) *The Views of the Public on Stop and Searches*, Police Research Series Paper 129. London: Home Office.

Stonewall (2007) *Workplace Equality Index 2007 – The Top 100 Employers for Gay People in Britain*, London: Stonewall.

StopWatch (2014) *Briefing: Schedule 7 to the Terrorism Act 2000*, London: StopWatch.

Storch, R. (1975) 'The Plague of Blue Locusts: Police Reform and Popular Resistance in Northern England 1840–57', *International Review of Social History*, 20: 61–90.

Storch, R. (1976) 'The Policeman as Domestic Missionary: Urban Discipline and Popular Culture in Northern England, 1850–1880', *Journal of Social History*, 9: 481–509.

Styles, J. (1987) 'The Emergence of the Police – Explaining Police Reform in Eighteenth and Nineteenth Century England', *British Journal of Criminology*, 27: 15–22.

Telep, C.W. and Lum, C. (2014) 'The Receptivity of Officers to Empirical Research and Evidence-Based Policing: An Examination of Survey Data From Three Agencies', *Police Quarterly*, 17: 359–85.

Thompson, E.P. (1968) *The Making of the English Working Class*, Harmondsworth: Penguin.

Tilley, N. (2003) 'Community Policing, Problem-Oriented Policing and Intelligence-Led Policing', in Newburn, T. (ed.) *Handbook of Policing*, Cullompton: Willan, pp. 311–39.

Trojanowicz, R. and Bucqueroux, B. (1990) *Community Policing: A Contemporary Perspective*, Cincinnati, OH: Anderson.

Turley, C., Ranns, H., Callanan, M. and Blackwell, A. (2012) *Delivering Neighbourhood Policing in Partnership*, Research Report 61, London: Home Office.

UN (undated) *United Nations Peacekeeping Operations*. Available at www.un.org/en/peacekeeping/ operations/ (accessed 1.8.17).

UNFICYP (undated) *United Nations Peacekeeping Force in Cyprus – Facts and nistry of justices*. Available at www.un.org/en/peacekeeping/missions/unficyp/facts.shtml (accessed 1/8/17).

Van Damme, A. (2017) 'The Impact of Police Contact on Trust and Police Legitimacy in Belgium', *Policing and Society*, 27: 205–228.

Van der Spuy, E. (2000) 'Foreign Donor Assistance and Policing Reform in South Africa', *Policing and Society*, 10: 342–66.

Waddington, P.A.J., (1982) 'Conservatism, Dogmatism and Authoritarianism in the Police: A comment', *Sociology*, 16: 592–94.

Waddington, P.A.J. (1993) 'Dying in a Ditch: The Use of Police Powers in Public Order', *International Journal of Sociology*, 45: 335–53.

Waddington, P.A.J. (1994a) 'Coercion and Accommodation: Policing Public Order After the Public Order Act', *British Journal of Sociology*, 45: 367–85.

Waddington, P.A.J. (1994b) *Liberty and Order: Policing Public Order in a Capital City*, London: UCL Press.

Waddington, P.A.J. (1999a) *Policing Citizens*, Abingdon: Routledge.

Waddington, P.A.J. (1999b) 'Police (Canteen) Sub-Culture: An Appreciation', *British Journal of Criminology*, 39: 287–309.

Waddington, P.A.J., Stenson, K. and Don, D. (2004) 'In Proportion: Race and Police Stop and Search', *British Journal of Criminology*, 44: 889–914.

Wakefield, A. (2004) *Selling Security: The Private Policing of Public Space*, Cullompton: Willan.

Wakefield, A. (2006) *The Value of Foot Patrol: A Review of the Literature*, London: Police Foundation.

Wakefield, A. and McLaughlin, E. (2009) 'Transnational Policing', in Wakefield, A. and Fleming, J. (eds) *The Sage Dictionary of Policing*, London: Sage.

Walker, N. (2008) 'The Pattern of Transnational Policing', in Newburn, T. (ed.) *Handbook of Policing* (2nd edn), Cullompton: Willan, pp. 119–46.

Walklate, S. (1995) *Gender and Crime – An Introduction*, London: Prentice Hall.

Wall, D.S. (1998) *The Chief Constables of England and Wales – the Socio-Legal History of a Criminal Justice Elite*, Aldershot: Ashgate.

Wall, D.S. and Williams, M. (2007) 'Policing Diversity in the Digital Age: Maintaining Order in Virtual Communities', *Criminology and Criminal Justice*, 7: 391–415.

Walsh, D. and Milne, R. (2007) 'Perceptions of Benefit Fraud Staff in the UK: Giving P.E.A.C.E. a Chance?', *Public Administration*, 85: 525–40.

Wambaugh, J. (1989) *The Blooding*, New York: Bantam.

Waples, S., Gill, M. and Fisher, S. (2009) 'Does CCTV Displace Crime?', *Criminology and Criminal Justice*, 9: 207–224.

Weatheritt, M. (1987) 'Community Policing Now', in Wilmott, P. (ed.) *Policing and the Community*, London: Policy Studies Institute.

Weisburd, D. and Braga, A. (2006) 'Hot Spots Policing as a Model for Police Innovation', in Weisburd, D. and Braga, A. (eds) *Police Innovation – Contrasting Perspectives*, Cambridge: Cambridge University Press, pp. 225–44.

Weisburd, D. and Neyroud, P. (2011) 'Police Science: Toward a New Paradigm', *New Perspectives in Policing*, Washington DC: National Institute of Justice/Harvard Kennedy School.

Weisburd, D., Telep, C.W. and Braga, A.A. (2010) *The Importance of Place in Policing – Empirical Evidence and Policy Implications*, Stockholm: National Council for Crime Prevention.

Westmarland, L. (2002) *Gender and Policing – Sex, Power and Police Culture*, Cullompton: Willan.

Westmarland, L. and Rowe, M. (2016) 'Police Ethics and Integrity: Can a New Code Overturn the Blue Code?', *Policing and Society*, (Early Access).

White, A. (2010) *The Politics of Private Security: Regulation, Reform and Re-Legitimation*, London: Palgrave.

White, A. (2013) 'The New Political Economy of Private Security', *Theoretical Criminology*, 17: 85–101.

White, A. (2016) 'Private Security and the Politics of Accountability', in Lister, S. and Rowe, M. (eds) *Accountability of Policing*, London: Routledge, pp. 172–91.

Whitfield, J. (2004) *Unhappy Dialogue: The Metropolitan Police and Black Londoners in Post-war Britain*, Cullompton: Willan.

Whitfield, J. (2007) 'The Historical Context – Policing and Black People in Post-War Britain', in Rowe, M. (ed.) *Policing Beyond Macpherson*, Cullompton: Willan.

Williams, C. (2003) 'Britain's Police Forces: Forever Removed from Democratic Control?', *History and Policy*, 5 November.

Williams, M. (2006) *Virtually Criminal – Crime, Deviance, and Regulation Online*, New York: Routledge.

Williams, M. and Robinson, A. (2004) 'Problems and Prospects with Policing the Lesbian, Gay and Bisexual Community in Wales', *Policing and Society*, 14: 213–32.

Wilson, J.Q. (1968) *Varieties of Police Behaviour*, Cambridge: Harvard University Press.

Wimshurst, K. and Ransley, J. (2007) 'Police Education and the University Sector: Contrasting Models from the Australian Experience', *Journal of Criminal Justice Education*, 18 (1): 106–122.

Winsor, T. (2011) *Independent Review of Police Officer and Staff Remuneration and Conditions*, London: Home Office.

Wood, J. and Shearing, C. (2007) *Imagining Security*, Cullompton: Willan.

Young, J. (1999) *The Exclusive Society: Social Exclusion, Crime and Difference in Late Modernity*, London: Sage.

Zander, M. (2005) *Police and Criminal Evidence Act 1984* (7th edn), London: Thomson/Sweet and Maxwell.

Zedner, L. (2006) 'Policing Before and After the Police – The Historical Antecedents of Contemporary Crime Control', *British Journal of Criminology*, 46: 78–96.

Index

British Association for Women in Policing (BAWP), 126, 278
British Broadcasting Corporation (BBC), 122
British Security Industry Assoc-iation (BSIA), 210–11, 214–15
Brixton riots (1981), 144–5, 161
Brodeur, J.P., 173
Brogden, M., 32, 96, 107–8, 180
Brooks, Duwyane, 146
Broomfield, J., 130
Bucqueroux, B., 94–5
Bullock, K., 263
bureaucratic tasks performed by police officers, 14
burglary, 194, 197
Burke, James Lee, 188
Burke, M., 128–9, 132
Burrows, J., 194, 197
Button, M., 191, 211, 214–15

Caldeira, P.R., 213
Camps, F.E., 198–9
Canada, 14, 201
capital punishment, 37
Caramlau, L., 239
Card, R., 50, 57
Carswell, S., 119
Certificate of Knowledge of Policing, 261
Chakraborti, N., 155
Chan, J., 76, 106, 133, 246, 260, 265
charging for certain police services, 216
Charman, S., 133
Chartist movement, 28, 36
chief constables, 33, 82, 278–9
Child Exploitation Online Protect-ion Service, 266
child protection, 194–5
'citizen-focused' policing, 104
'citizen in uniform' concept, 26, 46, 63, 159, 262
'citizen's arrest', 57
citizenship, schooling in, 4
civil liberties, 35, 63, 233–5, 239, 241
civilian staff in the police service and 'civilianisation', 215, 279
class divisions, 36–7
climate change, 270
closed-circuit television (CCTV), 9, 233–7, 248–52, 279
Cochrane, Kelso, 154
Cockroft, T., 122
codes of practice for the police, 49–55, 62, 76–8, 86, 149
Cohen, P., 32
Coleman, C., 197

collaboration between police and community, 101–3
College of Policing, 76, 110, 261, 264, 272, 279
Collins, Wilkie, 188
Colls, R., 3
Colman, A., 131
colonialism, 24, 168–9
Colvin, R., 130
common-law powers, 55, 57
'communities at risk', 159
community consultation and collaboration, 99–103
community-oriented policing (COP), 107–8
community policing model, 13, 81, 93–112, 133, 161, 253, 271, 273
    challenges for, 106–9
    definition of, 94–8, 111
    export of, 180
    as a means of recovering public consent, 97–8
    practice of, 99–106
    principles of, 95
    process-led approaches to, 94–6
    projects of, 106
    and reassurance, 103–6
complaints against the police, 70–5, 86
Comprehensive Spending Review (2010), 208
Compstat system, 243, 248
computer-aided dispatch (CAD) system, 244–5, 250, 253
Confait case, 48
consent of the public to policing arrangements, 61, 93, 111, 145, 149, 159–61, 234, 266, 271, 279
constable, office of, 279
consultation between the police and community, 99–101, 110, 112, 279–80
'contestability' policy, 217
'contracting out' of services, 215–16, 266
co-operation between police forces, international, 174–5
    macro, meso and *micro* levels of, 178–9
'cop culture', 121, 200
Copeland, David, 236
'cops and robbers' tradition, 117
Corbett, C., 239
Corcoran, D., 133
corruption, 71, 76, 147, 192, 202
Council of Europe Declaration on the Police (1979), 174
Counter Fraud Specialists, 191
County and Borough Police Act (1856), 33–4
craft model of policing, 262, 264
Crawford, A., 83, 100, 108–9, 218–19, 222, 266–7
Crawshaw, R., 79–80
Crime and Disorder Act (1998), 101, 111, 155, 218

Mark, Sir Robert, 46
'marketisation' of policing, 215
Martin, A., 237
Marx, G.T., 247–8
Matrimonial Causes Act (1857), 192
Mawby, R.I., 8, 25, 197
Mayne, Richard, 30, 34–5
Mazerolle, L., 219
media representations of police work, 5–8, 13–16,
    117, 122, 188–90, 202, 231–2, 235
Menezes, Jean Charles de, 10, 70
meso-level co-operation between police forces, 178–9
Metropolitan Police, 71, 126, 146–7, 150, 236,
    259, 272
  Commissioner, 279
  compared with earlier systems, 38–40
  historical development of, 24–40
micro-level co-operation between police forces, 178–9
middle-class attitudes, 240–1
Mika, H., 81
militarism, 30
military capacity for maintaining order, 27–8, 35–6, 39
Miller, J., 153
Millie, A., 271
Milne, R., 191
miscarriages of justice, 58, 76
missing person investigations, 194
Misuse of Drugs Act (1971), 54–5
'mixed economy' of policing, 84, 218
mobile phone use by drivers, 240
money laundering, 219
Morgan, R., 59
Morris, B., 197
motorists, criminalisation of, 240–1, 252
Mulcahy, A., 62, 149
multi-agency partnerships, 217–18, 282
'multilateralisation' of policing, 207–8; *see also*
    pluralisation
multinational corporations, 181
murder of police officers, 31; *see also* homicide
Muslim Police Association, 124

nation states, new role of 168–9, 172–3, 178–82, 212,
    223, 270; *see also* state sovereignty
National Crime Agency (NCA), 110, 126, 195
National Health Service, 191
National Police Chiefs' Council, 62, 126, 263, 272, 282
National Policing Improvement Agency (NPIA), 282
Neighbourhood Policing, 98–9, 104–11, 155, 247,
    270–3, 282
Neighbourhood Watch schemes, 102–3
neo-liberalism, 259–60, 271

networks of policing, 220–1, 225
new managerialism, 222
new public management, 216–17
New York City, 243
New Zealand, 179–80, 192–3, 209
Newburn, T., 59, 80, 109, 212, 222
Neyroud, P., 78, 120, 260, 263–4
Nijhar, P., 107–8
Norri, C., 234, 237
Norris, David, 147
Northern Ireland, 76, 80–1, 179–80
Notting Hill riots (1959), 154

offender management services, 217
offensive weapons
  categories of, 51–2
  definition of, 49
operational independence of the police, 9, 69, 72, 87
opposition to the police, 31–6, 40
Organisation for Economic Co-operation and
    Development (OECD), 176
Organisation for Security and Co-operation in Europe
    (OSCE), 175–6
organisational subculture, 282
Orgreave disorder (1984), 76
'orthodox' account of the history of policing, 34–40
Osborne, D., 213
outsourcing of police work, 211, 217
'over-policing', 119–20, 132, 150, 250, 252
Oxford, Kenneth, 48

Palmer, S.H., 32
Palmiotto, M., 193–4
'panda' cars, 145
'panoptical' prison design, 243, 247, 249, 253
Paoline, E.A., 122
paperwork, 15
paramilitary policing, 81
community participation in policing, 25
patrol work of the police, 11, 14, 30, 98, 104, 106,
    110, 119, 218–19, 246, 264, 285
Patten, Chris (and Patten Report, 1999), 80, 179
Peel, Sir Robert, 24, 27, 34–5
performance of the police
  micro-management of, 216
  monitoring of, 70, 78, 246, 271
persuasive skills used in policing, 61
'Peterloo Massacre' (1819), 28, 35
Pickering, S., 169
Pilkington, Fiona, 154
Pinkerton Detective Agency, 192
Pitchfork, Colin, 199

watchmen, powers of, 38
Weatheritt, M., 96
Weber, L., 151
Weber, Max, 10
Weisburd, D., 109, 263–4
West Midlands Police, 208, 266
White, A., 84
Whitfield, J., 123
Wild, Jonathan, 192
Williams, M., 129, 251
Wilson, J.Q., 119
Wimshurst, K., 262
Winsor, T. (and Winsor Review, 2011), 47, 261
women

in the police force, 125–8, 130–1, 136
role and status in society, 125–6
as victims of crime, 127–8
Wood, J., 220
workforce modernisation, 261
working-class activism, 36, 40
'working personality' of the police, 118–19, 126, 129, 136

Young, J., 212

Zander, M., 47–50
Zedner, L., 38, 223–4
zero-tolerance policing (ZTP), 180, 243, 285